BILLY GRAHAM EVANGELIST TO THE WORLD

BY THE AUTHOR

BIOGRAPHY

The Cambridge Seven
Way to Glory (Havelock of Lucknow)
Hudson Taylor and Maria
Moody
Billy Graham
The Man Who Shook the World (The Apostle Paul)
A Foreign Devil in China (Nelson Bell)
George Whitefield
Wilberforce

HISTORY AND TRAVEL

A Cambridge Movement
Shadows Fall Apart
The Good Seed
Earth's Remotest End
The Keswick Story
Faith and Freedom in Russia

Billy Graham

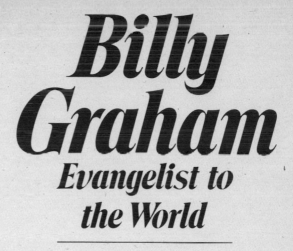

Evangelist to the World

by John Pollock

*An Authorized Biography
of the Decisive Years*

SPECIAL CRUSADE EDITION
Published for the
Billy Graham Evangelistic Association

**world wide
publications**

1303 Hennepin Avenue, Minneapolis, Minnesota 55403

Designed by Jim Mennick

Library of Congress Cataloging in Publication Data

Pollock, John Charles.
  BILLY GRAHAM, EVANGELIST TO THE WORLD.

  Includes index.
  1. Graham, William Franklin, 1918— 2. Evangelists—United States—Biography.
BV3785 G69P597   269'2'0924 [B]   76—62949

Contents

Preface　*vii*
Acknowledgments　*ix*

PART ONE

1　Hills of the Headhunters　*3*
2　The Kohima Miracle　*16*
3　Black and White Together　*27*
4　Land of Morning Calm　*43*
5　The Million on Yoido Plaza　*54*

PART TWO

6　European Linkup　*71*
7　London and "Moral Integrity"　*86*
8　Ireland: Mission of Reconciliation　*91*

PART THREE

9　"Not the Work of Man"　*105*
10　America's Spiritual Hunger　*118*
11　The Team　*134*
12　The Grahams: A Family View　*139*

13 The Man Himself   *147*

14 Graham and the Presidents   *164*

PART FOUR

15 The Road to Lausanne   *187*
16 July 1974   *200*
17 The Sleeping Giant Awakes   *216*
18 The Glory of Brazil   *236*
19 Post-Lausanne   *249*
20 Billy and Youth   *254*
21 The Rain Campaign   *263*
22 "I Intend to Keep On . . ."   *274*
23 ". . . And On"   *286*
24 New Fields   *296*

Appendix: One Man's Furrow   *313*
Index   *317*

Preface

BILLY GRAHAM is probably the best-known religious figure of the age. I have already told the story of his life and ministry up to 1969, twenty years after he first sprang to fame during his Los Angeles campaign when he was still only thirty years old. A biography of a contemporary cannot be more than an interim account, lacking the perspective of the definitive Life which one day must be written, but this earlier book remains available, and for reasons of space cannot be summarized as a prelude to the present book.[1]

What now follows is not a thin continuation of all that he has done from 1970. It selects vital and representative episodes and is based on the private papers of Billy Graham, which he generously made available together with his own comments; and on research at the chief areas of his ministry, mostly undertaken not less than one year after the events and followed up by correspondence. Those two sources, with the memories and reflections of his associates and many others, provide the essential material for an authoritative account of his work, his aims and his influence. My book therefore is both the "inside story" of Billy Graham and a history of his ministry.

---

[1] See *Billy Graham: The Authorized Biography* by John Pollock (1966, McGraw-Hill, New York; Hodder and Stoughton, London. Updated edition 1969, World Wide Publications, Minneapolis). Those who are entirely unfamiliar with the outline may wish to turn at once to the appendix of the present book to read an abridgment of my biographical article in the Billy Graham silver jubilee issue of *Christianity Today*, 13 September 1974.

At this stage in Graham's life a strictly chronological arrangement might confuse. My earlier book on his first fifty-one years fell naturally into a chronological pattern as, eventually, will a definitive Life; but unless a writer on Graham is merely to skim the surface he is faced with the fact that many matters are unfolding at once. In the present work, therefore, the order of events is secondary.

Another problem is the sheer weight of source material. For instance, even one percent of the more interesting or significant stories of converts of his ministry would fill the book several times, quite apart from anything else. I received or researched more evidence than I could possibly use, but nothing will be wasted and I am grateful for it all.

Billy Graham: Evangelist to the World offers a fully rounded account of the man and his ministry: I have not sidestepped any aspect and therefore I believe that it must be the necessary basis for informed discussion and assessment. The general reader will, I think, be absorbed by the story and will get to know Billy Graham in an intimate way.

JOHN POLLOCK

Rose Ash,
Devonshire,
England.

Acknowledgments

I WISH to thank the Billy Graham Evangelistic Association most
warmly for the cooperation I have received in the preparation of this
book and for making available the material on which much of it is
based, with no conditions except, of course, that my account should be
factually accurate. I am grateful to the Board of BGEA for making
possible the research and writing.

On our research tours in six continents my wife and I received a
very great deal of help and kindness in one way or another, including
interpreting and translating of tapes, often at considerable inconve-
nience for the people concerned. To list everyone is not possible. They
know, I think, how grateful we are.

I want to thank all those, including Billy Graham, his associates and
BGEA staff members, who gave me memories and impressions. As
before, I have received full cooperation and courtesy from the whole
Graham Team and I want to thank particularly those who helped me
organize the research and travel, especially George M. Wilson and
Esther LaDow in Minneapolis, Maurice Rowlandson and Jean Wilson
in London, Donald Bailey in Atlanta, Stephanie Wills, Elsie Brookshire
and Lucille Lytle in Montreat, Barry Berryman in Sydney and V.
Samuel Jones in Hong Kong. Billy Graham's personal associates, Dr.
T. W. Wilson, and Dr. Grady Wilson, have at all times smoothed my
path and encouraged me, and I would like to thank Mr. and Mrs. Fred
Dienert of Philadelphia for their help and guidance.

I owe much to the skill of those who transcribed tapes. A special word of thanks to Mrs. Alana Richards, now of New Orleans, and Mrs. J. G. Palmer of Hemel Hempstead, England, who undertook the difficult work of transcribing interviews and discussions, together with the following members of the secretarial staff at BGEA, Minneapolis: Dorothy Ander, Sharon Barr, Cheri Cooke, Terri Doyle, Pam Elston, Sharon Fluger, Jane Haas, Bobbie Hansen, Sherry Larson and Arlene Skaff.

I owe particular thanks to Mrs. J. E. Williams of Bideford, North Devon, who once again deciphered my handwriting and typed and retyped; this is, I think, the tenth book on which we have worked together.

Finally, I wish to thank those who have given me permission to quote from their private letters. If inadvertently I have failed to seek permission from any, I hope they will forgive me.

PART ONE

1 Hills of the Headhunters

BILLY GRAHAM heard a loud, peremptory knock on the door of his hotel room in Bangkok, Thailand, on a Sunday morning in November 1972.

He had hoped to be flying to Calcutta and from there to a crusade at Kohima, capital of Nagaland in northeast India. On his arrival at Bangkok the previous day, however, shattering news of rebel hostilities had forced a change of plan. He had since spent a restless night; never had he canceled a crusade.

The knocking continued. Opening the door, Billy saw an American who was a stranger to him; a young girl, evidently the American's daughter; and a Naga. The American, barely pausing to introduce himself as Neal Jones, former missionary among the Nagas, cried, "Billy, you've *got* to go to Nagaland!"

The Naga added his urging. "Oh, Dr. Graham, you will set the Christians back for years if you don't go."

As a result of the discussion that followed, Billy Graham, to his own relief, felt free to change his mind. He caught the next plane to India, and thus to one of the most extraordinary events in his ministry. "We call it," says one of the younger Christian leaders of northeast India, "'The Kohima Miracle,' because right from the start God was there working, opening doors and more doors. Although we had lost hope, it happened. So we praise God."

Far up toward the mountainous Burma border lies the Indian state of Nagaland. There on knife-edge ridges of dense jungle perch bamboo villages, which in former times were fortified independent communities at war with their neighbors and living in fear of demons. Headhunting was an integral part of religion. As a boy, Longri Ao, now Nagaland's foremost Christian churchman, had helped his father, an animist priest, to sacrifice pigs and chickens before the young men went on a raid. He had seen them carry back dripping heads to boil off the flesh. Skulls were hung outside the bamboo hut of a headhunter, who would call on them by their actual names, believing their spirits to be his protectors here and now and his servants in the next world. Such a man had authority and moral power in the village according to the number of his heads.

Fourteen Naga tribes lived in those hills, each with its own language and distinctive facial characteristic within the general Mongolian type. American Baptist missionaries entered to evangelize the Ao tribe in 1872, nearly ten years before British India began to extend a settled administration there. Very slowly a strong church emerged and became a byword for zeal. In Longri Ao's words, "Christ has created a new people out of these headhunters whom armies could not stop."

After the heroic British defense and relief of Kohima, which stopped the Japanese invasion, the independence of India in 1947 brought a movement demanding separate Naga sovereignty. Widespread rebellion turned Nagaland into a guerrilla battleground, and the government of India withdrew all western missionaries in 1954. Longri Ao and other pastors were trusted go-betweens in the attempts at reconciliation which led to the establishment of a peace mission and the granting of statehood in 1962. Agitation and sporadic warfare continued, however, and thousands of lay Christians absorbed their energies in a hopeless political quest.

The sorrows of war sharpened Naga spiritual hunger. The church grew fast with more than 10,000 adult baptisms a year, mostly of young tribal people, until Nagaland held the highest ratio of regularly worshiping Christians to population of any state in the world. "Our people," says Longri, "found that the peace, security, and joy they wanted so much would never come through political measures or social changes. So they started praying together."

As they prayed, they began to long for Billy Graham. They had learned about him from missionaries in his earliest days of fame. Since the intertribal language is English, many Nagas read *Decision* magazine and his best-selling book *Peace with God,* and listened to the Hour of Decision on the shortwave broadcast from Manila. Some had heard him preach at Calcutta during his Indian tour of 1956. "Billy Gra'm," as the tribal people pronounce his name, became to them God's man for the age. "We must see him in person. We must listen to him personally. Our lives will be deepened, our faith strengthened, and our vision widened. Nagaland is the right place for him to come." Yet the Indian government seldom gave a westerner a permit to enter the "inner line" it had drawn round the disturbed Naga Hills.

In 1967 Billy's associate Akbar Haqq, an Indian citizen, held a crusade in Kohima. At that time a truce was declared, so that as Akbar preached, the Indian army commander and his officers sat side by side with "hostiles." Akbar offered hope of Billy himself coming in four years' time. The Nagas who attended the Asia-South Pacific Congress on Evangelism at Singapore sent Billy a tribal shawl "as a token of our love" and extended a general invitation. This became definite when he was asked to come to the centenary of Christianity in Nagaland in November 1972; he cabled his definite "Yes" late in May 1972.

Nagaland was delighted, yet disappointed. The Baptist centenary would be held in the remote Ao village of Impur where the missionaries had first settled, and because of its small size the Aos had invited only twenty-five each from other tribes. The Angamis who live around Kohima thought it a "pity to let Dr. Billy Graham take the trouble of coming all the way to Nagaland and go back without meeting the bulk of Christians." They begged him to come on after the centenary "to a 'Dr. Billy Graham crusade' at Kohima for which our field will take all responsibilities," including the securing of inner line permits from New Delhi. Kohima, on the main road through the mountains, would be accessible from the other hill states too, each with great numbers of Christians. The Naga capital would be host to all northeast India, a plan warmly endorsed by the North East India Christian Council which deplored the relegating of Billy Graham to being a mere component in a Baptist celebration.

Graham and his advisers realized that the government of India was unlikely to permit a visit long enough to cover two separate occasions, and that a crusade at Kohima offered more strategic ministry, with dates that fitted better into his schedule. By cable and letter from Walter Smyth, his coordinator of crusades, he withdrew from Impur, accepted Kohima, and suggested a seven days' preaching which would open with Akbar Haqq and conclude with a three-day visit from Graham (three days being the most for which he could expect an inner line permit).

"The news spread like wildfire among all the churches of northeast India and brought a great sense of victory and joy for the people of God. Prayers in all churches and homes were intensified," recalls Longri Ao. An organizing committee drawn from all tribes in Nagaland began work at once. Longri Ao and Lhousuchie Mhasi, secretary of the Angami Baptist Church Council, wrote to Smyth adding "One more thing: Will you kindly send some top gospel soloists along with Dr. Billy Graham to sing at the crusade? Our people, too, do sing, and they love good gospel singing. We shall consider it a special privilege if you would kindly take this matter to God in prayer. Please consider the Kohima Crusade a major one which will have far-reaching consequences."

On August 8, little more than three months before the intended crusade, hostiles attempted to assassinate the then chief minister of Nagaland, killing his driver and two others and wounding his daughter in the hip. The government of India quickly withdrew the cease-fire agreement and disbanded the peace mission.

Two weeks after the ambush Charlie Riggs, Billy Graham's director of counseling and follow-up, and Walter Grist, Akbar Haqq's crusade director, arrived in Calcutta on August 22 expecting inner line permits for a two-day visit to Kohima to start counselor preparation. They met a blank wall of officialdom. Mhasi and two other Naga leaders had driven to Imphal airfield in Manipur state to meet Riggs and Grist at the plane. They hung around for two days, then sadly retraced their drive along the famous Imphal Road which passes some of the most beautiful mountain scenery in the world, historic from the heavy fighting in World War II. Back in Kohima they learned from a telephone call from Shillong in the Khasi hills, the former Assam capital and hill station, now capital of the new state of Meghalaya ("Home of the Clouds") that the Americans would meet them there, outside the inner line, on September 1. The call had come from the secretary of the North East India Christian Council, a thirty-three-year-old Khasi named Ricwch Robert Cunville.

One of the Kohima crusade's important consequences for India would be the profound change of direction it caused in Robert Cunville. The younger son of the director of the Pasteur Institute at Shillong, with both parents devout Christians, Robert had intended to go to England for medical training. Then a barefoot youthful evangelist stayed in their home and Robert soon knew that his own life must be spent in the ministry. His parents insisted that he wait three months before canceling the British trip. In that time, he recalls, "I became more convinced that the Lord had really called me. My mother wept, out of joy." He went to a famous Indian seminary, but its liberal theology shifted him into absorption with an almost wholly "social gospel." Pushed high into youth work associated with the World Council of Churches and UNESCO's International Voluntary Service, he became well known to church leaders throughout India as a preacher and administrator, and had attended many conferences overseas. By 1972 a Billy Graham crusade was hardly his idea of significant religious activity and he became involved only because of his post as secretary of the North East India Christian Council.

Six Nagas made the two-day motor journey to Shillong, arriving downcast because the crusade looked as if it would never take place. Then Charlie Riggs told them of other apparent disasters in the Billy Graham saga which had "worked together for good." He spoke of London in 1954: an uproar over a slip in a brochure nearly stopped the crusade before it had begun, but it made the little-known evangelist front-page news; Ethiopia in 1960, where the stadium had been denied them until the providential arrival of a Norwegian businessman who knew the emperor personally; a South American city in 1962, where an official order banned the use of a stadium after the first night, but the resulting controversy had brought thousands more to the substitute site.

When Riggs finished, Longri Ao stood. He is large for a Naga and he drew himself up until he seemed to dominate the room. "I've been moved," he said. "We are going to add another chronicle to these events of God." He led the pastors and laymen in prayer and then urged Riggs to give them ten days to renegotiate with the government. "Continue to believe that God is going to open the door," he said.

Inner line permits often took months of waiting and even then frequently were refused. It would need a miracle now, and Robert Cunville did not believe in miracles. While Christians redoubled their praying, a deputation, which included Cunville, took a personal letter from the chief minister of Nagaland, a staunch Christian like all the state cabinet, to the minister for home affairs, K. C. Pant, in New Delhi, who showed them great kindness. "You are the soldiers of peace," he said, "and a Graham crusade will help to bring peace in Nagaland. But Dr. Billy Graham is a very important international figure and his security is the responsibility of the government of India." He asked if the Angami Naga Baptist church would take responsibility for the maintenance of peace during the crusade. As the Naga historian writes, "This was an absurdity, but in good faith the church took the risk." Longri Ao went into the deep jungle to meet the underground leaders, who gave a written undertaking to preserve peace during the centenary and the crusade, and who solemnly bit on a bullet in recognized token of their oath.

Billy Graham, in America, had received more than one letter from Indians outside Nagaland urging "that I postpone the trip. They feel the situation is too politically tense. However, in my heart I do not feel inclined to cancel unless I am forced to." In the first days of October the Indian home minister, who had come to New York for the General Assembly of the United Nations, invited Graham to lunch. Their discussion proved decisive. The Team would receive permits, provided no incident had marred the centenary immediately preceding the crusade, but these might be cancelled at the last minute, even as they boarded the plane at Calcutta.

The risk remained that the Naga underground would shoot Billy Graham as a sure way to focus the world on their demand for independence, but he had received too many threats to his life, including a very serious one at Dallas only two months previously, to be troubled: "We will take all possible precautions, but if this is where God wants us then I think we must go."

Early in November Billy flew to Hawaii, where he stayed during the presidential election, and then to Japan. Away in northeast India the Naga Baptist Centenary passed without breach of the ceasefire. Thirty foreign Baptists were admitted briefly who, though they did not know it, had received their permits only because the government of India wished to test the sincerity of the truce promised for the crusade.

The tribal communities of six states began a great migration. From Sikkim and the foothills of Kunchenjunga, from Bhutan and the wild mountains of the China border, from Manipur in the south and the Khasi hills in the west, and from every tribe in Nagaland, groups converged on Kohima for "the day of the Lord," in Longri Ao's expressive phrase. "Many people walked five, six days, men carrying their food and bedding, and women carrying their babies on their backs," in the tapering baskets of the hill folk, secured by a strap to the forehead, "coming in thousands just to hear the word of God preached by Billy Graham."

Kohima is a small town scattered across steep-sided ridges, which make it look smaller except at night when the whole area twinkles with lights. Its mountainous isolation and the comparatively primitive conditions obliged the crusade organizers to provide accommodations, food, health, sanitation—and protection.

Virtually every house had agreed to receive guests. Public buildings and schools became dormitories, the Indian army's 8th mountain division loaned hundreds of tents at the general's own suggestion. People rich and poor donated 800 cattle, 600 pigs and tons of rice to be sold at a nominal price to those who had not brought their own food. Villagers cut firewood for free distribution to the thousands of fires necessary for cooking and warmth. Christians and non-Christians worked. Liquor shops promised to close for the duration. The town was repainted.

The Nagaland government gave the crusade committee a contract to build a scheduled four miles of jeep road up steep jungle-covered hillside to an airstrip so that the wages earned could swell the crusade fund. Longri Ao recalls how "Men and women, including high officials and their wives came out with their hoes, shovels, spades and axes to cut the trees and dig the road. It was an unusual scene, big and small working together singing and rejoicing. They carried their own food and drinking water as they worked for several days constructing the road. Our people love to work together in a great crowd. Everybody enjoyed it. Altogether over. 15,000 individual stints went into this work." The Indian army brought bulldozers free of charge to do anything beyond manual effort. The road earned the crusade 30,000 rupees (about U.S. $13,000, where the average daily wage equals about $2).

Just below the War Cemetery with its famous "tennis court" memorial, scene of the bitterest fighting of the siege, and its cherry tree which marks the farthest penetration of the Japanese invasion of India, lies the town football ground. It measures only 500 by 300 feet. It would accommodate 100,000 tribal people, who are small-boned, small of stature and love to sit close. The crusade committee had improvised seating for that number, leaving a counseling area clear, and had erected a huge rostrum, designed like a Naga chief's house, of timber and bamboo and dried grass, big enough not only for the platform but for a thousand-voice choir. All the choirs of Nagaland and many other places had been practicing. Everywhere, in churches, in family groups as they harvested the paddy or returned to their home from the fields, the Christians of northeast India had prayed.

On Tuesday 14 November disaster struck Nagaland. While Billy Graham in Tokyo fulfilled his last day of public engagements before going to Taiwan, an Indian army convoy ran into an ambush at Mile 35 where the Dimapur-Kohima road takes a sharp bend around a steep hill, with thick jungle above and paddy fields falling away below. The rebels killed a lieutenant and three sepoys, and wounded eight. Crossfire caught three cows and a big bull. The hostiles disappeared into the jungle. "The news spread all over the country like lightning," relates Longri Ao. "Our agreement with the central government had not been kept. The light was off and deep darkness came upon one and all. We were all at our wits' end to make any positive suggestion at this juncture. We were simply waiting for an order from New Delhi canceling the crusade." The army imposed a curfew on eleven villages in the immediate Kohima area, and the crusade committee sent emissaries to the rebels' deep jungle hideouts and fruitlessly demanded an explanation of why they had broken the truce.

Robert Cunville, who had been to Calcutta to deliver the Team's inner line permits to Akbar Haqq, arrived back "to find all of Kohima in a very sad atmosphere." The bazaars already were crowded with visitors to the crusade and 80,000 people had passed the town checkpoint. "For six months no such incident had taken place," he related after it had all become history. "The devil was trying to stop the gospel from being preached. We all prayed, 'God do a miracle and let us have this crusade.'" And then he adds, "Again God saw the tears of his own people and he overruled the power and affairs of men. No order came from the central government canceling the crusade. Yes, God was still on his throne, with the passing events of the world under his control."

Billy Graham and T. W. Wilson were then in Taipei, Taiwan, where Billy addressed the world congress of the Junior Chambers of Commerce ("Jaycees") on "International Morality," followed by a private audience with Mme. Chiang Kai-shek. It was "one of the most interesting talks I have ever had; our entire conversation had to do with spiritual things." The rest of the Nagaland Team[1] had arrived in Calcutta, where that Thursday evening in Akbar Haqq's room at the Ritz Continental hotel overlooking Calcutta's park, the Maidan, Robert Cunville, newly arrived again from Kohima, broke the news of the crisis.

They first called the home minister in New Delhi by telephone. He told them that the government would not withdraw the inner line permits, but because of the risk of ambush the Team must decide for themselves whether Graham should go in or not. Then a hotel bearer delivered a telegram from Kohima assuring them of the chief minister's continued support for the crusade, but this did not dissolve the Team's dilemma. Apart from the assassination risk the crusade might be manipulated for political ends—either by the central government, using Billy Graham's safety as an excuse for pouring in more troops, or by the underground, who might somehow turn the meetings into a demonstration for independence. Thus the crusade might embarrass the cause of Christianity throughout India. Yet, as Cunville, by now convinced of its importance, pleaded with the Team, 80,000 people had come to Kohima to hear Billy Graham in a spirit of expectancy and prayer.

For Akbar Haqq, due in Kohima the next day, the situation looked specially delicate. As early as 18 September he had warned Graham and Smyth that the Nagaland campaign might jeopardize his Indian ministry should it identify him, despite himself, with the rebel cause. Now, after they had prayed and discussed and prayed again, Akbar Haqq sadly reached the conclusion that he could not go to Kohima. Nor could he advise Billy to go. The other Team members accepted his advice.

---

[1] Cliff Barrows, Walter Smyth, Tedd Smith the pianist, Archie Dennis the black singer, Akbar Haqq, Walter Grist.

At midnight Cunville telephoned Kohima. It was a very bad connection but when this "shocking news," as Suchie Mhasi described it, came over, "the burden in our hearts was unspeakable." Longri Ao and Mhasi agreed to leave at daylight to beg the Team "not to abandon us at this last minute." In Calcutta, Robert Cunville retired to his hotel room and "I wept that night before God."

Since Billy Graham alone could make the final decision whether to go to Kohima, and needed all the facts, Cliff Barrows and Walter Smyth decided to intercept him at Bangkok. They flew eastward the next morning, Friday 17 November.

Billy Graham, unaware of the unfolding drama in India, flew southwest with T. W. Wilson from Taipei to Hong Kong, and on across Indochina through about two hours of major thunderstorms. (Despite his countless thousands of hours of flying, Graham does not particularly enjoy air travel. Before the days of jets he was inclined to be tense, perhaps the long-term effect of having been in a crash landing in Canada in 1947. On one Australian flight in 1959, by an old-type propeller plane, lightning severed the antenna which clattered along the fuselage to every passenger's alarm. Billy gnawed his fingernails. When a nervous stranger said hopefully, "With Billy Graham aboard we should all feel secure," Billy's spirit willingly agreed but the flesh felt more than a trifle weak.) At 4:30 in the afternoon they landed at Bangkok.

A counselor of the U. S. embassy, Edmond Corr, took them swiftly through immigration and customs and on emerging "we were amazed to see Walter Smyth and Cliff Barrows there." During the long ride to the city center the two briefed Billy and advised him not to go to Nagaland. "Billy was astounded," recalls Smyth. Billy said, "Walter, we've never cancelled a major meeting—we've come halfway around the world. We've never cancelled a crusade before."

Checking into the Busit Thani hotel, Billy and the other three immediately prayed in his room. He read to them from Acts 21, where Paul was urged in the Holy Spirit's name not to go up to Jerusalem and replied, "What mean ye to weep and break my heart? for I am ready not to be bound only, but also to die at Jerusalem for the name of the Lord Jesus." The risk of ending Billy's world ministry by death or serious wounds was certainly a factor, but uppermost lay the prayer, "What is your will for Nagaland?" That evening the Kohima crusade was opened by Naga preachers with much prayer for Billy Graham's safe arrival.

Billy recorded in the diary which he dictated daily during part of this tour: "As Cliff, Walter, T. W. and I discussed and prayed we began to realize that the crusade might take on serious political implications. In the meantime our hearts were bleeding for the Naga Christians in what must be a period of confusion and possible disappointment. On this Friday night I could not go to sleep. I rolled and tossed most of the night in agonized praying that God would show us the way."

The next morning, Saturday, he recorded: "I still am confused as to what the Holy Spirit would have us to do. Cliff, Walter, T. W. and I met and most of us seem to feel that we should not go to Nagaland unless the Lord very clearly directs otherwise. Therefore, we asked Walter to go to New Delhi with the possibility of making a public announcement in Delhi as to why we should not go to Nagaland. I wrote out the announcement that Walter was to make. In the meantime I was very unhappy in my spirit."

The press release which Graham drafted explained the postponement of the crusade, expressed his deep distress, and his prayer for peace in Nagaland. Walter left at once for the airport. Meanwhile, the embassy counselor sent cables to state department officials in New Delhi and Calcutta for advice.

Billy went to a lunch given in his honor by the U. S. ambassador, with "a number of interesting guests, including an Irish Catholic priest who sat across from me." Billy did not record the name of a Baptist missionary couple, the Reverend Richard E. Gregory and his wife, Marnie, who heard Billy mention sadly that he had canceled his visit to Nagaland.

In Calcutta that Saturday night the Naga leaders, with Cunville and Charlie Riggs, talked and prayed in the air conditioned hotel room, where closed windows shut out the unending clamor of Calcutta streets.

At half past midnight Walter called from New Delhi and read out Billy's press release, which could not be issued until offices opened on Monday. Billy had decided that no one should go. Robert Cunville seized the phone, "Brother Walter, God can still do a miracle!" Walter replied, "Amen."

The men turned to prayer again, and, recalls Charlie, "grabbed hold of the verse, 'The king's heart is in the hand of the Lord, as the rivers of water; he turneth it whithersoever he will.' And we said, 'Lord God, Billy Graham is the king in this case. His heart is in your hand. Turn it in the right direction, not in the way we want it to go, or the way all of his counselors want it to go, but the way you want it to go.' And we called the people up in Kohima, thousands of them, and said, 'Pray, pray, pray.' " But indeed all Kohima already was a sea of prayer.

The next day, Sunday November 19, Billy Graham recorded in his diary at Bangkok: "I spent a restless night still deeply disturbed as to whether to go to Nagaland or not. Ed Corr called from the American embassy to say that he had received a number of cables during the night from both Delhi and Calcutta. They all seemed to indicate that while there were risks involved and that some of the reasoning given me for not going to Nagaland was valid, yet it was their thought that the Indian government felt it would probably be better for me to go." Billy and Corr arranged to meet at Calvary Baptist Church before attending the 11 A.M. service.

While they had been talking on the telephone a car was weaving fast through the crowded streets of Bangkok toward the hotel.

It happened that an Angami Naga layman, L. Bizo, treasurer of the Council of Baptist Churches in northeast India and stationed at Gahauti in Assam, had stopped off on his way back from a conference at Hong Kong to stay with his predecessor. That man, a forty-two-year-old Cornell graduate, Cornelius (Neal) Jones, had spent thirteen years at Gahauti until the government banned missionaries from the entire Restricted Area. Bizo had been born at Kohima, where his father, a gardener at the deputy commissioner's bungalow (which later became the heart of the battlefield), had suffered much local opposition when he became one of the first Christians.

On that Sunday morning, a day of bright sunshine, Neal Jones introduced Bizo after the 8 A.M. service at the International Church to several friends. One of them, Mrs. Gregory, when she heard he was a Naga, mentioned Billy Graham's sorrow at the ambassador's luncheon that he had been obliged to cancel the Kohima crusade. Bizo and Jones were shocked. Bizo had imagined Billy Graham already in Nagaland since the opening day. These two men felt so upset that they decided to track him down. Taking Neal's fourteen-year-old daughter,

Grace, they drove to Calvary Baptist Church, found out the name of his hotel, and at about 9:50 A.M. drove up to the Busit Thani and demanded Billy Graham's room number.

Billy, getting ready for church, was about to exchange his pajamas for a suit when "there was a vigorous knock at my door." ("I shall never forget your knock on my door in Bangkok," he wrote to Neal Jones afterward.) Startled—for visitors normally are met by T. W.—he opened the door to see a young girl and the two men. Barely introducing themselves, Neal Jones cried, "Billy, I have come here as the servant of the Lord. You've *got* to go to Nagaland."

Billy, after "calming him down a bit," listened with T. W. as Neal Jones, "in the strongest possible terms," backed by Bizo, begged him to reconsider. God could look after him in any danger, said Jones. He emphasized the arduous preparations, the tens of thousands of eagerly expectant tribal people. Cancellation would undermine the authority of the church leaders, who had been the moving force in the peace mission, and thus would play into the hands of the underground hostiles by demonstrating their power. He had not been asked to cancel; the permits were not withdrawn; at the very least he should make his final decision in Calcutta, after meeting Naga leaders, said Jones.

"Oh, Dr. Graham," Bizo cried, "you will set the Christians back for years if you don't go."

After further discussion, which included Cliff Barrows, Billy exclaimed, "We are going to Calcutta!"

They learned that seats were vacant on the flight booked by Bizo, and, records Graham, "for the first time in several days I was beginning to feel peace in my heart. I knew we were doing the right thing. We had had so much negative advice, and now for the first time something positive was being said and done. Before leaving the room we had prayer together and all of us felt we were making the right decision in going to Calcutta."

2 The Kohima Miracle

ABOUT half-past two on that Sunday afternoon, Calcutta time, Charlie Riggs, Longri Ao, and Suchie Mhasi were again in Charlie's room at the Ritz-Continental, their faith waning, when the telephone rang again.

Charlie answered it and heard an unmistakable voice: "Charlie, this is Billy."

"*Billy!* Where are you? I thought you were in Bangkok."

"No, I'm in Calcutta. We're going to Kohima."

Charlie dropped the phone. "Praise the Lord!" Billy, in the home of the American consul-general, who had rushed from the golf course to Dum Dum Airport on receiving a message from the Bangkok embassy, heard Charlie shout, "This is Billy and he is in Calcutta." The two Nagas jumped up and down. They hugged Charlie and each other, praising the Lord, and when Cliff, T. W. and Bizo arrived, having come ahead with the baggage, they hugged them too. All were so absorbed in praising that they never noticed a bearer step in with a tray of tea which, when they noticed, appeared to have fallen from heaven like everything else just then.

They tried vainly to call Walter in New Delhi; but, having failed to release Billy Graham's press announcement of cancellation, he had gone to Agra with Akbar to see the Taj Mahal. Walter held the inner line permits, and the government offices in Calcutta which could issue duplicates were closed. The airline had reallocated the seats, yet no other transport could reach Nagaland in time. That night, more miracles brought duplicate permits and the release of nine seats for the early morning flight.

Meanwhile, up in the hills that Sunday afternoon, a dejected Robert Cunville rode a badly sprung bus up the hairpin bends of the Kohima Imphal Road. "I had hardly been sleeping and so I became blacker than ever! I had been praying all along on the plane that maybe it was God's will that another Billy Graham come out of northeast India. I was due to speak at the main service at 4 P.M. I arrived at Kohima at 3:30 P.M. and went directly to the crusade office where the committee wept to God in the basement of the office. We just prayed for a miracle. We asked God to forgive any sin that we had accidentally done, our pride, etc.

"We had just finished praying at ten minutes to four when a phone call came from the chief minister of Nagaland that I should contact Calcutta." Telephoning such a distance is difficult and slow except officially, but the chief minister got Robert a line at once and he heard Charlie Riggs shouting the news with joy: "Billy and the Team will arrive tomorrow!"

At five minutes past four Cunville mounted to the rostrum and saw for the first time the football ground packed to capacity with anxiously waiting people. On hearing his news the whole immense crowd of 100,000 gave voice. When tribal Christians pray, whether in a family group or in a huge crowd, each individual prays aloud, oblivious of anyone else. As the Kohima congregation poured out their thanksgiving, the sound, as one Naga said, was like the waterfalls of heaven.

Back in Calcutta at that time Billy Graham was briefly watching an inter-services cricket match. The American consul-general, Gordon Matthews, had suggested attending it as a means of meeting many distinguished Indians, including General Aurora, victor of the recent war which had led to the creation of Bangladesh. Billy was much amused when everything stopped for tea. "The British left forever upon the Indians the necessity of having tea in the afternoon." In the tea tent he met generals, politicians and social leaders. "One came up and said that he had been converted to Christ through the one meeting we held in Calcutta in 1955. At least a dozen people asked me why we didn't come to Calcutta for a crusade. One of the generals told me that if we came to Calcutta we could have a half million to a million people at each service. He said Calcutta is ripe, ready and waiting."

Ruth Graham had told Billy to be sure to meet Mother Teresa in Calcutta. The consul-general, who knew her well, took him through the crowded streets with their noisy traffic of ox-carts, buses, ancient cars, processions, wandering cows and ceaseless press of people, where the color and variety somewhat disguise the poverty. He turned up a dark and dingy alley to the Mother House.

"We went inside on a little veranda and there we were met by two warm, gracious and friendly nuns. They told us that the Mother was in but it would probably be impossible to see her. Mr. Gordon took a card out of his pocket, wrote a little note and asked if it could be delivered to her personally. He was assured that it would be. We waited in a little anteroom for about fifteen minutes and in came Mother Teresa. She was everything and more than I had heard. Many times you build up expectations in your mind about a person and then you feel a bit let down after you have met them. Not so with Mother Teresa. Her face is the face of a saint. Her eyes are piercing. Her face is lined with character and strength. . . . She told me she had heard of me for many years, had often prayed for me and hoped sometime to attend some of our meetings. I told her that my wife thought she was doing one of the most wonderful works in the world and that I agreed. I promised to pray for her and her great ministry as she helps bear the burden of so many people. She said that last night she had held five dying people in her arms and talked to them about God as they were dying."

Early in the afternoon of Monday 20 November 1972, toward the end of the long, twisting, dusty drive through the fine scenery of the hills in a convoy of ten rather aged cars, plus armed police vehicles, Billy Graham and his Team first saw Kohima, on a ridge ahead to their left, with mountains above it.

With eight miles still to go, Billy recorded the last entry he found time to make in his Nagaland diary. "We were met by one of the most colorful and largest crowds I have ever witnessed. They had built a large white arch that said 'Welcome, Billy Graham.'[1] On top of the arch was a cross. Tens of thousands of people lined the road for the next three miles, waving, smiling, shouting slogans of friendship. The Associated Press estimated that more than a hundred thousand people were there to welcome us. Tears came to my eyes. I felt rebuked that I had even doubted about coming to these mountain people to minister the gospel. I felt terribly unworthy."

He called a halt and jumped out of the car to greet these cheering, laughing tribal people, in their bright shawls, red and black and yellow, each tribe different, who now converged in a seething delighted mass to shake his hand. The police urgently shepherded him into the car again, saying they would otherwise never get him into the town. As the convoy drove slowly toward the state guest house, the streets of the bazaar looked one sea of happy faces.

A few moments before four o'clock the Billy Graham Team walked to the "chieftain's house" platform. A hush fell. It was a moment charged with emotion for the thousands who had waited so eagerly, and for the Team who had so nearly turned back. As the choir, 750 men and women in white shawls edged in red and black, broke into "Oh Lord, send a revival," sung in English, Billy and his six friends "stood there in wonder and amazement that we were in the place God had brought us, in a place where people who had prayed and, in such simple faith, knew Billy was going to be there; and God had answered their prayer." The football field looked like a vast multicolored flower bed. Each tribe, and the interpreter waiting in front, wore its distinctively colored shawl. Behind the terraces were cherry trees in bloom and then the jungle-green hills.

Robert Cunville stepped forward. "Let us all give thanks to God." Cliff Barrows had never heard tribal praying before. "It was as if a wave of ocean had broken about a hundred yards offshore and you heard them way in the back begin to pray. Then it swept toward you as others joined in vocally and it got to the platform and it swept over us and we began to pray out loud to God and the choir joined in. For five minutes there was an anthem of praise going up to God."

---

[1] The full message painted on the arch read "Welcome to the Billy Graham Kohima Crusade, Jesus Christ the Hope of the World."

No one present could forget the joy of the tribal people that day. Tedd Smith was astonished to find a grand piano, a little battered and elderly but finely tuned, on the platform at so remote a place. He saw "the eagerness as they listened" to him and to his music, and then to Archie Dennis singing and to Billy Graham preaching. "The joy and peace that their faces portrayed will be indelibly etched in my memory." The delays and uncertainties had created immense expectancy. As Cunville puts it, "God in his own way had tested us and had intensified the spiritual tempo of the Kohima Crusade. We have never before experienced such Spirit-filled meetings in northeast India." Longri Ao adds, "Everybody in the crowd felt the presence of the Spirit of God. The fellowship was deeply warm," not least because the tribal people recognized gratefully the Team's risk in coming.

When Billy Graham stepped to the podium an Angami stood beside him to interpret the sermon to the Angamis, who naturally formed the largest sector. On the field, nineteen other interpreters stood ready with megaphones or bullhorns. Billy spoke his opening sentence. There was a moment of dead silence, then a babel of sound as all the interpreters shouted at once, each in his own tongue. The sound stopped, Billy spoke another sentence, "and then the stadium was alive with the sound of the translations," recalls Cliff, "and for an hour that's the way the message went." From the platform it sounded cacophonous. But the human ear is very selective and each language group, whether from Nagaland, Sikkim, Manipur or points between, quickly forgot the other sounds as they listened to their own language. It was the Day of Pentecost, with a difference.

Billy Graham had learned early in his ministry the art of preaching through an interpreter. It had been taught him by the founder of the People's Church in Toronto, Oswald J. Smith, as they had traveled by Swiss train in August 1948 to a world conference at Beatenberg. Smith had used his method since 1924 in Russia, Latvia and Germany: very short sentences and no illustrations. Graham developed that skill, including however a use of simple illustrations. In December 1961 Billy had demonstrated this method to President Kennedy, who was then going to South America. Kennedy thereupon said he would drop the state department's recommendation of translation paragraph by paragraph. He used Billy's way (and Oswald Smith's) in his famous speech at the Berlin Wall.

At Kohima Billy Graham's sentences had to be direct, short and simple. One difference from his usual practice was his exclusion of humor and funny stories. The Nagas are a merry race with a great sense of humor but never in the pulpit. When Billy had asked Longri Ao's advice on the plane, Longri had replied, "When you are wrestling for the souls of men, how can you make it light? You must not be humorous; be very serious. Souls are dying and at all costs they must be saved."

Even Longri was not prepared for the astonishing response at the end of the sermon. Billy invited those who wished to decide for Christ to stand up, and nearly everyone stood. The next night he made precisely plain what he meant. He concluded, "If you've never trusted Christ before, if you've never asked Him to come into your life and into your heart, stand now in your section." Cliff Barrows, profoundly moved, watched as "hundreds of people, quietly, cautiously and carefully, stood." Counselors in each language, with materials printed for inquirers who could read, moved in. Those 269 counselors were not enough for the 838 decisions registered that night. In addition, many inquirers who were illiterate never had their cards filled in.

Billy Graham nearly froze in bed in the unheated state guest house at 5,000 feet, although the Nagas brought him three hot water bottles and he slept in most of his clothes. At least he had hot water in the shower whereas T. W. Wilson next door had to force himself under a cold shower, supplemented by a pail of piping hot water. He calmed his chattering teeth with the thought of his high privilege to be in Nagaland at all, and at such a time.

All the Team were impressed by the spirit of their Naga hosts. Barrows and Riggs were allotted a young man who lit their fire and insisted on shining their shoes. They learned he was Nihulie Angami, principal of Kohima Bible College. This was the man who had given the sermon at the crusade on Sunday morning before their arrival, on the theme of the lordship of Christ. Tedd Smith's memory of Nagaland hospitality, as of the crusade meetings, is of "faces that mirrored love, concern, kindness and selflessness on a level that I suppose I'll never see again. I don't think I've ever been with such gentle people." Billy Graham, moving among the chief men of church and state, recalls their "outstanding, dedicated evangelical leadership. . . . Men like Longri Ao impressed me tremendously." So did the stewardship of the tribal people. A collection for the Nagaland missionary movement totaled more than 12,000 rupees.

Security required that apart from a visit to the War Memorial, Graham's movements be narrowed to the route between the crusade ground and the state guest house. It was there that church leaders of northeast India conferred with him. "He seemed to be a very humble person," recalls the only woman, "and that impressed me very much." He was unable to address any special meeting for youth, and the ordinary people could not get near him, to their and his mutual regret.

On Tuesday morning when Graham and the Team were back on the platform for a Bible study hour with a congregation nearly as numerous as at night and hungry for teaching (most of them would have listened to a two- or three-hour sermon, had Billy's strength allowed it), an incident occurred that passed into the folklore of northeast India. The crusade leaders had received many requests from relatives of sick, wounded or dying persons that Billy should pray for them individually, and therefore had put out a big box for names, including those of "the sorrowful and the oppressed and sin-laden." They brought this box, full of slips of paper, to Graham. He was somewhat surprised though moved. He emphasized to the crowd that neither he nor prayer in itself had magic power. God heals, or does not heal, according to his will. Then he prayed publicly over the box while all the multitude joined silently.

Longri Ao ("I believe in miracles") and the committee made no inquiries. Months later in a village in the state of Manipur a retired Army captain came running to Robert Cunville to tell how he had put in the box the name of his nine-year-old epileptic nephew, "and from that day," Cunville wrote to Graham on 17 April 1973, "this boy was completely healed." Cunville gave three other examples. A Shillong woman too sick to travel to Kohima asked her husband to carry one of her dresses. He placed her name in the box and held the dress as Billy and the crowd prayed. He returned to Shillong to find his wife well.[2]

"Old Pastor Bendang of the Ao Church at Kohima got TB and became so bad he had to give up his pastorate and live near Dimapur.

---

[2] *Mrs. Glacefield Rosebud Jones:* TB and suspected appendicitis; surgery had already been scheduled. She left the hospital without needing it, and is living in good health in Shillong.

In November 1972 he was very ill; he could hardly eat. They brought him by jeep to Kohima and his name also was in the prayer box. From that day he has been eating well, and his health is so much improved that just a few days ago he was asked to be pastor of another church.[3] Brother Mhasi must have written to you about the wife of a pastor in a village near Kohima. Her family were waiting for her death; they were feeding her only with liquid. After that prayer she recovered completely.[4] In the same village a man suffering from tetanus and waiting for death was healed. *The miracle of Kohima continues*—praise His name and thank God for you, Billy."

The plane schedule for Thursday, when the Team's permits would expire, involved a 3:30 A.M. start from Kohima and an eight-hour drive to Imphal. The committee hoped the government of India might allow a stay until Friday's more convenient plane, since requests for helicopters had been rejected. That would, in effect, extend the crusade by a day. But during Wednesday morning's Bible hour loud gunfire shattered the peace. Graham called to the crowd to stay calm; not a soul moved. An innocent Konyak man, in Kohima for the crusade, had been killed by the fire of whatever extremist group again broke the truce. Later, troops and rebels clashed fatally at two or three places down the Dimapur road as the people were leaving at the end of the service, creating tension and concern.

New Delhi, learning of the incidents by radio, refused to extend the Team's permits. The early start, the tedious drive, seemed inevitable, but the crusade committee "felt ashamed to have to send off our beloved friends in this way; and so with prayer we placed another request for one helicopter for Dr. Graham. Unofficial sources indicated that this would be impossible, but we knew God who has overruled in all things so far will yet do another miracle."

The crusade, then, had to close that Wednesday afternoon. An estimated 115,000 squeezed into the football ground, thousands stood outside in the undulating ground above and below, and more would have come had not the curfew restricted eleven neighboring villages;

---

[3] *Pastor Bendang Ao:* Now pastoring a church in Kohima, March 1976.

[4] *Mrs. Kopralie,* wife of a pastor of Jakhama village, who had been kept alive by oxygen; she was found to be healed that same morning and subsequently left the hospital. Now living in good health, March 1976.

the shooting incidents had sharpened the Nagas' hunger for peace, for worship and teaching. Animists came by the hundred, impressed by the atmosphere of the past week, and so did Hindus from other parts of India who served in Nagaland, expressing their amazement at the peacefulness of so great a crowd, day after day.

Billy Graham preached from Luke 15 on the lost sheep, the lost coin and the lost son. Sentence by short sentence, as the hot sun bore down (no one put up an umbrella lest it block the view of those behind) his words were interpreted. "The Bible says, 'There is pleasure in sin for a short time' . . . Soon it becomes sour and empty . . . The sinner becomes restless and feels the loneliness of sin . . . One may look quite happy outside, but something can be missing in the heart . . . Man is made in God's image so there will be fellowship . . . But sin breaks the relationship. . . ." As he closed, Graham said again, "God is searching for you tonight, so you can repent of your sin, and be willing to give up all sins. He wants you to receive Jesus, and serve Him as you go back home."

The tribal people could not bear to let Billy go. While hundreds were being counseled, the people rushed toward him to touch his clothes or to have a closer view of his face, or simply to say thank you.

The last engagement was a farewell reception at the chief minister's home with its motto, "Christ is the Head of this house." "It is our custom to sing a hymn before meat," said the chief minister, announcing "My hope is built on nothing less than Jesus' blood and righteousness." After the hymn came dog-meat hors d'œuvres and among the main dishes were fried hornets. The sight turned American stomachs queasy as the host offered the dish. "This is royal food, the delicacy of chiefs." Only the valor of Billy, standing under a merciless movie camera, gave the others courage, fortified by prayer, to put spoon to mouth. But when they tasted fried hornets they voted them delicious, and Archie came back for a second helping. To top the pleasure of the evening a radio message came from New Delhi that helicopters, not merely one but two, for all the Team, would arrive the next morning.

Billy Graham flew from Kohima on Thanksgiving Day 1972 for his private interview at New Delhi with the prime minister, Mrs. Indira Gandhi, and westward to Iran for a private audience with the Shah. In two and a half days in remote Nagaland he had preached to more people than at any equivalent period in his ministry—though this record would be broken six months later in Korea.

He had made, in the words of a senior government official, "a tremendous impact on the minds of the people." Some 4,000 persons had recorded decisions for Christ, many more than expected, yet the crusade services were only the start of a revival which flamed across Nagaland. "They returned rejoicing to their villages," said Longri Ao two years later. "They returned different, completely changed men and women." In the official report of the Baptist Church in 1974 he wrote of his findings: "Dr. Billy Graham's coming to Kohima and preaching the Word of God changed thousands of lives and awakened the churches. As a result of this, every year several thousand people find Christ in this land. Many spirit-worshipers among our people have recently accepted Christ as their Lord and Savior. Men who had taken scores of heads in village raids were converted. . . ." These headhunters, whose names in their youth "were a terror among their own people" and had clung to their old religion, now had "become soul-winners."

The church leaders of Nagaland and northeast India who had organized the crusade were themselves profoundly affected. It taught some "that under any circumstances we should not turn back if God is making use of us." Others found a new desire to reach Hindus instead of despising them. Some planned to go out as missionaries.

Robert Cunville had been so impressed by the events leading to Graham's arrival in Nagaland "that I began to question my calling. But the preparation was just a prelude to the time I met Dr. Graham. Then my whole thrust in life changed, to saving souls rather than just trying to 'give a cup of cold water.' I had had enough of the 'wisdom of this world,' the social gospel. I'm no longer comfortable with anything except the real Great Commission of Jesus Christ." Shortly afterward, Cunville went to the School of World Mission of Fuller Theological Seminary at Pasadena, California, on a scholarship provided by BGEA. In 1975, after earning his doctorate, he returned to India as an evangelist.

The crusade became a decisive factor in bringing peace to Nagaland at last. Force of arms, as a way to fulfillment for the Naga people, looked less desirable now. The crusade theme, "Christ the Hope of the World," pointed to a better way of absorbing tribal energies. Support thus slackened for the hard-core underground as hundreds of hostiles surrendered their arms in the following months. Politicians began to recognize that if they believed in the Prince of Peace they should work out a peaceful solution. Others abandoned plans to seek an alliance with atheist China, though groups of young men still slipped across the border for training.

The former governor, B. K. Nehru, afterward high commissioner in London, doubts whether Billy Graham's coming had an effect on the insurgency either one way or the other, but among Nagaland Christians the crusade is regarded as a turning point. The way to peace proved slow and hard with many setbacks, but at length, in November 1975, three years later, the Shillong Agreement (in which Longri Ao played an important part) virtually ended the Naga rebellion. As a result, 1976 and 1977 became more than ever years of revival.

3 Black and White Together

UNTIL a crusade audience could be racially integrated Billy Graham refused to preach in South Africa. When the opening came at last in 1973 it was made by a man whose Christian dedication and service owed much to Graham's own ministry, Michael Cassidy. Cassidy was born in Johannesburg in 1936, son of a British engineer and his South African wife. His parents had met in Mafeking during the siege.

As a boy at Michaelhouse, the leading private school of Natal, Cassidy was a mixture of hearty naughtiness and a confused religious devotion. He won a place at a Cambridge college and went to England, vaguely intending to be a lawyer or teacher. Within a few weeks an undergraduate friend who had "experienced a very dramatic and profound conversion" during Graham's Harringay crusade the previous year, and knew that Michael wished to join the Christian Union, asked him if he had ever surrendered to Christ. "He had struck my Achilles' heel: that was the one step I had resisted through all my teen-age years." Before they left the room "We knelt in a simple act of faith and I invited Christ into my life. That very day I became aware of his presence." Almost immediately Michael Cassidy saw South Africa's problems in a different light.

A week or two later, in November 1955, Billy Graham came to Cambridge for a mission to the university. "Dr. Graham's message went home deeply to my soul and I had a new hero," relates Cassidy, who had now determined to devote himself to Christ and to Africa. When later he used part of a legacy to visit relatives in New York he found Graham's 1957 crusade in progress at the old Madison Square Garden. "I remember one night pacing up and down the corridors which flanked the arena. The meeting was over. Hundreds were being counseled. I had seen God at work in a wonderful way as the Spirit honored the proclaimed Word. I was seeing mass evangelism. Suddenly I found myself saying, 'Why not in Africa?' From that moment my calling was clear."

Cassidy entered Fuller Theological Seminary in Pasadena, California, and there, through his vision and Charles E. Fuller's generosity and guidance, Africa Enterprise was born, a small multiracial, international team of evangelists.

By 1971 Michael Cassidy at thirty-five had won recognition in South Africa and beyond as a lay evangelist who was at home in African locations, in white private schools, in cities and suburbs. He had joined forces, too, with Bishop Festo Kivengere, the noted Ugandan evangelist. Kivengere was a product of the East African Revival and the friend and occasional colleague of Billy Graham.

Michael Cassidy, an engaging personality with plenty of humor, had proved himself a builder of bridges between South African Christians of differing races and denominations. He had faced the complex racial situation, recognizing both the fundamental injustice of South Africa's policy of separate development for blacks and the absence of easy solutions. He ploughed rather a lonely furrow, since those Christians who were most vocally opposed to apartheid looked with scorn or suspicion on evangelism. White evangelicals, on the other hand, both the smaller English-speaking groups and the powerful Dutch Reformed Church, tended to accept apartheid however much they might hope to soften it. Cassidy's frank paper on "The Ethics of Political Nationalism" to the World Congress of Evangelism at Berlin in 1966 had seriously upset delegates who were members of the Dutch Reformed Church.

Four years after Berlin, Michael Cassidy had a vision for a Congress of Mission and Evangelism in South Africa. Recent chinks in the armor of apartheid led him to believe that this could be interracial on a scale not seen for many years. Soon a committee which included staunch evangelicals and representatives of the South African Council of

Churches, and which aimed to involve all major churches and smaller groups, had begun to plan it for 1973 at Durban.

When Cassidy was briefly in the United States he told Billy Graham about the forthcoming Congress. Billy said, "I would be open to coming out, if you'd have me." "If we'd have you, Billy," Michael exclaimed. "We never dreamed you might be available."

Michael wrote to Walter Smyth on 9 February 1972. "I cannot overstress how important Billy's involvement in the Congress could be for the country at this time. . . . you cannot imagine how much we would be encouraged." A few days later, however, the committee rejected an invitation to Graham by eight votes to seven. The "noes" feared that a man of such stature would dominate the Congress; the public might suppose they looked to him to solve South Africa's problems. (As the saying goes, "South Africa's savior won't come in a jumbo-jet.") Every black had voted for Graham to be invited, and as the committee members scattered to their homes several felt the decision to be wrong. John Rees, secretary of the South African Council of Churches (SACC) thereupon telephoned church leaders including the Anglican archbishop, who unanimously pressed the invitation to Billy Graham. In due course the committee reversed their vote and changed the date to suit him.

Graham insisted, "We will come only if it is clearly interracial and integrated. If I am asked point-blank whether I agree with apartheid or not, my Christian conscience will force me to say, 'No, I do not agree with apartheid.' "

The Congress would be integrated. Anglican synods and some similar meetings had continued to be interracial under apartheid but this Durban Congress would draw denominations and the varied races together. As John Rees assured Graham, "for the first time it will be multiracial in the fullest meaning of that word. We will be quartered together in one hotel, sharing, eating, living, experiencing together. This in itself is a milestone in the history of the South African Church." Cassidy looked forward to an almost unprecedented opportunity for Graham "to speak a strong Biblical and evangelical word into the major church power structures of an entire country." The Dutch Reformed Church, however, refused to come in officially, though individual members would attend.

Graham did not intend to get involved in politics. He would declare the gospel and talk on evangelism. Nor did he intend, because of a heavy schedule in that year of indifferent health, to remain throughout. "I think just two or three days would be sufficient," he told Walter Smyth on 9 August 1972, seven months before the Congress—significant evidence that his early departure was not precipitate, for one reason or another, as has been sometimes asserted since.

Graham had no plans to preach at crusade-style meetings in South Africa, until in September Cassidy suggested that an afternoon rally, on the Saturday of the Congress week, would "be a glorious and unprecedented act of witness for this country. People would come from all over to hear you, and the impact of the Congress would be multiplied a hundredfold around the country, even by that one meeting. If you approve in principle I am sure we can work it as a fully interracial occasion." There had been integrated rallies before, but nothing on the scale envisaged for King's Park rugby football stadium. Graham replied that he would be delighted to preach "if in fact it is interracial."

He and Walter Smyth were aware of some disquiet among the more conservative evangelicals lest the Congress might be theologically too "liberal." On 11 January 1973, therefore, after correspondence with Cassidy, Smyth wrote to Graham who was in the Mayo Clinic hoping to get fit enough for the South African visit. "As you know, I'm the last one to suggest additional engagements but if you decide to go to South Africa, I feel it would be significant to have a public rally—either Capetown or Johannesburg—sponsored by Youth for Christ either just before the Congress or right afterward."

Billy agreed, and the vigorous Southern Africa Youth for Christ leaped at the opportunity. Johannesburg was chosen. Time being short, a conference of 200 ministers and lay leaders willingly agreed to YFC staff's coordinating the arrangements. Their president, atomic energy scientist Louw Alberts, had already secured government consent to a fully integrated interracial rally on Sunday 25 March.

The Presbyterian structure of the Dutch Reformed Church enabled congregations to act without formal decision by church synod, and they began preparing at once. Still, some of the Durban organizers feared lest this Johannesburg rally should overshadow theirs, weakening the impact of the Congress on South Africa.

It was a unique situation for Billy Graham, and one that reflected the tensions within South African Christianity: he was being sponsored by two groups that mistrusted one another. The Durban people felt that the DRC and Youth for Christ were too content to evangelize all groups without challenging (as an African theologian puts it) "the heresy behind the system of dividing the races." The Johannesburg people were nervous about a Congress with such breadth of theological, political and racial outlook. This nervousness actually led to the absurdity of their attempting to suppress, by professionally sticking together the offending pages, the Congress information which they had agreed to insert in the Johannesburg rally program. It was a self-defeating ploy, since the day was hot and human nature is inquisitive.

Nevertheless Billy's decision to preach at both Johannesburg and Durban insured him in effect the sponsorship of the entire non-Roman church; and as events turned out, his impact on South Africa's future was far greater than if he had gone only to either.

The Johannesburg venture was rapidly getting the name of "the miracle rally." Wanderers cricket ground, the only arena of sufficient size, proved to be vacant that year on only one day, the day required. Further, the cricket club broke a hallowed rule and agreed to allow use of the turf, thus doubling the stadium's capacity. The Christian musical group with the highest standard, who traveled all over South Africa on a tight schedule arranged months earlier, was due in Johannesburg that weekend. Two famous sportsmen, Gary Player the golfer and Trevor Goddard the Test cricketer (who would also speak at the Congress), acted as press officers. In the words of Dennis House, the rally's director and YFC's secretary, "Never before had a religious speaker the sort of publicity that Mr. Graham was to enjoy in the coming weeks." The South African Broadcasting Commission offered a one-hour nationwide live broadcast of the rally on radio (television was still two years away) which would give unprecedented opportunity to a foreign preacher.

Hard work and use of the methods developed by the Billy Graham Team offset the shortage of time. Thus Dr. Jan Malan of the Dutch Reformed Church and his wife, Gabrielle, translated the counseling material into Afrikaans and trained some 350 men and women on three successive Sunday afternoons. "The Afrikaans people can all speak English, but you can never reach the heart and soul of anybody if you don't speak his or her language. . . . we thought very highly of the material." Altogether nearly 3,000 counselors were trained, using ten languages.

Down in Natal the same principles were followed, with the advantage of six months in which to make ready. Whites, Indians and Zulus were all involved, the Zulu preparations being led by Ebenezer Sikakane, an African Enterprise evangelist. Africans trusted Billy Graham because of his clear stand on the race issue. As Sikakane went around week by week to teach the classes of committed Christians he found them "absolutely excited," profiting from the lessons and already talking to their friends about the coming rally at King's Park.

One important preparation for the Durban crusade was the chain of integrated prayer meetings in homes throughout the area. Mildred Dienert from Philadelphia, wife of Fred Dienert, whose company sets up the Billy Graham telecasts and handles the Hour of Decision, had visited Durban. She travels all over the world, especially where a crusade is being prepared, to alert women to the importance and possibilities of prayer.[1] Compared with London, Tokyo, Sydney and many cities where Mildred Dienert had been, Durban was small, the crusade was to be a single rally and she did not expect a surprising result. But the crusade committee chairman invited Jean Goddard, wife of Trevor Goddard the Test cricketer, to be women's prayer coordinator. Although she had been a committed Christian for only a short time, her enthusiasm led to no less than 600 homes being opened for prayer. It was estimated that a total of between 5,000 and 7,000 women prayed regularly together in groups for the crusade, a very substantial figure for the area. No less important, most of the 600 groups continued to meet, receiving and nurturing converts from the King's Park Rally.

Then Jean Goddard founded a chain of women's prayer groups across South Africa to prepare for the Lausanne International Congress on World Evangelization in 1974. In 1976 she died of cancer, but by 1978 it could be estimated that between 340,000 and 370,000 women of all races in South Africa were meeting regularly in prayer groups which had their remote origin in her work in Durban five years before.

---

[1] For the origin and development of the women's crusade prayer program, see chapter 9.

On the lovely late summer afternoon of Saturday 17 March 1973 Ebenezer Sikakane and his wife drove toward King's Park, the Indian Ocean a deep blue in front of them. They could hardly believe their eyes as they watched the stream of buses, cars and crowds on foot, moving toward the stadium. It was a familiar scene in different parts of the world to Team members, but this was a rally with a difference. It was multiracial in a segregated land. Ebenezer, a Zulu, stood inside the stadium amazed, not simply by the people pouring in, but at white ushers showing blacks into seats, and blacks leading whites, and all sitting anywhere, not in separate stands—with Africans and Indians relegated to the worst. Ebenezer and other Zulus could not keep back the tears. "Even if Billy Graham doesn't stand up to preach, this has been enough of a testimony."

A crippled Indian entered, supported by an African and a white. A white pastor noticed, with a start, a black mother and child offer sandwiches to a white woman, who accepted as if it were the most natural action on both sides. So quiet and good-natured was the crowd that the police dogs, usually needed to separate brawlers when different races came in big numbers to a stadium, were soon returned to the vans. The police kept out of sight themselves, the absence of uniforms being particularly remarked on by the Africans, Indians and Coloreds. Apartheid had even been lifted from the toilets.

The friendliness of the races, their discovery of each other as being equally first-class citizens made a startling impact on Durban, especially because of the immense size of the integrated rally, spreading onto the grass of the rugby ground, leaving only an area for counseling. Left-wing theologians who dismissed Billy's sermon were nonetheless deeply affected, recognizing that only he could have brought it together in the South Africa of 1973. A Natal Indian photographer said to the American black, Howard Jones, who was one of three Team members at the Congress, "I never thought I would live to see this." Bishop Alpheus Zulu, a president of the World Council of Churches, said afterward, "The sight of black and white South Africa together in that field, singing and praying to the one God, was a foretaste of what future generations in this land are certain to enjoy if we today will be faithful."

One problem needed delicate handling. The committee had arranged simultaneous translation into Zulu to be beamed to a section of the stands. But to direct Zulus to a particular place would seem like segregation. The crusade director therefore announced over the amplifiers that Zulus not understanding English were welcome to move to that area.

Another announcement, during the service itself, inadvertently produced a furor some weeks afterward. In the Indian quarter of Durban the market had burned down the day before the rally. The mayor announced a relief fund, and the Congress had a collection. Billy Graham paid a visit to the site of the fire and prayed publicly for those who had suffered, promising to send a donation when he returned to the United States. At the rally the chairman, Noel Hudson, expressed sympathy, but no mention of the fire came in the treasurer's statement announcing the offering to be made for rally expenses. Yet the mayor of Durban, who had warmly welcomed the Congress and sat on the rally platform, somehow supposed that the offering was going to the market. On learning a week or two later what a modest sum (the Congress's collection plus a few public donations handed in at the rally) had reached his fund, he bitterly criticized Graham to the press. When confronted by the facts the mayor made a gracious public apology. Such is the spread of myth, however, that at least one transatlantic paper asserted that "a primary function" of the rally was to raise money for this relief (as if such a rally could be promoted overnight) and that Graham had turned over a mere $130 of the $13,000 he collected. The paper called it "Doing Well by Doing Good."

That brief storm belonged to the future. The outstanding moment of the rally's preliminaries came when the young Ghanaian evangelical leader John Gatu brought greetings from black Africa to all races in the Republic.

Billy's sermon was like sermons he had preached all over the world —in its almost artless simplicity, its breadth of elementary exposition about Jesus from his birth to the Cross and Resurrection and coming judgment. "One heard the whole range of preaching of the early Christians," a British theologian commented. "It was a simple straightforward message of the gospel," recalled the Zulu interpreter eighteen months later, "and made a tremendous impact. Even now when people meet me they remember what he said."

Billy's words touched the condition and hopes of blacks, browns and whites. Without ever mentioning apartheid or making a direct political point he rendered the whole concept impossible, as the applause showed when he emphasized, "We are all one in Christ Jesus." Different points of the sermon reached different people. One woman, who had recognized herself only too clearly as he spoke of human sin, heard him say how 10,000 angels had waited to rescue Jesus from the Cross if only he had given the word. She said to herself, "That's it. I cannot resist him now, I'll go forward."

The sermon held little for many of the theologians attending the Congress. Listening at the back of a stand, John De Gruchy of the University of Cape Town had expected great preaching. As Billy invited those who wanted to know Jesus as Savior and Lord to come forward in public confession ("Don't come unless the Spirit of God is speaking to you; but if God is speaking to you, you get up and come"), John De Gruchy turned to John Rees and said, "Well John, let's see if anything can happen. I must confess I'm a little skeptical." De Gruchy recalls, "And then I was totally flabbergasted by what happened."

Bishop Bill Burnett, soon to be archbishop of Cape Town, who was serving as an usher, recalls that the sermon "didn't come anywhere near me. But then he wasn't talking to me. What he had to say left me totally untouched. I was absolutely astounded when I saw how many people came forward to be counseled, because the way I was feeling, nobody would have moved." Michael Cassidy had seen great response in New York and Los Angeles, "but in conservative South Africa? My thought was scarcely formulated when I stood to my feet incredulous. A sea of humanity was surging toward the platform like a tidal wave. The whole stadium seemed to be moving."

"I can't remember what Billy said," records Nan Hopkins, a doctor's wife from Pietermaritzburg who had been seeking God for months. "I do know that when he gave his invitation to come forward, I was amazed that anyone remained seated. I felt everyone would feel as I did, that they wanted to be counted for Jesus Christ. Mind you, I remember hoping that none of my friends would see me and go home and tell my husband, but it didn't stop me going. I remember, too, the smile of an African man when our eyes met together in Christian fellowship." It was the start of a whole family's Christian pilgrimage.

Another Pietermaritzburg woman, who with her husband saw their two teen-age daughters go forward, also found it inconceivable that anybody could have remained unmoved by Billy's message. "My spirit just soared as he spoke about Jesus, and I experienced a real regeneration." Nan Hopkins afterward met many who remained unmoved, and she concludes that a hearer's previous preparation is a key to response. The sermon, however, may bring to a climax a spiritual search that has been entirely unconscious, or may bring a sudden awareness of spiritual hunger or of divine judgment.

Rally organizers had expected about 1,600 people to come forward —the usual proportion, by Team experience at that period, for that size of audience. But more than 4,000 were on the move, quietly, without hysteria or cryings out, and without pressure from Billy. That response not only amazed South Africa but disrupted counseling plans. Having trained too few, the organizers were overwhelmed. Many inquirers received follow-up literature and had their card filled out but were not properly counseled. Others would gather around a counselor in groups of two or three. Many blacks counseled whites. One white who had a black counselor devoted his life subsequently to work among Africans. Indians especially came forward in large numbers.

The rally dispersed with a quietness very different from the dispersal of a Durban rugby football crowd. The follow-up processing should have begun in the orderly manner laid down in Graham Team manuals. Instead, it would have collapsed had not a retired businessman offered his services to the rally chairman.

While the work began of referring inquirers to churches, and Durban's Sunday newspapers featured the rally with headlines such as "Apartheid Doomed," Billy Graham attended a Zulu church service in the company of Bishop Zulu and was touched by the warmth of welcome.

On Monday he addressed the Congress. Despite the spontaneous standing ovation, many were disappointed. Some, from the more Catholic wing, felt hit over the head with a blunt instrument (partly because the sound was turned up too high in the Methodist church used as Congress auditorium). Some felt it a powerful, enjoyable message but incomplete. Blacks had hoped that Billy Graham would highlight the issues of evangelism in an apartheid society, but Billy was a guest of all races, including Afrikaners. Whatever his strong private feelings, his public words would ring round the land: he was to some extent a prisoner of his fame. He knew, too, that South Africans whatever their color resent being lectured at by foreigners possessing no more than a superficial acquaintance with their problems. Billy made his attitude to the system plain by implication, whereas Leighton Ford, less famous, could speak to the burning issues in a forthright manner which gave his Congress addresses memorable force. Ford and Graham represented a joint united standpoint; without in the least having directed Ford's words, Graham said through him and Howard Jones, who as a black had previous personal experience of apartheid, what he could not say himself.

Having spoken, Graham vanished, to the frustration of many of the Africans and others who had hoped for open discussion with him during the remainder of the Congress. Feeling unwell, he needed a full day's rest before the exacting Johannesburg press conference. Delegates laid the blame on this, unaware that months before any Johannesburg program was arranged, Billy had planned to leave Durban on the day he did. On the other hand some who disliked the Congress affirmed that he removed himself early because of disquiet. They were wrong. "There was nothing about the Durban Congress that I was unhappy about," he states.

His early departure "left an acute sense of vacuum and frustration," Cassidy says, and precipitated a sharp debate between African delegates and the rest, so that in a sense Graham dominated the Congress by his absence more than by his words. Nevertheless many South Africans hold that he "made a great mistake" in not staying longer in Durban.

The Durban rally had created such an impression that the press and radio in Johannesburg bombarded the rally offices for the time of Graham's arrival. Billy and T. W. Wilson flew in surreptitiously, even Walter Smyth and Dennis House of YFC not knowing about their arrival until T. W. called from the hotel.

Billy had two important meetings with the press. One was a private discussion over morning tea with a powerful Afrikaner newspaper's managing director, a man who had been nettled by Billy's public disapproval of apartheid. Billy listened carefully and said, "I was greatly impressed with him; a great many of his views were far more progressive than I had been led to believe." This Afrikaner was one of many who recognized that social change had to come but wished for a smooth transition, slow enough to avoid the violence which had made millions in other parts of the world miserable. The Afrikaner, equally impressed with Graham, afterward told his friends he was a Billy Graham fan and arranged for his paper to print the entire Wanderers sermon translated into Afrikaans.

At the public press conference Graham let slip a casual comment which passed almost unnoticed in South Africa but created in his own country a storm that almost blinded Americans to the good he had done by his visit.

The conference in a hot crowded room had put many questions to him, mostly on the racial issue. "The situation in South Africa," he had said in one of his answers, "is far more complicated than in America. I don't have the exact answer and the exact formula. I don't think anybody has. The people I have met are crying out to be treated with pure dignity. They don't want to be told that because they have a dark face they can't go here or there. Or that they get less pay for equal work. These are things we learned the hard way. We had to go through the strikes and demonstrations and cities burning, before we suddenly woke up to the fact that this was true. *Now, we have not solved our racial problems in America*—don't get me wrong. We're still finding our way. We're still searching. *We're no model.* But we have in action the finest civil rights laws in the history of the human race. And at least *legally*, we are on the right footing."

Toward the end the reporter of *The Star* asked his views on abortion. "Do you see it as the taking of human life?" "Yes, I do," replied Graham, but conceded that it might be justified after rape. As he spoke, his mind momentarily recalled a news item of the previous day. A twelve-year-old girl had been raped by a whole group, and an African chief had commented to him that in his tribe they castrated rapists. Graham, saying he was for the strongest laws against rape, added half-jokingly: "I think when a person is found guilty of rape he should be castrated. That would stop him pretty quick." The pressmen all laughed, Graham continued on the subject of abortion, and the questioner put a further question about mother and child.

Out of the corner of his eye Graham had noticed a sleepy British pressman rouse his pencil after the word "castrated." Graham "thought to myself, I better get back to that because I've put my foot in my mouth. I didn't get back to it, I forgot it." (Time was short as the conference had nearly finished.) Castration for rapists did not represent his considered view, though some years later an eminent British psychiatrist propounded it in *The Times* as the best therapy for compulsive rapists.

The remark received the barest notice from South African journalists, including the hostile writer in the *Rand Daily Mail* who sneered at Graham for most of his views and activities. In the U.S. it was widely publicized. A *Chicago Tribune* columnist even committed the journalist's heresy of jumping to conclusions without evidence and published a bitter, sarcastic piece on the assumption that Graham had been merely on a sightseeing tour of South Africa's beautiful scenery with blind disregard for the injustices suffered by the black majority.

This was one of the few occasions when Billy publicly answered criticism. He wrote a humble letter to the columnist, which set the record straight about the remark and about his work for the blacks in South Africa. The columnist gave Graham's piece full prominence in the *Chicago Tribune*.

All this, like the lesser furor over the Indian market, lay far in the future, a footnote to the page about to be written in Johannesburg's history that weekend of 25 March 1973.

Michael Cassidy spent much of the Saturday morning alone with Billy in the Johannesburg hotel, having come up from Durban at the close of the Congress. He recalls how as they discussed his message for Wanderers, "I got a tremendous sense of a man who really believed that it mattered to God what he said on any given occasion; who wanted to declare God's Word because, as he said, 'I will answer to God at the judgment for what I declare tomorrow.' I also realized afresh that morning how deeply Billy believed in the lostness of human beings without Christ. Often in the church we mouth these Biblical teachings but do not believe them deep in ourselves. I felt with Billy that he really believed, and it added a deep sense of urgency to his proclamation."

Billy had slept badly and felt unwell. Michael praised his own doctor's prescriptions and Billy asked to try them. That afternoon, at a private integrated reception at Gary Player's ranch outside Johannesburg, Michael slipped a packet into Billy's hand when no one was looking. Michael comments, "The thought of two evangelists talking about their respective stomach pains has never ceased to strike me as incongruous and comic." The reception was notable in itself; to invite both colors to a party was highly unusual. T. W. Wilson recalls, "We sensed a genuine friendship between the races."

The next afternoon, Sunday 25 March 1973, Wanderers cricket ground gave South Africa an experience similar to that of Durban's but on a greater scale. It had not been advertised as a multiracial meeting. Thus the multitude had all the stronger surprise at finding every stand, and the turf, open to anyone regardless of color, with large numbers of Africans despite the stadium's being on the far side of the city from Soweto, the main African township. Every race mingled freely under the bright sunshine. Dr. Alberts, who is positive that a large fraction of the audience was completely unchurched, comments, "That we could have a gathering of 60,000 people from all colors, kinds and tongues in the South African situation without any incidents was a tremendous testimony, a historical testimony, to the fact that when we meet before the Cross the other problems just become insignificant."

To get Billy to Wanderers fresh for his preaching the committee had a helicopter, but when the rendezvous was bungled he continued by car, slowly through the crush of traffic. Although he greatly enjoyed mixing with the colorful crowd, he arrived hot and weary, only to be taken in error straight to the platform. There he sat alone in the sun, jostled by delighted autograph hunters and well-wishers, while two hundred ministers and distinguished guests waited to greet him in a shady enclosure. His suit was not light enough for the heat, having been chosen with an eye to the color videotape being prepared for television in America and then as a film. Beyond that, the preliminary service was overlong.

While he was preaching he almost fainted, Billy recalls, "not only because of the heat but because of the press of the crowd. It was one of the most physically exhausting afternoons I have ever spent in the pulpit." People using binoculars from the distant seats could see the sweat pouring off him.

That day Billy Graham preached before the South African nation. Although SABC radio frequently transmitted from churches on regional programs, when the preacher could be called to account if his sermon offended the state, no preacher (and certainly no foreigner before Billy Graham) had received coast-to-coast facilities. The sermon was carried by the English service with full previous announcement on the Afrikaans. "That hour," says Dominie Schmidt, head of SABC's religious department, "most listeners to the radio in South Africa listened to Billy Graham. Their reaction was very, very favorable." Only the funerals of Smuts, the South African statesman, and Verwoerd, the assassinated prime minister, officially rated larger audiences.

In Wanderers itself the conclusion of Billy's sermon brought an immediate response. Here and there in the stands and on the turf people quietly rose to go forward. What at first seemed a sprinkle of individuals became a slow floodtide of humanity. The platform where Billy stood waiting, chin on hand in prayer, had been set in the center of a counseling circle, fifty yards wide, reached by aisles kept open between the massed listeners sitting on the turf in front of the packed-out stands. (The visual effect during the service was rather like green spokes of a huge stationary wheel, with the platform its hub. When the inquirers, pressing forward, had nearly filled the counseling space, and still came down the aisles in a great flow of all colors of face and clothing, it looked almost as if the wheel were turning.)

Stadiums in many parts of the world had seen similar sights at Graham crusades but this day was different. Separated peoples, from every race in South Africa, mingled. The fear that lies at the root of apartheid was lost at the foot of the Cross. "For the first time in our lives," says Mrs. Sue Moll, a veterinary surgeon's wife who had organized a party of a hundred to travel in buses a day and a night from Cape Town, "we witnessed the mass movement of the Holy Spirit in men and women and children of all colors and creeds. God the equalizer, before whom every knee shall bow, was there in action."

After his usual brief word to the inquirers Billy Graham left immediately for the airport. Behind him, packed tight in the area round the platform, less than 3,000 counselors helped more than 4,000 people who had streamed to the front. Among the counselors Trevor Goddard, the former Springbok captain, was especially happy to bring someone to Christ on the turf where he had won his cricketing fame.

As in other crusades, the South African rallies at Durban and Johannesburg brought thousands into firm faith—especially, in that country of widespread churchgoing, younger people, who had considerable knowledge of religion but had lacked commitment to Christ. Jan

Malan, leader of the Dutch Reformed Church's youth work, could say eighteen months later that the follow-up had found "many, long after Billy Graham had left, who referred back to that day as the day when they really made their final decision." Christians were strengthened, like the shy Afrikaner girl who counseled for the first time in her life at Wanderers. The following month during the South African games in Johannesburg she was able to join the teams of 300 teen-agers who undertook street evangelism. Zulu students went back from the Durban rally to their school outside Pietermaritzburg, "and the whole school was really gripped by revival," says a Zulu evangelist. Hundreds enrolled in Bible correspondence courses, tapes of the messages sold out, the film of Wanderers was shown all over the land.

Yet those South African rallies hold a special niche in history for their contribution to racial reconciliation. "Apartheid gets three knock-out blows from Govt.," ran the banner headline on the 8 May 1973 issue of *Drum,* the Johannesburg African magazine (the third blow being the international games in April). South Africans of all social levels and all colors had a first taste of really large interracial gatherings and found it exhilarating. Billy Graham, through the opportunity given him by the people, churches, and government of South Africa, had helped forward the changes which must eventually come.

4 Land of Morning Calm

"DEAR Dr. Graham . . . I am writing a *most urgent letter*. For years the Korean churches have been praying for your coming here. We now feel *the appropriate time has come.* . . ."

Dr. Han, Kyung Chik,[1] the most respected Christian in the Republic of Korea, sat dictating in Seoul on 20 November 1970 in the vestry of Young Nak Presbyterian Church which he had formed in 1945 with twenty-seven refugees from the Communist North. In 1970 his church now had 12,000 members and an average Sunday morning attendance of 10,000 needing three services. Like many other churches in Seoul Young Nak held large early morning prayer meetings on weekdays and maintained a full program.

The "Land of Morning Calm"—with its beauty of mountains and valleys where the rice terraces climb high; its thrusting cities; its vigorous, polite and friendly people—had passed through great suffering during the half century that culminated in the Korean War. Suffering had deepened spiritual life. Since Protestant missionaries first set foot in Korea in 1884 the churches had become famous for their devotion, growth and vision, especially in the north before the Russians imposed the Communist regime. In the war of 1950-53 and its chaotic aftermath South Korea heard the Christian voice strongly. Christians

---

[1] Koreans write their surname first, followed by a comma and then their given names. Some, however, also use a Christian name in the western way: *e.g.*, The Rev. Cho, Dong Jin is also known as The Rev. David Cho.

formed a bare 10 percent statistically compared with the nominal predominance of Buddhism (many South Koreans admit no religious allegiance even if affected by Confucian ethics). Yet the Christian church doubled its membership every ten years, growing four times faster than the population.

Dr. Han held the affection and admiration of all, standing above the conflicts that obtruded between denominations and groups in the years after the war, and was recognized as a true man of God. He had interpreted in 1951 when Billy Graham, after visiting the American front-line troops, had addressed a large crowd of Koreans who stood in Pusan's bitter cold to hear him. "He was a young man at the time," recalls Dr. Han, "but he was full of spirit. He preached a wonderful sermon, simple but dynamic." At the Berlin Congress of Evangelism in 1966 Han and a group of Koreans had issued a formal invitation and then banded themselves to pray for Graham's return.

Thus in November 1970 Han was dictating, "If it is at all possible at this time of spiritual hunger in Korea we want you to come for two weeks. . . . A most interdenominational group met last night and were unanimous that we MOST URGENTLY ASK you to come. . . . In the Spirit of Christ, COME!"

Billy Graham replied, "As you know, I have a great love for Korea and would like very much to come." He suggested a date in 1972. His ill health caused postponement, but finally a crusade committee unanimously elected Dr. Han as chairman and began to plan for the spring of 1973. In six provincial cities a Graham associate would preach on six consecutive nights.[2] At the Koreans' request, the dates were to be staggered so that Billy might preach at the closing seventh night in each city. He accepted, but with some misgiving that his health might prevent him. For a climax, Billy Graham would hold a five-day crusade in Seoul, the world's eighth largest city.

The dates were set for 30 May to 2 June 1973. Later, all concerned believed that the year's delay had been providential. The churches were more united. The armed forces had experienced a revival and the reverent mass baptism of 4,378 soldiers.

---

[2] The choice was: *Pusan:* Grady Wilson; *Taegu:* John Wesley White; *Taejon:* Akbar Haqq; *Chonju:* Howard Jones; *Kwangju:* Ralph Bell; *Chunjon:* Cliff Barrows (Lane Adams, designated originally, but then took up appointment at First Presbyterian Church, Hollywood, before the crusade).

As crusade director, Walter Smyth appointed Henry Holley, a forty-five-year-old Texan, an ex-staff sergeant, U. S. Marine Corps, who had spent much of his twenty-three years' service in administration in the Far East. When stationed at Washington he had helped prepare Billy Graham's second Washington crusade, and his efficiency and spirituality led to an invitation to join the Team on his retirement from the Marines.

As Holley shared in the church life and traveled through a Korea lovely in fall colors, "I sensed from the beginning that God was going to do something significant in that country. It frightened me and it excited me." To Sherwood Wirt at *Decision* magazine Holley wrote on 9 October 1972, "Korea looks real good. God is moving in a wonderful way over there. This should be a great crusade, perhaps one of the largest Billy has had." Holley felt awed by the scale on which the Koreans planned. In a report to Walter Smyth he prophesied, "We may see the greatest ingathering of souls and the largest response—both attendance and inquirers—of any previous crusade. This could be the most significant event in the history of Christendom in the Far East." The Koreans worked in the spirit of their proverb, "Expect the unexpected, and in the unexpected, expect Christ."

It was to be a crusade planned by Koreans for Koreans. It would borrow Holley's experience but not be under his thumb. The crusade executive secretary, Mr. Oh, Chae Kyung, president of the Christian Broadcasting System, who had been a cabinet minister under both President Syngmann Rhee and President Park, was a masterful man of great decisiveness. Mr. Oh did not always appreciate that his countryman had asked for a particular form of mass evangelism, a Billy Graham crusade on principles developed over nearly twenty-five years. He had many ideas in conflict with Holley's, and both men tried one another's patience. Their American interpreter, Dr. Otto de Camp, recalls some of their discussions. "I was the ham in the sandwich. When the going got rough the ham got well browned on both sides!"

Henry would return to his own office "and pace around and bite his nails a little bit," recalls Carroll Hunt, a missionary who had been seconded to be Holley's secretary for liaison between the Team office and the Koreans' crusade office, "and he would say 'Well, let's pray.' Then he would call everybody together and we would have a time of prayer, and we turned the problems to the Lord. But that didn't mean to sit down and put your feet up and wait to see what happens. . . . I've never worked with anyone who was more conscious of detail and careful. He is a man of strong spiritual commitments" and, fortunately, a man who can laugh.

Holley tried to move sensitively in the rather rigidly stylized yet emotional relationships of Korean life. Tension rose, for instance, when the Koreans proposed fund-raising methods which the Graham Team could not encourage. A big explosion came after the chairman and secretary opened a letter from Smyth dated 16 February 1973, which stated that on the grounds of high blood pressure Graham's doctors had ordered him to curtail his schedule. To conserve sufficient strength for Seoul "We will have to cancel plans for his appearance in the other cities. I realize this will be a disappointment. . . ."

The three biggest cities were appalled. In Pusan, Taegu and Taejon, with a combined population of four million, outrage and anger swirled. Committees determined to cancel their entire crusades if Graham would not come. Holley cabled America: "Severe disappointment. Matter of chairman losing face because of previously announcing B.G. coming. . . . Situation critical." Mr. Oh wrote to emphasize "how deeply letdown both Christians and non-Christians in these cities feel," for as Dr. Kang, the interpreter designated for Pusan, commented in English: "Americans, they always follow medical doctor's way. But the Oriental, even though his health is a little bad, if we promise, then we should be there."

Since the doctors' decision could not be rescinded the storm died down and threats of cancellation were heard no more. The provincial chairmen, however, did not damage the anticipation of the people by any actual announcement that Graham would not appear.

Tensions served to strengthen the common will. Gradually deep trust and affection grew among Henry Holley, the Koreans, and the others, whatever their denomination, who actively prepared for the crusade.

Almost all Christians in South Korea were involved. Certain clergy in the Hop Dong branch of Presbyterians, affected by fundamentalists in America who boycott Billy Graham as a "compromiser," refused cooperation, although their laity swung strongly behind the crusade. The reaction of other clergy was expressed by a pastor in Pusan: "I had a troubled heart concerning some who refused to participate in the crusade. Their boycott seemed to ignore the fact that this crusade was not to push any particular position or denomination but called for our fullest cooperation."

Two large Presbyterian groups created by a split in 1959, who for thirteen years had declined to pray or act together, buried their animosities. In a strongly denominational though mainly Presbyterian land, barriers dropped. Dr. Han could state a year later: "It was really the first time that all the Christian people, not only in Seoul but also in a good many provincial towns, gathered together. In that sense, it was unique. When we knelt together we found we were all friends."

In the wide Ham River which marks the western edge of downtown Seoul lies the open space of Yoido island where, as it happened, Samuel Moffett the first missionary had landed long ago and was stoned. Yet one of the stone-throwers became a convert and was the first to go as a missionary to his own people. Yoido is linked to each bank by bridges carrying the main road to the airport. The island's chief feature is the new "May 16" People's Plaza, a long narrow paved runway, approximately one mile by 200 yards, formerly the famous "Quay 16" landing ground of the Korean War, and still of strategic importance for an emergency. Its use was confined to military parades and official rallies.

During Holley's fact-finding visit in the fall of 1972 the church leaders took him first to the National Stadium which they had tentatively booked. It seated only 25,000, however, with no standing or movement permitted on the turf, whereas the Koreans already were talking of 300,000 attending the crusade. Next they looked at the children's park on a nearby mountaintop, site of Easter sunrise services. Although this could absorb 80,000 people neither its shape nor location seemed suitable. Then Sam Choy, an American missionary from Hawaii and Holley's close friend, who would be his coordinator for the provinces, suggested a visit to Yoido island. Henry at once said, "This is where I believe God would have us."

Dr. Han gazed nervously at the vast expanse of a Plaza where, if estimates proved overoptimistic, a mere 100,000 people would seem like sparse attendance. Mr. Oh opposed strongly. Younger committeemen, however, grew excited, especially David Cho, an associate secretary of the crusade and chairman of the arrangements committee.

David Cho, born in a Christian home near the China border, at the age of nineteen had given himself to God after spiritual conflict lasting three days and three nights. He had escaped to the South in 1946. After seminary, as an independent evangelist, he was once reduced to such hardship that his wife sold her wedding ring to buy them food. In 1968 he founded the Korean International Mission which sends missionaries to other Asian countries. Now he is pastor of a Seoul Presbyterian church, his base for evangelistic tours abroad.

Argument continued through the winter. At length on a bitterly cold day in late February 1973 Cho invited the older leaders to accompany him to the Plaza. As they stood in a northern wind blowing straight from Siberian snows, David Cho asked the chairman to pray that "if the Lord is willing he will give us this Plaza to be the crusade place." Dr. Han prayed. Then in the spirit of God's promise to Joshua ("Every place that the sole of your foot shall tread upon, that have I given you"), they all walked, praying aloud and claiming that promise, the entire length of the Plaza.

Government officials were astonished when formally asked for Yoido Plaza, which theoretically could be used only for state-sponsored functions. Nonetheless, the Cabinet approved the request and leased it to the crusade for a nominal sum.

Cho went to work. The government intended to install a lighting system at some convenient time, but in March 1973 the place was not yet wired. Cho approached an elder of his church Mr. Hahn, Keysun, a Boston-trained acoustics expert who was chief engineer of the state broadcasting system, and handed him the problem of light and sound. Christians prayed, Hahn hustled, and one week before the crusade he switched on the arclights where all had been darkness. Hahn's sound system proved so effective that even those who on the last day of the crusade stood at the congregation's farthest edges, nearly half a mile from Billy Graham, could hear every word.

Cho installed water and erected more than 5,000 temporary toilets and washrooms. He built a platform and a stand for a 10,000-voice choir. He designed an ingenious marking system on the Plaza's asphalt, for crowd control and exact statistics (a matter that became of some importance). Every day he continued early morning prayer meetings at his church.

One vital decision still pended: who should interpret for Billy Graham?

Interpreting at mass meetings is a severe drain on anyone's physical and mental energy. Dr. Han declined because of age and his already heavy responsibilities. He suggested instead a man whom Holley already believed would be an outstanding interpreter: Billy Kim (Kim, Jang Whan). In the midst of directing several Christian enterprises along with his Baptist pastorate, Kim had offered Henry unstinted kindness, guidance and the benefit of his wide contacts with government.

Billy Kim, thirty-nine, was the youngest son of a non-Christian *Yangban* (noble) family with land near Suwon, thirty miles from Seoul. When he was sixteen, during the disruption and poverty of the Korean War, he had acted as houseboy at a nearby American camp. A Virginian GI taught him English and then, with his family's consent, adopted him, forfeiting his own further education in order to give Billy Kim an education in the States. Kim returned to his homeland with a master's degree, an American wife, Trudy, a deep personal faith and a determination to preach Christ in Korea. In personality a blend of East and West, a man who could be as direct as an American yet oriental in persuasiveness, Kim's strong character, engaging manner and high social standing made him a valued director of Youth for Christ, the Far East Broadcasting Company and other international Christian organizations.

Above all he had shown himself an evangelist. In a land used to a more gradual, Presbyterian way of bringing men and women to Christ, Billy Kim, a Baptist, gave at his rallies an invitation to immediate decision, similar to Graham's invitation at crusades. If Korean churchpeople regarded him as somewhat a maverick, "The Lord had opened many doors," Kim could say of those years, "the universities and the army bases and the high schools and regular open meetings. . . . He laid upon my heart to do some direct evangelism to unreached people. We were having some great meetings in a number of cities."

When, therefore, Henry Holley began to talk about interpreting for Graham, Billy Kim was attracted. One grave reservation checked him, however: his American education had been entirely at Bob Jones University and its related high school at Greenville, South Carolina, where the other boys in his dormitory had led him to Christ. Officials of Bob

Jones rated Billy Graham the arch-compromiser, to be shunned and testified against as a menace to the cause of evangelism. In Billy Kim's memory no man spoke from the Bob Jones chapel pulpit unless known to take a strong stand against Graham. Nor was it mere disagreement over policy: Billy Graham and his wife, Ruth, so Kim understood, were proud, impelled by pride.

Kim had heard Graham preach, admired him from afar, and had attended the Berlin Congress of 1966. In 1971, despite a residue of prejudice from college days, he had written to the Graham Association urging a preaching visit to Korea. But to come out in the most public manner with Graham, voice by voice, side by side on radio and television, to have their picture in American newspapers and then on film, would certainly cause a break with Dr. Bob Jones, Jr., for whom Kim felt gratitude and affection. It would probably forfeit financial and prayer support for the Korean Inland Mission from Americans who shared Jones's attitude. Some of Kim's friends suggested he quietly leave the country for the duration of the crusade.

On 27 March 1973 Holley wrote a formal invitation. Billy Kim and his wife spent the next three days in prayer and also telephoned one of their principal American backers. "You know how to pray," that person said. "You know the situation in your country. You're going to have to live with your decision. But whatever you decide, we'll back you."

Trudy Kim encouraged her husband to accept. As they prayed, Kim saw he would lose friends. But he saw even more sharply that his decision, either way, would have immense impact on Korea. Opportunity for saturating the country with the gospel did not come often. Who, then, could best transmit Graham's message to the Koreans? Many a fine Presbyterian academic could translate his writings, but "to convey to our people his feeling and his message, extemporaneously, precisely" was something else. Further, a Presbyterian was not accustomed to giving an "invitation": he might translate yet not share the sense of urgency that now, at this crusade service, is the time to come forward to make a decision. "It's one thing to translate, another thing to *communicate,*" mused Kim. He faced squarely whether his own background, training and ministry had not uniquely prepared him. The inward call grew more insistent, along with the dread that some interpreter less prepared would blunt the edge of Graham's preaching.

"Finally the Lord gave a clear indication. I believe God directed our decision and once that decision was made I had real peace of heart and mind"—though he could not quite still the questionings of his earlier prejudice.

On 31 March Billy Kim accepted the "great honor and privilege." He added, "I am praying that the '73 Billy Graham Crusade will be a highlight in the history of Christianity in my country." Holley set him to prepare thoroughly by listening to tapes of Graham and watching him on film, until he was imbued with Graham's voice and personality.

"What is unique in such a campaign," Elizabeth and Otto De-Camp of the Christian Broadcasting System wrote in April to their friends in America, "is the intense and extended preparations before the opening of the crusade." Twenty thousand laypeople, for instance, were in training as counselors. "This reservoir of personal workers alone will be a great boon to the ongoing witness of the church as a whole."

In the provinces it was the same. Thus Pastor Pak, Seung Wan of Pusan was impressed that counselors "received such an assurance of their own salvation and such a confidence in sharing their faith that this was a very special result of this crusade. In our church we have sermons, but we have not previously had people able to counsel another in accepting Christ." "I am much more ready to witness," said a Pusan pastor's wife. "I can use the Scriptures better."

Meanwhile in each crusade city a home visitation campaign, begun on 4 February, steadily moved to its completion, led by a Korean who was local director of World Literature Crusade's Every Home Campaign, which financed this "saturation" by nearly $75,000.[3]

The statistics of the visitation in Seoul alone were mind-boggling. In three months and one week every one of Seoul's million and more homes received a packet containing two Graham sermons, an invitation to the crusade with a map to Yoido, and instructions where to write for further spiritual help if unable to attend. These were distributed by 12,430 Christians drawn from twelve denominations. Thus Seoul's six

---

[3] Dr. Han's committee had intended to meet crusade expenses entirely from within Korea, but in view especially of the heavy cost of preparing Yoido Plaza, they accepted the offer by Every Home Campaign. In addition, the Graham Association paid their own travel expenses, as usual, and kept Graham's rule of refusing any payment or fee for his ministry or that of his Team.

and a half million inhabitants had the crusade brought to their doors, in addition to posters in shops and at street corners, and frequent mentions on radio and television. By that time the Koreans openly expected such huge numbers at Yoido that the Team office, then in Atlanta, Georgia, grew nervous.

On Friday 25 May 1973 Billy and Ruth Graham touched down at Seoul airport. Ruth described to their family how "the committee were there with garlands of flowers, little girls in their colorful dresses throwing flower petals in our path. There was a platform, words of welcome and response; a band played, a girls' choir sang, and we went around the crowd bowing and shaking hands."

Ruth, who had been educated at the American school in what was now North Korea, when her parents were Presbyterian missionaries in China, summoned from her memory the words for *Thank you*. After Billy's short speech of thanks, interpreted by Billy Kim in their first personal contact, Kim was introduced to Ruth. "She asked me, 'How many children have you?' I told her I have three. 'What are their ages and what are their names?' And I told her. She said, 'You better spend time with them. Because I'm speaking from experience, they grow up very fast.' That really stuck with me. And then my mind began to churn. I had heard a lot of bad things about this couple, and here they were, not only concerned in the propagation of the gospel, they are interested in you as a person. That spoke to me deeply, and I thought, 'If this is the type of person they are, they cannot be that bad. God must also speak to them about the ministry.' From then on I erased all the things I had heard in the days gone by. I made up my mind: 'They are choice servants of God. I will give every ounce of my energy to make their ministry successful.' "

The committee gave the Grahams a buffet dinner reception that evening in the secret garden of the Chang Dok Palace, to which many leaders in government, the armed forces and business came. As the Grahams and their small personal staff left the foyer of the Chosun Hotel, Billy Kim with them, they saw drawn up a convoy of four black limousines with uniformed drivers. At the front was a Cadillac. Its driver bowed and opened the door. "This is too big!" Billy Graham exclaimed. "I come to the mission field and ride around in a big car? Can you give me a smaller car?"

Billy Kim's heart went out instantly to Graham's spontaneous distress at such personal pomp, but he said firmly, "This is a courtesy of the Korean government. If you don't take it they will feel hurt."

"Well," said Billy Graham. "If that is the case I'll ride in it."

"Bill felt terribly embarrassed by it," Ruth remembers, especially later when they drove past Korean women walking to the crusade with babies on their backs. "After meeting and talking with you," Kim wrote to Graham after the crusade, "all the questions in my mind heretofore, were dispelled."

As Billy Graham arrived at Seoul the campaigns of the six associate evangelists were reaching their climax. Most of the Associates found themselves addressing the biggest crowds of their ministry.

On the night before the Seoul dedication service Walter Smyth, the Holleys, Carroll Hunt and her husband, Professor Everett Hunt, and others went out to the vast Yoida Plaza. It was dark and cold and empty but, recalls Hunt, "There was already a sense of excitement." Billy Kim had come out, too, and they converged on the platform. Someone asked Hunt to lead them in prayer. "And I could hardly pray. . . . It was as though we knew God was going to do a tremendous thing in this place."

5 The Million on Yoido Plaza

SEOUL traffic has a character all its own. Private cars being few, a street is a weaving traffic block of buses and taxis nose to tail, tangled with others going in the opposite direction. But on the opening night of the crusade, as the Team bus drew nearer Yoido, Carroll Hunt recalls, "All of the traffic, a stream of humanity and vehicles, was going in the same direction."

The crowd itself was a witness to the rest of the nation watching on television. Thus a layman in Pusan was "especially impressed with the way people would walk along together singing on their way to the meeting and on the way home after it was over at night. I was also impressed with the police officials who were astounded that there was nothing for them to do since the crowds were so orderly."

Billy Graham, driving slowly across the bridge with Ruth and Kim an hour before the first service, with a police motorcycle escort quietly clearing a way, exclaimed, "Man, this is even bigger than we had at Dallas for Explo '72!"[1] When Team and staff members looked from the platform at the crowd stretching away in both directions of the long Plaza, some wept openly as they felt "the waves of anticipation and joy and excitement pouring up from that huge crowd down below." Long-serving missionaries like Sam Moffett, son of that first missionary, had been expecting a multitude yet he was "stunned by the emotional impact of that many people on that island. It's still with me," Moffett commented nearly eighteen months later.

---

[1] The Campus Crusade Youth Congress of July 1972. See chapter 20.

Still they came, Christians and non Christians, despite the unseasonably cool and gusty weather. Koreans customarily sit on the floor, not on stools or benches. As each arrived he or she would select a small space and put on the asphalt a piece of paper or cloth or wicker, align the feet neatly at its edge though probably nudging the person in front, and sit.

To insure a smooth crowd-flow David Cho had marked the Plaza into a grid of white paper strips glued to the tarmac, forming thousands upon thousands of square *pyongs* (six feet by six feet) with every 250 *pyongs* roped and separated from its neighbors by narrow aisles. When a section had filled, its steward reported to a chief usher who radioed by walkie-talkie to Cho's control center with its chart. This center informed the access points where to direct the crowd to unfilled sections.

The police issued estimates based on previous experience of the Plaza but not derived from Cho's grid: one night they guessed too high, at the other services too low. Cho would report their guess, published well before the start of the service, and later give his own count. On the first night Cho saw his chart fill until the attendance figure soared above the much-foretold 300,000 which had made Billy and the Team nervous about overoptimism.

Shortly before the service Cho hurried to Billy Graham in the room below the platform and announced what the chart showed: approximately half a million persons waited to hear him preach. Graham had often said that statistics are totally meaningless in the sight of God but no preacher could fail to be moved at this news based on precise counting. A few minutes later he walked onto the platform and saw an unbelievable crowd under the arclights. Ruth wrote to her family, "It is one of those things impossible to take in."

The choir of 7,000 led the singing. Cliff Barrows, introducing the choral and congregational numbers through an interpreter, and George Beverly Shea with his solos, had learned to sing in Korean each first and last line. In due time Billy Graham began to preach, sentence by interpreted sentence. "We are very happy to be in Korea. We have had a wonderful time here during the last few days. This is the largest audience that I have ever preached to . . . the largest audience ever to hear a preacher in person anywhere in the world. I am glad that it happened in Korea. . . ."

After heartfelt compliments to a country and people which had deeply impressed him, Billy approached the heart of his message. "Tonight I want to talk on a very important subject. I want to talk about the greatest Man who ever lived. He is the One who can solve the problems of the world and solve your problems. . . ."

Very quickly the audience, hearing every word clearly however far from the pulpit, as well as those who listened or watched in their homes, became aware of the extraordinary aptness and brilliance of Billy Kim's interpretation. One little problem, the disparity of heights between the two Billys, had been solved by building a hidden box for Kim. Although a trifle hesitant about this pretense, Kim knew that his compatriots if confronted by the long and the short would think the sight funny and be distracted.

Billy Kim actually enhanced Billy Graham. In gesture, tone, force of expression, the two men became as one in a way almost uncanny. A missionary fluent in Korean who knew Graham personally thought that Kim's voice even sounded like Graham's. Some TV viewers, tuning in unawares, supposed Kim the preacher and Billy Graham an interpreter for the American forces.

Earlier each day the two prayed and worked over the message. Kim was impressed that Graham checked every illustration and allusion: "Will it fit the culture?" Kim recalls foreign preachers who threw in untranslatable Shakespearean allusions or started imitating southern blacks in the U.S., "but Billy Graham was so precise in his choice of language and words." However, one secret of Graham's ministry is a readiness to change to a different though equally prepared sermon if strongly moved to do so during his private time of prayer. On two of the five crusade days in Seoul Billy told Kim as they stepped into the car, "I've changed my message." Yet even when denied full preparation Kim chose words that kept the Korean, normally a more copious language, to the same length of sentence as Graham's English, thus maintaining momentum. A Seoul pastor commented, "The interpretation was done so well in both spirit and accuracy that it was in itself a tremendous blessing to all who heard. I even heard some say the interpreting was better than the original."

There were pastors who, in no fractious spirit, criticized Graham "because I did not have enough theological content to my messages." He kept deeper matters until his address to pastors at the School of

Evangelism. Yet intellectuals and common people were equally confronted. "The message spoke straight to the heart," was a missionary's verdict, "to emptiness, to loneliness, to hopelessness, to indifference, to the sinful."

Then Billy Graham reached his invitation to commitment. The solid mass of humanity which had pressed into the counseling area prevented his asking any to come forward. But at his call thousands stood up in their places, and a wave of sound crossed the Plaza as they repeated the prayer of repentance and dedication after Graham and Kim. Following his further talk to inquirers, the trained counselors stationed throughout the area were unable to reach everyone because there were so many.

Statistics mean little at this point for in Korea hundreds of Christians who heard an invitation such as Graham's would make a public act of commitment. Others, as pastors found when following up inquirers, had never known about Christ before; others had attended Sunday school or youth group or church but had fallen away.

From nine A.M. to five P.M. on four days of the crusade more than 6,000 pastors and laymen from all over Korea received training at the School of Evangelism which used the large Pentecostal church building close to the Plaza.[2] Meanwhile Graham associates spoke at dozens of subsidiary meetings. John Wesley White preached to "7,000 high schoolers at one time, all out on the ground. Many fainted or went to sleep. Some teacher would run down and bop them awake! Some of the meetings at military installations were unforgettable—seeing 3,000 men and maybe 500 of them make their confession of Christ by standing and saluting Jesus Christ as their Commander in Chief."

Lee Fisher had an unusual assignment: to sing and preach to two large groups of former "little flowers," young girls removed from night clubs and brothels, their ages ranging from eleven to seventeen. Country girls seeking work in Seoul are often tricked into prostitution. The police rescue many and put them into schools to learn a trade. "They seemed like innocent children," says Lee, "not former prostitutes. When I gave the invitation, like all Koreans they readily responded. It was a touching and rewarding experience."

---

[2] See chapters 10 and 18 for more about schools of evangelism.

Ruth Graham went to the famous EWHA University where Dr. Helen Kim had pioneered women's education and broken the Confucian tradition of subordination to the male. Her successor, Dr. Kim, Ok Kil had invited the crusade women's committee to arrange a special meeting. Ruth had expected, she told her family, "200–300 middle-aged Christian women. Instead it was in their outside amphitheater with 6,000–10,000 students and visitors, a strong wind blowing, the girls' choir in brilliant-colored dresses looking like a flower garden and singing like angels. Dr. Kim introduced me; my interpreter, Dr. Lee, was delightful, but the message, geared for another audience and rearranged at the last minute, was, to put it mildly, a homiletical disaster." Koreans did not think so, nor noticed Ruth's difficulty in speaking by interpretation nor that she felt a little distracted by the World Wide Pictures film crew, and by the local tendency for listeners to stretch their legs or wander around without loss of attention. They looked on Ruth Graham, educated in their land, as almost one of themselves.

What really won hearts was Ruth's going to the early morning prayer meetings. Koreans did not suppose Americans could get up so early. She much enjoyed these meetings at David Cho's Cho Dong Presbyterian church. T. W. Wilson, Walter Smyth and Ruth would meet at 4:15 A.M. in the hotel's all-night coffee shop "for a quick eye-opener," as Ruth describes it, "just when the all-night entertainers from the night club next door would be coming in for their breakfast. Those poor, cute little girls with their false eyelashes drooping down their tired little faces, white and exhausted; the young men leaning on the table, eyes half closed. . . .

"It is an unforgettable experience to be near the church in the pre-dawn darkness and see people hurrying along the sidewalks, Bibles under their arms. And to hear them sing! There was beauty and pathos in that hymn that morning—though I couldn't understand the words and was unfamiliar with the tune." After a full-length sermon and then a long prayer by the pastor, the people began to pray out loud simultaneously but individually, just as Billy had described the praying in Nagaland. With hundreds present, each continued until he or she was ready to depart, or wanted to rest or walk about before coming back again. Some of the congregation prayed for an hour.

Late night and early morning prayer meetings took place on Yoido during the crusade. The island being excluded from the midnight curfew, many people bedded down on the Plaza. They preferred to sleep out in the open, with scanty food, rather than to miss the crusade through distance. Instead of joining the extraordinary nighttime rush hour which turns every main Seoul street into a honking serpentine of headlamps struggling to beat the curfew, they would remain after the crusade for the prayer meeting ending at midnight; then they would sleep (or pray in groups or on their own) until the curfew lifted, and depart. Many who had gone home after the service would now be arriving back on the island for the early prayer meeting.

Three thousand, six thousand, and on Saturday night ten thousand sang and prayed together on Yoido island in the open under the arclights.

Ruth joined them. Billy Kim considers that Ruth "made a tremendous contribution to the overall success of Billy's crusade," especially since women outnumbered men at the service. "She was so genuinely humble, and people could see it." They sensed, too, that Billy Graham was warm and humble. "You don't feel any kind of haughtiness in him," was Dr. Han's verdict. In a land where pride is a national characteristic this received frequent comment as ordinary people discussed the crusade. A Korean girl in the crusade office, who happened to be by herself when Graham called from his room was found afterward in a state of euphoria. "She could hardly believe that Billy Graham knew her by name."

Koreans and missionaries alike seem to have been surprised by the Team's concern and courtesy, their lack of veneer. One missionary, closely involved, who had seen many visiting churchmen come and go, began the crusade "skeptical because of the bigness and the fame. I thought, 'Here comes a slick bunch of professionals who will do everything just right; but I wonder what they're like as people.' Before they had left, however, I was perhaps one of their most unconditional fans. I perceived that here were men and women who were really committed to the things of God. It became very obvious to me why he was blessing their ministry so richly: it was because they had no illusions but that it was all his. They seemed very careful, from Mr. Graham on down, to protect that aspect and not to get their eyes off Jesus—lest, like Peter, they sink into the waves."

The crusade became the talk of the city from cabinet minister to waitress, shop assistant and barber. It was a chief topic on talk shows and the news. Pastors stoked the fires, like Oo, Mun Sun: "I continued to emphasize three things in my church. First, prayer. Second, attendance by all members at the crusade. Third, I encouraged them to take their unsaved friends to the crusade." Friday was Army Night and Saturday Youth Night. Christians, excited at the huge numbers attending, began to aim at no less than a million for the closing service on Sunday afternoon. That would be a resounding witness to both parts of the divided nation. At the committee's request Billy Graham publicly suggested that for the glory of God it would be wonderful to have a million to hear the gospel face to face. "They took that personally," recalls Kim, "and worked hard to bring people from all over the countryside."

Sunday 3 June 1973 turned warm with only passing clouds. Two hours before the service timed for three P.M., Graham and Kim joined the stream flowing toward Yoido.

When Graham mounted the platform and looked out over the Plaza, as far as his eyes could see on either side and in the lesser space to the front, a solid block of humanity quietly awaited him. Every section, every aisle between, and away to edges of the Plaza hitherto unused, sat an unbroken mass of people, who throughout that service, unless singing, stayed incredibly quiet. In Kim's experience of Korean crowds none had been so still. Even children seemed neither to fidget nor cry. Statistically there should have occurred hundreds of faintings, dozens of heart attacks or other medical emergencies, yet the first-aid posts dealt with a mere 117 minor cases. Dissidents or protesters or cranks might have abounded, yet only one mental case made a brief commotion close to the platform.

David Cho's chart registered the figure of one million, one hundred and twenty thousand present. The earlier police estimate gave about 650,000, which the next day's newspapers printed alongside Cho's. This discrepancy created some controversy beyond Korea, with claims that "BGEA computers had made a mistake." In Korea, Cho's figure stood. His grid system was known to insure a high degree of accuracy although the use that afternoon of the aisles between the grids may have raised the precise figure higher than his estimate. Any doubts disappeared some months later when a government rally on the Plaza drew a crowd, officially announced as numbering 950,000, which had occupied distinctly less space than the crusade.[3]

The enormous concourse, which the unusual nature of the open-ended Plaza made physically possible, was the largest gathering in Korea for any purpose, and the largest known meeting for religion anywhere in the world. Korean Christians and Team alike felt that organization, publicity, a famous preacher could not have drawn that crowd and kept it so reverent. "It had to be the Holy Spirit." Many had waited all night and then through a hot morning. One bedridden old lady, nearing death and forbidden by her family to go, crawled out of her bedroom window and dragged herself to the Plaza.

For all who took part, that final crusade service is a dreamlike memory: the solemn responsibility of ministering to such a multitude, the visual impact of so many mortals in one place. "They came to hear the Word of God," muses Billy Kim as he looks back, "and there is no expression other than overwhelmed. You are wordless, you're speechless."

Billy Graham knew he had a special responsibility when he came to the invitation at the close of his sermon. With a million present it would have been easy to trigger a mass reaction. He therefore made his invitation harder than usual. As Walter Smyth describes it, "He didn't just ask people to stand, 'if you want to accept Christ.' He said, 'If you're willing to *forsake all other gods*' (and he bore down on this), 'stand up.' There was a hush upon the audience at first. Then one here and one there arose, until thousands were standing." Billy led them in the prayer of accepting Christ. He gave them, as was his usual practice, a brief word on the duties and responsibilities of a Christian. Then he said, "Counselors with your material, make your way back to those people who are standing." Over 12,000 cards came in that day. Thousands more followed by mail from persons contacted without time for proper counseling. And, as the future showed, a great many made genuine commitments who never were reached by a counselor at the Plaza.

The million did not move during the counseling. Many prayed as

---

[3] Figures given by Cho were 30,000 *pyong*, each seating 12 persons (360,000); 35,000 *pyong* seating 9 (315,000); 35,000 seating 7 (245,000) and 40,000 seating 5 each, on the edges of the Plaza (200,000). Total: 1,120,000.

they sat. Thousands upon thousands began to sing. Then a helicopter rose from behind the platform. Dr. Han put up his hand for silence.

Billy Graham was leaving Korea that afternoon and the committee, recalling that his car had been mobbed by hundreds eager to touch or speak to him, had borrowed a helicopter and pilot from the U.S. Eighth Army to take him to the airport. Dr. Han explained that since Billy could not say goodbye personally to everybody his helicopter would circle in farewell over the Plaza.

At Dr. Han's word, the entire million and more stood and waved their hymnsheets or newspapers or whatever they carried. It was unbelievably poignant. Billy found the breathtaking view of this waving multitude indescribable: "The only comment I have is, 'Thanksgiving to God for all he did!' "

As Billy left Korea he issued a public statement of his admiration for the nation and its churches. He paid warm tribute to the dedication of the Korean Christians. Then he continued: "The crusade in its depth and outreach is beyond anything I've ever witnessed. The sheer fact of its having gathered over three million people in five meetings with an additional million and a half in the extra meetings conducted by my associates, makes it by far the largest face-to-face presentation of the gospel, not only in my ministry, but in the history of the Christian church. This is the work of God. There is no other explanation. To God be the glory!"

Billy had preached to 900,000 more than in the entire sixteen weeks of his New York 1957 crusade. In five days the Koreans had broken his highest attendance record, the 2,647,365 who heard him in the six weeks at Glasgow in 1955. The statistics of inquirers are formidable, even allowing for thousands of Christians who filled in cards as a testimony to previous commitment. The number of inquirers registering in Seoul was 79,793, including 35,000 whose cards flowed in by mail in the weeks after the crusade. A further 37,146 were registered in the provinces, making a total of 119,939 inquirers to be sent literature and visited in the follow-up. The statistics are underscored by the facts. "The whole church here is on cloud nine in the wake of the crusade," wrote Sam Moffett to Billy on 13 June, "which is going to affect the whole future of Christianity in Asia." Many of the larger churches held additional Sunday services to accommodate the numbers, while in others the congregations increased and did not suffer the usual drop in the hot summer. Billy Kim's own church, in Suwon, increased its attendance by thirty percent.

The Graham Team were "keenly aware," as Walter Smyth wrote in August, "that it was a reaping which took place, without doubt because of the years of prayer and sowing of the Word." The crusade was the most dramatic moment in a steady growth, when evangelism received an impetus that put it into higher gear. Mr. Oh wrote to Smyth in the following September, "We feel strongly that the crusade prepared the way for a new era in cooperative evangelism with the goal of winning this nation for Christ. Several campaigns have been conducted this summer with outstanding results." Dr. Han drew attendances of 50,000 for a three-night campaign at Kumchun and then devoted a month to army camps. He and his colleagues from the committee formed a postcrusade nationwide evangelization movement to reach all main cities not directly touched by the Graham Team, and to organize schools of evangelism. They determined to complete the evangelization of the eighty-five to ninety percent in Korea who do not profess Christianity. "I think we have caught the vision that it can be done," says Billy Kim, "if all of our churches and Christian organizations get together and really go after that Great Commission. There's a potential, there's a possibility. I think it's exciting, and I want to be a part of that."

On a different scale of strategy, twelve students who had attended the crusade school of evangelism started a mission of help in one of the worst slums of Seoul, "where sewer trucks dump the city's stinking waste into the river all day long. Twenty-five hundred people live there. If the father of the house is sick and can't work for a day, the children don't eat that day."

Thousands among those at Yoido Plaza had brought their tape recorders and now played Graham's messages to teach themselves or evangelize others. "We have heard them on the buses, in the hospitals, in our homes, everywhere," wrote Billy Kim. Pastors found evangelism easier since the crusade. "Now when we witness to unsaved people they already know what we are talking about and they are much more ready to listen to what we have to say about the gospel." Many pastors and laypeople placed a new emphasis on direct evangelism, and on Christ. "Billy Graham's message was very Christocentric," comments a

Chunju man. "Our Korean church is often too church-centered, even building-centered."

Side effects were numerous. The spirit of cooperation did not evaporate. Within weeks a split within the Holiness Church (the denomination derived from the work of the Oriental Missionary Society) had healed, at least partly as a result of the crusade. And although the two churches formed by the Presbyterian schism of 1959 did not formally reunite, they worked together again. At the next Easter, 1974, they held a joint sunrise service for the first time instead of using separate sites. On the local level the crusade taught Christians how strong they could be when united for action.

As for Billy Kim, he had become a national figure overnight. Such was his exhaustion, and such the demands for media interviews, that he disappeared to a hospital and lived on toast and milk for three days, "thanking the Lord and praying and meditating." He had "a new vision, a new passion for the lost, and a new love for the Lord and his Word." Opportunities for ministry opened as never before. "I'm going through a tremendous new Christian experience," he wrote to Graham on 16 July. "I praise God for the influence you have had on my life personally. . . . I wish I could convey to you the impact of the ministry you have had here in Korea. Never a day goes by that someone is not saved or gets right with the Lord or is called into the ministry."

Conversion stories were heard on every side. A boy from a rich family had fallen in love with a poor girl. Forbidden to marry they had decided on suicide but went to Yoido first, then returned each night and gave their lives to Christ on the last day. The man's non-Christian family relented and they married to start a Christian home. Another youth, a wild college boy who had been arrested often for drunkenness, walked with long hair, unshaven face and filthy clothes into a pastor's study. "I don't know about the Truth," he said. "I know nothing of the Teaching, but at the Plaza I decided to become a Christian. Please show me how to live like one." He never missed a Sunday, and later began a daughter church in a rural area and formed a team of young evangelists.

One man from an atheistic home told his story eighteen months later, using Korean words that reveal his lack of previous contact with the church, though a deacon had witnessed to him. Mr. You, Ook Chun did not go to Yoido but listened on the radio: "The impression

I had from listening by the radio was all good. I was especially thankful to hear in the message that sinners could put their burden of sin at the feet of Jesus's cross, and this was a blessing to me. I felt a strong desire to be forgiven of my sins and to be able to lay my burden of sin down. I received Christ in my home. When the invitation was given I stood up and prayed the same prayer and received Christ into my heart as my Savior." Standing in his stocking feet on the *ondol* (heated stone floor) of his home, as if receiving an honored guest, he became one with thousands praying at Yoido.

"At first I had the feeling that the kingdom of God was far removed from anything that related to me, but as I continue to attend church and read my Bible I am finding that this is really the Word of Truth and it now speaks clearly to my heart. Before this experience my family was divided and we had much trouble among us. Now we have a happy family. As I study the Bible I am teaching what I learn to my wife and children and I am finding that we are more and more growing together."

Nationally, the crusade was a startling, overwhelming demonstration of the strength of the Christian faith eighty-nine years after the first Protestant missionaries had stepped ashore a few hundred yards from Yoido. Not in their wildest dreams could they have imagined that a million Koreans would worship Christ together on that island.

Before the crusade neither the Christians nor the rest of the nation had realized, despite the spires of the Seoul skyline, how strong the church had grown. Because the census rated only ten to fifteen percent in the Republic of Korea as believers in Christianity, non-Christians had tended to dismiss it as unimportant. Then they saw the rivers of people moving through the streets, and they began to ask what gave Christianity that drawing power. All over Korea pastors and laypersons found that the effect of the crusade was "to encourage people to see that the work of the Lord had grown that big, and thus to encourage others to join with us."

The effect was seen in the growth of church planting and lay training. Thus the Hap Dong branch of the Presbyterian church pledged themselves to start 700 new churches in 1974–75 and reached their target. Their present aim is 10,000 new churches by 1985. "There are numerous stories of explosive church-planting movements in Seoul alone," wrote David Cho in June 1976. "At least one new congregation has been formed every day since the crusade. According to statistics, in May 1973 there were 1,400 churches in Seoul. At the end of 1974 there were over 2,000. Before the crusade the church-growth rate was 10.3 percent. Now it has almost tripled to 28 percent."

The crusade also strengthened the fiber of a nation which lives under the threat of invasion from the North. The North's Communist government knew that many of their citizens had listened to the crusade on the radio and therefore attacked it bitterly. They claimed that the million had been ordered to Yoido by the government, or had been drawn by trickery or sorcery. A gathering of that size openly disproved the Marxist theory that religion everywhere was declining. Moreover the Communist authorities were embarrassed by the number of crusade leaders who had been born in the North.

The crusade caused the South Korean government to take the church more seriously. The political troubles which erupted in the year after the crusade brought Billy Graham "great anguish of heart" as he followed them from abroad. They "caused me to pray for the Christians of Korea even more."

Despite the uneasy times, the Christians determined to use their freshly discovered strength not only for their own land but for all Asia. Graham himself had suggested that "perhaps the gravitational center of the church is now moving here to the Far East," to Indonesia, the Philippines, Korea. Korea could be a power center of evangelization in Asia and the world. To that end Graham announced his support for a new graduate school in Seoul, the Asian Center for Theological Studies and Mission, and has endowed its library.[4]

The professor of church history and mission at Seoul Theological Seminary described the crusade as "certainly the most significant event in the history of Christianity in this land." Dr. Han said that "with the Billy Graham crusade the Korean church came of age." In its maturity the church looks outward, dreaming that as the proportion of Christians rises in the last quarter of the twentieth century, hundreds will

---

[4] The Koreans' outlay on the crusade had amounted to U.S. $200,000 and all bills were paid. Billy Graham through his Foundation initially gave U.S. $100,000 to the Asian Center spread over two years.

go as missionaries to China, to Indochina, to South America, to the secularized, urbanized West.

In the perspective of history, that broadening and deepening of Korea's sense of global mission may emerge as the crusade's most important effect.

PART TWO

6 European Linkup

A N OLD jeep driven by a helper would usually take the morning mail, sorted by secretaries at Billy Graham's office in Montreat, North Carolina, up the steep curves and hairpin bends to his mountain home. But in October 1968 Graham was out of the state. After two days at his Association's headquarters in Minneapolis he had flown to New York for a week of discussions and meetings with the committee and Team preparing his Madison Square Garden crusade of the coming summer; then to Tennessee and Texas, across to Los Angeles and back home to Montreat, where he arrived nine days after leaving New York.

An important letter from Germany therefore reached him on the road, from the German Evangelical Alliance, accepting a firm date for a crusade in the industrial city of Dortmund in the Ruhr for April 1970, eighteen months ahead. Writing in English, Billy's usual German interpreter, Peter Schneider, had more to say: "Yesterday I met with David Rennie in Frankfurt and went with him to a key man of the German post office," who had confirmed that a crusade in Dortmund could be extended by closed circuit television to other German cities. This would mean, Billy Graham read, "that practically the majority of all Germans would be within one to two hours' reach of one of your meetings."

In 1967 Billy had addressed crusade services in twenty-five British cities simultaneously by television relay to local halls from Earls Court in London. Peter Schneider saw the possibilities for Germany and he won the interest of David Rennie, an electronics expert. For a year they corresponded, planning an All-Germany TV crusade.

Then they met at Frankfurt for detailed discussion. At breakfast in their hotel on an October morning of 1968, Rennie doodled on a paper napkin to explain that the signal had best go from the television tower at Dortmund by microwave to Hamburg, the hub of the German system. "Once in that hub it is just a question of engineers pushing switches and they can send a signal anywhere across Europe—" Suddenly, as Rennie recalls, "the potential of this swept over me." Once in the main German television lines, it was easy to go north from Hamburg into Copenhagen and thus into all Scandinavia; to go west from Cologne to Brussels, and thus into France, Holland, the United Kingdom, all of which were in the Euro-Vision network.

Peter Schneider was excited too, as his letter to Billy showed: ". . . so the technical possibility would be given," he wrote, "to enlarge your Dortmund campaign to an actual European television campaign. And if you like, David felt that you could without great difficulty include in the closing rally even the U.S. by satellite. As eight P.M. in Dortmund equals two P.M. in New York, BGEA might buy some television time and broadcast this closing rally in color through various television stations in the U.S. You see, Billy, we have had a good time and have let our thoughts run. . . ." Indeed, writing to Billy some days later, David Rennie wanted the Pacific satellite to carry the service line to Australasia, "where the time would be early on Monday morning."

Billy's thoughts ran, too, when he read their letters. Just as John Wesley did not see why the devil should have all the best tunes, so Billy Graham coveted the latest technology for the gospel.

He replied on 1 November 1968 to Peter Schneider. "I am thrilled and excited about the possibilities of an all-European crusade by means of closed-circuit television." He was, however, dubious about foisting a crusade from Germany on Britain—and the dazzling transatlantic and Pacific hookups died a natural death from the vast financial outlay that would be required. But he did not flinch from the "gigantic undertaking" outlined in Schneider's letter from Germany. He told his director of crusades, Walter Smyth: "this might present us with the greatest opportunity we have ever had in Europe. We may have to give financial subsidy to this, but I think it might be an investment that would pay great spiritual dividends throughout Europe. It might be possible to have it in every major country of Europe."

Six and a half years later, and five years after the last night of "Euro 70," Graham commented: "I think the Dortmund crusade was among the most significant of our entire ministry."

Euro 70, like all crusades, involved a partnership between the Graham Team and great numbers of Christians in the countries concerned. Peter Schneider led in Germany. Nine years younger than Billy, Peter had once been an admirer of Adolf Hitler. The formal churchgoing of his youth had lapsed into a vague pantheism learned from studying Goethe, until as a prisoner of war in the coal mines of Belgium, with faith in Hitler shattered, Peter became interested in the Bible and Christianity. After his release in 1948, his studies of philosophy and contemporary German theology further whittled away his beliefs. But in 1951 on a six-month tour of church youth organizations in America he "met the Lord, and returned home with a definite desire to serve him no matter where he would lead me."[1]

In 1954, as YMCA secretary for Berlin, Peter was the youngest member and only layman on a committee that hurriedly arranged Billy Graham's Olympic Stadium rally, after the Greater London Crusade at Harringay and Wembley had made such impact on Britain. Because Peter had been to Harringay they made him responsible for training counselors.

Six years afterward, married to a young woman who had given her life to Christ at that Berlin rally and who now never grudges his absences from home to help Graham, Peter organized and interpreted for the 1960 crusades in Essen, Hamburg and Berlin. He doubted that Germans, bred in the Lutheran tradition, would get out of their seats to go forward in public commitment, and was nervously embarrassed lest none respond when he first interpreted Billy's words of invitation at Essen. Thus, with other Germans, he was overwhelmed by the sight of the many hundreds who came forward at Essen, and even more in Hamburg. There, with attendances ranging from 30,000 to 75,000 the tent proved far too small, and the campaign had "tremendous impact."

---

[1] Schneider was unable to trace the young man responsible for his conversion—so he never knew of the effect of his witness.

In Berlin the tent stood right beside the border, a year before the building of the Berlin Wall. East German authorities were annoyed to see thousands cross over to attend, and they built a barrier of tanks, cars and soldiers.

Following the 1960 campaign Schneider learned to give an invitation to commitment at his own meetings, as did other German evangelists. Thus the coming of Graham to Germany had left a mark already, especially as each campaign was prepared by Germans for Germans, in close cooperation with the Team.

Dortmund turned rapidly into Euro 70 as David Rennie translated his table-napkin sketch into a detailed plan. Rennie, like Schneider, had first helped a Graham crusade in 1954 when, as a young businessman, before going to Iran for three years in the oil industry, he had been deputy chief usher throughout Harringay. He especially remembers the Saturday when Roy Rogers and his horse Trigger delighted 40,000 children. Although that very morning David Rennie had become engaged to be married—he did not see his future wife again until ten o'clock that night, twelve hours later. In 1966 he rescued the Earls Court crusade from a defective sound system, and he masterminded the TV relays and extended television crusade of 1967.

For Euro 70 David hired the same British firm to engineer the telecasts, again using eidophor projectors, a European invention but still rare in Europe: he had to scour Holland, Britain, Germany and Switzerland for them. And he met other snags. Whereas the German post office, like the British, leased links to any professional prepared to pay, and the French ORTF cooperated with Rennie on the basis that good television should be supported, the Belgian system required sanction from the state Television Authority. In the atmosphere still then prevailing in a predominantly Roman Catholic country, its officials blocked plans sponsored by the Protestants of Brussels and Antwerp— until a senior British engineer at the Brussels headquarters of the European Broadcasting Union discreetly intervened. Yugoslavia, a Communist country and officially atheistic, refused to permit a live relay to Zagreb but allowed a videotape to be shown each following night. Sweden, self-appointed champion of freedom, argued that closed-circuit television offended basic liberties. No pleading by Swedish Christians, even up to cabinet level, could win consent for a relay to any city in Sweden. Worse, the lines to Norway depended on Swedish links. No less than nine projected relays were on the point of extinction until pressure from the European Broadcasting Union persuaded the Swedes to grant facilities.

Swedes themselves crossed the border in great numbers to attend Norwegian centers. Not until five years later, when Graham addressed a stadium rally in Stockholm in July 1975, did Swedish television make amends by carrying the sermon live across the nation.

While technological twists were unraveled, spiritual links were forged. They were all the stronger because the Berlin Congress on World Evangelism in 1966 had created friendships and sympathies across barriers of language, race and culture. Thirteen German cities, including Berlin, organized relays.

The idea of a linkup across frontiers met early hesitation, but after an inter-European demonstration at Frankfurt a total of twenty two centers in nine countries outside Germany went ahead. All organized and trained as for an actual crusade, and early in 1970 Cliff Barrows, with Tedd Smith and the black singer Jimmie Macdonald, toured the cities. They went also into Czechoslovakia, broken by the still recent Russian invasion. Eastern European television had no link with the West; Czech Christians therefore arranged two rallies for Cliff instead, and the Euro 70 team were astounded and heartened, as they walked from their plane into the Prague airport terminal, to hear "Only Jesus" over the intercom. They wondered what courageous Christian had risked his neck.

For a final check of the far-flung arrangements Walter Smyth revisited Europe, returning to America encouraged. "I believe," he said on the telephone to Sherwood Wirt, then editor of *Decision*, "God is going to give us something tremendous in Europe." Schneider and Rennie shared this feeling, although they knew that the complex operation now reaching its climax would remain mere technology unless electrified by prayer. Nine other countries echoed what Schneider wrote to North Carolina about his own loved nation: "Well, Billy, as the days of this historic crusade are coming nearer and nearer, you may be assured that there are many many Christians in Germany praying fervently for you and for all of us, that the Lord may bless this crusade and give us a great victory."

Billy, who had kept in touch with him during crusades in Australia,

New York and elsewhere, replied on 17 March 1970. "I am tremendously burdened and prayerful about the forthcoming crusade. I am convinced that God is going to do something on a scale that we have not seen before. Please pray for me in my preparations. I feel terribly inadequate and weak."

Right up to opening night several question marks hovered over Euro 70. Urban guerrillas had broken up public meetings in Germany, and violent anti-American feelings had been aroused by the Vietnam war. Since disruption in Dortmund could undercut the expensive and devoted preparations in other countries, the organizers designed a platform for the Westfalenhalle that would allow audience and cameras a clear view yet would frustrate invaders. Underneath it they constructed a security studio where as a last resort Billy and his interpreter could be televised alone across the network, should battles rage above. Billy urged that "the strongest possible measures should be taken to see that the demonstrators do not get inside the building. If they want to demonstrate outside the building, that probably would help the crusade, unless of course they block the people from entering the arena. However, I believe the Lord will overrule in all these matters."

Though opponents stay quiet and electronics prove perfect, the whole multilanguage operation could be spoiled if Billy Graham's preaching were not conveyed to the people of the Continent by the finest interpreting. Peter Schneider had never interpreted a public address before the 1960 campaign, yet his single mistake was to pick up a joke of Billy's and repeat it from memory, only to realize that Billy had told a different one which started the same. At Dortmund Peter was the one interpreter on the platform. The other six sat in booths, where they could watch Billy both in the flesh and by monitor, with direct transmission into the network. Europe saw and heard Billy, with Peter sometimes in focus. Outside Germany and Austria they heard their own interpreter instead of Peter. Tests had disclosed that no statement in Dutch, French, Serbo-Croatian, Danish, Norwegian or Welsh takes longer than in German; thus Peter was always fractionally slower and the rest did not overlap Billy. Intense concentration was necessary as the booths were not fully soundproofed from the nearby confusion of tongues. The Serbo-Croatian interpreter, Josip Horak, had an extra difficulty in that he knew German so well that his ear sometimes stayed with Schneider.

On the Friday before the crusade the microwave link at the top of the Jungfrau, by which the picture would go to Geneva while the sound took a different route, remained docile under the snow. In Norway one eidophor projector broke during testing. Jean Wilson of Billy Graham's London office secured another from the Pye Company of Cambridge, who put it in order overnight for delivery to Southend, just in time for her to squeeze it into the airferry space she had booked for her own car. After further adventures it arrived in time by cargo plane from Rotterdam. Meanwhile, in response to a cry from Zagreb, Jean had driven from Southend to London airport and caught a plane, carrying duplicates for the lost customs papers of their eidophor.

At Dortmund, Germany's largest hall had been turned into a crusade auditorium. In America, *Decision* magazine had wired to a hundred American colleges and churches, and to missionaries and overseas leaders, asking that the crusade's opening Sunday be designated a Day of Prayer for Europe. Billy Graham had already met the German press, which tended to be suspicious of his motives. He told them, "I am not here as a political representative of the United States. I'm not here to defend Christianity or the church because I can't, but I am here to talk about Jesus Christ and what he can do for people today."

Television teams had worked almost 'round the clock to prepare for Sunday 5 April 1970. David Rennie, who had taken a ten-day holiday from his business, made a last check of the equipment as the hall filled, then sat at the prewar manual switchboard which the Germans had dug out of a museum to enable him to talk direct with the European control centers.

Sound and vision came in on time. As David Rennie recalls, "At 7:30 Cliff Barrows stepped to the platform and off we went. One felt the wind of God behind one; one had a glorious feeling of relaxation as the professionals took over. It was running smoothly, and we'd got about twenty minutes into the program when suddenly we lost everything!" The Dortmund audience, singing under Cliff's direction, remained unaware of the frantic search—which led to a kindly senior lighting engineer from London, who, to help the tense German and British crews had plugged his coffee pot into a socket which blew the fuse box.

Transmission was resumed, apologies went over the air and in due time Billy Graham preached before 14,500 people in Dortmund. Yet he was seen and heard by five times that number, in eight countries, exclusive of those in their homes watching Dutch television or listening throughout Europe later each night to the shortened sound version on Transworld Radio from Monte Carlo.

Billy had preached about half his sermon when a bearded twenty-two-year-old law student from Munster University marched to the front with a banner of protest. In a secular program the director would have instantly aligned his cameras to transmit the excitement as good television. Rennie, keeping the platform and security authorities informed by holding one camera tight on the man, but not transmitting the picture, ordered the others to close up on Billy to give viewers a sense of greater involvement with him. "Billy is too much of a master ever to stop," says Rennie. "Billy kept going and Peter Schneider kept going and no one was aware of a demonstration in Dortmund." Stewards swiftly moved the protester outside, where one of the special counselors allocated for possible demonstrators could interact with him.

"I felt in Germany," Billy wrote to a friend after the crusade, "that I was in hand-to-hand combat with the forces of evil, though I believe the victory was the greatest in the history of our work." Physically it was exhausting. He was preaching for three crusades at once: one to Dortmund and the Ruhr; another to all Germany; a third to Europe beyond. In Dortmund itself he at first faced considerable hostility from some of the German churchmen. Support increased sharply after Westphalian clergy invited Graham to address their synod on the fourth day. It was a noisy meeting which included harmless heckling as well as another demonstration by the bearded law student. This time he seized the microphone from Graham and claimed amid cheers that money spent on the crusade should have been given to the poor. Graham's answers to this and other points swung the meeting, and that night the audience overflowed the arena into a television relay hall and two smaller halls that were wired for sound. On Saturday, with all seats taken, latecomers broke through closed doors to spill into the open space before the platform.

On Sunday morning, an old friend of Billy Graham's attended a Catholic mass at the church of one of Dortmund's largest parishes. He heard a priest confess to the congregation his newly learned realization that forgiveness of sins could come only through Jesus Christ himself, and not through a priest. Graham's friend discovered that he had attended the crusade the previous night.

The local Lutheran bishop publicly stressed that the crusade showed that the hour had come for evangelism. "Thousands of German young people are reacting to Graham positively. This is a great joy to me." It was a joy to many throughout the Federal Republic, including President Heineman and Chancellor Willi Brandt, both of whom told the American ambassador about their interesting and refreshing discussions with Graham at Bonn.

Except in Cologne, where the hall never quite filled, the response to the All-German television relays delighted clergy and laity, while cities that had refused to cooperate regretted their mistake and asked for another opportunity.

As a direct result of the television crusade the German Evangelical Alliance made a historic decision in 1972 to stop being merely a spiritual fellowship without a permanent office. They became an active evangelizing body in the service of the churches, with Peter Schneider as general secretary. "On my many trips through Germany," Schneider wrote five years after the crusade, "I'm continually meeting people or I hear of people who have been converted through Billy Graham's ministry, especially through Euro 70. The other day I visited the city of Freiburg in the Black Forest, where the Evangelical Alliance was brought to life by cooperating in Euro 70. They are gratefully tracing back their present activities to this experience."

As reports reached Dortmund from different countries of Europe, Billy Graham could tell that the crusade had gone "far beyond all expectations." In a statement issued immediately before the closing service on Sunday 12 April 1970 he could claim that the majority attending were young, to whom an evangelistic crusade was new. "Thousands of youth accepted the challenge to lead a new life and help build the Kingdom of God. . . . We have proven that European youth will listen to the old message of the gospel if it is presented with authority, simplicity and urgency. The gospel message has not changed and human nature has not changed in 2,000 years. Only the methods change. . . . We now hand the torch of evangelism and revival to the pastors and Christian laity.

"The crusade has made a great impact on me personally. I have rededicated my life to reaching as many people as possible for Christ before I go to heaven. I have learned new ways to reach more people. From many discussions with European clergy and laymen I have learned and profited. It has been an overwhelming experience. None of us who participated in this modern day technological and spiritual miracle can ever be the same."

Paris and Copenhagen were the only cities with relays that can be listed as failures. In Paris a city-wide effect is virtually impossible and evangelical leaders held back until halfway through, yet the area director can recall that "there was no sense of disappointment, even though the crowds were not there. Every night there were dozens counseled and everyone was encouraged." In Copenhagen the churches remained lukewarm and the hall less than half full. Those who came forward might be counted on the fingers, yet the organizers thrilled to "the Christian fellowship with Christians across Europe; that was wonderful for us in a country where only a small minority attend churches regularly."

This sense of closeness to foreign Christians left a marked impression on relay leaders of different nations, who conversed on the telephone and exchanged requests for prayer before the meetings began, and on their people. The singing of choirs and congregations separated by thousands of miles, fed back to the Dortmund arena and away across Europe, gave a special thrill of unity, and that unity took root. A week after the crusade sixty-two Christians from sixteen European countries met Billy Graham to plan the Congress of Evangelism to take place the next year in Amsterdam and which in turn led to further international cooperation for the Christian gospel.

Unity across frontiers matched unity in the regions of the relays. "Even in a city of 50,000 people," said a Norwegian shipowner, "you will meet people again whom you didn't know before the crusade. I'm a Lutheran and he was a Pentecostal, and here was a Baptist, so we don't go in each other's churches usually. But we meet in the street, and suddenly I get happy inside because I know 'here is one of my brothers—we are one.'" Years later the chairman of another of the crowded Norwegian relays claimed, "There has been a marked closing of ranks of all Christian associations in the town and surrounding areas. The campaign united all Christians into one fellowship which is jointly tackling the common task: to win others to Jesus Christ." Those comments were endorsed by a letter from Oslo in May 1973 which emphasized that Euro 70 was the first time Norwegian evangelicals had cooperated on a nationwide scale. "Since this event we have had a different spiritual climate here. The revival started during Euro 70 still continues. We have never had so many joint evangelical actions as we have had these last years since 1970."

At the opposite end of Europe, at Zagreb in Communist Yugoslavia, the professor of history at the Roman Catholic divinity school could write in 1975 in the Catholic illustrated monthly, *Veritas:* "Those were unforgettable days in April 1970, when the hope awoke in many hearts that ecumenism in our region will not remain just an empty word."

The Zagreb relay is a story in itself. The story began in the Albert Hall, London, in 1955 when Josip Horak, the future Serbo-Croatian interpreter for Euro 70, obtained a rare visa to attend the Baptist World Congress. He longed to meet Billy Graham but friends laughed at the idea until Horak got lost in the corridors. He opened a door into a little room and saw Billy Graham sitting alone, resting from the importunities of newsmen. It was a first encounter that greatly influenced Horak.

Horak, a bachelor of laws and doctor of science, worked as an economist because the state forbids any man to be a full-time pastor. In the early postwar days, with religion under virtual interdict, the Protestants of Croatia formed a tiny segment compared with Orthodox, Roman Catholics, Muslims, and the antireligious Marxists. Horak became president of the Baptist Union of Yugoslavia, and in 1967, knowing that many citizens of Zagreb would ignore other preachers, national or international, yet listen to Billy Graham, he arranged a brief crusade with Dr. Robert Evans[2] of the Greater Europe Mission, one of Billy's oldest friends. But only the personal intervention of Vice-President (now President) Tolbert of Liberia persuaded the Yugoslav authorities to admit Graham for a weekend.

Since, under law, neither the city stadium nor the public sports-

---

[2] Dr. Evans is working on a definitive study of Graham's work in Europe over the years, in which Evans himself has played a notable part.

ground could be used for a religious purpose, Cardinal Soper gave them the Catholic seminary football ground. There on the July Sunday when Graham preached, Catholics and Orthodox shared the conduct of the service. Several thousand—of all creeds or none—attended, despite the usual ban on posters or public announcement of religious gatherings, and despite the rain. Not one person left the drenched ground. At the windows of the nearby Catholic hospital patients sat or stood to listen. The Serbian Orthodox *Vesnik* (Messenger) called it "the first public manifestation of the ecumenical spirit and Christian love. The Christians of Zagreb will never forget it. It has opened up a new chapter in interreligious relations, and not only in this town."

One momentous incident never reached the Serbian Orthodox press.[3] The elderly Metropolitan of the Zagreb Eparchy, Archbishop Damaskinos, had eagerly welcomed and prayed with Horak about plans for Billy Graham's weekend, having read Spurgeon's sermons. Dr. Damaskinos suffered from a weak heart, however, and when the June war in the Middle East caused some anti-American feeling, a fear of hostile demonstrations preyed upon his mind. At length, a week before the Graham Team's arrival date, he telephoned Horak at the export-import company where he was employed. In the conspiratorial manner dictated by prudence in an atheist state Damaskinos gave no name, only his address, and asked for a visit. "You know who is calling," he said.

Horak hurried to meet with him. To his dismay the archbishop urged that the Graham meetings be postponed. "We cannot postpone it!" cried Horak. "Trusting in the Lord's help, we go forward!" He suggested that the archbishop attend only the indoor united service at the Lutheran church. Damaskinos excused himself, saying he would have another, fatal heart attack if demonstrations erupted.

On Saturday, Horak entered the church from the vestry with Billy Graham and saw a row of Orthodox clergy, distinctive in tall headdress, sitting at the front. The venerable archbishop had come after all. At the close of the sermon, when Horak translated Graham's invitation to commitment, asking for hands to be raised, Dr. Damaskinos' hand shot up. Horak visited him at his residence later. "He was quite a different

---

[3] This story really belongs to my earlier volume *Billy Graham* (1969), but I learned of it only in 1975 and it is too interesting to omit.

man. He had excused himself because of his lack of faith. Dr. Damaskinos was a really great man and newborn believer and we found in him such a good friend." He moved afterward to be the Patriarch of Serbia's deputy in Belgrade, where he died.

Graham's visit of 1967 created a new spirit of mutual understanding between Christians. They could not forget the spontaneous linking of hands on the platform at the rally, forming an unbroken circle as they sang "Blest Be the Tie that Binds": Protestants, Orthodox, and a Catholic theologian, Dr. Sagi-Bunic, who called out, "Dr. Graham is going to teach us ecumenism." Three years later, when the relay from Euro 70 needed more space than any Protestant church possessed, while cinemas and public halls were barred by law to a religious gathering, a Catholic parish priest who had rededicated his life to Christ at the 1967 open-air rally, offered his crypt (church basement) for the paraphernalia.

More than 1,000 people crammed in each night, including atheists attracted by the technological novelty, the excellent organization, and the discreet posters which this time were permitted. On the first evening the electric power failed throughout that section of the city. After a few minutes a dim glow lit the screen, and then the videotaped picture returned. All saw and heard Cliff Barrows announcing the first hymn, and Horak's translation into Serbo-Croatian.

What followed may be seen through the eyes of a young woman called Nada. Brought up in a Baptist home, she had listened to many sermons, which generally closed, as is usual in Eastern Europe, with an invitation to the uncommitted to come forward. She had never responded. Nada became champion woman high-jumper of the Croatian republic in federal Yugoslavia and, though refusing to join the Communist party, she dropped church. She determined that if at length she became a Christian, no one should know of it by her going forward or other public confession of faith.

Her mother told her about Euro 70. To see this technical miracle Nada went the second evening. "The hall was packed. I felt great tension, something mysterious. On the great screen there was the picture of Billy Graham. I heard his voice, the voice of the interpreter. I felt mighty words of God's servant speaking to me personally. My heart began to beat fast. I felt that I am at the crossroads of my life,

I have to make a decision that will be binding for all eternity. Then the invitation was given, but I didn't have the courage to go forward. It was too difficult for me, a sportswoman. I saw the others who went forward. I understood the message, and the invitation, but I didn't go. . . ."

That night Nada could not sleep. Her bleary eyes the next morning suggested to fellow office workers that she had spent the night drunk. "I felt sick, miserable. In my ears sounded Dr. Graham's words which I had heard last evening. I felt that they were directed just to me, not to hundreds of thousands throughout Europe.

"With the greatest expectation I waited for evening. When I entered the great hall, I couldn't find a seat, but only a little standing space near the wall. Again I heard mighty words from God's servant. I understood every word and this time I could not lend a deaf ear. I could scarcely wait for the invitation and, when it was given, I was the first one who went forward. I was very much afraid, but when I came to the screen my fear left me. Wonderful assurance and peace entered into my heart, my whole being. I stood there firm like a rock in spite of the thousand eyes who looked on a girl standing alone before a large screen testifying about her new stand for Christ. Afterward others joined me, many came forward; but I felt that I was alone with God.

"From that moment my life was quite changed. I can witness everywhere and to everybody my experience that life without Christ has no sense. I know to whom I belong, and that all successes in this life without him are just great failures."

Nearly eighteen months after Euro 70 Josip Horak wrote in English to Billy Graham on 30 November 1971, on return from a visitation in different parts of Yugoslavia. "Everywhere they love you and ask about you. O how they long to see you! Everybody asked me when you will come again to our country, because they expect it will be easier to come here. So they and we pray. . . ."

Horak had frequently broadcast the Dortmund sermons over Transworld radio to Yugoslavia and throughout Eastern and Western Europe where many Yugoslavs live as temporary workers or as exiles. That same autumn of 1971 Dave Barr of World Wide Pictures brought to Zagreb the first four prints of the Euro 70 film, *We Hand the Torch to You*, with Serbo-Croatian sound track. Once again the crypt-hall of the

Roman Catholic church of Blessed Marks Krizevcanina (a Catholic martyr of the Reformation) was packed with a thousand people, Protestants and Catholics and Orthodox, despite the cold.

When Billy Graham came on the screen, they gave him a standing ovation.

7 London and "Moral Integrity"

Two chartered accountants from Belfast sat among the five thousand leaders of British business who had secured balloted places for the conference of the Institute of Directors at the Royal Albert Hall, London, early in November 1970. These annual one-day conferences, which include more men and women of top caliber in commerce, banking and industry than any other gathering in the United Kingdom, always selected five of the six speakers for their fame and importance in the business world. Each prime minister spoke during his term of office. The sixth address traditionally came from a man of eminence such as the Duke of Edinburgh, the Prince of Wales, the mayor of New York, or Peter Scott the naturalist. From time to time the director-general, Sir Richard Powell, invited a religious leader such as the chief rabbi, the cardinal archbishop of Westminster, or the archbishop of Canterbury.

As the two Irish accountants left the hall, one of them, J. R. Johnston, remarked to his partner, William Fitch, that it would be wonderful if Billy Graham could be invited. He then wrote to the director-general, who replied favorably, although Johnston's letter left no lasting impression on him. Back in Belfast, Johnston mentioned this reply to Fitch, who knew Sir Richard personally. Fitch's father, Dr. Thomas Fitch, a prominent Presbyterian minister, had been one of Billy Graham's earliest Irish friends and hosts, and William himself had come to the final point of dedicating his business life to the service of God through reading Billy Graham's biography.

Graham was due in London for a two-week visit centered round a pageant and set-piece oration at the Albert Hall to celebrate the 350th anniversary of the Pilgrim Fathers. Dr. Fitch was taking a small deputation to plead with him for a crusade in Belfast, which had been torn by civil strife since the summer of 1969. Bill Fitch decided to clinch his directors' conference idea, secured his father's permission to join the deputation, and telephoned Sir Richard Powell, who responded with enthusiasm. Fitch assured him that Graham, while not compromising his message, would suit the speech to the occasion.

In London on Tuesday 17 November Graham received the Irishmen. On hearing about the Institute of Directors, he made a perceptive comment. "If Sir Richard needs me to go and see him at his office I would be delighted to do so." Fitch knew of Billy's crowded schedule and was surprised at that offer. A time was arranged for the two to meet, sandwiched between Graham's being interviewed by the Sunday *Observer* and a long afternoon of radio interviews and televised discussion at the BBC.

"I expected him," Sir Richard related, "to be staying at the Savoy, but to my surprise he was staying at a very modest hotel in a back street in Kensington—and in a small room at that—and this immediately endeared him to me. I spent a memorable hour with him, talking of everything under the sun." At the end of that conversation, Sir Richard gave, and Graham accepted, an invitation to speak at the next year's Institute of Directors conference.

Powell has one final memory of their talk, "which I think illustrates Billy Graham's innate meekness, modesty and lack of swank." Powell had suggested that Graham lunch at the Institute's headquarters in Belgrave Square the next day. Billy replied that he would have loved to, "but I'm afraid I have another luncheon engagement I simply mustn't get out of." Sir Richard Powell afterward learned "by chance, that he had in fact been going to lunch with the queen! How many of us, frankly, could have resisted saying 'I'm sorry I can't lunch with you because I'm due at Buckingham Palace'? But not Billy."

Graham set about preparing for the Institute of Directors in the way he had used for years. In January 1971, ten months ahead, he outlined his preliminary thoughts to several of his staff and added, "This will be the most distinguished audience of Britishers that I have ever addressed, and my message will have to be professionally written, extremely clever, humorous, and with evangelism brought in very subtly." He also consulted one or two friends at the top of the business world in the United States, and after considering all suggestions he dictated his draft.

He decided to speak on integrity. "The major theme I would like to get across," he told an American industrialist when sending the draft, "is that both Britain and America need moral and spiritual renaissance. This has been said by many people on many occasions. Now, it is not only urgent but essential for our survival. It is going to have to start by someone making their commitment and lifting the torch. Of course my particular view is that it can start only with a personal relationship with Christ, that this relationship becomes the foundation and cornerstone of the restoration of moral integrity."

He sent a copy to Bill Fitch, begging him to be brutally frank. He sent one to Ernest Shippam, head of Shippam's Paste company in Sussex, a member of the Institute. Because Shippam had been an alcoholic before his conversion through Billy's 1954 London crusade, he wanted the directors to hear "an evangelical talk delivered with the fire of the Holy Spirit," like the one that had brought him to trust Christ on 12 April 1954 in Harringay arena. He feared Billy might hold back from "challenging each one of us as to what we are really like in God's eyes."

"Beloved friend," Billy replied, "we must keep in mind that I cannot possibly take advantage of a situation and give a straight-out evangelistic address. That would probably close the door for any evangelical contact in the future." In a burst of metaphors Billy went on: "I must be as wise as a serpent and harmless as a dove. At the same time I must not lower the flag or pull my punches. Everything I say on that day will be directed toward causing men and women to think about their personal spiritual condition—and their need of personal faith in Christ. However I must approach the situation in a totally different context than I would have at Harringay or Earls Court. I have given hundreds of such addresses in the past and somehow the Lord has honored them."

In contrast with Shippam, Sir Richard Powell felt that the draft was too sermonic in parts for the sophisticated and unsentimental audience which would include Jews, agnostics and atheists as well as Christians. He did not want Graham to compromise, but a broader, less personally emotive approach would tune in better.

After sending his reactions Powell "thoroughly expected a furious letter from Dr. Graham telling me that he wasn't used to being instructed on what he should say. Not a bit of it. I had a charming letter agreeing with all my proposed alterations." Powell liked the revised draft. The *Daily Mail* afterward printed a story that big business had "censored" Graham, a leak that grieved both Powell and Billy. The culprit was never traced.

On the Friday before the directors' conference Billy Graham fell suddenly ill of severe abdominal pains and fever while filming at Wembley television studios with Cliff Richard. He had not fully recovered by the Tuesday morning when he took his seat on the platform of the Albert Hall on 2 November 1971.

The opening speaker, Lord Goodman, outlining the day's program, made a gracious reference to Billy Graham. "He brings to his eternal verities a quality that is unique." A series of speeches by prestigious men preceded Billy—a long day. "I found that I was a bit weaker from my illness than I had anticipated and was extremely weary by the time I stood up," he said.

In contrast with the tones of optimism of earlier speakers, Billy Graham, after two funny stories and some gracious impromptus, sounded a note of warning as he discoursed on integrity. "Whether we survive or not as a civilization is going to depend on our attitude toward the moral laws instilled by the Creator of the Universe. . . . When a society loses its moral and spiritual moorings a vacuum is created, and it inevitably falls victim to alien ideologies and tyranny." By allusions and examples Graham made the point that the root of contemporary trouble is not economic or military but, as always, the human heart. "No matter how far man advances scientifically, his heart is exactly the same as it was in Jeremiah's day: 'the heart is deceitful above all things and desperately wicked.' "

The directors listened intently as thirty-five minutes sped by. In Powell's opinion, "It is no exaggeration to say that Billy Graham electrified his audience—tough, hard businessmen though they were." Throughout the address one director (who had drunk too much) interrupted and heckled, a unique experience for that august annual occasion. That increased Graham's exhaustion; he felt he was doing less than his best. His hearers were unaware of any strain. The few to whom he had shown the script listened astonished at the contrast between the written draft and its delivery. Bill Fitch, whose enterprise had opened this opportunity, thought the address "masterly." "Might I say," he wrote afterward to Billy, "that I would not have believed it possible that you could have been given such liberty in delivery and such authority in the presentation of your address." Ernest Shippam, who had criticized Billy's refusal to give a crusade-style sermon, gladly recalls, "I thought the address quite splendid for the audience. . . . what he said undoubtedly was governed by the Holy Spirit."

Graham spoke of the dehumanization of life and the need to restore moral and spiritual values. "When Britain was in danger of moral decadence in the 18th century, a small, unknown man walked across the pages of your history. His name was John Wesley. He talked in the open fields about the God of grace and forgiveness; he demanded a personal experience on the part of his listeners." Billy spoke of John Newton and William Wilberforce. Returning to the title of his speech he reminded his listeners that the word *integrity* comes from the Latin for "whole." "Our Lord often said to the people of his day, "Wilt thou be made whole?" He was called the Great Physician and he taught that men and women not only need but must have a new birth if they are to be made whole for this life and be prepared for the life to come. . . . it is only by having experienced this new birth that a nation or an individual can be born again morally or spiritually."

As he reached his peroration, he told a story about Winston Churchill's words to the boys of Harrow: "Never give in! Never! Never! Never!" He ended, "The torch of moral and spiritual power has been handed to you by other generations. If it flickers and goes out, no matter what your economic power is, or your military power, we are finished. But I say today, Let us hold the torch high, let us make it a moral and spiritual drumbeat that marches out of step with the permissiveness of these times. And as we march, let us never give in. Never! Never! Never!"

He sat down exhausted, to a standing ovation. That evening, while Billy began his journey home through an airport strike, delay, diversion, and fog, Sir Richard Powell wrote in his own hand: "I feel I simply cannot let the day go by without writing you this note, on my return from the Albert Hall, to thank you for what you did for us today. Your inspiring address lifted us all way up above the level of our everyday lives. We are deeply grateful to you."

8 Ireland: Mission of Reconciliation

NORTHERN Ireland's grievous troubles, with much destruction and loss of life, had continued for more than two years when William Fitch, during the London visit in November 1971 for the address to the Institute of Directors, discussed once again the urgent conviction that Billy Graham could fulfill a valuable ministry in Ulster.

Graham had promised long ago to hold a crusade in Belfast but in January 1970 he had written to a friend, "I just do not feel led in my heart at the moment to accept an invitation." In the late summer of 1971 he again gave it serious thought yet doubted the wisdom of it. "I do not want to give the impression that I am coming to take sides in a political issue." Walter Smyth told Fitch on September 30 of Graham's anxiety, so that his motives in coming might not be misunderstood. "When he comes, it will be with the hope that God will give him both a saving and a healing ministry and he does not want, in any sense of the term, to be the means of causing a disturbance   Right now, Mr. Graham feels the check of the Spirit." Consultations at the highest government levels in the United States and the United Kingdom were almost unanimous in advice to Graham "that this is not the time for me to come—but a visit later might be most helpful."

By mid-March 1972 the situation had so worsened that the British cabinet prepared to impose "direct rule" from Westminster. In both the communities of Ulster, the Protestant majority and the Roman Catholic minority, many believed that political moves could not alone create a climate in which violence would cease. After renewed pleas from Ireland, Graham's British Board sent a fact-finding mission of five laymen to assess whether his coming would be wise or welcome in Belfast or Dublin, either for a crusade or for a private visit to meet leaders and invited groups.

The London staff also approached a senior member of the government, a man not directly involved with Northern Irish affairs but a personal friend of Graham. He replied in strict confidence that he would support the view that Graham should go to both capitals on a private visit, and that a crusade should be held, provided it excluded political reference and took reconciliation as its theme. He doubted the physical possibility of a crusade in Belfast at the present, and suggested waiting two or three weeks to see the results of the British government's anticipated initiative. Direct rule was actually announced during the visit of the five laymen to Belfast, who returned to London after exhaustive consultations with political and religious representatives and with private individuals, Protestant and Catholic. On March 27, after talking with London by telephone, Walter Smyth reported to Graham "that the consensus was you should visit both cities for private meetings with leaders as soon as possible. In fact, it was mentioned again and again that the 'only man in the world today who could help both sides at this time was Billy Graham.' " One figure in Northern Irish politics had stressed that the population of both communities was frustrated, bewildered and tired. A time would come when hard attitudes would be abandoned and the people would want to draw together again. If a crusade hit that moment, he said, Billy Graham "could do incalculable good"; meanwhile a private visit as soon as possible, to include appearances on television, "could produce fruitful results." One recommendation of the British Board of BGEA was that Graham should aim to leave behind him a thousand dialogue groups, each comprised of five Roman Catholics and five Protestants.

Thereafter Walter Smyth, in close accord with William Fitch, was in and out of Belfast and Dublin making arrangements. Walter had a special interest: both his parents, of Presbyterian stock, had emigrated from Ireland. Though he was born in Philadelphia, he had spent eight years of his boyhood in Belfast; the First World War had prevented his father, temporarily resident in Ireland on business, from taking the family home to America. Walter's gift for human relationships and for discretion eased the delicate negotiations with both communities in each city. The secretary of the Dublin Committee, Mrs. Neill, described him as "that gracious and gentle ambassador."

Two weeks before Billy Graham arrived in Ireland he held a seven-day crusade in the Deep South of the United States, at a place, Birmingham, Alabama, which demonstrated the power of Christ to heal social differences as deep and historic as those in Ulster. On Easter Day 1964, following a serious outbreak of racial conflict, Billy had held a rally which proved a turning point in local race relations—so that when Billy held a crusade to celebrate the centennial of the city, from 14–21 May 1972, the change in the intervening eight years was one of the factors in the great happiness of the interracial preparations and of the crusade itself. Billy therefore left Alabama for Ireland, having witnessed how a community of conflict may become a community at peace.

A trivial change of plan plunged Billy Graham at once into the heart of the suffering. The original schedule had him arrive from the Continent on Sunday. Since this might wound Protestant susceptibilities, he arrived instead on Saturday evening, 27 May 1972. The extra time enabled him to accept an invitation to preach on Sunday evening the farewell sermon for his old friend, Dr. Thomas Fitch, William Fitch's father, who was retiring from his long ministry at Ravenshill Presbyterian church. Billy had preached there as a young unknown in 1946.

Sunday morning, however, had no engagement. It happened that Arthur Blessitt of the "Jesus People," a young "way-out minister of Sunset Strip," whose personal evangelistic tour, carrying a tall cross, had created a profound impression in Britain, was then in Northern Ireland reaching both communities. Billy told Graham Lacey, the twenty-three-year-old businessman who had arranged Blessitt's tour, that he wanted to go, without publicity, into the heart of the troubled area. "Arthur Blessitt," relates Billy, "carrying his cross from one area to the other had made friends with people in some of the more difficult parts of Belfast. He asked me if I had the courage to go with him on a Sunday morning down the most famous street which is more or less a dividing line between the so-called Protestants and Catholics. He said before we started, 'You will be watched by field glasses from upstairs windows—and if they accept you, you won't feel anything; and if they don't accept you, you won't feel anything because it will be a bullet in the back.' "

Graham Lacey recalls how "we sat in the car and had a time of prayer, committing the lives of Arthur and his wife and Billy into the Lord's care. They were to enter what are undoubtedly the two most dangerous roads in Northern Ireland, without any police guard or special security arrangements. Then Billy, in great humility, turned around and said, 'Now, you're going to have to treat me as a student of personal evangelism. I don't consider myself to be a man who's gifted of God just to deal with an individual.' "

Walking down the Protestants' Shankhill Road, the two evangelists "met a young man and talked with him, and this young man," continues Lacey, "got down on his knees with Billy Graham and Arthur Blessitt and made a total commitment of his life to the Lord. Although his heart's ambition had been to meet Billy Graham, he hardly expected he'd come face-to-face with him while walking to church that morning.

"We then walked along the Peace Line, which is an Army barricade dividing the Protestant and Catholic roads which run parallel with each other." Right on the Peace Line, amid the bomb damage, they knelt down and prayed for peace and for a revival to bring that peace. Billy recalls: "We could see on one side a Catholic church with a cross, and on the other side a Protestant church with a cross. Since it was Sunday morning we could see worshipers going in and out. It seemed to me weird and strange and incongruous that people who looked alike, spoke alike, and had the same culture, could be so divided. Yet I realized that the problems go far back into history and involve deep social and political divisions."

In the Falls Road, the extreme Catholic area where the IRA are dominant, "We walked along handing out tracts and speaking to people about the Lord. We stopped at a pub that was going full blast. The men in the pub recognized me, and both Arthur and I had an opportunity to preach to them. They laughed loudly at our jokes and gave us a great round of applause after our testimony." The pub was a *skabena* (unlicensed, illegal tavern) in the back of a hairdresser's shop. Many of those drinking were members of the IRA. Lacey remembers how "one man, the worse for drink, decided he would like to sing. So Billy Graham made a deal with him that when Arthur was through speaking about the Lord he could start singing. And at the end of Arthur's message, which was dynamic and of God, the drunk man started to sing 'The Devil in the Deep Blue Sea.' "

Lacey had been moved by the way Billy Graham talked about Christ to individuals in the *skabena* and to the man on the Shankhill Road. Billy's disclaimer of any gift for personal evangelism struck him as humility in the extreme.

They went next to Anderson Road, where early that morning a powerful bomb being carried by terrorists to a car had exploded prematurely, killing residents asleep in the small houses beside the street. Lacey continues, "We walked with a great feeling of shock, as it was evident that a dreadful tragedy had taken place. Billy went in with me to one of the houses where a bus conductor's wife had been killed and he'd been left alive. Standing in that utter bewilderment, it was remarkable to see the magnetism, almost the presence and beauty of the Lord, that seemed to shine from Billy's face, that drew the people to him to talk with him."

The two and a half hour visit to this danger area gave Billy an understanding and empathy that greatly helped his ministry in Belfast. Early on Monday morning, however, all that might have been compromised by a chance telephone call from the president of the United States.

The president was then in Moscow, and wanted to tell Billy, supposing him in North Carolina, that he had followed his advice and had attended the Moscow Baptist church (to the great encouragement of Christians in the Soviet Union). The call, through the White House, reached the switchboard of Billy's hotel in Belfast. The night porter refused to accept it because he had been ordered not to disturb Mr. Graham. The White House persevered, however, and Graham was awakened to take the call. He, Smyth and Fitch realized that some, refusing to believe that a call that had passed twice across the Atlantic could be simply about going to church, would ascribe it to presidential interference in the Irish situation, and would thereafter resent and mistrust Graham. The staff attempted to keep the call secret, but it leaked. Still, the truth of it was told.

In the next two days Billy Graham addressed a dinner for 200 leaders of the province; a breakfast for 1,000 arranged by the Christian

Businessmen's Committee; and met individuals and smaller groups. He had insisted that, with the obvious exception of the Ravenshill church service, all meetings must be fully integrated between Catholics and Protestants. Thus the dinner for 200 political and civic leaders included unionists and republicans who had never sat together before. That evening the Official IRA suspended military action (the independer more violent Provisional IRA did not follow suit for another three weeks, and soon broke off their truce).

Billy was regarded as an effective peacemaker by many in Ulster and received urgent requests to return for a crusade as soon as conditions allowed. Yet scores in the Protestant community rejected him because he reached out also to Catholics. He felt no surprise that Ian Paisley the hardliner had denounced him from the pulpit (not knowing that two of Billy's associates, T. W. Wilson and John Wesley White, were in the congregation listening to the tirade). Billy gladly prepared to meet Paisley but no meeting materialized. "I suppose the thing that surprised me most," Billy comments in retrospect, "was what I felt was a spiritual hardness and bitterness in Northern Ireland among some people, and the overwhelming enthusiasm and warmth that I felt in Southern Ireland. Yet it might have been a misjudgment, because the people in Ulster had gone through so much suffering and turmoil. I was treated with great hospitality in both areas and met many wonderful dedicated Christians on both sides." Ulstermen who were the closest concerned do not consider that a misjudgment. They know that Billy Graham's bid to reconcile Protestants with Catholics met rejection and antagonism, even from some who otherwise support his evangelism. The history of the following years shows that a broad movement of Protestants toward reconciliation and friendship with Catholics might not, in itself, have brought peace at that time, since the IRA, with substantial foreign financial aid, aimed to destroy the union with Great Britain which the Protestant majority were at that time determined to preserve.

Billy's Northern Irish friends sensed that he was aware of his rejection. They felt, too, his constraint, his anxiety lest he say or do anything to worsen the Irish problem. Yet one memorable occasion was "a wonderful time of discussion and prayer" in strict privacy at the archbishop's palace at Armagh, with the four church leaders of all Ireland: Archbishop Simms, the Anglican primate; Cardinal Conway, the Roman Catholic primate, the Presbyterian moderator and the Methodist president. The four leaders, who had been conferring regularly since the troubles began, had just issued a joint statement following an earlier statement and a Day of Prayer on Good Friday, calling on all to reject violence and to pray for a just solution. Cardinal Conway remembers the meeting with Graham as "a very pleasant occasion," noting especially that he "appreciated how delicate and complex the situation here was." Dr. Simms recalls that Graham's "readiness to listen as he went from place to place, and to be in touch with a very complex problem, even though there were no easy answers, impressed us all." Graham left Armagh aware more than ever that politics, not religion, were causing the violence in Ulster.

Another "highlight of my visit" was his warm and enthusiastic reception by the students of The Queen's University of Belfast, at a meeting, packed to capacity, arranged by the four chaplains, Roman Catholic and Protestant. Graham talked about the spiritual movement then sweeping American universities and urged that a revival, transforming the tragic condition of Northern Ireland, could break out among his listeners, the students. He spoke of the dangers "unless we can swing around and let Jesus Christ be our God and our Lord and our Master. God can give you the love and the understanding so desperately needed at this hour."

Billy sat down to an ovation. "He put it over with such a sense of love," said one student. Another said, "I think he really expressed what Jesus Christ means. For young people today this is really what we need. We need to get turned on with Jesus and then all the hate and fighting and bigotry will stop."

When Billy went to Ulster Television (the independent channel), they laid on a tea before starting the recording, to introduce people whom otherwise he might have missed. His visit made a deep impression on the television staff. The studio manager even sent a telegram after him to Dublin: ". . . You have helped give me a closer awareness of God, which I have always wanted but could never easily find before. I shall be forever truly grateful to you. . . ."

The discussion within Ulster TV's "Billy Graham's Prayer for Ireland" hardly gave Graham, again conscious that a word out of place might hinder efforts for peace, the openings he had used for apostolic witness in the BBC discussion chaired by David Frost in London during the 1966 crusade. But when the Ulster program was screened throughout the United Kingdom, few viewers would have endorsed the sneers of the critic of a London Sunday paper. Watching in the security of an England not yet afflicted by IRA bombs, he wrote, "The Preacher projected an unedifying image: a man of self-confidence and vast energy without sensitivity or real intelligence: a man obsessed with his own 'goodness.' "

In contrast, a Belfast resident wrote after watching Graham on the other (BBC) channel: "The visit of Dr. Graham to our strife-torn community came as balm to Protestant and Roman Catholic alike. All who listened to him must have been impressed by his graciousness and sincerity. His message to all sections of the community was 'pray and study the Bible together.' I should be pleased to hear from anyone— Protestant or Roman Catholic—interested in following the great man's advice."

The writer, a Protestant, immediately heard from the Cistercian monastery at Portglenone asking if the monks might come and pray. William Fitch later visited that monastery, and they prayed and studied the Bible at the first of monthly meetings. The monks' initiative led to similar moves across the religious divide.

The railway train crossed the border into Eire. Graham relaxed, becoming almost a different man. Yet he scarcely expected the warmth of his reception from both communities in the capital of a country predominantly Roman Catholic. "I was absolutely overwhelmed."

The visit had been organized by the Irish Council for International Christian Leadership, whose president was J. F. Dempsey, founder of Aer Lingus and a director of the Bank of Ireland, a Roman Catholic. The vice-president, Margaret Hamilton-Reid, a Protestant business-woman, had tried in person to give Graham an invitation to Dublin after the Institute of Directors meeting at the Albert Hall. When the dates of the visit to Ireland were fixed, however, Billy Graham's staff worked with the ICL in preference to others because of its broad base: Catholics and Protestants, business, the professions and government. Representatives of the Roman and Anglican archbishops and of other bodies joined the special committee. They had three weeks to prepare, with a host of willing volunteers, irrespective of denomination, "from the young P.R.O. [public relations officer] who arranged the press conference and all other related matters, the secretary who rolled off hundreds of hymn sheets, the businessman who lent and installed an organ and 20 TV sets for the relays, the lawyer who recruited volunteers to provide transportation, the other secretary who arranged the printing of tickets, the Jesuit priest who planned for and sent out invitations to a meeting for clergy. . . . There was little time for organized prayer except in small groups, so we prayed as we went, and the Lord heard and answered."

At Connolly station, Dublin, on Wednesday 31 May, as the ICL leaders escorted Billy down the platform some reporters blocked the way. Since the press had promised not to bother him but rather to wait for the press conference, his hosts tried to brush them off. "And he said," recalls Mrs. Neill, " 'As they have been good enough to meet me, I will say a few words to them.' The police had provided an escort for his car, and as they shot through the lights and kept the roads clear of traffic, he said: 'Are they doing this for me?' When they stopped outside his hotel, he went over to them, shook hands and thanked them for their help. These and many other small acts of graciousness endeared him to people and were a good prelude to his message—as when, after luncheon at the home of friends, he took time to seek out the housekeeper and thank her personally for her good cooking; she traveled miles from her remote home to attend his meeting."

In Dublin, Billy Graham had an engagement to meet the leader of the Official IRA in strict secrecy; he refused to disclose details at the time. Walter Smyth had been approached by a go-between a few days earlier in Belfast and had reacted with suspicion. Billy was doubtful, too, at first but they looked into it. "The Dublin police," Graham recalls, "had been contacted and were against the meeting, but I decided to go anyway, because of, first, curiosity; second, to learn what I could about the situation; third, I thought I might be a spiritual witness, fourth, I suppose the element of surprise, the possibility of danger, all challenged me.

"Walter and I were taken out the back door of the hotel, through the kitchen and into a car driven by two bearded men. They drove us to another spot in Dublin. We transferred cars and went straight to a working-class community. We were taken in the front door and were met by a lovely European-accented woman, who took us to a surprisingly affluent living room, where I met Mr.—." This man, Walter tells, was clearly glad to meet Billy Graham, though at the beginning "a little standoffish. But Billy has a way of disarming people very quickly." The IRA chief surprised them by his brilliance, his well-informed, reasoned flow of conversation. Billy says, "He talked for three quarters of an hour before I said anything, giving me a brief history of the background of the fighting in Ireland. I left there with the distinct feeling that the issues involved were not religious but political." Billy spoke of Christ's power and what Christ had done, for him, stressing his conviction that Christ himself was the only solution to Northern Ireland's problems. The two men had tea together before Billy returned to his planned engagements.

Those engagements demonstrated enormous good will toward him. The *Irish Times* commented on the breakfast meeting for 450 chaired by Chief Justice O'Dalaigh, afterward president of Ireland: "There are not many people in Europe, even the world, who could have attracted such a prestigious assembly from Irish life, as Dr. Billy Graham did. . . . The guest list was startling for the brains and wealth and influence it represented." Tickets, all free, were so sought after that they changed hands in a kind of black market. William Fitch, who had come with Graham from Belfast, heard of four business meetings "that could not be started following the breakfast because the men who were there couldn't stop talking about what they'd heard. I know of men who were killed in an air crash shortly after, who were at that breakfast. Some of them had appointments arranged to discuss spiritual matters when they got back. The whole visit to Dublin was extraordinary."

A smaller lunch included the prime minister, the two archbishops of Dublin, and the provincial general of the Jesuits. There was a meeting for clergy, Catholic and Protestant, and another for an invited cross-section of the public from near and far, of all ages: 2,000 came to the Royal Dublin Society. As Billy entered the hall, a Catholic priest ran up and shook him warmly by the hand, saying he was in the priesthood because of hearing him at a crusade. "And what shall I give them tonight?" asked Graham. "Oh," replied the priest, "they will want a crusade-type message." And that, one of those present recalls, "is what he gave, with simplicity and power, to a quiet and receptive audience."

When Graham went afterward to speak briefly in the two overflow halls which had heard by closed-circuit TV, one of the chairmen, another Catholic priest, told the audience that he had come to Christ through reading Graham's *Peace with God.*

A disc jockey the next morning made snide remarks about buckets going around for the collection and Billy Graham driving off in a cream-colored Rolls Royce. The disc jockey publicly apologized on the air the following day, saying the switchboard had been jammed with callers, none representing the committee, who had told him the facts: no collection, a volunteer driver in his own car (not a Rolls) and the Royal Dublin Society halls paid for by a student. That young man and his wife had dipped into their pockets as a means of bringing their spiritually unsympathetic relatives to hear the gospel. As a result, the student's father, sister, two brothers and their wives all entered part-time Christian work.

Billy Graham left Dublin in the rain on Friday 2 June and flew to London, thrilled by Eire. "I felt a sense of revival, and I had the feeling that if Ireland is going to be saved it is going to come from spiritual revival that is now taking place in South Ireland." "It was a historic occasion," wrote the mother superior of a Sacred Heart convent who had attended the VIP lunch, "and I am sure that the presence of Billy Graham in Dublin at such a time will do much to shake us all into the realization that we have to *pray* more earnestly for peace. Demonstrations are of little avail. . . ." The tape of Graham's breakfast was played in a convent in Donegal to all the nuns. The Holy Ghost Fathers in Dublin started a weekly ecumenical prayer meeting; more than 150 were attending three months later when William Fitch told Ruth Graham that the increasing interest in the Roman Catholic community, the desire to discuss spiritual matters with Protestants, "has been overwhelming." Interchurch relations in Eire had been friendly for years but hardly ever had involved open spiritual contacts; seventeen months after Graham's visit one of his associates, Akbar Haqq, could hold a united crusade in Dublin.

From embattled Belfast, Fitch told Graham a year later that they continued both "to hear of people who have been saved as a result of your being here" and to receive pleas to continue what was started. "The meetings that you had with the leaders, religiously, politically, and commercially, undoubtedly stimulated a concern which we have found very difficult to satisfy."

Perhaps the most apt summing-up came from a Church of Ireland rector in a private letter written in the immediate aftermath of the Dublin visit. "It was truly a wonderful experience and a spiritual encounter with Christ through his Servant Billy Graham. It was a challenge to my own personal life and also to my ministry. He has left me much to think about and pray about. Billy Graham has gone away leaving all of us a challenge regarding our *personal* and *collective* commitment to the cause of Christ in Ireland, which I believe is a commitment for *Love, Joy* and *Peace* among all Christians in Ireland regardless of their denomination. The only solution to Ireland's problems and the world's problems is to be found in the Cross of Christ."

PART THREE

⑨ "Not the Work of Man"

O N 22 May 1970 hundreds of buses converged on Neyland Stadium outside Knoxville, Tennessee from as far away as one hundred miles. Months of planning, cooperation and prayer were about to culminate in a crusade which Billy Graham looks back upon as one of his happiest. He reached Knoxville exhausted from Dortmund, without his usual time for rest, meditation and study, and spent much of each day before the service resting in bed.

Knoxville, a city of 174,000 people, tucked away in the shadow of the Great Smoky Mountains, was an unlikely candidate for a crusade at a time when much larger centers of population throughout the United States were clamoring for one. Lane Adams, however, once a fighter pilot, nightclub singer, but now a Presbyterian clergyman and associate evangelist on the Team, lived there. He knew that this region of great natural beauty and scattered industries (including Oak Ridge atomic energy plant) could create a crusade to touch the nation. Long ago he had presented the city key to Billy Graham, conveying the mayor's plea that "you will come to Knoxville and use this key to open many hearts to the Lord Jesus Christ."

Billy could make no promises. Three years later, at a ceremony at Montreat, he received letters of invitation from twelve denominations, eleven mayors and five college presidents, backed by a mile-long scroll containing 129,000 signatures. Using petition forms printed on paper donated by the manufacturers, people had signed in shopping centers, restaurants, factories, banks, until the names represented a cross-section of Eastern Tennessee.[1]

Two events give the Knoxville crusade historic importance. One was the emergence of Johnny Cash as a force in evangelism. This country singer's songs voiced the feelings and hopes of the poor, the prisoners and downtrodden. In boyhood the generous and kindly Cash had been an openly committed Christian, but now his slavery to drugs and drink had been so recent that the advance announcement of his coming to the platform worried some Knoxville citizens. Billy and T. W. Wilson, however, had met him privately. Cash "gave God the glory for delivering him," Wilson assured a correspondent, "and he told us personally what the Lord had done for him." He shared with them the story he made public some years later in his autobiography, *The Man in Black.* Billy believed that a testimony before the stadium crowd might lead Cash to commit himself totally to Christ, and that Johnny and his wife June "could be a great force for the Kingdom of God in this particular period."

So it proved. In the bright sunshine of the first Sunday, 24 May 1970, Johnny Cash sang with the entire cast of his television show. In a brief speech he warned young people to stay off drugs. "Take it from a man who's been there, who knows what he's telling about. . . . I escaped. I was lucky beyond measure. Don't try it. It ain't worth it." His words sounded a solemn prelude to Billy Graham's evangelistic address. For Johnny and June Cash that experience opened a path of strong Christian witness and began a deep friendship with Billy.

Four days later, on Thursday 28 May, for the first time in history, a president of the United States spoke from the platform of an evangelistic mass meeting. President Johnson had attended a Graham crusade but was not on the platform. A proposal to invite President Nixon to the Memorial Day service (Saturday 30 May) had been conveyed to Billy at Dortmund. He replied to the crusade committee that "under no circumstances would we be able to publicize such a thing if he should be able to come. . . . If it's possible it would be great," but it was highly unlikely because of the international and domestic situation.

---

[1] For the presentation, with the media in attendance, the leaders came to Montreat in a bus, the scroll in a car which arrived very late owing to a traffic jam. Rushing in, the two men carrying the heavy scroll tripped on the carpet and spilled it dramatically across the room in front of Billy.

Graham forwarded the suggestion to the White House.

Despite their long friendship,[2] Graham had had contact with President Nixon in office less than he had with President Johnson. Although he disagreed with much in the politics of both, his convictions about Nixon in 1970 were positive. The president discussed the Knoxville invitation with Billy Graham at Montreat on the telephone, stressing a fear that his attendance might be given a political interpretation and that he was not free on Memorial Day. Billy was then surprised and pleased when the White House suddenly announced that President and Mrs. Nixon would stop off at Knoxville and drive to Neyland Stadium, where the president would make a brief speech and then listen to Billy Graham's sermon before flying on to California.

The president's speech would be nonpolitical, yet every public act in a controversial presidency is open to political interpretation. When Graham learned that the Republican challenger to Tennessee's Senator Gore (D) would be in the presidential party, he at once invited the senator, whose presence would show the crusade to be neutral. Gore was unable to come. Nixon was genuinely anxious to support Graham, yet he would also have an unusual platform, in a Republican area in the Democratic South, for his first public utterance on a college campus since ordering troops into Cambodia at the beginning of May. Graham for his part would have the entire nation focused on the preaching of the gospel.

On 28 May, Eastern Tennessee appeared to be moving en masse toward Neyland Stadium to hear the president and Billy Graham. The stands and aisles were packed with 75,000 persons; an estimated 25,000 sat on the banks and approaches and in parking lots listening by amplifier. Thousands reached no farther than the traffic jams and heard the crusade by radio. It was the largest public meeting in the history of the state and, being a crusade Youth Night, the greater proportion of those in reserved seats were young.

Billy Graham rose to welcome the presidential party, which included Henry Kissinger, "to the campus of the University of Tennessee where, during the last six days 325,000 people have attended this crusade and thousands have marched across this famous gridiron to give their lives to Jesus Christ as Savior and Lord. In a day of student unrest,

---

[2] See chapter 14.

here on the campus of one of the largest universities in America, tens of thousands have been demonstrating their faith in the God of their fathers. . . ." For the president to visit a religious meeting, Graham continued, was a reminder that "ours is a crisis of the spirit—that only the Spirit of God can heal us and bring us together." With obvious reference to Cambodia, Graham referred to agonizing and unpopular decisions by former presidents. "All Americans may not agree with the decision a president makes—but he is *our* president—" Great applause swept the stadium. "Mr. President, we welcome you and your family."

Suddenly a distant yelling rose. Some two or three hundred had come to this crusade service to demonstrate against the Vietnam war. At once counter-cheers and clapping drowned their yells. The president stood to speak. The small corner chanted an antiwar slogan, answered by boos and handclapping by the majority. Billy and Ruth looked on with a trace of anxiety, but the president, elated by the support from the rest of the audience, smiled broadly. Police were pulling out ring-leaders and making arrests, and a few Tennesseans lent muscular support.[3] The football players surrounded the platform. The crowd sang hymns in a volume of sound. Cliff Barrows recalls, "It became a contest between the choir plus 74,000 people, and the small group."

The demonstrators having been booed and sung into temporary silence, the president started to speak. Immediately they yelled obscenities, then stood up and chanted "Peace *now,* Peace *now.*" At that the whole stadium gave Nixon a standing ovation. Even then, the demonstrators refused to quiet down completely. The president eventually spoke above the chants.

As befitted a government official he did not deliver a religious address. In the memory of the crusade chairman it was very appropriate to the occasion but some others felt it left much to be desired. The president was extremely tired that night and carrying many burdens, but they had hoped he would have been a little more forthright in his own witness for Christ. He went no further than saying that a nation must be sterile, however much the improvements effected by government, "unless we have the spirit, a spirit that cannot come from a man

---

[3] According to one source, one of the protesters, who unwittingly was carrying a police "bug" in his clothing, was heard to say, "Let's get out of here before these Christians kill us!"

in government, a spirit that will be represented by the man who follows me."

The president ended with an assurance of respect for "those who disagree with me." Despite thunderous applause, the obscenities and chants continued.

Immediately Ethel Waters rose from her place on the platform. That veteran black singer and former stage star, who sang at crusades until her death in 1977, wagged a finger at the demonstrators. "Now you children, listen to Mama." They quieted. "I love you and I'd hug you. But if my arms were long enough I'd reach out and *smack* you." The roar of laughter defused the situation. The majority of the demonstrators left the stadium, not waiting for Billy's sermon. The president later wrote to him that the evening had exceeded the Nixons' expectations "by a wide margin."

When Billy gave the invitation and hundreds moved forward, about thirty of the dissenters joined them, some to give the peace sign and silently continue their protest, one or two intending mischief until stopped by ushers. Eight, genuinely moved by the sermon, decided for Christ; at least one of them entered the Christian ministry.

That evening Leighton Ford noticed another demonstration. Among those coming forward he saw a Christian at prayer in the charismatic way, with arms upraised. His arms began to tire. Then two men nearest, one white, one black, spontaneously held them up, as Aaron and Hur had held up the arms of Moses.

In the university the demonstration made the crusade even more a matter of controversy. No one could avoid taking sides. In dormitories and classes the cause and claims of Christ were debated from varying viewpoints. Many students were among the 12,308 decisions for Christ registered in those ten days of May 1970. The president of the University, A. D. Holt, told an outside audience the next month that the coming of Billy Graham was the best thing that had happened in his recollection. To Billy he wrote, "Tennessee is a better State, U.T. is a better school, and I am a better guy because you came our way. Eloquent evidence of your good work may be seen in the improved church attendance, happier homes, and more dedicated Christian lives throughout our region." Nearly seven years later, at New Year 1977, Dr. Holt wrote to the author, "We are still enjoying the benefits of the enrichment that he gave to our lives."

A few weeks before the Knoxville crusade its chairman, Ralph Frost of the University of Tennessee, had written to Graham, "Many of us feel that if the crusade never became a reality, much good has already been accomplished in preparation and that we would feel fully repaid for our time and efforts."

Those words are echoed again and again throughout North America, as in other parts of the world. Tom Landry, head coach of the Dallas Cowboys, wrote four years after he had been chairman of the Dallas (1971) crusade that "The Billy Graham Team do such a tremendous job in their pre-crusade preparation that I'm not sure that we don't have as many conversions at that time as we do when Dr. Graham speaks during the crusade itself." At Cleveland (1972), the preparation team, in the words of Katie Williams, the chairman's wife, "gave us a tremendous lift in our Christian walk. We frequently said before the crusade, 'Were Billy Graham never to make the trip to Cleveland, we still could never be the same.' "

Such comments demonstrate that a crusade is far more than a series of meetings in a stadium or arena; most of it takes place before or afterward. "What most people see," says Sterling Huston, director of crusades in North America "is the high visibility part, the nightly meetings when thousands gather in a much-prayed-for setting to hear the clear proclamation of the gospel, and hundreds and often thousands respond to make their commitment to Christ. But evangelism is occurring in many ways in fulfilment of the immediate objective," which is to win men, women and children to Christ by many different means through thousands of Christians over a wide area. "The ultimate objective," Huston continues, "is that the local church will be strengthened in its work of witness long after we have left the community."

Graham and the Team stress that, in the New Testament, evangelism always builds up the church. Likewise a crusade must begin, continue and end with local churches. If they are not left stronger, the Team has failed. Many already would be much concerned for evangelism or they would not desire a crusade, but a time had come when they wanted to focus their entire region upon the claims of the Christian faith by the preaching of Billy Graham, backed by methods of preparation and follow-up developed over the years by him and his Team, and still evolving.

Invitations to hold crusades pour in from the four corners of the earth and from every part of North America. Acceptance of a particular place involves numerous factors and assessments, but the most important factor is prayer. Sterling Huston says, "We have tried to build a strategy in crusades that makes prayer the rudimentary activity. We start when a committee writes to us, by replying 'Yes, find out who is interested, get a broad scope of people involved, and pray.' When they say, 'When can we have a date?' and we're not able to give an answer, we say, 'Pray.' When they ask, 'What can we do next?' we say, 'Pray.' That is not just 'spiritual' comment; it is a conviction on our part that as they pray, God will ripen an area, prepare the Team's heart and the hearts of local leadership so that we'll come together at the right time and the right place."

The final decision where to go is Billy Graham's. It is largely subjective, after prayer and discussion with Walter Smyth, Cliff Barrows, Sterling Huston and local leaders. Graham takes advice, as in all aspects of his ministry, "but I reserve the right," he says, "to make the final decision."

Once a crusade is accepted, directors are appointed from the Team. "We go into a city," recalled one former director, Harry Williams, "and a sense of desperation and urgency fills my heart. When you find yourself in a hotel room in a large city, and you look out of that bleak window to a mass of concrete, buses, and teeming thousands of people, and you look over a stadium that has 70 or 80,000 seats—the sense of aloneness that somehow comes over you is overwhelming. But at the same time you sense the undergirding presence of God, who has called us there."

Another director, Larry Turner, adds, "Fresh from the victories in a previous city, you are awe-struck and you wonder how in the world are you ever going to fall in love with this city and how are you going to do the work properly. But within a few short days you begin to know people. You sense their heartbeat. It is the greatest privilege you can imagine to become close to people in many, many different parts of the country—to see the Lord's family with the same objectives, the same fervent burden for people who are outside of Christian fellowship."

The first task is to mobilize the many hundreds of churches and their congregations. Every minister is invited to the meeting where the principles of preparation are explained. The crusade director does not poll the clergy as to whether they will support; a refusal is hard to reverse, whereas the misinformed or reluctant, if left neutral, may join in later. Nor does anyone probe their theology. A few may hold aloof because of that: they condemn Graham's refusal to censor belief before he invites cooperation. Billy appreciates their dilemma but rejects the view that "because we have people on the committee from liberal institutions we are endorsing the theology of those institutions. The theology we endorse is the theology I will be proclaiming from the platform. If they want to come and endorse what I am saying, thank God! . . . I will never go anywhere where there are strings on my message. I ask all to attend and cooperate who wish to, regardless of what identification they may have. Who serves on what committee seems to me to be rather incidental. It is what is proclaimed from the platform that counts." Many a liberal theologian has rediscovered the Bible while helping in a crusade.

The preparatory meeting elects the chairman and the executive, which includes the heads of up to fourteen working committees to plan the varied aspects: Arrangements, Choir, Counseling, Finance, Follow-up, etc. The entire region, which may cover thousands of square miles and many millions of inhabitants, is alerted and guided by the simple expedient of the "pyramid" structure which is normal in American secular management.

For a crusade, four lines of mobilizing committees—ministers, laymen, women, youth—go all the way down to the huge base of the pyramid, until every congregation is preparing as though the crusade were to be held in their own sanctuary, every household is aware of it, and many have enrolled to learn more about the Christian faith or to help in one way or another. Thus a web is weaved of activities and Bible studies, in order to deploy resources of every kind, to train multitudes in evangelism and enthuse them. Sterling Huston heard a Presbyterian pastor say to a ministers' meeting, "If you get your people involved in a crusade, be prepared to run when it's over to catch up with them!"

The effectiveness of the preparations will much depend on the choice of right leaders at every level. John Corts, a crusade director, reckons that in the early days he spends much of his time praying about people and guiding the sponsoring committee in how to choose them. The world, he says, may rely on organization "but God depends on people."

At one time the structure included a prayer committee. During the nineteen seventies the Team integrated the responsibility for prayer into the four principal and mobilizing committees to make sure (in Huston's words) that "a part of their regular meetings is prayer—not just token prayer but meaningful, committed prayer that binds their hearts together toward a common purpose and calls upon the resources of God which alone can accomplish a spiritual result." Walter Smyth said in 1974, "I have been with Billy Graham almost 25 years, and I'm more convinced than I have ever been that 'Except the Lord build the house, they labor in vain who build it.' We can waste a lot of time and effort, we can promote, we can do all kinds of things; but if we don't have the blessing of almighty God, our work's going to be in vain."

Graham puts the greatest possible emphasis on prayer, "the first thing we rely on." Through *Decision* magazine and Hour of Decision broadcasts he insures that millions know where he will hold his next crusade. There have been those who set themselves to pray constantly for his ministry, like Pearl Goode, who prayed faithfully from the time of the London Harringay crusade (1954). She would travel by bus to the place of a crusade in America; friends sometimes raised money for her to fly. "She came to every crusade" is Ruth Graham's memory. "She never bothered Bill, but she would pray, all night some nights. In Copenhagen she had to sit in a tub of hot water to keep warm, but she prayed." When Pearl Goode died in 1972 Ruth gave an address at her funeral. Pointing to the casket she said, "Here lie the mortal remains of one of the secrets of Bill's success."

Another of the secrets of his success is that all his Team, as they prepare with efficiency and energy, are men and women who pray. On the morning of the opening day of the Chicago crusade of 1971 the fire marshal, conscious that the previous McCormick Place had burned down, condemned the way that 40,000 folding chairs had been tied together in rows by volunteer trades unionists. He told Charlie Riggs, who was directing the crusade, that it could not start that night.

Charlie called the crusade office downtown. Jack Cousins, Norman Sanders and the staff immediately gathered in prayer, claiming Charlie's favorite promise in Proverbs, "The king's heart is in the hand of the Lord." In this case the fire marshal was "king" and they prayed that his heart would be turned in the direction of God's will. Without explaining his change of mind, the fire marshal OK'd the chairs. The crusade opened on schedule.

The next morning Mayor Daley's secretary called to announce that he would attend the crusade on Sunday, "and if there is anything we can do to help you, you have only to let us know." Hardly had she hung up when Walter Bennett, whose advertising company had arranged all crusade telecasts for many years, called with the devastating news that McCormick Place had condemned the television cables as too hot, although they had been used at Madison Square Garden and elsewhere. It would cost $4,000 and too much time to replace them.

Riggs, Cousins and Don Tabb went to prayer at once. Then Riggs tried to let Mayor Daley's office know that indeed they could help, but the line was busy. They held another prayer meeting, got through, and within thirty minutes were told that the cables were not too hot after all.

Prayer suffuses the whole vast operation of a crusade. Prayer groups meet in every setting—factories, offices, schools—but nothing has been more important than the Women's Prayer Program. Women's prayer rallies had been held since the early days of Billy Graham crusades, and no one did more for them than Mildred Dienert, daughter of Theodore Elsner (the Philadelphia pastor who had encouraged young Billy Graham to go on radio) and wife of Fred Dienert. In 1966 Mrs. Dienert went to London to speak at rallies to promote prayer for the Earls Court crusade. There the prayer chairman, Jean Rees, put forward a plan which Mrs. Dienert soon adopted as standard crusade practice. Instead of inviting Christian women to come to the center of a city to pray, rallies were held at key points on the circumference, and they were shown how they could open their homes for prayer—until every woman in the vast metropolitan area and its hinterland, whatever her personal attitude to the Christian faith, had an invitation to a home near her own to pray regularly for the crusade for a few minutes.

Bonnie Barrows, Cliff Barrows's daughter, joined the Team until her marriage, going wherever a crusade was in preparation to expound and strengthen the women's program. Bonnie would encourage prayer in the context of the family and church, and would see church life transformed as the prayer campaign blended with "Operation Andrew." The idea behind Operation Andrew is that Christians will invite friends to the crusade for whom they have prayed individually.

Churches hire buses and reserve seats so that much of an entire neighborhood is present, either being prayed for or praying. "A crusade is not just mass evangelism," Bonnie would tell the women, but their God-given tool for personal evangelism. "It is thrilling," she says, "to see them really grab hold of prayer when they realize that 'It's not Billy Graham who's the missionary, it's *me*, where I live—praying for my neighbor and then bringing that person to the crusade.'"

The prayer program in North America is geared to short daily broadcasts. At Dallas the crusade of 1971 was scheduled to be the main opening function of the Texas Stadium, new home of the Dallas Cowboys, whose head coach, Tom Landry, was the crusade chairman. But when the plumbers' union went on strike throughout the Dallas area, the stadium remained unfinished. On a Friday four weeks before the opening day, the crusade executive could no longer delay a decision on whether to transfer to the less convenient and smaller Cotton Bowl. Union leaders rejected a plea to resume work at the stadium so that the crusade could start. John Corts, associate director under Riggs, thereupon called Tom Landry, who was in Buffalo with his Cowboys, and was told to make no move until Landry's return on Monday.

That Monday morning the women's prayer program opened. As Landry flew south, thousands of women were gathered in groups beside the radio in homes all over the Dallas-Fort Worth area. Charlie Riggs described the problem and they began to pray. Later that morning the crusade office received a call that the plumbers' union would return to work at the Texas Stadium, but nowhere else. The crusade opened on time.

Many other stories emerge from the prayer program wherever it spreads across a region. At Jackson, Mississippi (1975), the women praying on one block decided that all its children should be prayed for. Soon their forty-two names hung inside every refrigerator so that, whenever opened, its owner would pray for a name on the list. At Lubbock (1975), young people at Texas Tech wanted the entire faculty, students and staff, a total of 24,000 prayed for by name. They divided the list, typed names, addressed envelopes. The several thousand prayer hostesses each received a quota of names for prayer through the mail.

In another city a prayer hostess's visits to every house on her block brought in nobody. She therefore began to pray by herself. Late one night the telephone rang. A neighbor asked if she might come at once for a talk. She poured out her burden, saying she had no one to turn to but had remembered the woman's call. The prayer hostess led her to Christ.

A story from Seattle (1976) specially delighted Mildred Dienert when she met prayer hostesses after that crusade. One of them had timorously asked her husband, who hated Christianity although he had once been a full-time church worker, if she might hold a group in their home. He consented, as long as she chose a time when he was out. She wrote the invitations along the lines provided by the crusade office, she prepared coffee and cookies, and only one woman came. As they talked, the hostess learned of this neighbor's resentment toward God because her husband was dying of cancer, just as she herself had resented her husband's venom toward his former faith until she had learned Christ's way. Out of her experience she could help. They prayed, and the neighbor came to a trusting faith. The next meeting, another woman joined them, this one in desperation because her husband had deserted her and their two small children. The others shared their discoveries of Christian victory. The group grew until in the last weeks eight women were meeting to pray.

The hostess went to the opening night of the crusade at the Seattle Kingdome. When Billy Graham gave the invitation she was astonished to see, across the aisles, her husband going forward. She rushed down, maneuvered her way through the crowd converging on the counseling area, and they had a tearful reunion. He told her how the day of her last meeting he had returned home unexpectedly to find the prayer group still in session. From the kitchen he had overheard the two neighbors each telling of their discovery of Christ's love and his answer to their problems. Greatly moved, he had asked God's forgiveness.

With the prayer groups, the Christian Life and Witnesses classes and all the other preparations for a Billy Graham crusade of the nineteen seventies, some 20,000 to 50,000 people may be involved in one way or another before the meetings start. "But 'involvement' is only a tool in the hands of the Spirit of God," says Sterling Huston. "The fundamental source of our confidence is in the power of God in response to prayer."

Thus great crowds flock to the stadium. Many who are not yet committed Christians will have been drawn by Operation Andrew, others by interest aroused by the media and publicity. Walter Smyth is often asked whether he thinks a great many come out of curiosity. "I am quick to say Yes, I do. But they *think* they're coming out of curiosity when in reality many of them are coming because a friend, relative or neighbor prayed for them. . . . Many remain to commit their lives to Christ. That's the important thing. So it is not the work of man —it's the work of the Spirit of God."

10 America's Spiritual Hunger

THE SURGE of spiritual movements in the United States of the nineteen seventies created a climate favorable to evangelism, a climate to which the earlier Billy Graham crusades had contributed. Throughout the fifties and the turbulent sixties they had, as it were, placarded the gospel across the country, making men and women more conscious of the Christian message.

"God is reaching out today in a tremendous new way," Leighton Ford could say to the Billy Graham Team in December 1971, "opening people to Christ, perhaps as never before. We have seen it in all of our crusades this year; every one of the evangelists I've talked to has said, 'This year there's been a new dimension and a new response.' " Then, disillusionment over Vietnam and Watergate, along with the subtle but growing influence of the news media and the entertainment industry, induced widespread questionings about the nation's moral foundation and sharpened spiritual hunger.

The crusades, twenty-five and more, which Billy Graham conducted in the U.S. during the seventies nearly always revealed deep expectancy. The audience, as varied as the character and religious outlook of its region, would be attentive and quiet as George Beverly Shea sang the last notes of his solo and Billy Graham stepped briskly to the podium.

"Always to limit oneself," writes David Barnes of Paris, "to the preaching of what is essentially the same message must be a very humiliating thing for a man who is well read and intelligent. One of the greatest evidences of Billy Graham's commitment to Christ and his humility is that he sticks to that to which he has been called."[1]

Because of the telecasting of most crusades, many of his audience will have heard him before. Thus he is denied the easy use of old sermons, dear to the heart of evangelists. He believes that one reason for the great growth of his television audience is "more preparation of sermons."

Huge stadiums, as Graham commented at one press conference, are "exhausting for all of us—Cliff Barrows trying to get the big crowds to sing, me trying to reach those people in those upper stands. I stand in so many of these stadiums on second base and I cannot see the reaction of the people; it is an exhausting experience. An indoor auditorium is an easy situation compared to a huge stadium." Year by year as he grows older Graham states that he will go less to big stadiums, but year by year he accepts the opportunities they bring.

Before 1973, with its "Key 73" national emphasis on Evangelism, Graham had wondered, "Should I stop the big stadium crusades while we seem to be at a peak, or should they go on and possibly begin petering out?" But after 1973 he knew he must not stop while he had the physical strength; that year he had preached to more people face to face than any previous year in his ministry. Thus, as a Lutheran pastor wrote, recalling the Upper Mid-West crusade for the Twin Cities of Minneapolis and St. Paul: "Hundreds of thousands of people heard the claims and promises of Jesus Christ presented in an articulate and clear proclamation seldom heard today from either the covered or the open-air pulpit. Once that is done, the Holy Spirit probes the conscience, bringing one face to face with the ultimate question that Jesus asked in his day, 'Who do *you* say that I am?' "

An evangelist is preaching for a decision. That is his heaviest burden. As Leighton Ford says, "If you know you're going to preach and give an invitation, you're going to preach to the point of commitment and response. It takes more out of you: not just the invitation, but the whole message. Because it's just not 'Take it or leave it'; it's not just giving a little talk, or teaching, or simply preaching a sermon. *You're going for a verdict.*"

Billy Graham is equally emphatic that "especially at the invitation

---

[1] Billy's comment on this remark was that it was not humiliating but exhilirating to preach the gospel.

there is a great spiritual conflict. This is the part of the evangelistic service that wears me out physically and psychologically and spiritually more than any other. I sense that Satan is battling for the souls of men and women." At the moment of invitation the gathering in the stadium or auditorium becomes more than a mass meeting or a climax to months of preparation: the evangelist and his audience are caught up in the primeval, elemental conflict of the universe, between good and evil, the forces of darkness and the God of light. At that moment, there will be people who turn from darkness into light, from the power of Satan to God.

The associate evangelists have noticed that when they give the invitation, a smaller percentage of the audience come forward than respond to Billy Graham. "All of us would recognize the unusual gift that God has given to Billy." During the later part of the Harringay, London, crusade of 1954 one of the British organizers remarked that if Billy Graham ended his sermon by reading out the multiplication table and then gave the invitation, the people still would come: the expectancy, the desire for Christ had spread so deep, and Billy had been entrusted with this special gift. Yet it is no professional knack but a deep-felt urge. The late Joe Blinco once recalled how in Australia in 1959 Billy Graham, arriving early at Adelaide, had attended Blinco's meeting and had commented afterward: "Joe, when you gave the invitation, I wanted to stand up where I was and plead with the people and say 'Come!' "

Graham expects them to come. He steps back, knowing that no pressure or pleading by himself is needed because the Holy Spirit is at work. In 1975 Graham commented, "I believe the statistics will show that we are now reaching more unsaved and unchurched than ever." A significant development in the seventies has been the increased response. At Chicago in 1971 the total attendance was proportionately slightly lower than in 1962, yet the response considerably higher. At the Upper Mid-West crusade of 1973 the crowds were a little larger than at its predecessor at Minneapolis in 1961, but the response nearly double. At Albuquerque, 1975, seven percent responded to the appeal. At Seattle, 1976, out of a nightly audience of some fifty to sixty thousand, between 2,000 and 2,500 inquirers came forward each meeting. Each one was joined by a counselor ready, after Graham's brief final word of instruction and the benediction, to help the person understand and confirm his or her decision, and to start the process by which the convert may become a lifelong disciple of Christ.

The Billy Graham Team accept fully that Christ's great commission to his church is twofold: not only to win converts but to teach them. Therefore a crusade must not only evangelize. The follow-up and integration of converts with the local churches are as much a part as the preparation and the mass meetings.

The counselor, before parting from the inquirer, introduces him or her to a pastor or other experienced person waiting nearby, as an adviser, and gives a booklet for a Bible correspondence course; if a name somehow slips out of the follow-up process he or she would at least have the printed page and an address to contact. But the Team and the local committee make sure that few, if any, slip out except at their own desire: the objective is to help these thousands find answers to their immediate questions and then to become fully part of the church life of their neighborhood and to grow in faith and Christian character.

Decision cards, whether in hundreds or thousands on a particular night, go at once to the Co-Labor Corps. Trained young people and adults waiting in the back parts of the stadium, "they were dedicated, courteous, interesting and interested," recalls the leader of the 200 volunteers at the Hampton Coliseum part of the Tidewater crusade, 1974. "I had never before been involved with people representing so many denominations. The workers developed a deep Christian love for each other." They check the cards, tracing and correcting incomplete addresses lest literature or calls go astray. A panel of responsible men and women allot a minister to follow up, should the inquirer have named none. Another group sorts the cards statistically. If that night there have come forward from scattered parts of the stadium ten doctors, fifteen lawyers, thirty workers in a big local corporation, six women from one neighborhood and a dozen youth from a particular school, they can all be invited to appropriate Bible study groups.

The cards go through but "we constantly encourage the Co-Labor Corps," says one of the Billy Graham Team, Bob Williams, "that it is not a piece of paper. It is a person. We are doing the mechanics to initiate processes that we hope will cause real growth—and sometimes birth." There have been many born again, not at their coming forward but during the follow-up.

The Co-Labor Corps works into the small hours, and by special arrangement the post office stands ready. Therefore the next day, or as quickly as the mails can manage, every inquirer receives a letter from Billy Graham while the appropriate minister receives notification and a request for pastoral contact. Because of the work that night, lists will have been compiled to insure that the inquirer receives spiritual help through the mail at appropriate intervals along with an invitation to a nurture group Bible study, and that he is not neglected by the church.

Thus the crusade is both evangelism and the start of a teaching ministry. The Team has continually improved its means to this end. A method developed in the later nineteen seventies is the One-to-One, which encourages the convert to use a "read-through" series of Bible studies in company with a more mature Christian whom a local pastor will have trained.

Another tool is the telephone survey, which Charlie Riggs and Jim Mathis introduced after noticing the use of telephones by canvassers in the presidential election of 1972. In the Chicago crusade a million people had received a telephoned invitation to attend and, earlier still, informal telephone surveys of some of the inquirers had followed both New York crusades. Atlanta 1973 saw the first, rather haphazard, attempt to make contact with everyone who had signed a decision card. The scheme steadily improved. Five to seven weeks after a crusade, specially trained counselors, calling from their homes to people within their own areas, discover the state of the follow-up, give encouragement and counsel, and if necessary suggest joining a Bible study group. They report back to the crusade office, which takes appropriate action. "It requires a lot of work," says Mathis, "but gives us contact with the inquirers we were missing before. The best way would be to sit down at home with them, but the second-best way is to visit them by telephone, because it is still a personal contact."

Stories abound. In the survey after St. Louis, Jim Mathis called a forty-five-year-old vice-president of a famous firm, who was working late in his office. The man broke down and sobbed, because someone had cared enough to call. His counselor had made no contact, and the church to which he had been referred had ignored him. He was in despair, for his decision had been deepfelt yet since the crusade no one had helped solve his problems. The two talked for half an hour. After Phoenix, Mathis called a woman and discovered that she and seven of her children had come forward on different nights; a divorcee, she longed for guidance on bringing up the family as Christians. One of the choicest stories comes from the Tidewater follow-up. A man counseling students by telephone told his wife about a young fellow who had implored help in finding his estranged wife; in their separation she knew nothing of his decision for Christ and his desire to mend their home. The telephone surveyor's wife asked the name, then exclaimed that she had counseled that young woman at the crusade six weeks before and knew her address. The two soon met again.[2]

A convert put into words what many thousands all over America might say: "I asked Jesus to take over control of my life at Billy Graham's Upper-Midwest crusade on July 16, 1973. At the time, I thought it was a simple step, and indeed it was, a simple step in faith toward Christ. Since that time, however, the full impact of that step into Salvation has begun to come to me, and the impact is sometimes staggering. I still don't fully comprehend Salvation. I probably won't until I stand in the presence of God, but as each day goes by, I realize that that step was the single most important decision I had made to that point in my life. As I learn to give up more and more of myself to Jesus, I can sense his quiet power within me. At last I have peace of mind, I'm contented, and my life has meaning. . . .

"What part did Billy Graham play in my rebirth? He played a big part, but so did the friends who took me to the crusade and those people who befriended me and helped me grow in the days and months that followed. Dr. Graham and these friends all fit perfectly into the plan that God has for me. This plan is unfolding now and will continue to unfold throughout eternity. To give the credit to any person for what happened to me would be dishonoring God who is the Creator of us all. All the credit has to go to the Author of that plan for my life. Dr.

---

[2] As an example, the 1977 Cincinnati survey (6,251 inquirers aged 12 or over) reached 6,032. *Q.1:* 87% said their step at the crusade helped their relationship to Christ; of the rest, 77% asked for more counseling. *Q.2:* 90% had mailed or were working on their Lesson One of *Knowing Christ;* 10% showed no interest. *Q.3:* 79% had been contacted by a church; the rest were referred to the Follow-Up committee, for action. *Q.4:* 83% were attending church regularly; of the rest, 89% wanted more help. *Q.4:* 62% were involved in nurture or Bible study groups; of the rest, 92% indicated a desire and were put in contact.

Graham is a man used on a fantastic scale by God, but he is a man. The same applies to my friends, although they are used by God on a much smaller scale.

"Each time I hear Dr. Graham preach and invite people to come forward and receive Christ, and when I hear the crusade choir sing, I remember my walk forward, and tears come to my eyes because that is where life began for me."

The Greater Chicago crusade of June 1971 took place in McCormick Place, the largest indoor exhibition hall in America, twenty football fields wide. Since Graham's 1962 crusade which had culminated in a great rally in sweltering heat on Soldier Field, a vigorous local committee had kept up the momentum. Nevertheless, recalls Graham, "Chicago has always been considered a very complex city religiously. Many people felt we could not come back to McCormick Place and fill it night after night, but the Lord did it and many thousands responded to the appeal."

During the second night Billy Graham spoke strongly against Satan worship. During the fourth day he learned that some 150 young Satanists intended to break up the meeting. That night, he recalls, "I used for the first time a technique that I believe the Lord gave me in controlling demonstrations. I warned the Satan worshipers publicly from the platform ahead of time that if they did start to come and take over the platform, there were 30,000 of us present; that I was sure the overwhelming majority of the people wanted to hear the message, so I was asking the congregation to stand at the beginning of their demonstration, sing to them, love them, and gently push them out. It worked. It worked again in the next crusade in Oakland, California, and it's been working ever since."

But during that June evening in Chicago Billy had no certainty that it would work. The Satanists sat at the back, and the bulk of the audience barely noticed their hoots and shouted obscenities. The dangerous moment would come when he gave the invitation. The Satanists intended to move down and create a roughhouse at the front.

Jack Cousins remembers the "spirit of prayer on the platform. All we could do was to turn the problem over to the Lord." As Billy began the invitation T. W. and Grady Wilson, with Cousins, walked down to block the disrupters. Grady grabbed two long-haired youths. "Where are you fellows going?" he asked. One of them replied, "We're going forward to trust Christ." Grady, not relaxing his grip, said, "You're not going to cause problems?" "No, sir. We want to trust the Lord."

Grady let them go, and to his surprise no more Satanists came down the aisle. Then the associates saw what had happened. Large groups of "Jesus freaks," or "street Christians," much in evidence in the Chicago and Milwaukee of 1971, who before the meeting had been cheerfully sticking *Jesus loves you* labels on people entering the hall, had converged on the Satanists. According to *Christianity Today*, they had "surrounded them and blocked the way, praying, rapping about Christ, and outchanting the Satanists with Jesus cheers."

Most of the Satanists left peaceably but two students let off a large cherry-bomb firecracker—at which the Chicago police broke the nose of one of them as they chucked him into their van. The crusade chairman and two committee men, concerned at this violence, immediately visited the students at police headquarters. They counseled them on subsequent nights, too. Months later one of the two youths came forward in public confession of faith in Christ at McCormick Place, when the crusade follow-up committee (the Greater Chicago Evangelistic Association) showed the Billy Graham film, *Time to Run*.

Although the historical perspective is too short to judge which crusades of the seventies will prove most significant, each region has special memories.

Cleveland, Ohio, with a population about half black and half white, with high unemployment and thousands of empty houses in its center, was known as a graveyard of evangelists. Even the Beatles in their heyday had filled only 14,000 of the 80,000 seats of the huge baseball stadium of the Cleveland Indians, right in the heart of the city on the waterfront. "You cannot expect anything better in a Graham crusade," said one newspaper man.

"But," Billy now can say, "we had the cooperation of almost everyone in Cleveland, especially the newspapers and the television stations. We had excellent attendance and a marvelous response."

The chairman was a businessman, Howard Williams. Eleven years earlier, in 1961, he and his wife and their young daughter Christie were aimlessly watching television when a Billy Graham telecast came on. They stayed to watch. Each had been seeking God without telling the others. Each sat absorbed by the message. "As Billy spoke," Katie Williams records, "it was as though God reached down and lifted a huge curtain. . . . When Billy gave the invitation to receive Christ, I stood in our family room and acknowledged Christ as my Savior and Lord. Miracle of all miracles, as I opened my eyes there stood my husband and twelve-year-old daughter. We were one in Christ that night."

Billy began in exceptionally hot weather (July 1972) which added to the strain of preaching under the Kleig television lights. One evening it rained hard and only 27,000 came. In the offering that night the treasurer found a check in an envelope with a scrawled message addressed to "Howard Williams or Billy: Here is $5,000.00 to make up for 10,000 *chickens* who are afraid to get their feathers wet. *Don't* mention my name." Billy shortened the service and his sermon, yet hundreds came forward to be counseled in the rain. Clarence Agard, the man whose initiative many years earlier had finally led to Billy's coming to Cleveland, and who was engaged in the follow-up, wrote three years later that "it was significant how many of the real converts dated their conversion to that Tuesday night service."

Even Billy could not quite fill a stadium not filled since a baseball game in 1963, but 19,000 people came forward and, adds Agard, "the crusade gave many churches a new life and purpose, with thousands converted, not only during those days but in the months that followed, with marvelous transformation of lives."

Of particular significance was the breakthrough to blacks. Although well represented on the executive, the blacks of Cleveland at first distrusted Graham. As he mentioned to the editor of *Ebony* the following year, "I find great ignorance in the black community concerning my long-time efforts in race relations and civil rights."

Graham held his first fully integrated crusade in the South, at Chattanooga in 1953, a year before the Supreme Court's decision. In the following years he went at personal risk to flash points in the racial conflict—Little Rock, Clinton, Birmingham—to hold integrated meetings of reconciliation in the aftermath of violence. He wrote against segregation and publicly supported civil rights reform. But he would not march, convinced that he could contribute a better way. "Both the Right and the Left attacked me because I stood for racial understanding, racial reconciliation, at a period when many people on both sides felt that one should go further, either to the Left or the Right."[3]

In 1960 Martin Luther King and Billy Graham went together to the Baptist World Alliance at Rio de Janeiro. In the course of long conversations Graham told King, "I'm holding integrated 'demonstrations' in the big stadiums of America. You feel that you must march and even go to prison. I respect your views." At a Rio banquet King said in his speech that if it were not for the Graham crusades in the South, "my work would be much harder." As Daniel Moynihan wrote to Billy in 1973, "You and Rev. King, more than any two men—and, surely, with God's help—brought your own South out of that long night of racial fear and hate."

Graham had integrated his Team as early as 1957 when Howard Jones, then a Cleveland pastor, joined it during the first New York crusade. "Many times," states Howard Jones, "I know that Billy Graham has been acutely conscious of the problems I would face as a black person in dealing with those whites who were antagonistic to me because of my race and were not too happy about my being on the Team. However, Billy's humble and Christlike spirit created an atmosphere of love around his Team which made it uncomfortable for those with race prejudice to do anything that would destroy the bond and unity holding us together.

"There have been occasions at receptions when Billy would introduce me first, before other Team members, just to establish the fact that I was as much a part of his Team as anyone else. But in all my years with the Team Billy has never exhibited a paternalistic spirit, nor have I received any preferential treatment from him just because I was the first black with the Association. My ministry with the Team has been a spiritual fellowship with those who love the Lord and each other. Therefore when people ask me if Billy Graham is a friend of blacks, I am compelled to say yes, on the basis of my personal associations with him."

Billy brought John W. Williams, a Kansas City pastor, on to the BGEA Board as its first black member; supported a black congress on evangelism (1970); and accepted an invitation to be preacher at a black led crusade in Watts, the Los Angeles suburb which had been the

---

[3] For further details on Graham and the race question until 1969, see *Billy Graham* (1969 ed.) pp. 106–109, 278–282.

scene of race riots. That crusade did not materialize, as local leaders concluded that extremists might make it an excuse for violence. But the man behind this invitation, the Watts pastor and civil rights leader, Edward V. Hill, was the black who turned the tide at Cleveland.

Ed Hill, whom Graham describes as "a man of God and a mighty preacher," had been a co-founder of Southern Christian Leadership, had nominated Martin Luther King as its president, but had drawn away from him when King diminished the gospel element in his ministry. On 1 June 1972, five weeks before the Cleveland crusade, Hill was one of the speakers at a meeting for pastors and laypeople, black and white, in the ballroom of the Sheraton Cleveland hotel. "It was a thrilling message in support of Billy Graham, and a turning point in growing support from the black pastors."

Graham's impression during the crusade was that half the faces of those who came forward each night were black. That probably was not borne out by statistics, but black participation was far higher than had seemed likely. In the words of the chairman, writing three years later, "The probably disproportionate amount of time, effort and money spent in promoting the crusade in the black community was worthwhile. The crusade was such a mountaintop experience for both blacks and whites that Cleveland remains a better city because Billy Graham and his Team were here."

A year after Cleveland, the Upper Mid-West crusade met vocal resistance from black leaders in Minneapolis and St. Paul. Graham's response, although in recent years he usually needed to forego any physical strain beyond the nightly preaching, was to tour the hospitals in the black sections, and the problem areas of crime and poverty, and to visit blacks in the state prison at Stillwater. His chief black opponent entirely withdrew his antagonism and gave the closing prayer at the final crusade meeting at the Minnesota Fairgrounds. Carl Lundquist, president of Bethel seminary, wrote, "Your thoughtfulness in going far beyond the call of duty to deal patiently with the black community has left behind you a great spiritual bond that strengthens life for all who serve the Lord in this area."

Often a crusade shows evidence of lasting influence on a particular section of the community.

When Graham came to Raleigh in 1973 it was at the urging of his daughter Anne and her husband Daniel Lotz, a dentist in Raleigh. The meetings were held in Carter stadium of North Carolina State University and within a few miles of two other famous Southern campuses: Duke University at Durham and the University of North Carolina at Chapel Hill. Seven lesser schools were in the same region. President Terry Sanford of Duke welcomed him to the university's large chapel. The crusade committee was chaired by a professor of computer science at Chapel Hill and included several academics. A professor of psychiatry at Duke gave a strong testimony at one of the meetings.

As *Christianity Today* commented, "The most vocal and influential critics of Christianity are found in the universities. Thus it was a joy to see the other side of the coin in Raleigh." Of the 10,568 inquirers who came forward, three quarters were under twenty-five. Billy wrote, "Thousands of students participated and thousands responded to the appeal to receive Christ. We didn't have a single demonstrator, which came as a surprise to me. There was a depth to the meetings that was very encouraging."

Carter Stadium was the first in America to refuse permission for a telecast, fearing damage to their Bermuda turf by camera installations. That at least enabled Billy to feel completely relaxed as he preached and to enjoy the entire Raleigh crusade. For his daughter, Anne Lotz, the crusade brought many opportunities. She arranged two "coffees" for leading women of the area, at which they could hear about the crusade and meet those taking part. Far more women came than had been expected. Most attended the crusade and Anne has since been teaching a regular Bible class numbering several hundred women, known to have a strong spiritual influence on the city.

The Greater St. Louis crusade that same year was notable for the support of the numerous Roman Catholic community. Twenty years earlier Catholics had shunned Billy Graham but in the aftermath of the second Vatican Council he and his Team attracted their support and good will in many places. At the Charlotte crusade (1972), the monks of Belmont Abbey sent their "felicitations, good wishes and, more important, fervent prayers. . . . We accept you as friend, brother and alumnus." A White House secretary once wrote to Billy that although a traditionalist Catholic she never missed his telecasts and "would rather read your *Decision* than most Catholic periodicals today."

Graham received an invitation from the Protestant churches of

Central Italy to hold a crusade in Rome during 1973, for which, he discovered, "quite a number of Catholic clergy are privately very enthusiastic." He learned from a very high source that the Vatican did not object, that he was free to preach in Rome as elsewhere and that his attitude was deeply appreciated; such a mission would offer an opportunity for all Christian communities to pray together. But the Protestants of Central Italy failed to bring their plans to fruition.

In St. Louis the official newspaper of the archdiocese gave unqualified support in a long editorial, saying, "Nothing but good can come from his famous crusades." It applauded his focus on "the person of Jesus the Savior who is both God and Man and on the sacred Scriptures which speak of him and his message. . . . If ever there was a time when all Christians should join together in giving witness to the beliefs they hold in common it is now."

Although no one could assess the proportion of Catholics in the audience of over 20,000 which jammed the arena each night, more than 700 Catholics recorded decisions and were referred to one of the 2,000 interdenominational nurture groups. St. Louis was a milestone on the road toward the Billy Graham Michiana crusade held in 1977 in the stadium of the most famous Catholic university in America, Notre Dame.[4]

History may reckon that the single most important segment of the Billy Graham ministry, other than lasting decisions for Christ, is the School of Evangelism held during each crusade. In the early twentieth century, in the United States, departments of evangelism were maintained by the Federal Council of Churches, the YMCA and several of the main denominations, especially Presbyterian; and some 300 evangelists would attend an annual convention at Winona Lake. During the nineteen twenties and thirties many churches dropped the study of evangelism and it was almost unknown as a university subject. Despite the work of faithful individuals here and there it had acquired a disrepute that gave some substance to Sinclair Lewis's character, Elmer Gantry. By the mid nineteen sixties the impact and integrity of Billy Graham crusades had changed the situation again, yet thousands of clergy and theological students lacked training in evangelism, and less

---

[4] See also *A Catholic Looks at Billy Graham,* by Charles W. Dulles S.J., Paulist Press, New York, 1973.

than fifty Bible schools and Christian colleges taught it. Then a prominent California layman had a vision from which sprang the crusade schools of evangelism.

Lowell Berry, of Oakland, California, had rededicated his life to Christ in the Graham San Francisco crusade of 1958; previously a liberal churchman, he was president of the Northern California Council of Churches. He now wished to help forward the cause of evangelism. Berry had started in the fertilizer business in 1932 with little money and a limited knowledge of the business, but "One of the things that helped me most was to find out how others who had been in the business longer than I went about their work and with what kind of equipment." His willingness to learn, together with his energy, persistence and flair, had made him a leader of the fertilizer industry in California and Texas. Aware of the great impact of the Graham crusade on his life, Berry realized that similar principles could apply. If seminary students saw evangelism in practice at a crusade, and were taught by men of experience in the context of a crusade, they would enter their ministries with an understanding and skill they might otherwise lack. He put the idea to Billy Graham.

One of Graham's associates, Lane Adams, had already tried it on a small, informal scale with seven students from his own alma mater. Lowell Berry's insistence and generosity brought twenty-seven seminary students to a school of evangelism organized by Robert Ferm during the Chicago crusade of 1962. The schools grew in numbers and scope. At first open only to seminarians, they were extended to young pastors, then to all pastors. This brought in a wealth of experience, especially to the seminars which had been added to the program of lectures at the suggestion of Victor Nelson, in charge of administration. Later schools and programs were geared to include laymen, and then ministers' wives, thus increasing the value to the life of the church. Expanding greatly from 1970, the schools drew all ages, races and denominations. The numbers who enrolled in North America at any one school varied from 500 to 1,600 according to the location of the concurrent crusade. The faculty, which in later years was brought from far and wide, always included several Graham associates; Kenneth Chafin, dean since 1967, had become very aware of "the enormous insight, experience, resources and abilities of the different men on the Team."

Ken Chafin, a Houston pastor who had previously been Billy Graham professor of Evangelism at the Southern Baptist seminary in Louisville, did the most to mold the schools which Bob Ferm had pioneered. By 1976 Lowell Berry had given more than half a million dollars in scholarships for students and ministers, in North America and overseas.

Billy Graham regards the schools as his special tribute to the local church. "They are very close to his heart," says one of his associates. Graham wrote to Berry in 1974, "We shall move forward with ever greater vigor on these schools." Graham does not want them to be too diffuse. "If we try to cover the entire range of the church ministry," he warned, "we might find ourselves hopelessly bogged down. . . . If we limit it to the subject of evangelism then it becomes a very narrow rifle shot on a subject on which we can speak with some authority."

He always addresses the school, especially enjoying the opportunity to share his experience. Many of the students, as Chafin told him after Atlanta (1973), "say that the most helpful thing at the school was your 'pastoral sharing.' I think this is a good kind of message for you to bring. They hear you preach every night, so they really do not need another address from you. This is probably the only time in their lifetime that they will have an opportunity to be this close to you and for you to share with them some of the convictions that guide your life."

By 1978 thousands in North America had attended crusade schools of evangelism, and even greater numbers abroad. Chafin finds that the most rewarding part is what the school does to the students. "We have had individuals converted at the schools, we have had individuals clarify their call; we have had people who were preparing to drop out of the ministry have their call renewed; we have had ministers who were defeated revived; we have had people who were in moral difficulty get right with God. I have never seen one week have such an impact in the lives of individuals." It is in effect a traveling seminary, and many students say they learn more in a school of evangelism than in a whole year at seminary.

The fruit of a crusade will not be fully ripe for at least five years but, in the short term, region after region shows a basic similarity. The Raleigh chairman, computer scientist Frederick Brooks, six months later in a letter to Billy Graham described the situation which is typical: "The persistent effects of the crusade delight the heart. Every participating church recognizes the presence of new converts and 'rededi-cations,' for some of whom Christ is real for the first time. The laypeo-ple and preachers know each other and love and respect each other in wholly new ways across our divided denominations, races and geogra-phy. The evangelical student groups on our campuses are continuing the fruitful cooperation that itself proclaims Christ. Most joyful to me, however, are the changes in boldness and seriousness brought about by the counselors' training classes and crusade experience."

Another point is added by the vice-chairman of the Birmingham, Alabama, crusade of 1972, Pastor Dotson Nelson, writing three years afterward. "The chief significance, apart from the changes in individual lives, lay in the fact that over a period of six weeks literally the whole area was talking about religion in general and the Christian faith in particular."

11   The Team

"**I**T HAS been a Team effort," Billy emphasizes, "not just a Billy Graham effort." Among those who have been his associates from the first, three may be singled out as indispensable. A fourth, the singer George Beverly Shea, has been invaluable to the Graham ministry from earliest days but not so closely involved with administration and developments.

Cliff Barrows has worked with Graham since 1945. The public knows him best as master of ceremonies and song leader at crusades. He plans the program and controls the strict timing required for the telecast to millions across America and to many parts of the world. The worship service which precedes the preaching is difficult to arrange because staunch older church people hope for a traditional program, yet the younger and generally larger segment of the audience want their kind of music. Billy Graham says, "I feel we should go back to the old tunes of the thirties and forties, which would be new today, but apparently Cliff disagrees and I bow to his wisdom." Cliff tries to keep a balance between choir, solos and hymn singing but critics often accuse him of having too long a service before the sermon, since most people have come to hear Billy Graham.

Cliff Barrows is far more than a song leader and director of music. Before any invitation is accepted for a city or a country, Cliff is among the two or three assessing the situation for Billy Graham's final choice. Cliff keeps touch with the committee during the preparation, and throughout the crusade he is the clearinghouse for most problems that arise. He can work very long hours, has great physical stamina and can sleep at any time of day or night, awaking refreshed after the shortest rest.

With Ruth Graham, Cliff takes a major share in the oversight of World Wide Pictures, the Billy Graham film organization. He has chief responsibility for the telecasts. The weekly radio Hour of Decision is produced at his home under his supervision, and his touch is felt in most of the multifarious activities of the Graham Association. In Billy Graham's words in 1977, "Cliff's temperament and spirituality have probably been one of the most cohesive forces holding the Team together all these years. Everybody loves and respects Cliff."

George M. Wilson, like Cliff Barrows, was close to Graham before the founding of the Association. In September 1950, at Graham's request, he filed incorporation papers with the State of Minnesota. He set up an office in one room of about 600 feet in Minneapolis, helped in the first year by Frank Phillips of Portland, Oregon. Then George Wilson took over fully, at first under Graham's almost daily supervision in person or by telephone.

George Wilson became famous as manager of an office handling one of the biggest flows of mail in the United States. Billy had long ago determined "that if ever I had an organization of my own it would be built on the prayers and gifts of many people rather than a few." George and he were agreed that the money should not be raised at crusades. The returns from listeners to the Hour of Decision and from the growing mailing list increased day by day. All who wrote were added to the list and their contributions receipted and recorded in the Minneapolis office. George made himself an expert in the field, seeking out the latest equipment. As the ministry grew, so grew George Wilson and the efficiency of his office. His handling of more than 40,000 letters a week, rising to 100,000 a day after a telecast, has been named by the United States Post Office as one of the best mail operations in America. Wilson's business principles and office practices have been studied widely.

When Frank Coy of Cleveland, with his experience as head of a retail business and in banking, manufacturing and many philanthropic and welfare organizations, was invited by Graham in 1973 to join the BGEA board of trustees, he insisted on first reviewing their business methods, probity and efficiency. "I came away from that review feeling that the BGEA was one of the best-run business operations. I was greatly impressed by the control and integrity exercised in the financial as well as in the spiritual aspects of the Association." As Graham says, "George has built an extremely efficient and spiritual organization in Minneapolis that has caused me a minimum of problems over the years. Without his intuitions, leadership, and God-given gifts I do not know what we would have done."

Graham and Wilson both emphasize how much the ministry of the BGEA has profited from the board of trustees and the executive committee of leading businessmen and women who give time, experience and spirituality to direct and control the financial side, reviewing the budget strictly. The size of the BGEA operation, with its films, radio and telecasts, its *Decision* magazine gaining a circulation of nearly four million monthly, its other literature and activities, involves very considerable sums of money received and spent. The board, George Wilson, and Graham's determination from earliest days that his activities should be able to stand the closest scrutiny, have insured that, in the words of the *Charlotte Observer* in February 1977, after prolonged investigation, "Unlike many other well-known evangelists, Graham's organization and Graham himself have avoided even the hint of scandal."[1]

The third of Graham's indispensable close associates from earliest days is Grady Wilson (no relation to George) who with his brother T. W. Wilson, who joined the Team much later, was a boyhood friend from Charlotte.

A notable evangelist with a strongly Biblical message, whose force and friendliness have always appealed especially to the Southern states, Grady Wilson's bonhomie, wit and massive size sometimes mask to the casual observer the fact that he is a man of acute intellect and judgment. When Billy Graham's personal secretary retired, her successor for a few years was an intellectual, who moved afterward into an academic career. At first, Billy recalls, she "could never figure out why

---

[1] For the *Charlotte Observer*'s attitude later that year to Graham's funds for world relief, etc., see chapter 22.

I had a fellow like Grady Wilson around. But she had not been with me a year before she was astounded at Grady's balance and ability to solve problems. 'More and more,' she said, 'I depend on his counsel and advice.' "

During the Association's first fifteen years, with its problems of growth, organization, and shortage of funds to meet the expanding opportunities, Grady Wilson's wisdom and horse sense, and his gift for making and keeping friends, were most important to Billy Graham.

To these three, the core of the Team, Graham would add Walter Smyth and Charlie Riggs, two who joined in the early nineteen fifties, whose roles have been mentioned in earlier chapters. Behind them are Team members, whether associate evangelists, crusade musicians, directors, office workers, business executives, or technicians, all committed to evangelism. Although men and women of different races, colors and ages, and varied in cultural and denominational backgrounds, they work as a family. The chairman of the Phoenix crusade (1974) eulogized to Billy, without exaggeration, "their infectious enthusiasm, dedication and love for each other. . . . You have no prima donnas on your Team."

Service on the Team is a sacrifice. Walter Smyth, linchpin of the Team's worldwide arrangements, whose ministry takes him from home more than any, speaks for all of them: "This matter of travel—there is not one of us who would continue to do this for any other purpose. I would not be away three weeks out of the month for any amount of money or for any kind of job in the world." He adds, "Behind every Team member, there is a woman of God; and I don't think enough has ever been said about Ruth Graham or any of these wives. Any of us will admit that we couldn't possibly have done what under God we were privileged to do, without them." The wives endured loneliness, brought up the children, taught the family to share in the absent husband's ministry.

Two motives, along with the basic motive of love of God and response to his call, keep the Team going. One, described by Walter Smyth, is "meeting people all over the world whose lives have been completely changed in a Billy Graham crusade. You see the reality of the thing, that it affects people, that it is genuine. Some people say, 'It's superficial. It won't last. It's a racket. People are moved for the moment.' But then when you come back to Britain and talk to men by the score who were converted in 1954, went through theological training and are now ministers; or you go to Australia, and learn that ever since 1959 a certain percentage every year of candidates for the ministry, and applicants to the Bible schools or theological colleges, dates their conversion back to Billy's meetings—when you see God at work like that, you don't mind putting your whole self behind it. I have been privileged to have a little part of all this. And I can't go to bed at night without thanking him."

The other motive is personal affection and loyalty to Billy Graham. Sterling Huston seems to sum up the Team's attitude: "All of us have had the public image of a great prophet and a great evangelist; and there is a certain aura about him which, on first meeting, with that tall stature, penetrating gaze and dynamic personality, seems to be overwhelming. Yet, as you spend more time in close contact, you are conscious of his humanity . . . but you are more conscious of his total integrity and his single-mindedness of purpose, that he wants to serve Christ and please Christ and to be true to his calling of preaching the gospel. You are conscious of the great demands upon him and the tremendous challenges and temptations that face him as he decides where to use his time and how to respond as a public figure.

"Again and again you see him listening to what the Holy Spirit says, admitting his uncertainties about what to do and where to go, then turning to God in prayer with that open and loving heart available for God to lead. Most important, you are conscious of the fact that he wants God alone to get the glory."

12 The Grahams: A Family View

ONE OF Billy Graham's three daughters, all now married and mothers, says, "He has been such an idol and such a standard for us that we can't look at him objectively." Nevertheless the memories and impressions of Billy Graham's children provide a valuable insight.

The elder son, Franklin, comments, "History has shown that many public figures live two lives: one for the camera, the other behind closed doors. Not so with Mom and Dad. Their lives are the same before the public as they are behind closed doors."

The eldest child of Ruth and Billy Graham, Virginia, known always by the Chinese nickname Gigi (Mrs. Stephan Tchividjian) was five years old when her father shot to national fame in 1949. Anne (Mrs. Daniel Lotz) was one year old. Ruth, or Bunny, as their third daughter is always known (Mrs. Ted Dienert), was born in 1950. William Franklin, Jr. (Franklin), followed in 1952 and Nelson Edman (Ned) in 1958. Thus they grew up during the years of Graham's advance to a world prominence greater than that of any previous evangelist, even D. L. Moody, and subject to pressures that modern media can apply ruthlessly to a public figure and his family.

Apart from strict orders to refuse interviews, the children were protected from fame so well that they were unaware of it. The Grahams had made a vital decision when they settled in remote Montreat, a country community around the conference center and school of the Southern Presbyterians, where Ruth Graham's parents, the Nelson

Bells, had lived since leaving China. In the house on Assembly Drive across the road from the Bells, and later in their mountain home, the children spent a normal childhood, out of the limelight. "The home atmosphere," Ned recalls, "was not really affected by my father's position as an evangelist as far as I could tell." It was a normal home, with parents "who never let me down."

The Bell grandparents, with their understanding and happy characters, gave the children extra security and love. They encouraged and helped Ruth during Billy's absences on crusades. The Montreat people were another aid to normal growth. Tourists in early days might gape and in return be victims of pranks by the Graham children, but the neighbors, mostly retired missionaries or college staff, treated them casually however much they enjoyed a young family around. The mountain folk, as one child says, "are so kind and wonderful in North Carolina. Some of them did not know that Daddy was famous, and for those who did, it really didn't matter, except that he was a man of God doing what God called him to do. They would holler out, 'Hey, Rev. Billy,' or make some comment about their respect for him, but there was no awe and adulation."

The Graham home was not elegant or pretentious and was a veritable Noah's Ark. Together with the Pyrenean sheep dog, Belshazzar, and afterward Heidi the St. Bernard, they had sheep, flying squirrels, rabbits, even a skunk, a horse, a mule, and a pony. A goat named Khrushchev could be smelled a mile away, until they had to get rid of him. "We took him in the jeep," recalls Anne, "and drove and drove until we felt we had confused him enough that he would never come back home. We let him off. And as we were driving up the driveway, there he was, welcoming us with sort of a knowing grin, much to the glee of all of us children."

Anne's first German Shepherd puppy, the runt of a litter, and rejected by everybody, died of a rattlesnake bite. "I was crushed," she recalls, "so Daddy decided to get me a 'good dog' this time and ordered me another German Shepherd from a South Carolina kennel. The dog arrived—gorgeous and pedigreed. After a month, he became horribly vicious to everyone but me. He adored me and I him. He would go around the outside of the house, determine which room I was in, and then lie down outside." Billy sent him to an obedience school. It seemed to improve the dog, and Anne took him on a leash to see her father, who was reading in bed after returning from a preaching tour. "For the first few minutes everything was fine—then the dog lunged for him and would have killed him except that Daddy put a pillow over his head and Mother helped me drag the dog off. Of course, we had to get rid of the dog. But I'll never forget Daddy calling me into his study the next day, letting me cry on his shoulder and tell him how horrible I felt. Then we knelt in prayer together."

Anne comments that this was an instance of her father's teaching them to take heartbreaks and fears as well as everyday needs to God in prayer, and to seek the blessing or the lesson which God hid in every setback ("in this case to lean on him, making him my dearest Friend and putting him first"). Her father's teaching meant much to her a few years later when she came down with mononucleosis, in which the physical misery was compounded by her disappointment at being unable to go on to college. "Daddy reminded me to look for God's blessing —it didn't take long to find it. The blessing turned out to be six feet six inches tall, weighed 230 lbs. and was an athlete-turned-dentist who visited each weekend while I was confined to the house. Of course it was Danny, whom I fell in love with and married a year later."

In their childhood, discipline stayed firm but not because of parentage. The children were never featured as public examples of a Christian family but had a healthy sense that home, in Franklin's words, "is private and personal; it is not for the world to see." Once their father took several of them to church at Ridgecrest, the Baptist assembly ground a few miles away and, Bunny recalls, "Franklin was quite wigglesome and chewing gum loudly and whispering and whatnot. After church a lady sitting behind us said, loud enough for us to hear, that Billy Graham's son should not behave that way in church. We were sort of indignant that she should think we should act any different from any other children."

Their parents did not consider themselves out of the ordinary. Ruth never emphasized their father's renown. They heard about luncheon with the queen or the president; the vice-president or other famous people came to the house, but it all was accepted casually. A young Team member staying at Montreat, who wondered how much the children realized, asked five-year-old Anne what kind of work her father did. "Well, Uncle Bill," she replied, "I think he preaches sometimes, but I really wouldn't call that work!"

Occasionally came a brief visit to a crusade, New York in 1957 being specially remembered for the great joke played by their mother as the train approached the Hudson River tunnel. She warned them it might leak, and they all wrapped themselves in towels, "and Mother was just laughing up a storm when we finally discovered that in fact the tunnel was perfectly dry."

For their schooling they bounced down the mountain in a rickety old jeep with hard seats to the local public school. But when Gigi and Bunny each went away south to a Christian private school the staff treated Billy Graham's daughters like royalty. Though Gigi graduated, Bunny suffered from being placed on a pedestal, until her parents saw their happy easy-going daughter growing tense and decided to try a northern school. There, the staff's exertions to avoid special treatment made Bunny feel herself "something undesirable." Even when her father was off to minister to the front-line troops in Vietnam, where he might have been killed, the school refused to allow her to go home for Thanksgiving.

Later the children inevitably derived much interest, enjoyment and travel from their father's position, yet sometimes they were over-protected even as adults. Their father asked them to be present when his native city honored him on "Billy Graham Day" (1971) but without consulting him the officials barred the lot from the reception attended by the president. When Graham was grand marshal of the Rose Bowl Parade, all but Ned converged on California—only to be excluded from most of the functions. Again, their parents had no say in the matter.

One of them thinks that "this protection has led people to feel Daddy really didn't care greatly for us." Nothing could be farther from the truth. "Daddy was a wonderful Daddy" is the verdict of each. "He was loads of fun," telling absurd jokes and stories. He would hike with them in the mountains, including a hilarious occasion when they stayed in Switzerland as guests of the family who afterward became Gigi's in-laws, and they climbed together to a high Alpine village. Billy had bought a new shirt and, as he walked, all the flies in the district came too. "A little black cloud hung over him, swarming everywhere he went. We thought it was a scream—he was so embarrassed and just began to walk faster and faster, trying to get away from them. Then he had an idea and took off his new shirt. Sure enough, when he put it on the ground and walked away, the flies stayed all over the shirt. It must have been something in the material."

For Billy, each of his five children was his favorite. He treated them according to their characters, playing ball or teaching the boys to shoot; teasing Gigi, playing rough with Bunny, being very loving with Anne. "He was always loving and affectionate with each of us—always hugging us girls. Even if he were just taking us shopping, or to a meeting or to church, he would hold our hands and walk beside us, as proud as though we were sweethearts instead of daughters." When they grew older he still held their hands but would introduce them to everyone from bellhops to presidents.

But he was away for long periods, and they missed him dreadfully. Yet however frustrated they felt at not having him around when needed, their childhood memories are dominated by the fun of his presence rather than by resentment at his absence. They ascribe this to the sterling character of their mother.

Ruth missed her Bill even more than the children missed their Daddy, but she never wept in front of them when he went or complained while he was away. "She stamped on our minds at a very early age that he was going for Jesus' sake, to tell others the good news of the gospel of Jesus Christ, and we never questioned his having to go." She would deliberately distract them so that he slipped away without fuss, and soon they could count the days to his return. The daughters learned from her "not to look to our husbands to be what only the Lord Jesus could be," always available to protect, guide and cherish. Ruth had a special gift for making the household revolve round Billy even in his absence: he was head of the household. Looking back on those days, the children are sure, too, that the extraordinary sense of his presence when not physically there should be attributed to his faithful, constant prayers.

The Bell grandparents[1] formed an essential support, but one of the girls says, "I don't believe Mother has ever been recognized and honored for what she has done; because without her, Daddy's ministry would not be what it is." In childhood they knew nothing of their parents' early decision, contrary to the usual practice of evangelists,

[1] See the present writer's biography of Dr. Nelson Bell, *A Foreign Devil in China.* Dr. Bell died in August 1973, aged 79, and Virginia Bell in November 1974, aged 83.

that Ruth should stay at home for the children's sake. Nor could they appreciate the cost to Ruth of the strain of controlling a family alone for much of the year; nor the cost to Billy of knowing what that strain must be; and for both, the rawness of separation. Gigi at the age of twelve or thirteen had a glimpse of the cost to her father, then about thirty-eight. "I had been very rude, and he spanked me. I then asked him in anger what kind of a father he thought he was anyway, always being gone. Tears filled his eyes; it was the first time I had seen tears in Daddy's eyes. Afterward we talked it over, and I have never forgotten that experience. It was the first time I began to realize as a young adult just how much he was giving up by being gone. Now as a parent I understand quite fully the anguish he must have gone through at times, wondering if he was making the right decision by leaving."

Billy's return would be a gala day. In the first years, when usually he arrived by overnight train, they would drive down to Black Mountain railroad station, standing excitedly by the tracks in the early morning dampness with the mist hanging on the mountains.

"And then," records Anne, "he would be there, smiling, hugging, laughing, and our whole world turned bright, even on the rainiest of days. He usually brought us home some sort of present—more often than not it was a stuffed animal. (Even after I got married, he brought me home a little koala bear and kangaroo that he had picked up in Australia. On one visit to my home in Raleigh, he brought our little son Jonathan a stuffed bear and a flight bag; with a grin, Daddy said he would always be crazy about stuffed animals and just couldn't get over the habit of bringing them home.) We were allowed to take his hat and overcoat back to his closet—usually snuggling it on the way and it was *so good to have him home!*"

Soon they would gather together in the living room or around the table and he would describe some of his experiences. He would spoil the children a little, bringing the dogs into the house (forbidden) and giggling when Ruth glared in pretended disapproval. Rules like bedtime tended to relax, and pocket money would increase. He was generous, too, with time. Even then, however, he had a habit of suddenly returning to his sermon preparations or correspondence or reading, or to making decisions by telephone.

The children always had an open door to their parents. "It did not matter who they were with," says Franklin, "or where they were. If I wanted to talk they always were ready to stop and listen." No rule was ever imposed that the children should not interrupt their father at his desk, but they hardly ever did; they feel a little resentful when heedless strangers impose on his time for the mere pleasure of it.

Only once did Bunny interrupt him. He was at the 1971 Chicago crusade and she had a serious worry on her mind. About an hour before he was due to leave for the meeting after returning very tired from Washington after attending Tricia Nixon's wedding at the White House, she poured out her trouble, weeping on his shoulder. "Busy as he was, he spent time, he loved me, he prayed with me, he cried with me. That will always be a very special memory, that Daddy would take time from his busy and tiring schedule to share his daughter's burden."

The Grahams brought up their children to have a deep sense of right and wrong, a sensitive conscience, and an instinct of courtesy and thoughtfulness toward others They taught them how to make decisions irrespective of the eddies of public opinion. The Grahams never were disapproving parents but understanding and forgiving in the occasional lapse, such as Anne's celebrated though unintentional public endorsement of Barry Goldwater during the 1964 campaign, when Billy greatly desired his family to submerge private feelings to public neutrality.

Gigi says, "Because of their example, I respected them and listened to their advice. I saw Daddy live what he preached. I saw them making Christ their life, not just their religion." "I was able to see Christ in my parents," says Ned. "Their love *and prayer* have guided me all my life, including my own commitment to Christ." "When you see the truth, why tamper with something less?" comments Bunny. "There was never any question in our minds that Jesus Christ was the only way. Mother and Daddy showed us in their own lives that Christ was real. You could see that it was really what made their lives go, and that their whole life was centered around the Lord Jesus." Franklin points to the influence of their "dedication to serve Jesus Christ no matter what the cost or price. Christ was and is *Lord.*"

Anne writes, "They set the tone for our lives by the way they lived theirs. Their depending on God was obvious—Mother's light would be on late at night and early in the morning as she studied her Bible and prayed. And Daddy, even though the world acclaimed him as a great man, and so many sought him for advice, would still get on his knees and humbly ask the Lord for his guidance. Through all of this we learned that seeking God was not a sign of weakness but a sign of strength and knowledge of ourselves—we are not complete persons until we allow Him to take control; then we become that for which we were created. This wasn't taught to us dryly and piously, but with abundant joy and happiness."

It is not surprising, therefore, that the Grahams saw, in Ruth's words, "the Lord graciously work in each child's life; with deepest gratitude to God we have seen each one respond to Him." It was not always easy. But Billy and Ruth do not feel it is fair to air one's children's problems publicly, and are quick to speak of God's faithfulness and to give him the glory for laying his hand upon each child. They know that each one is now his.

13 The Man Himself

SHORTLY after President Johnson retired, Billy tried to call him and then wrote from Montreat that "I am thinking about you and praying for you during this period of transition. I am sure that it has been a very difficult time for you after so many years of public service to find yourself suddenly a private citizen. Even in my small way I experience it from time to time. I have often gone on three to six month crusades abroad in the midst of a whirlwind of activity. I jet home to the quietness of this mountain and for the first few days I hardly know what to do with myself. There even come times of depression. However, that all soon passes."

Difficulty of adjustment, pressures when on tour, responsibilities that do not cease wherever he is, all contribute to Billy's tendency to insomnia. He goes to bed by eleven or twelve and rises by seven or eight. Always a light sleeper, he often wakes in the night or very early, when his mind clicks alert at once.

That at least gives more opportunity to nourish the devotional life which is vital to any Christian. Ruth, an early riser, says, "In the morning, I'll go to take in the mail, and he's sitting on the bed reading the Bible. He reads long passages of it at a time. He's always at it; but it isn't as if 'From 7–7:30 this morning I have Bible reading.' That's not Bill's nature, he's not that organized a person. But he does read the Bible continually, and every day, and large portions of it." Away from home the pressure of a tight schedule offers less opportunity, but

Graham comments, "I take time each day in the morning and evening to read passages of Scripture and ask the Lord to speak to me through them—apart from any preparations of sermon material." He is only too aware of the Tempter's robbery of time, but at the very least Billy reads five psalms and a chapter of Proverbs daily, a habit of many years picked up from Leland Wang, the great Chinese Bible teacher. In 1967 he had these compiled in a monthly book for daily use, in the *Living Bible* version, and sent a handsomely bound copy to every senator and congressperson. He gave away more than a million copies of the entire *Living Bible* to those who wrote in after a telecast.

His own preference is for the Revised Standard Version and the King James Version. He has used up at least thirty-five copies of the Bible but wishes he had one copy with all his own annotations. Instead, he has many translations partially marked up. He has a habit of making notes on scratches of paper, transferring his thoughts and ideas to a dictaphone to be typed by his secretary and then throwing the scraps of paper in the wastebasket. He has never been much of a Bible marker.

As for prayer, "I have learned, I believe, to 'pray without ceasing.' I find myself constantly in prayer and fellowship with God, even while I am talking to other people or doing other things." Sometimes his prayer is an unexpressed longing that an individual should come to Christ or find Christ's answer to a problem. It may be a flash thought, barely expressed as a prayer, when reading a newspaper or watching television news—Billy has friends in almost every country in the world, and news of crisis or violence will instinctively focus him on individuals. His prayers go especially to countries once open to the gospel and known from his personal visits there, where Christians suffer persecution.

Billy Graham prepares sermons and speeches with exceptional thoroughness. He is a voracious reader, especially of biography, history and current affairs. Having cultivated a nearly photographic memory for the printed word, he can assimilate a page swiftly. He subscribes to the *New York Times,* the *Washington Post,* the *Christian Science Monitor* and three London daily papers: *The Times,* the *Daily Telegraph* and the *Daily Express.* When he is home he thumbs rapidly through each one to see if there is an article of particular interest to him. Ruth extends his range, being an even more dedicated bookworm who distills for him her browsing in C. S. Lewis, Solzhenitsyn, Pascal,

Chesterton, George MacDonald and much else: poetry, literature, theology, Bible studies and other areas. Often as they lie in bed at night she will tell him what she has read during the day.

Billy likes the quip that to borrow from one writer is plagiarism, but from many writers is research—saying that in this sense he is a great researcher. Two or three of his staff, including Leighton Ford, John Wesley White and Ralph Williams, regularly offer material for his articles and messages, while part-time researchers may receive specific themes to work up.

Billy says, "Among all of those who have helped me, next to Ruth, I suppose Dr. Bell gave the greatest aid. He was a prolific writer and always had an apt illustration and concise outline to give me in time of need." But Billy's father-in-law was a very busy man as surgeon, then as executive editor of *Christianity Today* and denominational leader. Of those actually on Billy's staff none did more than Robert O. Ferm and Lee Fisher. When Billy Graham was an obscure student, Lee conducted evangelistic campaigns, preaching and singing; a composer, author, very athletic individual and excellent golfer, who helped teach Billy to play, he can also "cook as few men I've ever met," remarks Billy.

In 1950 Lee suffered a physical and nervous breakdown and loss of voice, caused by anemia and the untimely loss of his first wife. From that experience came his well-known hymn, "A Christ for Every Crisis." Billy Sunday's song leader, Homer Rodeheaver, asked Fisher to help build up his Ranch for Boys, in Florida, where Lee slowly regained his strength.

At that time Billy Graham, then in his early thirties, was president of Northwestern Schools, a Bible school/college with a total student body of 1,200. Every week he was giving one of the few national radio broadcasts live on the American broadcasting system, writing a daily newspaper column for the *New York News*, *Chicago Tribune* Syndicate, and answering hundreds of letters himself. His secretary of those days, Luverne Gustavson, said, "I don't know how we did it except God gave the strength." Rodeheaver recommended Lee as an aide in preparing the radio script. Graham was a little reluctant, having always done his own writing (he had already written *Peace with God*, which was to become one of the world's most translated and best-selling books). However, finding it difficult to keep fresh and up-to-date with so many other responsibilities, he asked Lee if he would give part-time help, while running the Boys' ranch. Eventually Lee Fisher moved to Montreat in the capacity of Research, with the understanding that his new wife Betty would assist with the children when Ruth was away.

Billy continued to write most of the radio scripts himself but would send copies of other sermons, as he prepared them, for additional illustrations or Scripture verses. Fisher would also work up subjects Billy gave him or submit material. His experiences and knowledge of leading figures of the past made him a mine of ideas. Billy would always study, revamp, put in his own matter and make the piece his own, yet Lee's assistance, especially during the 1950s, was, as Billy says, "extremely helpful, together with the suggestions from Team members and other clergy who were always sending ideas or comments for sermons and articles."

During the 1960s Lee helped with Billy's syndicated column "My Answer" along with Dr. Bell and Bob Ferm. Each year Billy writes at least one column explaining to the people that he does not write them all himself. He personally edits every column, and the syndicate will not take one without his own handwriting on it. But he does not disguise the fact that he gets help, like practically every other syndicated columnist in the United States. Some have a research staff of five to ten people. One of the better-known radio preachers in America has three separate staffs so that early every week he has three to choose from for the next Sunday. Billy never has had anything like that. He has always felt he could not preach another person's sermon—except on a few occasions in the midst of extreme activity, such as the extended New York Crusade of 1957, when he borrowed from John Wimbush, then pastor of Calvary Baptist Church.

Bob Ferm has worked longest in this area of research, beginning in the late 1940s when a professor at Northwestern Schools during Billy's years as president. "Bob and Lois, his wife, joined our Team to help me in any way possible. Bob has gone to many Bible schools, seminaries, pastors' conferences, etc., telling about the work of the BGEA. As well as organizing and directing the schools of evangelism for a number of years, he has gone into almost every city I've been to, ahead of time, and collected facts, figures, statistics, stories, anecdotes to help me to become more acquainted with the area before I get there.

He usually appraises me of the church situation and the various theological crosscurrents in the city."

Bob also fills in when Billy's schedule prevents background preparation. Once Billy had promised to preach the farewell sermon at an old friend's retirement from a pulpit in a large American city, immediately following a busy schedule in Europe. Bob Ferm spent three weeks in correspondence, telephone calls and literary research, so that when Billy stepped into that pulpit he had at his fingertips the history of the church and city and plenty of little-known anecdotes, humorous and otherwise, about the pastor. "It's a matter of providing him with the raw material," says Bob Ferm, which Billy then turns into his own product, dictating, rewriting, absorbing.

Before major events, like his Lausanne keynote speeches, he gets special advice from friends. From time to time Calvin Thielman, John Akers, Don Barnhouse, Bob Featherstone and Eric Mayer have helped in his research both officially and unofficially. "Incidentally," comments Billy, "I have found that there is a vast difference between preparing a message for delivery and writing an article: two different approaches and two different styles. That is the reason I have never been able to find anyone who could write for me in speaking. The sentences must be extremely brief, paragraphs brief and extremely simple. The average American has a working vocabulary of 600 words; the average clergyman has a vocabulary of 5,000 words. As I have grown older I have had to study to be simple."

In all his preparation Billy takes great pains to be factually correct. "He made so many blunders in the early years," says Grady Wilson, like mixing up a football allusion so that football fans flooded him with notes of correction. Yet he can still be caught short. In one country he wondered why the people looked puzzled at the parable of the sheep and goats. He said later, "I found they only had goats and they didn't know what sheep were. That would be something culturally that I ought to know."

"I am amazed at his attention to detail," says researcher Bob Featherstone. "He is very concerned about a word or a phrase, or that he be effectively related to the group or organization to whom he speaks." Sometimes he overprepares. A set piece like a centenary address, thoroughly researched, submitted beforehand to those concerned, with their corrections dutifully absorbed, may read in print better than it sounded when delivered, because he did not depart from his prepared text. In London in 1970 his Pilgrim Fathers oration, preached in the Royal Albert Hall, was less effective than the relaxed off-the-cuff address he gave the following night in the same hall to an enthusiastic rally of Anglican youth.

Delivery matters to him as well as material. In early days he practiced each sermon on an associate, sometimes "preaching" it several times until he had it well fastened in his mind. He may try out something humorous on Grady or T. W. Wilson. Humor is often provided by Grady, who finds that Billy for all his great sense of humor can be slow to catch the point. And he exercizes his vocal chords. On the way to a meeting he will roll up the windows of the car and yell, "Yes! Yes! Yes!" Ruth will playfully yell back, "No! No! No!" And Grady, unless driving, begs to be warned so that he can plug his ears.

Even with the sermon thoroughly prepared, the script typed in large print and the voice duly exercised, there is that other element without which, as Billy has often said, his lips would turn to clay. He wrote to a Team member who had helped with a speech, "Now pray that the power of the Holy Spirit will descend upon me for that occasion."

Ernest Shippam, a British manufacturer converted through the ministry of the Harringay crusade from a life of alcoholic defeat, was due many years later to preach, as a layman, from the Oxford pulpit where Billy Graham had stood the previous Sunday. The rector sent him a transcript with a note, "I have never heard Billy preach more wonderfully." Shippam began to read with appropriate awe, but "I could not see anything in it that the ordinary evangelical would not have preached; which just went to show that it was not the actual words but the presence of the Holy Spirit talking to people's hearts." When Billy heard of that comment he recalled George Whitefield's reply when asked if a sermon might be printed, "Yes, if you print the lightning and thunder!"[1]

Preparation, personality, the cumulative effect of world fame on the expectancy of the audience: these factors would effect nothing without the Holy Spirit's apostolic gift.

---

[1] In the original incident (Boston, September 1740) there actually was a storm while he preached (see the present writer's *George Whitefield*, Doubleday, 1972 p. 161)

"I am most anxious that whatever days I may have left, my life will have more 'depth' and less 'surface,' " wrote Billy to John Stott in 1970. The years have tightened the tension between Billy's desire to use the increasing opportunities that his past ministry has won for him and his desire to hide away and study. This man who, for millions, has made Christianity simple without cheapening it is, as George Cornell says, "a highly sophisticated, sensitive and imaginative thinker." If he had his life to live over again, Billy would give more time to study. He knows, too, that one of his strongest temptations has been "to try to do too much. Jesus moved with a serenity and quietness in his ministry, and yet at the end of his ministry he said, 'I have finished the work that I came to do.' He did not heal all the sick, feed all the poor, or raise all the dead. He did what he could. Perhaps I have attempted to do too much."

Billy has never found it easy to discriminate between claims on his time. A visionary, he has grown increasingly impatient with administrative responsibilities, yet knows they are a key to wider usefulness. One problem is where to set the limits to the BCEA ministry. Another is the increasing flow of invitations to speak, many of which will open superb opportunities for a clergyman's ministry, often in a secular setting. He wrote half jokingly to a friend whose institution wished to honor him, that "there seem to be more than 10,000 awards in America every year (each involves a major speech of response) plus every type of celebration and convention you can possibly think of—and sometimes I think I'm invited to all of them!" He can take only a handful each year and then is obliged to explain to personal friends, worldwide, why he cannot come to their special event. As he wrote (in 1972) to one, "The spirit is willing but the calendar is limited and the body is weak. . . . I would appreciate your prayers that the Holy Spirit will teach me how to give priority to the right things and the courage to say no to the rest."

If he ties himself down with too many engagements, he cannot seize sudden strategic openings. "I want to be flexible," he says, "so that I can change plans at the last minute if necessary, to go and do what I believe the Holy Spirit would have me do—like Philip, preaching in great evangelistic meetings in Samaria, who was suddenly whisked away by an angel to talk to one man, the Ethiopian nobleman —which was not in his date book!" Such flexibility is a part of his nature. Walter Smyth, in their long experience together, has become very conscious that "somehow, out of all these changes which from the human standpoint seem sometimes a bit distracting, eventually comes God's plan. I think it's because God knows Billy better than we do, and has made him the way he is. I've seen again and again where I thought: Goodness! Not another change! And yet it was the very thing needful."

As for crusades, it is one of Billy's little eccentricities that as he faces another he will complain to Ruth that he cannot possibly get through the heavy list of engagements. Press conferences, ministers' meetings and the school of evangelism; countless interviews, perhaps businessmen's or governor's prayer breakfasts; and every night to preach to a huge stadium audience, knowing he will be heard and viewed by millions on TV—the crusade looms before him like a black cloud. Afterward he will enthusiastically state that it has been the greatest opportunity ever. Together with his dislike of dark and rainy days and his worrying about the weather (with some reason, in view of the number of rain-drenched, windswept stadiums he has preached in), his groans disclose how human he is. "We tease him about being like Jeremiah, the prophet of doom," says Ruth. "And yet when it's all over it has worked out fine and he is always glad he went."

Billy, however, does not let any fear spoil for long the happiness that is a marked feature of his character. Occasionally he gets discouraged but very soon, as Walter Smyth says, "The Lord comes along and gives him what he needs to overcome it. Very rarely is he ever sharp with anyone. Yet when he gets overly tired this begins to show up, not publicly but privately. You know then that he needs some rest. And," commented Smyth in 1976, "the pressures upon him are not getting lighter, they're getting heavier."

Billy adds to his burden by the intensity of his absorption in the ministry. He has inherited his mother's intensity (his father was more relaxed, with a dry humor) and feels deeply the moral decline of his country, the sufferings of persecuted Christians, the shortness of time before free speech and free worship may be extinguished in yet another part of the world. Friends or relatives may find him relaxed, delighted to learn how they are; he will have them talking about themselves and will be thinking of ways to help them. "And then after a little bit," said one relative wistfully, "you've lost him." He will be off on some aspect of the ministry or a book he has read, or will fall silent, his mind back on a problem or winging far away to an associate who is engaged in a spiritual battle. Even when his own family gathers at Christmas and he is enjoying every minute's chat and playing with the grandchildren, he will suddenly disappear to his desk, to rejoin them later in the evening before slipping away again.

One evening shortly before Christmas 1972, when the Nixon administration had ordered the resumption of bombing in Cambodia, Jim Wilson, a rising young evangelist, was staying at his parents' home in Montreat. He came into the dining room to find "Uncle Billy" signing letters at T. W.'s table. "Jim," said Graham, "let me read you something."

It was a letter from a churchman of some prominence, whose home Billy had visited many years before. The minister attacked Graham in anger and bitterness for not condemning, with all his vast influence on the nation, the Vietnam war. He ascribed his silence to base motives: "his lust for famous friends" . . . Graham was "a prostitute of the administration" . . . "consumed with desire to boost your ego even if you do not realize it," and so on.

Jim thought "how unjust it was, how unfair, and how I wished in my own heart that I could take this man to task."

"Now, Jim, let me read you my response." After a warm, friendly opening Billy's reply went on, "I can easily understand the harshness and outrage of your letter. I accept your rebuke with all the humility I can muster. If I were in your place and from your vantage point I might have written a stronger letter. . . . The tone of your letter in no way diminishes my own personal admiration for you and my affection for you in the Lord."

He pointed out, gently, that it was impossible for that man to know all the facts about Graham's relationship with the president, and added, "You may not believe it, but I deplore the continuation of the war in Vietnam as much as you do. I hope and pray that there will be an early armistice." He gave a few facts without rebutting the unjust accusations and expressed the hope that they could discuss the issues in person when opportunity came. "I am deeply grateful that you made this a private exchange. I admire your courage and frankness in writing a harsh letter. Your criticism is not taken lightly by me." He ended with strong good wishes for the man's own ministry.

Jim Wilson exclaimed, "Uncle Billy, how can you be so unjustly criticized and react so calmly?"

"Jim, when I was your age, I suppose I wanted to fight all my critics. Now, I just leave them with the Lord. If I tried to answer every critic, that's all I would have time to do. But God has called me to preach and be about the business of winning the lost." Jim Wilson comments, "I think I learned a great lesson then about what it means to walk in the Spirit and depend on God for every detail of life."

Billy Graham once remarked, "I am blamed for just about every mistake in the evangelical camp. But, although I do not enjoy it, I have learned to live with it and endure it." He likes a quotation from Abraham Lincoln which George Wilson hung in the Minneapolis office. "If I were to try to read, much less answer all the attacks made on me, this shop might as well be closed for any other business. I do the very best I know how, the very best I can—and mean to keep doing so until the end. If the end brings me out right, what is said against me won't amount to anything. If the end brings me out wrong, ten angels swearing I was right would make no difference."

If Graham learned early to live with praise and criticism, he confesses that "it is sometimes a conscious battle" to accept graciously a violently unfair verbal assault; but "most often it is just my natural way. I have really never been a fighter at heart and do not like to engage in sharp answers. I believe that a soft answer turneth away wrath," although, as Ruth remarks, "sometimes a soft answer makes them furious!"—particularly those extreme conservatives who abuse him, with bitter name-calling, for his willingness to accept cooperation from those who do not subscribe to their theology.

David Kucharsky, now editor of *Christian Herald*, who has attended scores of Graham press conferences and had seen him at *Christianity Today* briefings and board meetings, has found his generosity of spirit "a wonderful example, because I cannot ever recall him being the least bit cynical, even in private conversation. There are not very many people (Christians or otherwise) about whom that could in truth be said." At home the same spirit pervades, as Anne Graham Lotz recalls. Many a man who is gracious in public will explode in a sympathetic family circle, but "as Daddy shared his experiences, I cannot remember one single time that he criticized someone or made a disparaging remark about any particular person. Even those who were outright in their hatred of him, when we asked him about it, he would just say that perhaps they needed our love and prayers more than others."

On the other hand, states Graham, "Everybody needs some friends around him who will say, You are *wrong!* And that includes me. I really value the friendship of people who'll just tell it to me like it is, even though I may try to defend my position for a while." Many of the developments and changes over the years in the crusade ministry and in Billy's personal attitudes have followed public or private criticism. Thus when Reinhold Niebuhr criticized him in the 1950s for not taking a stronger stand on the race question, although Graham already had integrated his crusades, in advance of churches and schools, "I thought about it a great deal. He influenced me, and I began to take a stronger stand."

The Billy Graham ministry has not been powered by a fit man's energy. Billy has paid a high price in strain on his health. For years he had a succession of "physical problems from time to time that have either weakened me or been irritating enough to humble me." The kidney trouble and eye trouble of earlier years have not recurred, but in February 1971 surgeons at Mayo removed an infected salivary gland. Later that year he suffered a slight heart valve problem which prevented his preaching in Korean provincial cities. He learned gradually to live more within the limitations of his strength until his health was better, with occasional setbacks, in his later fifties than five years earlier. Billy's friends worry about his health, especially because his father and uncles died of strokes in their sixties following hardening of the arteries, and he dreads a diminishing of strength while opportunities for service continue to widen.

Thus, he exercises more than when he was younger. He has almost abandoned golf but he jogs regularly. At Montreat he has measured the only level stretch of his mountain drive; back and forth ten times is a mile. When in Honolulu for a convention address he measured a stretch between two points in a parking lot in Kapiolani Park and faithfully jogged a mile before going on to visit his radio station. His practice around the world is similar as local conditions permit. He has a moderate appetite, enjoys vegetable and salads, fish or chicken. He loves olives but rarely eats dessert. For breakfast he likes an egg (eating only the white), orange juice and coffee.

Anne Graham Lotz has a story, dating back to her later schoolgirl years, about an incident that her father does not remember. She had ridden in the car to see him off at Asheville airport. "It was rather crowded, and as usual, he had to shake just about every hand out there. He finally got his bags checked and was waiting to board the plane. I had stayed with him during all this, trying to look inconspicuous, not wanting any of that curious attention to land on me, yet also wanting to stay close, since he was leaving. The plane came in, and he turned, shook my hand, said it was nice to have met me, and boarded the plane! I stood there stunned, but then had to laugh. Poor guy, he had been meeting so many people and was so preoccupied (as only he can be) with the upcoming meetings, he was just more or less mechanical. . . . Bless his heart, how we love him!"

Billy himself remarks that "one of the greatest prices I have to pay now is the fact that I am instantly recognized by so many Americans and foreigners. This means that I am actually a prisoner in a hotel room or in my home. . . . It is impossible for me to go out for a quiet meal with my wife or family, to stroll down a street, to walk in a park. This is why I would like to be abroad a great deal of the time in countries where I am not well known, like Japan—or even Russia. You have no idea what it is to lose your privacy, until you've lost it. Always being recognized gives me a great opportunity of witness, but it is also physically draining."

In a plane returning from Dallas he had to sign autographs and answer questions for what seemed to him at least a couple of hundred giggling schoolgirls going to a swimming rally. He enjoyed it but arrived home exhausted. "It certainly isn't a glamour life," comments a Team member, Irv Chambers. "I've seen Mr. Graham try to eat in a public eating place and not be able to get through a meal without standing up five or six times to shake hands with people." Gigi says, "I've never seen him rude to anyone when the line has been ten or twelve long for autographs during one meal. With all the hectic schedule and the pressures during a crusade, I have only seen him be gracious and Christlike."

He will not tell a lie when asked point-blank if he is Billy Graham, but he can often sidestep gracefully because a face seen on television, or from a seat in a stadium, never looks quite identical with a face met unexpectedly at close quarters. A man followed him into the restroom of a Howard Johnson restaurant in Charlotte. "You look so much like Billy Graham," he said. "Have you been told that before?" "Oh yes, people always tell me I look like him." The man said, "Well, after seeing you close up, I realize that you are not." One day a stranger approached Billy and Ruth in the street. "You wouldn't happen to be Billy Graham?" he inquired. Then, without waiting for an answer, he said, "No, of course not. Billy is not as tall as you." And off he went.

Billy was touched to receive (May 1974) a letter from a Trenton, New Jersey, businessman who had assisted, with sensitive courtesy, after a hired helicopter had force-landed at Mercer county airport. ". . . When you responded that quite often you are taken as Billy Graham, at first I was satisfied with your reply; however, as you continued to speak to your helicopter pilot I knew you were Billy Graham. I well understand your reasons for not wanting to be recognized, especially when tired after possibly many hours of traveling. . . . My wife and I follow your telecasts closely. I look upon our chance meeting as not chance but prearranged by God. I feel that I have come face to face with the one mortal I most admire, and I must say that my admiration has grown considerably stronger as I was able to observe you at a time of some difficulty and to see that your faith in God is exhibited in your everyday life."

Billy was amused once in a British railway dining car, when he was traveling alone with Grady to the Keswick Convention centenary. He ordered cider, the west country's strong drink, in the belief that it was nonalcoholic like American sweet cider. The waitress said, "I had thought you were Billy Graham, but as you are drinking that, you can't be!"

"There are many times," Billy comments, "when I find myself actually hiding and withdrawing." Thus he often sits with the hotel blinds half drawn, and on a sunny day Grady Wilson will firmly draw them back. Yet Billy loves to be with people. He suffers from the loneliness of his position where too many either fawn on him or seek advantage, even if for some good cause.

He craves deeper companionship than he can obtain except from very few outside his own family and his close Team associates, with whom he can relax totally. He longs, too, to minister personally to many more individuals than his heavy schedule allows. One burden is "the constant request for appointments from hundreds and thousands of people each year whom I cannot possibly see. If I were ten people I could not see them all. Many of them just do not understand. Most of my closest friends do understand." When it was announced that he would be briefly in London in May 1976 he received several hundred requests for five minutes of his time. Cliff Barrows, in their association of more than thirty years, has "always been tremendously encouraged and impressed by his personal interest and love for people and his desire to accommodate them any way he could. I think this desire has been one of his greatest problems; perhaps it has been mine as well, our inability to say no."

As well as ministering to ordinary men and women, Graham has the unique opportunity to minister to those at the top of their professions or in public life. Every year he spends a few days in Washington while Congress is in session. Senators and members of the Cabinet treat him as an equal and he has held private spiritual conversations with governors throughout the United States, with ambassadors and heads of state around the world. Douglas Coe, who arranges his Washington schedule, mentions that "if Billy Graham knows a man has just come to Christ, he often takes time out to call that person, sometimes long distance or under difficult circumstances, taking great pains to track him down in order to encourage him and tell him he is praying for him."

One year Billy spoke in Washington eleven times in four days, with numerous individual conversations. In pursuing this ministry among the prominent he is well aware of the dangers. President Johnson might write of him, "All of us—Democrat and Republican alike—are nonpartisan in our feelings about Billy Graham," but others might misconstrue motive as vanity or a thirst for secret political power. Some who acknowledge his sincerity will charge that Billy is not always blunt enough in counseling, or that he allows politicians to use him. Doug Coe emphasizes the temptations and problems a man encounters working with the powerful, the rich and the wealthy, while still keeping his life right before Christ. He adds, "When place and position are so prominent in our culture, when people want to wine you and dine you, to touch you, to get your autograph, to take you on their yachts, to fly you in their planes,.to give you a place of honor, and you still desire to remain a humble servant of Christ, it takes the power of the Holy

Spirit to accomplish this. This is one of Billy's great challenges, and yet as much as any man in an equivalent position he has handled it admirably. The credit goes to God, and to Billy's genuine desire to know Christ in the most intimate way."

Billy likes to believe the best about people and is deeply disappointed when any public figure whom he had admired is uncovered as a hypocrite. "Unfortunately," Billy once wrote to a friend, "some of us are inadvertently and unwittingly used politically—I am expert on that subject! I hope I have learned my own lesson!"

Eminence, however, is not a necessary passport to Graham's concern. A Tennessee pastor, whose marriage had been saved after Billy had led the wife to Christ, wrote to him many years later, "You have always acted as though every little Christian was as important in your sight as in the sight of Christ."

Graham's warmth and concern bring out the best in those he meets. When he made a special trip to Oberlin to dedicate a center for retarded children which Mrs. Howard Jones supports, the Joneses held a reception in their home for friends black and white. They recall how "his presence made everybody feel so good; he was humble and down to earth with everyone, open and friendly and warm." His warmth and tenderness make him thoughtful of those around him. Sometimes a conflict of schedules or strategies, or one of Billy's sudden changes of plan, may leave calloused feelings and a sore heart, but if the aggrieved person manages to get through, a distressed Billy will take pains to bind up the wound. That thoughtfulness is aided by his even temper, not always found in a man of Billy's passion for punctuality, and by his good memory for faces. In a crowded room he will greet old acquaintances who barely expected to be recalled or noticed. His alertness is the admiration of his staff. When Graham was grand marshal of the Rose Bowl procession, one of the BGEA overseas associates and his family were among the crowds packing the streets. Billy did not know they were in Pasadena. The associate was astonished, as the procession rode by, that Billy should spot him and wave.

Billy's manners are those of the Old South. "When our teen-age daughter walks into the room," says his sister Jean (Mrs. Leighton Ford), "he stands up. He doesn't have to do that because he's at home, but he does it. This is just Billy! He is one of the most courteous, polite, individuals I've ever known." He is appreciative. Wherever he goes he invariably writes to all who helped or entertained him, a courtesy the more welcome because many Americans are not ready writers. A crusade director is always told to provide an address list of those who carried responsibility or gave a personal service, and Billy dictates his personal thanks.

"No man," writes George Cornell, "could be so continually surrounded for so many years with so much adulation and criticism, and still remain the plainly decent, good-humored, thoughtfully kind man he is, without being of quality timber." The adulation might make for pride in a lesser soul, and the criticism for vindictiveness, but "Graham can laugh at himself, and does, which is the mark of honest humanity."

Graham's sense of humor is one of the qualities that endeared him to former British prime minister and foreign secretary, Lord Home (Sir Alec), who in his memoirs (1976) names Billy Graham as one of the great influences on his religious life. Their friendship began when both were in Rhodesia in 1960, the one for constitutional talks, the other for a crusade. Lord Home recalls[2] a meeting "attended by thousands of Rhodesian Africans. Words of one or two syllables held them spellbound. . . . I have always been attracted by Billy Graham's open and easy manner, and by the natural way in which he talks about Christianity and in particular that part of the teaching which relates to man's contact with man. . . . Christianity is made by him a happy religion and this is what it is meant to be."[3]

Humor goes hand in hand with humility. Billy Graham has faced the temptation of pride, as in 1957 when a decision to extend the Madison Square Garden crusade might incur a sharp drop in attendance. "It took me a whole day to make up my mind and to tell the Lord, Yes, I was willing to preach to a few." His lack of self-importance shows impulsively. Coming off a train at Toronto with Grady, he saw two nuns burdened down with bags, which he carried to their car. In Atlanta he had entered a pre-Lausanne committee meeting late and sat down beside Paul Little at the back, when a waiter passing outside upset a tray of crockery with a resounding crash. Paul Little recalled,

[2] Letter to the author, 2 February 1975.

[3] Relating other examples of Graham's humor, Lord Home writes of Billy's riposte "when I told him that the only thing which made me doubt the omniscience of the Almighty was the extraordinary places in which he put oil. He said, 'But how could he have known that the British would be so foolish as to give up their empire?'"

"Like a shot Billy was on his hands and knees handing the dishes to the fellow out in the hallway. His spontaneous and unself-conscious response is a measure of the man. His humility continually amazes me."

Gigi says, "I have grown to realize that Daddy is a truly humble person. In fact, he's so humble that you know it's God-given. It's not something he strives for or puts on. God has clothed him with true humility and gentleness." Billy would dissent a little. "I am not as humble as all that; I have plenty of temptations to pride." It is true that like most persons of achievement, he dislikes having time wasted by casual unpunctuality or frittered away in trivialities. At the other end of the scale he has a natural pride in wanting his contribution to be recognized at the bar of history. Nevertheless, he is prepared to let others take credit, he does not obtrude a sense of his own importance, and he learned early the Scriptural commandment, *Walk humbly with thy God.*

His emphasis in the early days of fame, that if he reached up to take any of God's glory "my lips would turn to clay," has been an abiding attitude to his life and work. An Irish woman journalist, who had failed to secure an interview during his crowded Belfast visit of 1972, caught him at last by panting down the railway platform just before he stepped into the train. As the guard blew his whistle she shot a final question. "As head of a large organization with an attendant media, do you ever feel you have got bigger than your message?"

"Oh no," he said, his gentle drawl quite horrified. "I hope the Lord would let me die if it ever got like that."

14 Graham and the Presidents

PUBLIC interest has a natural focus on Graham's relationship with successive presidents of the United States. Such a contact has been unique in history among American clergymen, for its length of time and closeness—despite President Truman's first summons to the White House being also his last. Billy, young and newly famous, committed the faux pas of yielding to an importunate press corps what he and the president had talked about. Truman's annoyance taught Graham a lesson he has never forgotten.

Truman at the age of seventy-seven is reported to have included Billy Graham among the targets of his gritty salvos at figures past and present. "Graham was never a friend of mine—all he's interested in is getting his name in the paper." Not long before Truman died in 1972 he summoned Billy, who was holding a crusade in Kansas City nearby, to Independence. "Billy," said Truman as they shook hands, "are you still giving those Republicans hell?" After that they conversed on matters more appropriate to Billy's ministry. As for that celebrated gaffe of 1950, "He told me that he thoroughly understood that I was young and had not been properly briefed."

The first encounter with General Eisenhower came through a mutual friend by the name of Sid Richardson in Fort Worth, Texas, an oil man. Billy Graham was suggesting that Eisenhower declare himself for the presidency, although Billy was not particular about which party. After the Washington crusade in 1951, Richardson, who had already met Graham in Texas, called and asked if he would be willing to go to Europe and meet Eisenhower. Richardson said, "I'll pay the way for you and your wife. I think he needs to get to know you." Graham agreed to go because it meant a brief vacation for him and Ruth. Eisenhower received Graham at SHAPE headquarters and kept him for nearly two hours. During the course of the conversation he asked Graham what he preached and what he believed. He looked out the window for quite some time and said, "You know, that's what my father and mother believed. I'm afraid I've gotten away from it in the army." That was the beginning of a long friendship which Graham probably cherishes as much as any friendship he has had. Later Eisenhower wrote him a letter expressing "not only my congratulations on what you are doing, but my hope that you will continue to press and fight for the old-fashioned virtues of integrity, decency and straightforwardness in public life. I thank the Almighty that such inspired persons as yourself are ready to give full time and energy to this purpose." The general said he had no objection whatever to having it known that he applauded Graham's efforts.

Immediately after Eisenhower's nomination for president he had Senator Frank Carlson call Billy to the Blackstone hotel in Chicago. Eisenhower wanted to know if he had any suggestions. Graham told him that the country was in great need of spiritual renewal and that this should be one of the themes of his speeches.

Eisenhower invited Graham to Denver a few weeks later and asked him for some ideas for his speeches. There, Eisenhower introduced Graham to Conrad Hilton, who was later to play such an important part in the early prayer breakfast movement in Washington.

During the time at the Brown hotel in Denver, Graham presented to Eisenhower a red Scofield Bible which years later the press reported as at his bedside. In that conversation Graham urged Eisenhower to join a church and attend it regularly. During his years in the army he had not belonged to any church. Eisenhower said, "I promise I will join a church, whether I win or lose the election." Then he said, "If you went to Washington, which church would you belong to?" Graham said, "What denomination would you like to join?" He said, "Well, my wife was a Presbyterian. I suppose I would like to go to a Presbyterian church." Graham said, "There are two churches I could highly recommend—one is the National Presbyterian in Washington and the other is the New York Avenue Presbyterian." The president eventually joined the National Presbyterian Church and was baptized by Dr. Ed Elson, who led the Eisenhower family into a deeper walk with God.

After the election Graham went to Korea with Bob Pierce. The war was at its height and Graham had Christmas lunch with John Eisenhower, the president's only son, who was on the front lines in Korea. When Graham returned home Eisenhower invited him to the Commodore hotel in New York five days before he was to be inaugurated president of the United States. He went over to the window and, looking out over New York, said, "I think one of the reasons I have been elected is to help lead this country in a spiritual revival. I would like to quote a passage of Scripture in my inaugural address. Do you have any suggestions?" Graham gave him three Scripture verses, one of which the president used. The president did not discuss the prayer that he led the the nation in at the inauguration. Some people gave Graham credit for it but he was totally unaware of it until he heard it himself.

Mutual respect and friendship grew during the Eisenhower presidency. In those years, when Graham had to battle against the "Elmer Gantry" image of mass evangelism, the public endorsement of so highly respected a president gave him valuable support abroad and at home. Thus, on his way to start the first New York crusade, although Graham spent only a few minutes with the president at the White House, the national press coverage was enough in itself to help the crusade that was to be a turning point in Graham's American ministry. Earlier, in March 1956, Graham had 45 minutes with him, reporting on his evangelistic tour to India. They also discussed the race question in the South, including (as the president wrote to him two days later) "the opportunity open to ministers of promoting both tolerance and progress in our race relations problems." Graham worked quietly and effectively to carry out the president's mandate to help change attitudes among Southern clergy, white and black.

When facing a second term, Eisenhower wrote, "I count heavily on your friendship and support now, as I have in the past." Altogether, including the years of the general's retirement, they had sixteen sessions together. Graham's affection ran deep, and Eisenhower counted Billy Graham as one of his "dear friends." In Walter Reed hospital during his final illness Eisenhower spoke of heaven and they prayed together. The general said, "If my experience can help anybody else, make good use of it."

President-elect John Kennedy is reported to have groaned when his father, Ambassador Joseph Kennedy, told him that he must certainly ask Billy Graham to see him, but over the years of his presidency an interesting friendship developed. Five days before he was inaugurated president, Kennedy invited Graham to play golf with him. Driving him in his own convertible, Kennedy first of all asked Graham to "Tell me all about the second coming of Jesus Christ. Do you believe it's going to take place literally?" Graham had an opportunity to witness concerning the Biblical teaching of the coming again of Christ. They discussed religious matters vigorously, though the difference in church loyalties restricted mutual counseling in depth.

In 1962 a curious incident occurred at the White House. Graham was about to embark on his South American tour of brief crusades in several countries to which, by coincidence, Kennedy soon would pay state visits. The president said, "I'll be your John the Baptist."

"Mr. President," replied Grady Wilson, the associate with Graham, "remember what happened to John the Baptist!"

"All right. I'll be your forerunner then." Graham and Grady Wilson recalled the exchange after November 1963.

Graham was placed among the family friends at the funeral, and Robert Kennedy wrote a handwritten card of thanks for Graham's letter of condolence: ". . . Hearing from you who has accomplished so much good for so many people around the world is greatly appreciated. The president greatly admired you and what you are doing."

Billy was strongly drawn to Lyndon Johnson from the day in the early nineteen fifties when he first met him in Texas. Billy appreciated Texan individualists "who were movers and doers." The two men had already drawn fairly close before November 1963. That again was the result of the activities of Sid Richardson in Texas. Sid Richardson had become one of Graham's friends and confidants. It was through Sid Richardson also that he met a young Texas lawyer by the name of John Connally, who was later to become a good friend. When Graham preached at Richardson's funeral there sat Speaker of the House Sam Rayburn, Lyndon Johnson and Richard Nixon.

Shortly after he assumed the presidency Johnson called for Billy Graham to visit him privately at the White House for prayer. On 9 December 1963 the president wrote to Billy, "Your message met the need. The knowledge that one of God's greatest messengers was seeking divine counsel in my behalf provided me with a strong source of strength, courage and comfort during the extremely trying days immediately after the tragic event in Dallas. I shall cherish this in the days ahead." In late December Billy stayed in the White House for the first of many visits which gave him an insight into the "almost unbearable responsibilities" of the presidency and a growing affection for the Johnson family. He learned something of the pressures, the cascade of advice and criticism from all directions which are a president's daily lot, the agonizing decisions and moral dilemmas posed continually by the demands of national security.

Billy's interest in politics and government, always strong, was increased by his glimpses inside the presidency. But he sought, not always successfully, to restrict counsel to fundamental moral issues and to strengthen President Johnson's faith. "As God was with Washington at Valley Forge and with Lincoln in the darkest hours of the Civil War," he reminded the president in the early days, "so God will be with you. There will be times when decisions come hard and burdens are too heavy to bear—that is when God will be nearest to you." Billy Graham upheld the presidency even when he did not understand or personally agree with a particular policy.

President Johnson tried to draw Graham into offices such as being chairman of the citizens' committee to help implement the civil rights law of 1964 (the crusade schedule would not have allowed time). On another occasion he asked him if there were any place in government he would like. Yet he accepted his refusals ungrudgingly, telling him that his greatest contribution to America was to continue working for the spiritual and moral awakening without which no reform could bear fruit.

Ruth Graham played a big part in holding Billy to his rightful sphere. When they were dining alone with President and Mrs. Johnson the weekend before the Democratic convention of 1964, the president asked Billy whom he would recommend as vice-president. Under the table Ruth kicked her husband. Instead of taking the hint he said out loud, "Why did you kick me?" The president, his curiosity roused, echoed Bill's question. Cornered, there was nothing for Ruth to do but reply to Bill, "Because you are supposed to limit your advice to the president to moral and spiritual issues."

The president graciously conceded, and the conversation was changed. Dinner over, Ruth followed Mrs. Johnson to the family sitting room. The president hung back. Once safely out of earshot, he turned to Bill and demanded, "Now, what do you really think? Who *is* your recommendation?" Graham answered, "Hubert Humphrey." Graham had first met Humphrey when he was running for mayor of Minneapolis in the mid forties, and they were personal friends.

Graham valued the Johnsons' example to the nation in their close family ties and their faithful churchgoing, but—though he and Ruth prayed the more incessantly for the president because of his responsibilities—"I just happen to love you because you are you," Billy once wrote to LBJ. Billy found him a warm outgoing personality who confided freely, often on secret matters. The president included Billy's close associates in his affection. Grady Wilson recalls a meal when Mrs. Johnson rebuked the president for his table manners, and the president replied, "Bird, now let me eat the way I want to. I just have a couple of country boys here." When the president was recuperating at Charlottesville, Virginia, after a heart attack, T. W. Wilson stayed dutifully outside when Billy went in. A few minutes later the Secret Service man summoned him. "T. W.," said the president, "I thought you came here to see me." T. W. answered that he had not wanted to intrude; Billy would represent the whole Team; they all were praying for the president's recovery. The president replied, "Sit down over there. I have no secrets."

Johnson attended the Graham crusade in Houston, the first president in office to attend a mass evangelistic meeting; 65,000 were present.

Sources close to the president say that the prospect of Billy's coming would always lift LBJ's spirit, and their conversations would leave him with a widened horizon. "My mind went back," LBJ wrote shortly after laying down office, "to those lonely occasions at the White House when your prayers and your friendship helped to sustain a President in an hour of trial. . . . No one will ever know how you helped to lighten my load or how much warmth you brought into our house. But I know." One of the president's former staff wrote to Billy after the funeral: "He was greatly affected by your care of him. Through many a dark passage your remembrance of him stirred his hopes and better instincts. You were one of those few people who caused him not to forget certain things he had learned in his mother's lap, certain things he would occasionally call 'the unforgettables.' " Mrs. Lady Bird Johnson shared with the present writer her feelings of affection for Billy and Ruth Graham. "I know how much Lyndon treasured Dr. Graham's counsel. He found solace in him both as a religious adviser and a friend in good times and in times of trial and anguish. My appreciation for them has grown through the years—for the ways in which they have touched and enriched our lives and the lives of people the world over."[1]

During and after the election campaign of 1968, Billy Graham was able to perform confidential nonpolitical services for the nation which helped to make the changeover of administration one of the smoothest. On the last night of the Johnson presidency he stayed at the White House. After the ceremony, at which Billy Graham prayed the Nixon inauguration prayer, both the Johnson daughters crossed the platform to give Billy a kiss. Billy was unable to go to the airport to say goodbye, since he was President Nixon's guest in the presidential box to witness the inaugural parade. No clergyman in history had been so close to two successive presidents of differing political parties.

In the years of President Johnson's retirement, after one visit to the LBJ Ranch Billy urged him to take a strong public stand in the gospel his great grandfather, Samuel Baines, had preached: he would reach millions. The former president replied rather vaguely, but he made a point of attending the Dallas crusade and of endorsing a resolution of the Texas legislature inviting Billy to hold a crusade in Austin.

Billy delivered the invocation at the dedication of the Johnson Library at Austin. Later, at the ranch in the hill country, LBJ took him down to the oak trees by the river and said, "Billy, one day you're going to be asked to preach my funeral. You'll come right here under this tree and I'll be buried right there. You'll read the Bible and preach the gospel, and I want you to, but I hope you'll try to tell some of the things I tried to do." They spoke together of the brevity of life, "and the fact that every person will some day die and stand before God to give an

---

[1] Letter to the author dated 13 March 1975.

account." They discussed the resurrection at some length. A few months later the news of Johnson's death reached Billy fifteen minutes after he walked into his mountaintop home upon returning from President Nixon's second inauguration.

Graham's address and prayer of committal by the oak tree on 25 January 1973, with the nation watching on television, came from a full heart. He spoke of the man he knew, his compassion for the underdog, his friendship for children of all races, his strong family life, and his faith. He spoke of death, judgment and the Cross. "Lyndon Johnson understood that . . . for the believer who has been to the Cross, death is no frightful leap in the dark, but is the entrance into a glorious new life. . . . For the believer, the brutal fact of death has been conquered by the historical resurrection of Jesus Christ. For the person who has turned from sin and received Christ as Lord and Savior, death is not the end. . . ."[2]

Richard Nixon and Billy Graham had been friends for some eighteen years at the time of the presidential election of 1968, having been introduced to each other by Senator Clyde Hoey of North Carolina. Graham was having lunch with Senator Hoey in the senate dining room when the senator said, "There goes young Richard Nixon from California." Graham immediately said, "I know his parents. I would like to meet him." Senator Hoey called Nixon over to the table and during the conversation Nixon said he had often heard his parents speak of him. Then he suddenly asked Graham if he would like to join him in a golf game. Graham said yes. They played golf that afternoon at the Burning Tree Golf Club near Washington, and that was the beginning of their friendship. Billy Graham had already met Nixon's parents two years earlier in California at an evangelistic meeting. "The friendship is well rooted," the Nixons' daughter Julie writes,[3] in a letter to the author, "and stems from the days when my grandmother first began to follow the ministry of Dr. Graham. Nana is the great spiritual force in our family. I am sure that part of my father's feeling that he can trust

---

[2] The text of the address printed in the *Congressional Record* (5 February 1973) is evidently taken from Graham's prepared script, not from a transcript of his actual words. For instance, it records him as quoting from a poem of John Oxenham but in fact he quoted from the hymn "Abide With Me."

[3] In a letter to the author dated 2 July 1975.

Billy Graham as a man of God stems from his knowledge that Nana believed with all her heart in the Graham mission."

Julie Nixon Eisenhower has a vivid memory of the day in 1967 when Billy Graham preached at her grandmother's funeral. "My father, up until the moment we all had to file past the coffin to leave the church, had been composed and strong for Tricia, me and the other members of the family. But as he prepared to thank Dr. Graham for being with us, he broke down momentarily. Sobs racked his body and he buried his face in Dr. Graham's shoulder. This lasted for perhaps only five or ten seconds. Because we all loved Nana so much I feel that the true cementing of the Nixon-Graham friendship came at that moment."

Late that year, when Nixon debated whether to run for the Republican nomination of 1968, Billy Graham's counsel, as they walked the sands in Florida, was a strong factor. Graham believed Nixon to possess great moral character and personal integrity, and to be blessed with an ideal family life. Graham also knew, at first hand, General Eisenhower's view that Richard Nixon was better qualified for the presidency than any other individual. Later, Nixon invited Graham to be one of his guests on election night, but Graham declined because he did not want to be seen publicly on such a partisan and emotional evening. He stayed in a nearby hotel, however. He had told Nixon, "If you lose I will be ready to come over and have a prayer with you." The next morning when Nixon realized that he had won by a hairbreadth, he called Graham on the phone and invited him to his hotel suite. He called his family together and asked Graham to lead them in a prayer before he went down to meet the press. Billy thought this rather significant because the president-elect, of Quaker background, had been reluctant to talk openly about his personal faith—though Graham believed it to be deep.

Nixon once half-jokingly asked Billy Graham if he would be willing to run as his running mate for vice-president. Graham looked him in the eye and said, "God has called me to preach the gospel, and I consider that the highest calling in the world." This was during a conversation in his New York apartment when he knew he had the nomination sewed up and was thinking of a number of names for vice-president. Later Graham urged Nixon to choose his long-time friend, Senator Mark Hatfield. In later years Graham has often wondered if things would have been different had Nixon followed that advice. After Nixon was elected he asked Billy Graham what job he would like in his administration, and once again Graham said, "You could not offer me a job as an ambassador, or a cabinet post, that I would give a second thought to. When God called me to preach, it was for life." Nixon said, "I knew you would say that, and I respect you for it."

Richard Nixon understood and strengthened Billy's resolve that he should stay out of politics. Over the years before and after November 1968, as Billy relates, "in our casual conversations on the golf course or around the dinner table I have often discussed politics and world affairs with him, especially my experiences overseas and my knowledge of the mood of America. For example, in the 1960 election I was out of the country most of the time, but when I did see him I told him I felt it would be better if he did not comment on the religious situation that had arisen as an issue in the campaign. Mr. Kennedy was the first Catholic to come close to the Presidency. I felt it would do Mr. Nixon only harm if he answered back. . . . There was a time in the 1960 election when it was rumored that I was about to endorse him. He called me and said, 'Billy, your ministry is more important than my election.' That was always his position." Paul Harvey, one of those who urged Graham to keep out of the Kennedy-Nixon race, has said on Paul Harvey News that "your personal friend lost by the margin you could have delivered."

In the first months of the Nixon presidency the press built up Billy as if he and his ideals were a major influence behind the White House ("the President's Preacher," *Newsweek* called him, and *Life* wrote of the "omnipresence" of Billy Graham). The buildup was embarrassing: in the first three months Graham received hundreds of requests for his intercession with the president for jobs, pardons, and so on, which he declined on principle—even when White House personnel tried to reach the president through him. The buildup was also potentially damaging for the Graham ministry, by positing a situation in which he could supposedly do and say more in the White House than was possible.

His influence in fact counted for less than was popularly supposed. He was one of a wide range of clergy asked to preach at White House services. He saw President Nixon on fewer occasions privately than he had President Johnson, who in his five years had received him twenty-three times, including five overnight visits. He knew less of what went on during the Nixon administration than during the Johnson years. In course of time the Grahams were given to understand that some of President Nixon's staff were anxious to restrict and frustrate any influence he might have.

Nevertheless the two men remained friends in spite of the inevitably changed relationship when a private citizen becomes president. Like millions of Americans, Billy Graham's feelings toward the Nixon of 1969–72 were positive. More than a year before the President's reelection he summarized some of them in a private letter. "I am certain that he has brought a sense of ethics to the Presidency that has been largely derived from the Christian faith as believed and practiced by his parents." As to whether the president should state his own Christian convictions more explicitly, Graham pointed out, "This has been rather difficult for him, with his Quaker background. He has also been extremely reticent to speak out about his personal faith for fear that people will think he is using it politically. He is very sensitive at this point. On several occasions he has urged me to stay out of politics. He has also been hesitant to attend our crusades for fear that people will interpret it politically," as they had at Knoxville.

One of the high spots in the Nixon-Graham friendship, other than the president's attendance at the Knoxville crusade, followed a visit by the president of the Chamber of Commerce at Charlotte, North Carolina, to the White House. Charles Crutchfield, one of the best-known television personalities in the South and head of the Jefferson Broadcasting Company, had invited Nixon to come to Charlotte on the day the city would publicly honor Billy Graham as its most famous son. The president replied that "nothing would please him more than to be on hand when we honored Billy, but that coordinating dates would be a problem." Charles Crutchfield immediately called Billy Graham. Billy was reluctant. He did not feel he could accept such an honor, since the city had already honored him several years earlier. Graham continued to refuse in several phone calls from Crutchfield. One day the telephone rang, and it was President Nixon stating that he wanted to come and that he would like to do this to honor their years of friendship. Graham said, "If this is your wish, Mr. President, then of course I accept. I am deeply honored and flattered but in my life and ministry all the glory should go to God." After months of negotiation with the leaders of Charlotte, 15 October 1971 was named Billy Graham Day, with a public rally at the coliseum. Among those sitting on the platform to honor Billy that day was Senator Sam Ervin, who was later to play such a crucial part in the Watergate affair.

On the previous night the Grahams attended a reception at a nearby country club. Billy's sister, Jean Ford, recalls "how honored he was, and how he stood in the receiving line for hours and talked to every person just as if they were his best friend. He loved it because he was seeing people he had not seen for twenty-five or thirty years, since high school. . . . He loves to see old friends. Billy likes to reminisce with second, third or fourth cousins whom he hasn't seen for years."

The next day Billy and the president and their wives rode together in the motorcade through cheering crowds, including children given the day's holiday from school. At the coliseum the inevitable group of anti-Nixon protesters were barred, or quietly removed, and went away to begin the inevitable lawsuits; but unlike Knoxville they did not disrupt the program which had been organized by the hard work of Crutchfield and the chairman, Edward M. O'Herron, veteran business-man and state legislator, and hundreds of voluntary workers. The president himself had insisted on a strict exclusion of political overtones, to the annoyance of some local Republicans.

Charles Crutchfield rates Billy Graham Day 1971 as "probably the most memorable day in the 200-year history of Charlotte. The over-whelming majority of people responded enthusiastically," and tele-grams of congratulation came from all over the world. The president, then at a peak of achievement nationally and internationally, "gave one of the finest nonpolitical addresses I've ever heard," Crutchfield writes. "The president spoke without notes and quite obviously from the heart in a moving tribute to Billy."

"Early in 1972," recalls Graham, "Mr. Nixon asked me if I had any advice for him in the campaign. I said, 'Yes. Let others run your campaign and you just keep on being a good president.' In hindsight, I wonder if that was good advice." During the campaign Graham stated publicly (for the first time in a presidential election) which way he would vote, but otherwise took no part.

Late in 1972 Graham saw "a slight change beginning to take place in the president—and especially in early 1973. I was chairman of the symphony concert at the Kennedy Center for his inauguration in January 1973. I told my wife later, 'The president does not look himself. I've never seen him look or act that way.' He was terribly preoccupied and seemed hardly to know we were present. I could tell by his eyes that he was under some severe strain. At that time I had no idea what was about to come, nor did any of his other friends."

By the time Billy Graham returned from his integrated South African rallies that spring of 1973, the Watergate revelations were pouring out. Flying up from North Carolina shortly after the Charlotte crusade, he drafted a feature article at the request of the *New York Times*. It appeared on the editorial page on Sunday 6 May. Graham also used it, slightly expanded, as his Hour of Decision broadcast a week later. He had spoken earlier to George Cornell of Associated Press and had been interviewed on the television *Today* show on 27 April. His views were widely quoted in America and around the world, making clear his attitude to the scandal as it had unfolded to that point.

"Of course, I have been mystified and confused and sick about the whole thing as I think every American is," he told the television interviewer. He did not then think the president knew about it, believing that "his moral and ethical principles wouldn't allow him to do anything illegal like that. I've known him a long time and he has a very strong sense of integrity." But "we're demanding too much of our presidents," so that it was almost impossible for them to keep a finger on everything.

Graham called for punishment of the guilty and replacement of "everybody connected with Watergate," but deplored trial by the media and by rumor, and leaks of confidential evidence. He saw the scandal as "a symptom of the deeper moral crisis. . . . On every level of our society, public and private, deceit, dishonesty and moral looseness seem to be increasing. America has condoned amoral permissiveness that would make Sodom blush. . . . We live in a society that is too often dominated by selfish interests and expediency. The time is overdue for Americans to engage in some deep soul-searching about the underpinnings of our society and our goals as a nation. For decades we have been brainwashed into thinking that there are no absolute moral standards."

In calling for a national soul-searching and repentance he urged that Watergate be put in historical perspective. "No political party can claim the title of 'Mr. Clean.'" Passion for social justice should include not only concern for the underprivileged and oppressed but "a new determination to strive for an honest, and efficient government at all levels." Watergate could teach the nation to "take the law of Moses and the Sermon on the Mount seriously."

During the summer of 1973, after his return from the Korean crusade, Graham found the political situation "so discouraging that it has almost made me physically sick." "I have been dismayed and shocked by the revelations of Watergate," he wrote in September. At the same time, "while I cannot defend the Nixon administration's wrongdoing, I am disturbed by the 'overkill.'" He believed that America harmed itself by a loss of proportion and by a double standard which condoned lawbreaking by those who had more popular causes.

Throughout the rest of 1973 Graham was attacked by those who held that "though supposedly a 'moral leader,' he failed to cut bait with the immorality of the White House until it was too late and any criticism of Nixon would seem to be like kicking a friend when he was down." Some said that his refusal to denounce Nixon proved he was a ward of the Oval Office, in such debt to the presidency that he could not make critical appraisals. A crank letter sent to one editor, who forwarded it with an amused note, suggested that the paper had better drop Graham's *My Answer* column: "He was wrong about Nixon, and he might be wrong about God!"

Many who deeply admired Graham were puzzled by his refusal to condemn; at the same time he was being urged by those who stood by Nixon to rally publicly to his defense. "He was criticized severely by saint and sinner alike," writes one of Graham's oldest friends, "but once again it was his love for a man he was seeking to win, and to counsel in his onerous task as President of the United States of America." Associated Press writer George Cornell comments: "He generated a lot of pop derision for his reluctance to denounce Nixon as the Watergate mess emerged. When the facts became clear, Graham did repudiate the behavior, but he did not disown the man nor renounce a friendship. . . . As I understand the classic meaning of friendship, a real friend remains one in a pinch, particularly so then; and any friendship is hollow and a sham if it doesn't stand up under pressure, when trouble comes. Personally, my hat is off to Graham for continuing to be a friend when being so was rough and when expediency was against it. A weaker character would turn tail when a friend starts going under, afraid of getting bruised himself in the downfall."

All those months Billy Graham was unable to get through to the president. During the 1972 campaign, as William Safire relates in *Before the Fall,* a White House staffer had suggested arranging a debate between one of the opposition candidates and Graham. The president killed the idea: "No. It may hurt his ministry." "That was his general attitude throughout my years of friendship," comments Graham, who believed that for such a reason Nixon deliberately kept aloof as the crisis deepened. On 27 July 1973 Graham replied to an old friend who had asked him to put to the president some suggestion (unconnected with Watergate), "Unfortunately I have very little contact with the White House at the moment."

Graham recalls, "I tried to get in touch with him a number of times, to assure him of my prayers and urge him to seek the Lord's guidance in a very difficult situation. . . . Mr. Nixon was a personal friend and at no time did I consider him as a parishioner. I seriously doubt if he looked upon me as his pastor, though having a pastor's heart (even though I am an evangelist) my feelings could not help but go out to him in his times of suffering and sorrow. There was little I could do for him except pray."

Graham was in Switzerland early in December for a planning session for the forthcoming Lausanne Congress when Mrs. Nixon called to invite him to stay overnight, with Ruth, and to preach at the White House service on Sunday 16 December.

After that Sunday sermon, Senator Helms wrote to him, "Your message was powerful, and it was obvious that you touched the hearts of everyone present." Senator Hatfield, asking for a copy of the full text, called it "powerful and significant." Graham had a long, private talk with the president; as always, Graham did not comment on its substance, but he spoke frankly on spiritual issues.

Julie Nixon Eisenhower was staying with her parents. "I was feeling the strain of over six months of Watergate," she relates, "and, more important, I was facing the fact that after years of searching I still did not have a deep spiritual base in my life. Ruth Graham and I met for an hour in the little sitting room off her White House bedroom and I asked her how I could read and study the Bible so that it had meaning and so that I could understand and apply what God was saying. I remember that she encouraged me, but most of all I remember her Bible. It was incredibly worn and heavily underlined; there were written notes in the margins on almost all the pages. I saw immediately that Ruth Graham drew strength from the Word of God. And I knew already from earlier encounters that she led the kind of life I wanted to lead. Looking into her eyes I realized once more what a source of inspiration she must be to her husband in his life's work." The Grahams put Julie Eisenhower in touch with a congressman's wife who held a weekly Bible study in her home. "Since that time," she says, "the Bible study has given new direction to my life."

During the visit to Washington Billy Graham recorded a long discussion with the editorial staff of *Christianity Today*, published in the issue of 4 January 1974, which revealed his sense of unease, his regret for the president's lack of frankness to the nation, and his determination not to prejudge or denounce him from the pulpit. "In America a person is presumed innocent until proven guilty. As far as I know, the president has not been formally charged with a crime. Mistakes and blunders have been made. Some of them involved moral and ethical questions, but at this point if I have anything to say to the president it will be in private."

Graham again condemned and deplored the Watergate break-in, but suggested that a modern president was too isolated; he expressed his belief that the men around the president had a "magnificent obsession" to change the country and the world which led them to unethical behavior. He pointed out, as he had forcefully pointed out in the *New York Times* article six months before, that this was partly a result of the "situation ethics" taught by a school of modern theologians. "We are now reaping the bitter fruits of that teaching." He stressed that moral judgments must be absolute and urged avoidance of hypocritical and self-righteous glee at the evil done. "There is no blinking at the fact that Watergate has become a symbol of political corruption and evil. But let us hope that by God's grace we may turn the corner. Let's hope we realize that there is one crisis more urgent than the energy crisis and that this is the crisis in integrity and in Christian love and in forgiveness."

Graham looked for Watergate to lead to a cleansing of the political processes. Meanwhile he expressed his continued regard for the president. "For a person to err in his judgments is not wrong, or sin. I also think there is a difference between judgment and integrity. Until there is more proof to the contrary I have confidence in the president's integrity—but some of his judgments have been wrong and I just don't agree with them." He revealed something of the agonies that Richard Nixon had endured six years before. "During 1967 and early 1968 he really did not want to run for president. He almost decided not to. He was actually afraid that what is happening now would happen to him. I think his running for president came partially as a result of ambition but mostly as a result of sheer patriotism. He really felt he could make a contribution not only to America but to the world, especially in foreign affairs. He seemed to feel the mid-seventies would be very dangerous for America and the world."

The *Christianity Today* interview, widely quoted and reproduced, upset some of the president's friends, mildly though Graham had criticized. After reading a wire service summary, a close friend of both men wrote to express his sadness that Graham appeared to be trying to cut away and not stand by the man for whom he professed friendship. Another correspondent talked of rats leaving the sinking ship. But Senator Hatfield wrote, "Your comments in the *Christianity Today* interview were most perceptive and thoughtful. You were courageous and right to share as candidly as you did."

The president saw Graham once and they talked on the telephone a couple of times in the six weeks following publication of the interview. "I am sure," wrote Graham, "that he understands that we cannot condone the things that are wrong, even though we love him as a friend and respect him as a world leader. At the same time I am well aware of the forces that are arrayed against him. I am convinced that he will survive."

In May 1974 the publication by the Watergate committee of the tapes revealed a man who was a stranger to Graham. It seemed almost as if there were two personalities in one skin: the man he had known and the totally different man of the tapes. Graham repudiates the view that Nixon fraudulently hid his character to maintain their friendship; and he has no concrete evidence to support any theories as to what changed Nixon so swiftly and so radically. Graham says, "I think it was something spiritual and psychological, that could even have been caused by medications prescribed for him, or a demonic assault. St.

In Dortmund, Germany, the Euro '70 crusade draws a massive audience.

Billy joins celebrities to honor America on the fourth of July. (From left: Connie Stevens, Jack Benny, Glen Campbell, Bob Hope.) (1970)

Billy and Ruth greet crowds at the Rose Bowl Parade in Los Angeles. (1971)

Billy and Johnny on the
Johnny Cash Show.
(1971)

Billy Graham Day is celebrated in Charlotte, North Carolina, on October 15, 1971 as Richard Nixon presents Billy with a plaque. Mrs. Nixon, on the left, looks on with Mrs. Graham.

Billy visits the plaque in place in Charlotte, North Carolina. (1973)

Part of the integrated crowd at the Johannesburg, South Africa crusade. (November, 1973)

Billy dons traditional costume in Nagaland. (1972)

Billy visits war-torn area of Anderson Street in Belfast, Ireland. (June, 1972)

A spirit of unity sweeps the crowd during Billy's crusade in Dallas, Texas. (1972)

Billy and Johnny share a light moment on the Johnny Carson Show. (September, 1972)

Billy Graham closed his five-day Seoul, Korea, crusade at Yoi-do Plaza on the banks of the Han River before a crowd of more than 1,000,000. This was the largest single crowd in the history of his ministry. (1973)

Governor Jimmy Carter and his wife, Rosalynn, join in the hymn during the opening ceremonies of the Billy Graham crusade in Atlanta. (June, 1973)

Billy with Vice President Gerald Ford at the Kemper Open in Charlotte, North Carolina. (1974)

Billy gives the keynote address at the Congress on World Evangelization in Lausanne, Switzerland. (July, 1974)

The Hollywood Bowl is the scene for the Silver Jubilee Anniversary Celebration in 1974. The festivities marked twenty-five years for the Graham's remarkable world-wide ministry.

Billy, with Trisha Nixon and his wife Ruth, pays tribute to Ethel Waters at a testimonial dinner in her honor. (October, 1976)

Billy and Ruth share a contemplative moment at home in Montreat, North Carolina.

Paul says, 'We wrestle not against flesh and blood but against principalities, against powers, against the rulers of the darkness of this world, against spiritual wickedness in high places.' " Graham believes that Satan was somehow involved in the downfall of Nixon. "On my infrequent visits with him since his resignation I have found him more and more his old self."

When the tapes became public "the embarrassment," says Ruth Graham, was the "hardest thing that Bill has ever gone through personally." With great reluctance Graham issued a statement on 28 May 1974, read over the telephone from Montreat to Associated Press and reported on the front page of the *New York Times:* "While we have no other president's transcripts by which to compare these, I must confess that this has been a profoundly disturbing and disappointing experience. One cannot but deplore the moral tone implied in these papers, and though we know that other presidents have used equally objectionable language—it does not make it right. 'Thou shalt not take the name of the Lord thy God in vain' is a commandment which has not been suspended, regardless of any need to release tensions.

"What comes through in these tapes is not the man I have known for many years. Other mutual friends have made the same observation.

"Now all these matters are in the hands of the judicial process set up by our Constitution. The law will take its course." He urged prayer for all concerned in the judicial process, and for "a sense of judicious patience" to govern all in America, including the news media. "Our repudiation of wrongdoing and our condemnation of evil must be tempered by compassion for the wrongdoers. Many a stone is being cast by persons whose own lives could not bear like scrutiny. Therefore we dare not be self-righteous."

Graham repeated several of the points made in his broadcasts and article the year before, including: "I believe that our nation will survive as a strong and united power. But if we do survive, it will be because we have maintained our moral compass, the law of God. It is by God's moral law that someday we will all be judged. Therefore God commands all men everywhere to repent while there is yet time. America needs to repent and turn to God for forgiveness, for correction, for direction, and for healing.

"While I have had little contact with the president during the past eighteen months, yet the president is my friend, and I have no intention of forsaking him now—nor will I judge him as a man in totality on the basis of these relatively few hours of conversation under such severe pressure. But I would be neither his friend nor God's servant if I did not point out what the righteousness of God demands at such a time as this."

Graham remained a target of criticism. "Naturally," he wrote on 7 June, "I have gone through a very agonizing period in regard to what is going on. The pressures on me from all sides have been extremely great!" The press corps traveling with Vice-President Ford grilled him almost viciously when he and Ford were golf partners, but he refused further comment. "I have already spoken from my conscience as strongly, boldly and forcefully as I can." Shortly afterward he left for Europe to prepare for the Lausanne Congress. Away from the crisis he waited for the full public explanation he was sure the president must possess, whatever his faults and failures. When Graham returned to America in August, a few days before Nixon's resignation, he was obliged to enter the Mayo Clinic because of an acute problem with his jaw that had plagued him throughout the Lausanne Congress. Thus, hard at work abroad and then in the hospital, he was spared the deepest agonies of the president's personal friends.

He urged the American people to pray for the former president in his "almost unbearable" suffering, even those who felt betrayed. Graham approved the presidential pardon because he believed that the trial of a former president would be destructive of the best interests of the nation. He thought a one- or two-year trial would tear America apart, that Nixon might not live through it and that Ford would be unable to govern.

"I will always consider him a friend," he said privately and publicly. But he was unable to make contact. Efforts to speak personally or on the telephone were rebuffed. To an acquaintance who expressed his heart's burden that Graham should be given opportunity to meet the former president's spiritual need, Billy replied in mid-November from Montreat that he had had no personal contact at all, merely a few words with Mrs. Nixon since Nixon went into the hospital. "I stand on 'ready' to go to him at any time for spiritual ministry. . . . I can only imagine from 2,500 miles away the terrible struggles that must be going on inside."

At length, on Thanksgiving Day that year, they spoke on the

telephone. In March 1975 shortly before the Albuquerque crusade, Billy Graham was invited to San Clemente. "The purpose of the visit," writes Julie Eisenhower, "was simply to reassure both of my parents of his complete love and faith in them. The lack of hypocrisy and absence of a 'holier than thou' attitude had always impressed me tremendously. Dr. Graham's capacity for friendship and his eagerness to love make him stand apart from other men."

Graham is convinced that no full or fair judgment on Richard Nixon will be possible for many years.

Some expected the fall of Nixon to bring a diminishing of Graham's influence and ministry. In the early 1970s the two men had seemed to be the civic leader and the religious leader of the "new majority," those Americans who did not follow the libertarian trends sweeping the country yet were not rigidly conservative; with one leader broken, the other might lose his high position in the hearts of fellow countrymen. Even more superficially, some supposed that Graham's national stature was little more than a projection of press photographs of his golfing with the great.

By the crusades that followed Watergate, Billy Graham's strength was quickly proved to be undiminished. In some respects it was increased. Evangelicals had never before been as close to the White House as they had appeared to be in the Johnson-Nixon years, and perhaps they had begun to depend (as one younger leader suggests) "on our political and social influence and prestige, rather than on the Lord." Billy Graham had been regarded uncritically as their hero who could do no wrong, who succeeded in all he attempted, the friend of presidents and able to gain for evangelicals a hearing. After Watergate they were prepared to criticize him yet acknowledge his unique gifts and contribution.

With the nation Graham's high standing was shown to spring from his personal integrity. The strength of his ministry lay where it had always lain, in his uncompromising dedication to the gospel. In the Gallup Poll published in late December 1974, Graham was second only to Kissinger as the man America admired most; apparently Graham had not been hurt. Three years later *Christian Century* polled thirty-five editors of religious publications and religion writers in secular journals, for the "ten most influential persons in the field of religion in the U.S. today." *Christian Century* reported in the issue of 18

January 1978 that "The clear winner, receiving almost unanimous support, is evangelist Billy Graham." It seems that the Watergate experience cured Graham of any hankering for a political role. His great interest in politics had always been a danger; the crisis helped straighten his priorities. Watergate was a valley of shadow. Ruth says, "It was one of the greatest disappointments in his life, and a personal hurt, because he really loves the man. And he is concerned for this country."

But Watergate, in Graham's life story, must be seen in perspective. It finished and was past just as Billy Graham reached a new plateau. Through the Lausanne Congress on World Evangelization and all that followed it, he was beginning a world ministry on a wider scale than ever before.

PART FOUR

15 The Road to Lausanne

Taking a taxi to Washington airport after an appointment with President Kennedy on 12 September 1962, Billy Graham picked up Carl Henry, founding editor of *Christianity Today*, for a few minutes' conversation.

Carl Henry had attended a small conference that Billy Graham had convened at Montreaux in Switzerland two years earlier, to discuss the urgency and issues of world evangelism. Some time after that conference a former Team member suggested that Billy follow it up with a larger world conference on evangelism. That planted a seed in his "heart and mind which began to germinate." He discussed it with several of his associates and with his father-in-law, Nelson Bell, then executive editor of *Christianity Today*. Next, Billy wrote to friends throughout the world. Their replies urged unanimously that only he could call such a conference and get worldwide response. Therefore, the early planning assumed that BGEA would be the sponsor. Then it occurred to Billy that if some other body were to be the official sponsor, while BGEA organized and financed it behind the scenes, the world conference would command more intellectual response. He finally decided on *Christianity Today*.

In the taxi Billy told Carl "that he had been recently burdened for a great international gathering whose objective would be the Great Commission." The World Council of Churches was increasingly preoccupied with social and political action which downgraded the

Biblical concept of evangelism and excluded it from serious debate. Billy (who had attended, except when illness prevented, every WCC Assembly, including its formation at Amsterdam in 1948) wished to restore the balance. Carl willingly agreed that *Christianity Today* should sponsor a world conference and suggested that it could mark the tenth birthday of the magazine in 1966.

Graham next raised the matter at a meeting of *Christianity Today*'s board, of which he was a member. The board agreed to be the nominal sponsor, provided that the magazine had no responsibility for finance or organization. He then formed an *ad hoc* committee composed largely of BGEA personnel plus Robert P. Evans of the Greater Europe Mission, Clyde Taylor of the National Association of Evangelicals and Carl Henry. Henry agreed to arrange the program. Billy asked Stan Mooneyham, then his press relations officer, to go to Berlin to organize the congress, under Graham's personal supervision and that of the *ad hoc* committee, and sent Victor Nelson ("such a meticulous, detailed man") to assist Stan.

Thus the Berlin congress was essentially a BGEA project throughout, with *Christianity Today* lending its name and its editor as chairman. The fact that BGEA paid all the bills was kept quiet at the time lest it damage the effectiveness. Billy Graham had a direct part in all decisions such as speakers and program, retaining the right of absolute veto which he did not hesitate to use. Thus, some of the *ad hoc* committee wished to exclude Oral Roberts. Graham used his veto and also urged Roberts to come, with impressive results; it gave Oral Roberts a broader view of the church and was a factor in the founding of his university. In his letters to Graham he gave full credit to Berlin.

Twelve hundred delegates gathered at Berlin in October 1966 for this World Congress on Evangelism.[1] They reflected the pattern of the times, the majority of the participants being born in the West although many of them now served developing nations. They explored the intellectual, theological basis of Biblical evangelism, they discussed methods; and, with a somewhat gingerly touch, they looked at evangelism's relation to social action. Whatever the weaknesses in retrospect, the results of Berlin swept the world.

---

[1] See *Billy Graham* (1969 edition) pp. 233 ff., and the two-volume official report, *One Race, One Gospel, One Task* (1967).

At Billy Graham's urging, against the opposition of other members of the committee, Berlin had ended with no clear plan except to encourage regional congresses; at that time Graham felt "that Berlin should be a once and for all conference and let the Holy Spirit do his own follow-up work."

The regional Congress for Asia and the South Pacific, at Singapore in 1968, was financed and organized by BGEA, with Stan Mooneyham and Victor Nelson playing a crucial role, but as in other congresses the regional leadership planned and conducted the proceedings. Graham kept away. "Time after time I was urged by Asian leaders, as well as members of my own Team, that I should go. However, I felt that it was important for the Asians to do it as much on their own as possible, with us staying in the background. I believe that, in hindsight, this proved to be effective and God-directed. The Bogata Conference, which had such tremendous impact on all of Latin America, was also organized and largely financed by us. Again, I felt I should not go for fear that they would think I was in a dominant role."

In January 1970 Graham brought a number of international evangelical leaders to Washington to discuss a possible second world congress. Most of those present wanted one soon. Billy Graham and Bob Evans, almost alone, saw things differently. "Since," recalls Billy, "I was the convenor and chairman of the meeting, I vetoed the idea, in favor of going to Europe first." The European congress took place eighteen months later in August 1971 at Amsterdam, where once again Victor Nelson and the Association made the organization and finance possible without intruding. Graham, reluctant to take part, and the only non-European participant, was persuaded to give the opening keynote address. He "did not want to inject myself in any way and had never at any stage planned to stay for the entire conference. I felt it was better for the Europeans to do it themselves and discuss their own problems without my presence."

In the weeks before Amsterdam Billy had consulted by telephone and letter "a number of my friends including Harold Lindsell, Harold Ockenga, Clyde Taylor and members of my own Team and staff. All of this 'input' confirmed my own conviction that the time had come for another world congress." His conviction was reinforced by a letter he received from Australia, setting out the reasons why the time was ripe. The writer, Bishop Jack Dain, an Englishman who was formerly a missionary society executive based in London and who now served as co-adjutor to the archbishop of Sydney (Marcus Loane), had been Graham's close friend since 1956 when he had arranged his meetings in India. Jack Dain had become widely known as a missionary statesman. He was an organizer of formidable energy and skill, combined with notable gifts of diplomacy.

In his letter Dain pointed out that since January 1970, when he had shared Graham's reluctance for another congress, the World Council of Churches had moved yet further into radical theology, political action, and a passion for humanitarian service devoid of any proclamation of the gospel, until many of the ecumenical leaders themselves recognized its decline in spiritual authority. Parallel to this "sad development" had come massive evidence "of the movement of the Spirit of God, both in evangelism and in renewal," across the countries of Asia, Africa and South America. National leaders were emerging; evangelical cooperative agencies were flourishing; the Billy Graham ministry itself was only one of the Spirit-authenticated ministries that were disclosing the revitalized sweep forward of Biblical Christianity.

All this had "produced one new and significant feature all over the world": responsible church leaders from other traditions now welcomed the ministry of evangelicals whom not long before they had shunned. "The ball is at our feet," wrote Dain, "provided we are prepared to act with humility, with wisdom, with courtesy and with our emphasis on a positive ministry of evangelism and renewal rather than trying to organize a counter-ecumenical organization." He suggested that Billy summon a further consultation. "I cannot see anyone but yourself being raised up by God to take an initiative at this time in this direction."

Graham, however, moved slowly, and Dain is convinced that their "slow and careful approach" created one of the chief factors in the ultimate success. In December 1971 when he was on vacation at Vero Beach, Billy called a group of Team members, including Jack Dain, to discuss a possible world congress. Graham then sought opinions from some 150 church leaders throughout the world. Not a single reply opposed the idea on principle, though many, like John Stott, British theologian and evangelist and Billy's close friend, set out constructive cautions.

"After many discussions and telephone conversations with friends and advisers," Billy recalls, "we finally made the decision to go ahead. At the Greenbrier in West Virginia at another Team retreat, I asked Jack Dain if he would be willing to take responsibility of being chairman of the conference. He said that he would under certain conditions. One was that the archbishop of Sydney would give him permission. Second, that we would assume the financial burden. Third, that we would furnish personnel and fourth, that he would always consider me the 'leader' and that it would be understood that I was in charge and that he would fulfill this function only to carry out my personal instructions. I reluctantly agreed, especially to the last part. I was determined from the beginning that the next congress would be set up on a far more representative scale and with much more democratic representation than Berlin had. I had set a figure of approximately 3,000 coming from every country of the world, with a wide variety of speakers, representing every conceivable viewpoint within what is normally called evangelicalism."

Graham, Dain, and the 120 "convenors"—international, interracial, and interdenominational—whom Billy called to Los Angeles in August 1972, announced an International Congress on World Evangelization to be held two years hence. Their vision went further and deeper than before. In Dain's words, "This is not another congress on evangelism. We thank God for Berlin and for every one of the other regional congresses, and for the dozens of national congresses on evangelism. This is not a congress on evangelism: it is a congress on *evangelization*, and there is a difference." They would be concerned with the implications of Christ's Great Commission in its fullness: to "make disciples," to "baptize" and to "teach."

"I began to pray as to who should be the executive director," continues Billy Graham. "I talked to Stan Mooneyham about it, but he felt he could not do it because of his new duties as president of World Vision. I contacted Victor Nelson next and he felt that his age and flagging strength would not allow him to undertake such a responsibility. I had recently been in contact with my old schoolmate, Don Hoke, and I began to think about his various qualifications. Without discussing it with anyone, I wrote him a 'feeler.' "

Donald E. Hoke, a Wheaton alumnus, founder-president of Japan (afterward Tokyo) Christian College, was a man of intellect, vision and drive who had shaped numerous missionary enterprises in Japan. He wrote back somewhat positively because he felt that his ministry in Japan was almost finished and his college ready to be turned over to nationals. "I immediately felt," continues Graham, "that we had our man as director. As I look back, I should have consulted Jack Dain at this time, rather than acting on my own, but since the idea of the conference had been mine and there was no organization as yet, I felt I had the authority to go ahead."

Billy wrote about Don Hoke, "His total commitment and dedication to the work of the Lord have been proven to me a thousand times over. He has the historical and theological knowledge that we need in a man in that position." He was decisive, even dictatorial at times, but could debate decisions without rancor, and if his background had made him less familiar with the mainstream churches, he overcame this weakness quickly in the course of the traveling involved in Congress preparations.

Leighton Ford accepted the chairmanship of the program committee and gave nearly a quarter of his time over two years, "one of the great experiences of my life. My outlook and ministry have been profoundly affected." Graham wondered who should be full-time program director. "My first thought was to get Carl Henry but in conversation with Leighton Ford on the telephone, the name of Paul Little came up."

Paul E. Little of Illinois, whose death in a road accident one year after Lausanne deprived the church of one of its most able younger lay leaders, had served with Inter-Varsity Christian Fellowship and its Urbana conferences, and had led the student evangelism for Graham's 1957 New York crusade and several of Ford's crusades. He was theologically alert, a gifted writer and speaker, a thinker who was an evangelist. Billy doubted that "we could find a person in the whole evangelical world who would have more ability and would command more respect." "I had tremendous admiration for Paul," Billy recalls, "not only as a theologian and student worker but also as an administrator. I called him on the phone and 'put the burden on his heart.' He promised to pray about it." He accepted later by telephone.

On the day the planning committee met for the first time, at Los Angeles in August 1972, Paul heard that his father, for many years on the staff of Moody Bible Institute, had died. "I retired to my room for a time of prayer and meditation after receiving the word and on returning to the meeting, Billy saw me in the hall, and threw his arms around me, almost crushing me since he is considerably taller than I He expressed his love and concern and prayer, telling me that he had received word of his own father's Home call in a meeting similar to this and could understand what I was going through. His spontaneous reaction and loving concern meant a great deal to me."

Warwick Olson, the Australian who looked after all the relations with the media, says that "Paul Little made a greater impression on my life than any other single person. No matter where he was or who he was talking to, you knew within five minutes' casual conversation that he was a Christian and where he stood and why The combination of Paul Little and Leighton Ford was a very powerful tool."

Hoke and Little were full time. Bishop Jack Dain, executive chairman, continued to carry much of his normal diocesan load in Australia, but thought nothing of writing fifty or sixty letters a day for the Congress and worked his best at full stretch. At meetings of the planning committee he drew together men and women of different cultures and kept them to the point, gracefully stopping those who spoke too long, "and when things were heated, Jack always had that ability to bring things back to a point where everyone was happy."

Once, several members including Billy clamored for the floor. "Gentlemen, gentlemen," cried Jack. "We must have order. Now," he said, pointing at someone or other, "You, I think, were first; then you, then you, and you. And Billy, then I think it will be your turn." Billy sank back with a grin but some of his own people, one committee member recalls, "were rather shocked that Jack would make Billy number five!"

Billy had insisted that Bob Evans, Bill Bright and some others should be on the planning committee. He asked Leighton Ford to represent BGEA "as I would not be able to give to it the time I should. The planning committee was in charge. I attended most of its sessions, but took only a minimal part in the debates, though I gave them a major address in Switzerland outlining the reasons, challenges, hopes and dreams that I held for the forthcoming Congress.

"During the entire preparation period, Jack Dain made it clear to me both by letter on many occasions and in verbal conversation that he looked to me as the convenor and leader of the conference. I had to remind him constantly that I wanted no such position. It was understood between us that, in any crisis situation, my word would be final but none ever arose before or during the Lausanne Congress."

Bishop Dain's verdict is that "the Congress could never have been conceived or carried out without Billy's own primary role." Following his original initiative and his writing to the church leaders, "it was Billy and his Association who made available initially the staff and the finance, through which alone it was possible to mount the operation long before other sources of funding could be secured.[2] There was the total involvement of Billy, and the Congress stands under God indebted to him.

"At the same time I would equally make clear that Billy himself insisted from the outset that neither he nor his staff should control or dominate the Congress. Billy himself took very great care to insure that this was carried out, and those of us who were involved at the Congress were frankly amazed at the way in which so many senior members of the BGEA team quietly worked in the background. . . . He constantly insisted that it was an international Congress called into being by a group of international church leaders, controlled by an international planning committee and an international executive committee, and he insisted on this being recognized by others throughout the whole of the planning." Bill was the hidden, yet effectively sovereign, Congress leader. His close identification was the key to its progress. As Robert E. Coleman of Asbury says, "No other person could have brought together so varied and esteemed a group."

Throughout the preparations, which coincided with the busiest years of his life—Nagaland, South Africa, Korea, and numerous crusades in the United States, with much ill health—Billy provided, writes Dain, a "warmth of personal support and encouragement, time and time again. There were obviously moments when I was under very, very heavy pressure and at times frankly discouraged, but I found constant encouragement from Billy himself." Nor was this mere sympathy, for Billy had twenty-five years of experience in bringing men together, with all the related issues of finance and organization. He had a grasp of world affairs and a vast range of personal contacts, and he had learned

---

[2] A total of three million dollars was raised, partly by Maxey Jarman of Tennessee on Billy Graham's behalf, but largely from an enormous number of small donations contributed by supporters throughout the world on the BGEA mailing list.

to balance urgency and reality, the desirable and the possible.

The first problem was to find a site which provided the three essentials: an auditorium for at least 3,000; sixty small rooms so that the entire Congress could divide into small seminars and discussion groups; and adequate hotels and dormitory space, all at a point convenient for travel from anywhere in the world.

They wanted to place the Congress in Asia, Africa or Latin America but at that time no city met the requirements. Billy then rather hankered for Rome, believing that the world press would pay more attention and that almost every potential participant (as delegates were to be called) longed to see the Eternal City. But he yielded before the possible embarrassments and confusions. In August 1972 Walter Smyth and Don Hoke visited four sites and chose Lausanne, which proved ideal. Don Hoke set up an office there in April 1973, at the modern congress hall known as the Palais de Beaulieu. The city of Lausanne already ran a special conference bureau in liaison with the hotels, and Hoke brought in "a wonderful Chinese Christian" named David Tam, experienced in international transportation, who negotiated favorable charters with Swissair. A nice touch about Lausanne for Billy and Ruth was its nearness to the summer home of Gigi and Stefan and five of their grandchildren.

The worldwide selection of participants did not go easily. The plan was imaginative: every nation in the world should send true leaders and potential leaders, those who were doing, or shaping, evangelism in its widest sense, rather than ecclesiastical bureaucrats or status holders. Of each delegation twenty percent should be under thirty; not more than ten percent should be over sixty, although this might rule out some with exalted rank; ten percent should be women, and lay participants should number thirty percent of the whole. If every land followed those guidelines approximately, the entire participation would be balanced for a working, not merely a listening Congress. A fundamental change of atmosphere and direction was intended, not a passing euphoria and a large stock of unsold reports or papers.

But many national committees failed to follow the guidelines, especially with regard to youth. They narrowed the selection to the obvious individuals or chose their own friends. The whole selection process started too late and thus many potential participants, who had made other commitments, were lost.

Nonetheless, the chief planners fulfilled two hopes. They were particularly anxious for strong representation from mainstream denominations, whose links with organized evangelical bodies were often tenuous. A letter to Billy from a bishop of one such denomination echoed his own feelings. "My anxiety is that the very great opportunity presented by the Lausanne Congress may fail to accomplish its redemptive role in the life of my own communion unless that communion can feel that it is involved in a significant way in the Congress." In this at least the intention was amply fulfilled: Lausanne saw bishops and archbishops of every race and color from the various episcopal churches, including the archbishop of Uganda who was martyred in 1977.

The planners also insisted that the larger delegations should come from countries where Christianity was on the move. Jack Dain wrote to Billy, "One of the most important factors to be borne in mind is the speed at which the Christian church is growing around the world. It is unthinkable to my own mind that we should have large contingents from many of the European countries in which the church is largely static and dead, and small contingents from some of the countries of South America, Africa and Asia where the church is vibrant and growing rapidly." Crossing that very letter, Billy Graham wrote to Jack, "It seems that the great movements of the Spirit of God are centered in such places as Africa, Latin America, some places in the Philippines and Indonesia, and most certainly on a thrilling and unbelievable scale here in the United States. While there are encouraging signs here and there in both Europe and Britain, yet there have been few bursts of revival fires."

Britain presented a marked contrast to the rest of the world. Britons of judgment and integrity, including personal friends of Dain, opposed the Congress. A vocal group of younger evangelicals, whose presence would have been beneficial, derided the very idea and created a distrust which was a prime cause of refusal from more than half the British invitations. The most vocal opponent refused to attend Bishop Dain's London press conference, which would have removed his published misconceptions.

To compensate for the disappointing British, the executive received letter after letter from countries seeking larger participation because so many wanted to come; and in the end, to use a simile favored by Hoke, the Congress did indeed have "the right type of atomic fissionable material through which God could start a great chain reaction around the world."

Paul Little wrote to Billy Graham, "I am getting more and more excited and enthused about the congress. I believe this can be a really historic event with the prior preparation which is going into it and with some of the ideas that are developing for disseminating the information far beyond the participants themselves." The program planners had decided at first that the Congress should focus on strategy rather than theology, since they could build on the theological foundations of Berlin. But in October 1972 Graham urged them to give it a strong theological basis, and that became the more necessary when the WCC Bangkok conference, at the turn of that year, reduced *Salvation Today* to a liberation almost exclusively social and political. The Lausanne planners sought to keep "a dynamic tension" between strategy and theology, with full awareness of social problems.

It was to be a working Congress. In Paul Little's description: "Hence we decided to send the study papers out in advance; people had to respond within fourteen days or their place would be given to someone else. This was a tremendous attention-getting mechanism! No other single thing was as effective in getting people involved in advance and bringing them thoroughly prepared. I'm convinced the impact of the Congress was much, much greater because we did this. We wanted also to bring people together from all over the world who were concerned with particular theological issues and particular evangelistic strategies. This worked out very well, and having all speakers submit their papers in advance for review at the planning plenary, and by sending them clear instructions in advance, we improved the quality of presentation immeasurably," although at a cost of many headaches for Little as he struggled to keep translations and printing to the deadlines.

Thus Lausanne was conceived less as an event than a process toward the evangelization of the world. Experts in the theory of evangelism, who had spent years studying principles and methods, would meet Christians from the world's mountains and cities, savannahs and suburbs, who had no theory in their fingers but had brought their hundreds or their thousands to Christ. Teachers, pastors, elders, healers, helpers, would learn together. Whereas at Berlin the thinking was of evangelism within each culture, Lausanne would break down the walls of partition.

Much care therefore went into the design and leadership of the small demonstration groups and seminars, as well as the national strategy groups; these would all help mix the theological and the practical.

With nine months to go, the energy crisis with its rocketing prices brought the whole enterprise into question. Airline fares, including charters already negotiated, rose three times in one year. "There were a number of times when I was tempted to cancel Lausanne because of the rising prices," recalls Billy Graham, "but constantly Ruth would tell me 'Don't do it. This may be the last world Congress ever held. Go forward even if you have to borrow the money.' She was of great encouragement."

When the administrative committee met in Lausanne in December 1973 they faced whether to cancel or to shrink the Congress, "or whether we should in faith go ahead." They decided unanimously "that the very crisis only underlined the relevance of our meeting and the urgency of the unfinished task of world evangelization." They economized where possible, reducing each country's allotment of participants by 10 percent, though honoring every invitation already accepted. Since participants, from wherever they came, were asked for only U.S. $80 (equivalent) for their share of Congress expenses, in order to include their hospitality and travel, the subsidy reached high figures. David Tam, who had left his family for fifteen months to serve the Congress, had put his original travel budget at nearly half a million dollars less than that of a commercial agency, and despite the crisis he saved fifteen percent of that.

Billy Graham wrote to Jack Dain three months before the opening date, "I recognize that there are still many hurdles to cross, and the greatest problems, obstacles, difficulties and tensions probably lie ahead of us. Satan is not going to take such a world impact lying down. We are engaged in a gigantic spiritual struggle. The attacks will be fierce at times as he comes as a 'roaring lion.' However, it is those subtle attacks that will be the most dangerous, when he transforms himself into an angel of light. I was so delighted that you put so much emphasis on prayer during the recent meeting. This meant a great deal to me personally." More than a million people had covenanted to pray, thanks to the selfless work of Mildred Dienert in encouraging prayer groups. As Billy says, "She traveled to every part of the world at her own expense and organized probably the greatest chain of prayer that evangelicals have ever known."

Dain had been distressed by the number and nature of attacks on the Congress. He declined to answer press criticism but took pains to reply to every personal letter. Patiently he would explain why no small, cheap assembly could provide the fertilization that a larger number of people from each culture and country would make possible; and how the money had been raised by widespread efforts that did not divert funds from the churches. He justified to one type of critic the inclusion of Christians from Communist countries, and to another the exclusion of leaders of important Christian bodies, unless they came as individuals thoroughly committed to the Biblical gospel. And he could easily refute the charge that the Congress had been imposed on the world by Billy Graham or anyone else.

By now, however, many thousands on every continent, whether participants or not, had begun to appreciate the potential and the purpose of Lausanne—not least because of the enormous success, numerically, of the worldwide women's prayer campaign. When millions of women throughout the world are praying for a coming event, their husbands soon learn about it.

16 July 1974

CORRESPONDENCE poured onto Jack Dain's desk in Sydney, urging that Lausanne produce "a worldwide strategy, and the possibility of a worldwide evangelistic fellowship, functional rather than structural."

A decision on that could not be imposed on the participants, though there was some temptation to do so; it must emerge from their own convictions and discoveries. But Graham shared the attitude expressed by Harold Lindsell in a letter (3 July 1973) to Bishop Dain. "The worst strategy in the world would be for Lausanne or for post-Lausanne to be put in a position of accenting the negative. This is not an enterprise which is designed to produce eyeball to eyeball confrontation with the World Council of Churches. I conceive of Lausanne as being a positive, irenic gathering which does not have for a major purpose knocking down the World Council of Churches or anything else. We go there to affirm what we believe. We go there unfurling a positive banner and telling all people everywhere that our purpose is to seek the fulfillment of the Great Commission in our time. We ask for any and all people everywhere who believe as we believe to join us in the fulfillment of this great objective."

Billy Graham, in "private off-the-record remarks" to an early meeting of the planners which he expanded into a long extempore address to a later meeting, defined the aims of Lausanne.

"The task," he said, "is to relate the changeless gospel to a changing world." First, "to speak with a strong and clear voice as to what evangelism is—what is its message?" Second, he looked for a challenge to the world church to complete the task of world evangelization "by the end of the century." Graham deeply regretted the absorption of the World Council of Churches since the Edinburgh conference of 1910 in important but secondary matters. "What would have happened had all of that energy, time and money been spent on Biblical evangelism?" He wanted a return to the road they had lost. Nevertheless, the Congress must "think through the relationship between evangelism and mission" and examine the relationship between evangelism and social responsibility. He hoped, too, that Lausanne would lead to a new sense of oneness across a world shrunken by modern technological progress, whether by a new structure or not.

Above all, he hoped there would develop "what I will call 'the spirit of Lausanne.'" . . . From Lausanne could come a new love, a new fellowship, a new song, a new slogan, and the whole world church could look back and talk about the spirit of Lausanne.

Billy reached Lausanne early, with Ruth, after a visit to the Tchividjians, Gigi's parents-in-law in the south of France, "an opportunity to get a bit of sun and relaxation."

He arrived, he recalls, with "an infection in the lower jaw bone that was causing extreme pain. The doctors advised it would take at least three weeks' treatment. I felt I could not spare the time and decided to endure whatever pain there was to be and go to the Mayo Clinic afterward and get any work done that was necessary."

On 16 July 1974, as the culmination of three years' work and prayer, nearly 4,000 people from more than 150 nations gathered in the Palais de Beaulieu. The opening fanfare, specially composed by Tedd Smith, rang through the convention hall, which displayed in six languages the motto of the Congress, *Let the Earth Hear His Voice*. This theme was taken up by the Congress hymn, written at the invitation of Cliff Barrows by Margaret Clarkson, a schoolteacher from Ontario well known for her hymns, and translated into the other five languages. Originally the motto was to be longer—too long: *Praise the Lord, Let the Earth Hear His Voice*. By an "inspired lapse" the committee forgot to tell Miss Clarkson when they dropped the first phrase, before she had written her hymn. Her "Praise the Lord, sing Hallelujah," set to the magnificent, familiar early nineteenth-century tune *Regent Square*, gave Lausanne a song that lingered in people's minds.

The climax of the opening convocation came with Billy Graham's address, "Why Lausanne?" He had begun discussing it six months earlier and had worked on it for six weeks, submitting ideas and drafts to experts such as Donald McGavran, Harold Lindsell and Arthur Johnson. "On occasions like that," Billy afterward wrote, "I feel a little bit like a fish out of water. I am used to the rough and tumble of platform evangelism and do not consider myself an 'address' maker." This was unnecessary self-depreciation, since he had delivered hundreds of such addresses though none before was of such significance. Billy knew the urgency of the hour. He believed in the possibility of world evangelization by the end of the twentieth century. This speech could help Christ's church on earth recover, in the century's last quarter, the thrust and passion that had been lost in its first.

That speech has been called by Christian world leaders who heard it one of the best he had ever given. "It raised high the banner of true evangelical, Biblical Christianity. It made very clear the issues of our day, and what Lausanne was and where it was going. Everyone was thrilled with this bold, forthright declaration of contemporary evangelical truth."

Immediately after his address Billy Graham, with Bishop Dain, went to the concourse outside the hall, and while the congress watched by television they switched on the "Population Clock." Created by World Vision International from statistical information, and placed in a huge illuminated map of the world, it clicked up the net number being born. Even before the end of the benediction a few moments later the figure had reached 25; by 9:55 P.M. that evening it showed 163,569. Remorselessly, day and night, the clock emphasized the evangelistic task. When formally switched off at the close, it had registered that over 1,800,000 persons in need of the Christian gospel had not been born when the Congress began.

The participants had arrived in a spirit of expectation. The days fulfilled and deepened that expectation in an atmosphere of discovery and joy, aided by the smooth running of the administration. Most of them knew little of the hectic hours, from early until late, spent by Dain, Hoke, Little and their team, helped by the corps of young stewards and by the attitude of the permanent staff of the Palais de Beaulieu. Tony Höfliger, its managing director, told Hoke "that in a way he had not experienced before, his whole staff wanted our Congress to succeed. They did many things beyond the call of duty," and every man and woman employed there attended, voluntarily, the final Holy Communion service.

Problems came and went, needing wisdom and patience and oil for troubled waters, of which Jack Dain possessed an apparently inexhaustible supply. In the first two days the food, catered by the Palais's usual subcontractors, brought complaints for its tasteless, skimpy resemblance to the fare of a poorly organized youth camp in the mountains. Dain, Hoke and Bruce Ogden, the Australian arrangements director, asked for an emergency meeting with Palais representatives. "Bishop Dain forcefully told them the food wasn't good enough for his dog!" The Palais put pressure on the subcontractor and the food became ample and varied.

On the third day the participants from Taiwan spotted among the flags flying on the forecourt (kindly left by a Postal Union Conference, and representing all their member states) the flag of Red China. They refused to enter the hall again unless it was removed. That prompted the Koreans to notice the flag of North Korea, with the same reaction. Since, regrettably, no Christian from mainland China or North Korea had been in a position to come to the Congress, the offending flags could quietly disappear.

An American minister who is inveterately opposed to cooperative evangelism—and to Billy Graham—began holding meetings on the entrance steps during the lunch break, distributing tracts that threw doubt on the Congress and attracted knots of puzzled participants. Whereupon the two Palermo brothers, Italian-Americans well known for their musical evangelism, secured Hoke's approval for a counterplan. With guitar and accordion electronically amplified they entertained on the steps with their jokes and Christian songs, leaving the would-be disrupter without an audience.[1]

A more serious problem arose from the Congress program's being

---

[1] In 1950 one of the Palermos was a "third golfer" with Billy Graham and Cliff Barrows in the diner near Ocean City, New Jersey, when Theodore Elsner first put to Billy the idea that led to the Hour of Decision. See *Billy Graham* (1969 edition) p. 88.

too full, as the planners recognized in hindsight. "One runs the risk of scheduling the Holy Spirit clean out of the picture," a South African participant commented. He now confesses his secret pleasure at the breakdown, on the second evening, of the finely produced screen feature which was to bring home the Great Commission's meaning by "a massive and spectacular display, the last word in Western man's technical achievement." They ran it later in the cinema with great effect, but that evening, in the plenary session, "there was something rather splendid about this earth-shaking Congress starting off with an electronics catastrophe! I almost felt it was a challenge from God to us about the direction of our dependence."

Problems and deficiencies were outweighed by the immediate, decisive impact of the Congress on those who came. From the outset they sensed that it ushered in a new epoch. The division between missionary-sending and missionary-receiving nations had gone. Whites were outnumbered by other colors; skin color was insignificant in this totally interracial Congress "magnificently obsessed" with reaching the unreached in a spirit of love.

The Third World was not looking in on the deliberations of the West, as at Berlin, but was giving counsel and inspiration equally: a person's contribution, not background, counted at the Congress, which brought home to the participants as never before the strength of the Christian church. Those who lived in spiritual backwaters like Britain and Western Europe were amazed to realize how fast Christianity grows elsewhere. A Bolivian bishop wrote afterward to Billy that he and his countrymen had "not only received inspiration and challenge and a large amount of materials for our task today, but also the evidence of the amazing renewal of the churches of Christ around the world."

Halfway through the Congress four Cubans stopped Don Hoke in the lobby. The Castro government surprisingly had allowed them to attend, even lending money to two, whereas East Germany refused visas to all their forty. The Cubans "were almost dancing with joy. Each of them took my hand in two of theirs, pumping it up and down. Through an interpreter they said how thrilled they were to be there, how much it meant to them, how the spirit of liberty and unity and fellowship was enriching to them after almost twelve years of exclusion from the world community. The Congress would almost have been worth it for what it did for those brethren."

Bishop Festo Kivengere of Uganda, looking back a year later, summed it up: "Lausanne, to me, was a joy! Here were Christians who belonged to different denominations, different experiences, different characters. Yet you didn't have to say 'They are one.' You saw it! It was a demonstration of how Christians can be one in spite of their different backgrounds.

"Lausanne helped people to reexamine what they were doing already. And then to learn what, perhaps, in their evangelization they hadn't yet discovered. Through others! It was an exchange of what can happen, what can be done, and an eye-opener to what was happening in other parts."

The plenary sessions, with the speaker's head shown on a huge closed-circuit television screen above him as he spoke, and his words simultaneously translated into the five languages other than his own, provided learning and inspiration. But the heart of Lausanne lay in the prayer cells in dormitories and hotels, the friendships formed or renewed at meals, and the group activities in which the Congress spent half its time. Kenneth Chafin emerged jubilant from his first session on mobilizing a denomination for evangelism. "I have never addressed a more significant group of men," he said. "All but one of the ninety-nine were directors of departments of evangelism in their own denominations."

National strategy groups probably provided the most lasting foundation for the continuing thrust of world evangelization. Because the selectors of participants had avoided a narrow interpretation of the term "evangelical" the groups could not be dominated by one point of view, or by one denomination or geographical area. Thus the Scandinavians, meeting as an entity, included Norwegians and Swedes who in their own countries would not or could not combine. At Lausanne their arguments, tension and struggle resolved into a common mind, until members of the group said that now they would be able to work together in their own lands for the first time in history.

The multiracial South African group was shadowed by differing attitudes to the country's fundamental social problem. That obtruded also on their discussions about asking Billy Graham for a nationwide crusade. When some of the Africans opposed it, one or two of the whites suspected that the real reason lay in a conviction that Graham would promote racial reconciliation on a scale even greater than at the

Durban and Johannesburg rallies of 1973, whereas these Africans regarded racial tension as their one hope. They produced a document condemning racial inequality and made the impossible demand that every South African present should sign.

The India strategy group, numbering no less than 210, divided into smaller geographical sections for part of the time. Their plenary sessions tended, as one younger participant complained, to go "round and round" and did not face the possible long-term consequences of the political changes which, it turned out, were less than a year away; but much detailed planning quickened the pace of the evangelization of India.

An African bishop from a small nation exclaimed early in the congress, "I am bubbling over with ideas. I cannot wait to get back to my country. I believe our whole nation will be changed as a result of what I have learned here." A British missionary doctor put into a letter to Billy Graham what many felt. "Those of us from Uganda were able to share together so much of the burden for our own land and were able to get to know each other in a much deeper way.... I think many of us were able to stand back a little from our normal situation and see the world from God's point of view a little more clearly and to realize more deeply the desperate need of a lost world without Christ and the task of world evangelization which lies before us. I think many of us were encouraged by Lausanne both to go on deeper with the Lord in our own lives and to share the wonderful gospel of the saving knowledge of Christ with others."

The participants found that this Congress was their own, molded by their own hard work and deliberations. Unlike many international church conferences, no secretariat sought to impose on them theologies or conclusions which had been decided upon already, nor did they need to wrest its direction from the hands of any dominant faction. Lausanne achieved a fusion of minds, hearts and aims, because it was not afraid of tensions.

One such tension arose when young radical evangelicals got together, a development that disturbed some of the older leaders. Jack Dain, however, welcomed it and knew that it could not be swept out of sight. He gave them facilities and was rewarded by good will where resentment might otherwise have grown—and though they produced their own document they did not oppose the Lausanne Covenant.

Again, as one younger leader, Os Guinness, wrote, "it was profoundly encouraging to see an evangelicalism emerging with such balance between evangelism and social concern." John Stott rejoiced particularly "at the new spirit of maturity which refused to dodge difficult issues but debated them openly, candidly and charitably."

The chief tension lay between those who were accustomed to working within the World Council of Churches, however much they might deplore some of its trends or activities, and those who rejected the WCC. A subsidiary tension lay between members of mainline denominations and the numerous smaller churches, many of the latter having originated in secession.

A Tamil bishop of the Church of South India wrote, "At Lausanne I was amazed how the power of the Holy Spirit held us together and made us to shake off all the unwanted barriers, even the so-called theological problems, and had drawn us to a level of thinking which only the Living Lord can do. I personally felt at the beginning there was what may be called a tendency for creating artificial dichotomy between the ecumenicals and the evangelicals. I was watching how this division was going to build up. But I think the entire man-made structure collapsed and the Almighty overruled it and within three days I had realized that there was no more of that kind of tension and feeling, and we were all of one mind. The Holy Communion service without any denominational tinge and reservation, participating in the broken body of the Lord, and drinking his poured-out blood was more than a symbolic power of the Holy Spirit, it was a sacramental unity."

The world press which awaited the birth of a rival to the World Council, and wrote already of Lausanne versus Geneva, found instead that every participant and observer had the opportunity of stating his or her view of what should emerge formally from the Congress: a new world structure to unite evangelicals; a simple endorsement of existing structures; or a low-powered committee to continue the aims of Lausanne. The third choice prevailed.

In no area, however, was participation more evident than in the creation of the Lausanne Covenant, a term chosen deliberately. "We wanted to do more than find an agreed formula of words: we were determined not just to declare something but to do something, namely to commit ourselves to the task of world evangelization." As statement about evangelism, from a strong theological base, the Covenant must be a mainspring of action, not merely a historic document.

The planners intended the Covenant to emerge genuinely from the Congress, yet be weighty enough to command world attention. If hurriedly produced by a small committee and imposed on the Congress, as at Berlin, it would pass unnoticed. On the other hand, the Congress must not be diverted into hours of debate on the wording of a document.

The planners chose a middle course. Three months before Lausanne the administrative committee selected key ideas and emphases from the plenary papers and rated them in an order of priority. J. D. Douglas, Scottish theological journalist, an editor-at-large of *Christianity Today* and the last editor of the *Christian,* created a first draft out of relevant statements. After slight revision, the committee circulated this to consultants throughout the world. A month before the Congress Douglas wrote a second draft in the light of their replies.

On arrival at Lausanne the planners appointed John Stott, who was not a member of the planning committee, as chairman of a small drafting body. From then on, Stott and Leighton Ford, each with many other calls on their time, became virtual prisoners of the Covenant for hours on end in a small office at the top of the Palais, while Jim Douglas as well seldom left it. On the opening day of the Congress this committee produced a third draft. A team of translators went to work at once, followed by young men and women volunteers of the print shop under command of Barry Berryman, director of Billy Graham's Australian office, who turned night into day throughout the Congress to keep abreast of the flow of papers, notices, news—and the Covenant. On Friday July 19 (the day of Stanley Mooneyham's powerful audiovisual address on "Acts of the Spirit '74") every participant received a printed copy with an invitation to submit comments of substance not later than Monday morning.

Much debate took place in national groups, hotels, dormitories. The Germans, for instance, argued hotly among themselves, and were specially happy to discover that in the end every one of them could sign.

On Sunday and Monday Jim Douglas and his secretary stacked, by language and subject, some 3,000 replies, passing them to selected readers, one for each of the six official congress languages, who culled and sorted the significant comments and trends according to Stott's guidelines. They reported to Stott on each of the Covenant's fifteen paragraphs, and all Monday, as the reports reached him, he engaged in numerous consultations with representatives of particular viewpoints. At last on Tuesday morning he could give the drafting committee a summary.

That evening a fourth draft of the Covenant went to the thirty-strong planning committee for line-by-line discussion. "No one will ever know except the members," wrote Dain afterward, "the agonies through which we all passed before we were able to present the document that virtually had the total endorsement of the planning committee. Several sections in that Covenant were very, very sensitive areas for certain members, particularly those who dealt with the problems of culture. I can only marvel that after grappling for hours with these matters we did come to a common mind. Here I would pay a tribute to John Stott, who not only spent many hours of the night working on this but whose wise insights carried us through those difficult passages in the planning committee itself."

From the start, Billy Graham had entered into the making of the Covenant "with energy and seriousness," reading each draft "carefully and prayerfully, approving or disapproving here and there. I think it should be pointed out that while Jim Douglas, John Stott and Leighton Ford did a magnificent work—yet that Covenant represented the entire planning committee phrase by phrase, and sentence by sentence. Hours were spent changing a phrase here, deleting a sentence there. Finally, on the night before it was to be distributed, it was brought to me by Leighton Ford. I read it out loud in front of him and made only minor suggestions which he graciously accepted, though I had made a number of suggestions in the planning committee as it was read sentence by sentence. There is no doubt in my mind that the greatest 'input' in the drafting of the Covenant came from John Stott—yet much of the Covenant came from the entire planning committee."

The final revisions were, in the end, comparatively few. As each paragraph passed the planners John Stott sent it to the panel of translators, who worked literally all Tuesday night. It was "a tough bit of work," Ford comments, "and would have been impossible without tremendous dedication."

On Wednesday morning the Covenant went back to the print shop, and by late afternoon all participants had a copy in their own language. In the evening plenary session John Stott expounded the main revisions to the Congress, with that lucidity, intellectual courage and spiritual wisdom that had already made him in effect the theological leader of world evangelicalism. He invited them "prayerfully to consider the possibility of signing if God so led them."

On the last morning, after the Communion service, Graham and Dain signed the Covenant as a symbolic act and as the expression of their individual commitment. When the number of signature slips were counted it was found that nearly all at the Congress had signed. The staff released the figure but not the names on the slips, which were destroyed.

Thus the Lausanne Covenant was an authentic act of those gathered there. For that reason it was taken seriously and studied carefully, despite its length, at Geneva, Lambeth, Rome and throughout the Christian world. Evangelicals were acting on it already, as Billy Graham could comment four months later: "It seems that God inspired the Committee to write a historic document that could well be a theological watershed for evangelicals for generations to come."

For most of the eight days at the Palais de Beaulieu Billy Graham stayed in the background. Dain writes, "He was always available for consultation, guidance and advice without ever seeking to intrude his role into that of the Congress itself. He was the honorary chairman and yet he was very, very rarely seen on the platform. In itself this is a remarkable tribute to a man of God who has wielded, under God, such power and influence and yet who quite deliberately chose to adopt that minor-key role."

More than 600 persons requested interviews but he could see few, and hardly any of his personal friends, for "I was absolutely swamped with unscheduled meetings and scores of appointments that kept me going from about seven A.M. till eleven P.M. every day," including press and television interviews. Many participants had arrived with authority from their countrymen to beg Graham to hold a crusade in their land, like the president of the Supreme Court of Cambodia, who had been converted from Buddhism by reading Billy Graham's book, *Peace with God.* (That man almost certainly lost his life in the Khmer Rouge conquest the following spring.) Christians from the half-explored West Irian part of New Guinea brought a present which Walter Smyth accepted on Billy's behalf. Months later, notes were passing between

Montreat and Atlanta: "We have received the two stone axes mailed from Lausanne, but I don't believe the bow and arrows have arrived yet. . . ."

All the BGEA men and women worked hard, equally in the background. Thus Walter Smyth, on the floor of the lobby between sessions, smoothed out problems amid the din of hundreds of voices in dozens of languages. Above this the tones of the paging announcer's pleasant, gentle voice were amplified to penetrate the partitions of the upstairs seminar rooms. Leighton Ford helped Paul Little as minor crises arose with steady frequency in the program department; George Wilson, Victor Nelson and dozens from the Association had their tasks.

Franklin, the Grahams' eldest son, helped the travel department; the Congress proved a turning point in his life. Meeting so many Christians from the Third World (he had already worked for a time at a mission hospital in Jordan) and realizing what some of them had suffered or might suffer for their faith, he ended his hesitations of years and, alone in Israel shortly after Lausanne, dedicated himself fully to Christian service. He married, and he and his bride enrolled at a Bible school and later for a business degree at a university. In vacations he became a valued and well-loved member of the preparation team for his father's crusades, specializing in encouraging the widespread prayer program.

Ruth Graham was responsible for one of the high spots of Lausanne, when guest speaker Malcolm Muggeridge addressed the Congress on "Living Through an Apocalypse." The planners had always intended to include one speaker of world prominence from outside the ranks of evangelical theologians or strategists. Ruth suggested Muggeridge, whose pilgrimage of faith from agnostic cynic to Christian apologist she had watched from afar, reading all he wrote. His address brought a freshness and with that delighted the participants as he illumined the urgent need of humankind and his own discovery of Christ. At Muggeridge's request the Congress sent his honorarium to Mother Teresa in Calcutta.

On Sunday afternoon, when the weather turned warm and the Alps showed clear beyond Lac Leman, came the Laustade in the Olympic stadium, the evangelistic rally which was the one public meeting of the Congress. It was prepared by the Graham Team, with the thoroughness of any Billy Graham rally, yet even the Team showed surprise that the stadium was packed. At one time the planners soared to global horizons by investigating the possibility of live television by satellite. That proved too expensive, but the whole world would have heard the testimonies from a Japanese, born a Buddhist; an Indian, born a Hindu; and an African, born a pagan. Those testimonies were a high point, yet when Billy had proposed to include them the Lausanne committee had debated the idea vigorously and accepted it only when Billy personally advocated them.

All who attended the Congress sat in a solid block in one part of the stands. Hundreds of them had never attended a crusade. When they saw such crowds come forward immediately on Billy's invitation after a sermon more simple than most would have delivered themselves, they were humbled and heartened. The Laustade therefore had a significance beyond its actual evangelism. Peter Beyerhaus, professor of missions and ecumenical theology at Tübingen University in Germany, looking back two years later, regarded "the Laustade evangelization as the climax of the whole Lausanne event which put all our talking and thinking into actual practice!"

So the days passed, as participants mobilized their skills and prepared themselves to complete the evangelization of the world. Billy now knew that Lausanne had "accomplished far more than I had ever anticipated or dreamed. The enthusiasm, unity, openness, frankness, candor—the universal reception of the Lausanne Covenant—even the overwhelming success of the public meeting, which many people said could not be held, all testify to the hand and blessing of God upon it."

In his statement to the press conference on the last full day Billy recalled that during his opening address he had suggested four things he hoped would emerge. He now could fairly claim that they had done so, "and so much more than we ever dreamed or our small faith would ever dare let us hope for.

"First, I said I would like to see the Congress frame a Biblical Declaration on Evangelism. I believe we have done that. The participants mentioned frequently that the Congress has had a strong theological foundation, and appreciated the solid restatement of the great themes of the Bible. In an age of theological relativism, this has been not only good but a definite encouragement to many. Further, there was an appreciation of the fact that the Congress dealt with difficult issues theologically. . . .

"Second, I said I would like to see the church challenged to complete the task of world evangelization. We are leaving here more deeply entrenched in more countries and more truly a world church and more able to evangelize, than any other period in history. We have been challenged over and over again to fulfill the Great Commission in our generation. The vision of the whole world in need of Christ especially extended to people in their own cultures.

"Third, I said I trust we can state what the relationship is between evangelism and social responsibility. If one thing has come through loud and clear, it is that we evangelicals should have social concern. The emphasis on the Lordship of Christ in all areas of the Christian's life and witness has been healthy. The Congress has avoided the temptation of being obsessed with social action, but has also given it a balanced place.

"Fourth, I said, 'I hope that a new koinonia or fellowship among evangelicals of all persuasions will be developed throughout the world.' . . . We have heard from the participants, loud and clear, that they do not want a structured organization, but they do want a continued fellowship." He added two more points, that Lausanne had brought its participants the refreshment of being with other Christians, and "a new appreciation for the work of God in all parts of the world."

Jack Dain, exhausted as were all the staff, had found the whole experience "very moving, for one could not cross the Congress floor without finding one was constantly stopped by people who wished to express their profound gratitude to God for being there, and for the Congress itself."

The gratitude and dedication reached a climax on the last morning, Thursday 25 July 1974, at the service of Holy Communion, with Festo Kivengere, Anglican bishop of Kigezi in Uganda, not yet exiled by Amin, as the preacher. He had a struggle as he prepared his address, for "I had a funny feeling that perhaps it would be boring, an anticlimax." It was to be devotional, on the Cross, and early that morning he and his hotel roommate, George Duncan, Scottish Presbyterian preacher well known for his addresses at Keswick, who was to preside at the service, prayed and talked it over. "We felt that God wanted this service to be a melting experience."

When the time came the preacher and his hearers equally sensed the power of the Spirit. The bishop was caught up in the realization that the Cross of Christ "was the only possible answer to what we had been discussing." Festo kept closely to his prepared theme, though overrunning his time, but, as he wrote to Billy several months later, "that message on the Cross so overwhelmed my soul that when I stopped I had the most awkward feeling that I was not sure what I had said and how I said it!"

"Festo was long," in Stephen Olford's opinion, "but he gave one of the most powerful and necessary messages of the Congress. Ultimately, all is solved at the foot of the Cross, and we needed that word."

The distribution of the bread and wine to more than 4,000 people took far longer than intended. Graham, as he rose at last to give the closing address, "The King Is Coming," felt himself somewhat an anticlimax, though no one shared that feeling. He was suffering much from his infection and "While I was speaking it was difficult to keep my mind on the message because of the pain. I was afraid to take a pain killer for fear I would not be alert." Since it was already late in the morning he shortened his address.

He stressed the urgency to evangelize because of the certainty of Christ's return, and in calling for rededication and recommitment he did not hesitate to confess his own need. "You know what God has been saying to you these past ten days, I know what he has convicted me of, and what I must do." This public remark, which in fact referred to his private determination to cut out any lingering desire to play a political role in his own country, made a strong impression, especially on participants from the Third World. "Dr. Graham confessing his own weaknesses—we thought we were the only ones that had problems like that. This was the most moving message for us!"

Closing his address with what Harold Ockenga called "a great thrust," Billy touched on eight characteristics needed in a man or woman who would be an instrument that God can use. He ended, the final words of the International Congress on World Evangelization: "The problems with which we wrestle as we go back to our places of service are in many cases not intellectual. They lie deep down within the will. Are we willing to deny self and to take up the Cross and follow the Lord? Are you willing? Am I willing? . . . The King is coming!"

After delivering his address Billy went outside and stood on the steps for an hour or more, shaking hands, signing autographs, and posing for pictures with groups or individual participants as they dispersed throughout the world.

Lausanne 1974 had become a date in Billy Graham's life comparable to 1949 and 1954. The Los Angeles campaign in the tent at the corner of Washington and Hill Streets in 1949 had made him a national figure. Five years later the Greater London Crusade of 1954 had brought him world fame. Twenty years after London, Lausanne showed him to be far more than an evangelist: he was a world Christian statesman, a catalyst who could bring individuals and movements to a fusion that set them on a new path for the glory of God.

17 The Sleeping Giant Awakes

TWO MONTHS after Lausanne, Billy Graham returned to California for a nostalgic occasion in the area where he had sprung to fame a quarter of a century before. To celebrate this silver jubilee *Christianity Today* sponsored a brief crusade in the Hollywood Bowl in September 1974, televised nationally the following December. Billy wrote to a friend, "I can hardly believe that twenty-five years have passed since that memorable eight weeks at Washington and Hill Streets. If someone had told me then what the next twenty-five years would hold in store, I would probably have had a heart attack from fright! I still run frightened—always in trembling and fear that I will do something or say something that would bring reproach to the name of our blessed Lord."

Immediately after the Hollywood Bowl Billy Graham flew to Brazil. The next period of his life was about to open with a crusade which, if Billy could surmount the challenge that Rio de Janeiro presented, could have enormous effect on a nation likely to play an increasingly important role in world affairs because of its vast natural resources and rapid economic growth.

He had been to Brazil twice. In 1960 he had addressed an evangelistic rally to close the Baptist World Congress at Rio, which remained for nearly thirteen years his largest meeting anywhere (143,000). In 1962 he had held a brief crusade at São Paulo.

In June 1973 Charles Ward, the Team member responsible for

South American affairs, invited the comparatively young president of the Brazilian Baptist Convention, Nilson de Amaral Fanini, then on his way home from a meeting in Portland, Oregon, to confer with him at Miami airport. They were old friends. After greeting each other with a Brazilian hug, Ward told Fanini that Billy Graham felt the time was right to accept the long-standing invitation to return. Fanini replied delightedly that in Brazil they felt the same.

They talked for three hours, first in the lounge and then in the restaurant, where curious diners might have noticed an unusual sight: two men, their meal finished, kneeling at their table and praying in Portuguese.

Ward reported to Walter Smyth that Fanini, "a very personable man of high caliber with real spiritual insights and understanding is definitely our key man if we are to develop a crusade in Rio next year. He is interested, yea more, thrilled at the possibility of Dr. Graham coming to Rio in 1974. He is praying for revival in Brazil, deeply desiring that his homeland might be won for Christ. He feels that Dr. Graham's coming could have a catalytic effect in initiating the revival he longs to see."

The time was ripe. Since the almost bloodless revolution of 1964 Brazil had become politically the most stable state in South America. Ordinary Brazilians, unless suspected as Communists, could say and do what they liked in a land free of racial and color barriers, where a mixed population, nearly all talking Portuguese whatever their origin, had developed a peculiarly Brazilian spirit.

Unlike other South American nations, the Republic did not give the Roman Catholic church an official position. Religious freedom has been a characteristic since the days of the empire and Brazil now had its first Protestant president, General Ernesto Geisel, grandson of a Lutheran pastor and himself an active Christian; in 1973–74 the chief of the armed forces, who in Brazil is almost as powerful, was also a Protestant, the late General Humberto Melo, who had preached in Baptist churches.

Though the majority of Brazilians were Catholics in name, their Catholicism formed a social rather than religious attitude. To fill their spiritual vacuum thousands had turned to a spiritism akin to African voodoo. More than 25,000 spiritist centers existed in Rio, whether promoting *umbanda* (white magic) or the fearsome *macumba* (black magic). Spiritism had spread through all classes, often side by side with outward allegiance to the Catholic church. Candles burning on beaches or roadsides, crowds pouring in to be exorcised of their problems or ills by spiritist practitioners, were eloquent of Brazilian hunger of soul.

Meanwhile Protestants, or Believers *(Crentes)* as they termed themselves, grew in numbers twice as fast as the Brazilian population. Evangelical missions had worked in Brazil for more than a century but in the past thirty years the membership of the denominations they had founded had risen dramatically, with the Pentecostals being the fastest-growing church in the world. When Laurence Olson of the Assemblies of God had first worked in the interior of Minas Gerais in the early nineteen forties he and his Pentecostal Believers had been stoned and his life had been in danger more than once. "Now, we are winning so many hundreds and thousands of people that are coming into our churches that the Catholic Church can't stop us." The bulk of the Believers were from the poor, but by the sixties the Presbyterians, and the Baptists in the big cities, were enrolling many members from the professional classes and even a few from the aristocracy.

Spiritism and materialism, as a byproduct of a vibrant economy, ate the hearts of the people. "Brazilians were starting to look for material things only," says Fanini, "and the Catholic church is losing control of the people. When the people have no religion, it is tragic for the nation. So the crusade came right at that point when people were looking for something, when there was this vacuum in the Brazilian heart. And then came the bread of life."

But the evangelicals had a weakness which might nullify their hopes. They would not work together, each denomination being an island entire in itself, separated by a sea of prejudice from the others. Such disunity was a strong reproach in the eyes of their countrymen. Some of the churches had cooperated in enterprises led by others, or in social service, but never in the history of Brazil had they come together as equal partners in a nationwide evangelistic campaign.

As soon as Nilson Fanini arrived home in Niteroi, the city across the beautiful harbor from Rio, he called on his friend and neighbor Harold Renfrow, an American missionary who was secretary-treasurer of the Baptist evangelism board. Their South Brazil mission became the first to pledge themselves formally to a crusade, should it be born, with Renfrow seconded as crusade secretary-treasurer.

The day following, the two friends and another Baptist called on a Presbyterian pastor, Isaías de Souza Maciel, chief of an interdenominational social service organization, at his hospital on the outskirts of Rio. They asked him to be chairman of the committee of ministers. "That day," says Maciel, "we placed at their disposal all of our work, everything we had. We gave to them the assurance that we would go from church to church, and county after county, from city after city, from village to village, asking them to give their support: the pastors, people, and churches, asking them to participate in the great crusade which should come to pass."

Benjamin Moraes, Presbyterian pastor in the rich area of Copacabana beach, and professor of jurisprudence and former minister of education in the state cabinet, who had listened to Graham preaching in New York in 1957, also pledged his influence. The Episcopal bishop of Rio, Edmund Sherrill, swung behind the crusade when he discovered that of seven Englishmen on his staff, three were converts through Billy Graham. When 200 ministers and laymen met Walter Smyth and Henry Holley at Bible House in August 1973, the speech of a Pentecostal pastor, Laurence Olson of the Assemblies of God, persuaded those who hesitated.

The Bible society's hall, on the first floor, could not seat all who came to this meeting with Smyth. Harold Renfrow stood by one of the windows above the narrow street with its noisy traffic. Dozens stood around the walls. David Gomes, president of the Bible society, the man who had led Fanini when a boy to personal commitment, presided. Smyth sat on his left, Fanini on his right. After much discussion Fanini, highly respected as pastor of First Baptist Church in Niteroi and as an evangelist, summed up, "challenging my people for this crusade. Then came the time for the decision. Before we decided, we knelt down, all the leaders, to pray. As we started to pray, most of us started to cry. We cried more than we spoke. Then when we finished, we felt that the Holy Spirit had touched us. We knew it was God's will. So unanimously we voted for the crusade. And then a fire started to burn in our hearts, and we started to work."

They elected Fanini president of the crusade. His fervor, charm, efficiency (he was a former army officer), his gift for winning confidence, which opened unlikely doors, made him a popular leader who never allowed anyone to forget that the sole aim of the crusade was the glory of God.

From the start it was the Brazilians' crusade. Nothing upsets them more than a suggestion that it was imposed from the outside. As Pastor Maciel says, "We did it in our way, and the success could be attributed to the Brazilians." Further, the crusade established something new and extraordinary in Rio de Janeiro: the coming together of evangelicals and their growth in mutual goodwill.

There were many difficulties and trials in the year of preparation. For six months the chairman of the finance committee, a devoted Christian but immersed in business, did nothing about raising funds. No undue alarm was sounded until almost too late, when Walter Smyth, having rightly treated Brazil as a developed country requiring no BGEA subsidy except the normal $10,000 loan for starting off, nearly postponed the crusade for a year. Edward Payne, "Brother Ted" as he was known affectionately, an American international banker resident in Rio, took over the financial end of things, and with Fanini and others pledged that the money would come. Walter knew that the difficulty was solely financial. The spirit was great.

They were hindered, too, by a widespread belief that Billy Graham would foot the bill. Several churches did nothing about finance or other matters because the pastors forgot to pass on the various requests made in the occasional newsletter. Then Lawrence Olson, who had his own radio program, suggested going directly to the public by radio—for almost no Brazilian home, however poor, lacks a transistor. "Get the people to work on the preachers," he said. "Not the other way around!"

Fanini promptly appointed him to publicity. Olson first made up a five-minute program, transmitted four times daily, with a few seconds' recording of Billy Graham's preaching at São Paulo in 1962, then news, requests and information, which immediately alerted all Greater Rio and the cities and communities bordering the Bay of Guanabara.

As for finance, Fanini lost weight and sleep, but never faith. Twice only were bills not paid on time. If there was nothing to meet an immediate need, the people always responded when told. From a church for the blind came a gold watch and other jewelry to be sold for crusade funds. Another problem arose when a senior Baptist pastor urged, "No collections in the stadium!" Since Roman Catholic priests had a reputation for demanding payment for every service, the crusade should avoid the slightest reference to money. Others on the committee knew that without collections the crusade would end in debt. That man gracefully conceded the point and, when the time came, the treasurer put his requests from the platform in such a way that the people gave gladly.

After it was all over, a small indebtedness remained. But the Believers still gave until, like Moses during the making of the Tabernacle, Fanini begged them to bring no more. The surplus was sent to BGEA, which used it to show Billy Graham telecasts in Brazil a year after the crusade.

Henry Holley, director of the crusade, found Brazil a culture shock after Korea. The charming but time-consuming courtesies tried his Marine-trained attitudes. The Brazilians greatly admired him but were amused by his sergeant's manner, however much he hid his feelings: when Henry started combing his hair, Fanini knew he was "getting warm inside his mind." Walter Smyth made an inspired choice in sending as Henry's assistant Norman Sanders, married to Howard Jones's daughter, Cheryl. This black American couple won Brazilian hearts by their easy manners and flow of talk, their charm, their fine singing voices, and above all by being young enough to learn and speak a little Portuguese and to sing some of their songs in it. Holley and Sanders made an excellent pair. Edgar Hallock, an experienced missionary, joined them as office director on his return from furlough. Frequently Hallock found himself "batted around like a ping pong ball" since Holley and Harold Renfrow, executive secretary-treasurer, often gave opposite orders. He would thereupon go to Fanini, whose decision was final.

The organization of the crusade impressed ordinary Brazilians. Nothing like it had happened before, and the defects were trivial beside the achievement. Facts of life in Rio made for difficulties. A single telephone call might require twenty or even forty minutes before achieving a connection. But it would have been no quicker to transact the business in person. The amount of traffic and numbers of people squeezed between the mountains and the sea; the tunnels, bottlenecks and roundabout routes caused by the *morros* or rocky outcrops separating many of the districts from each other; together these make Rio one of the slowest cities in the world to drive across.

Local problems were illustrated in the organizing of the counseling and follow-up training. According to normal crusade preparation, Holley had suggested eight or ten classes of 300 or 400 each for the Christian Life and Witness course, located in different parts of the city, on which people in outlying parts should converge. But most Rio people live far from their employment; every day thousands upon thousands get up very early in the morning to make a two- or even three-hour journey by bus and train to their work in the center. The return in the evening may take longer. They could not afford the time or the fare to come back again to a central church. After some persuasion the planned number of classes was increased, first to forty and then to seventy-five locations. Instructors were imported from São Paulo.

The hunger of the Believers put all plans out of joint. The number of locations expanded to 125 and there should have been more, but too few instructors had been trained. As Harold Renfrow says, "our planning was very small in meeting the desires of the people."

The Christian Life and Witness course, as in many other cities when a crusade is in preparation, had the effect of beginning the evangelism long before Billy Graham's arrival. Thus at one church a married woman believer, Dona Zerda, inspired and taught by the classes, began to speak of Christ to her neighbors. The woman next door, Dona Helza, a backslider, returned to her faith. Soon Dona Helza's three daughters and two nieces, all living in the house, were converted, followed by Dona Zerda's youngest son.

Dona Zerda's husband, Senhor Serafim, was the leader of a spiritist center. Practicing black magic *(macumba)* with its blood offerings of sacrificed chickens, it promoted hatred and fear. Through the prayers of his son and the church, and the witness of his wife, Serafim abandoned *macumba* and accepted Christ. His first convert was Jaedemilto, fiancé of one of their daughters, who later brought in several of his own family.

The sick mother of a neighbor living opposite was converted next. She began to pray for her daughter who years before had left the church to practice white magic *(umbanda)*. The daughter was one of the women, dressed in white, who blew cigar smoke and snapped their knuckles over patients, then went into paroxysms signifying the transference of evil spirits from the sick person to the practitioner. She, too, was reconciled to Christ. Her married brother, Senhor Anibal, seeing the change in his sister, followed her from *umbanda* into Christian baptism with his two little daughters. Later his wife experienced a transformation so profound that friends failed to recognize her. At that point, fifteen conversions and two restorations had resulted from Dona Zerda's attendance at the classes—and the chain reaction continued.

The most sensational individual consequence of Greater Rio's preparation for the crusade was the conversion of Brazil's favorite film and television star, Darlene Gloria, who had recently received an award as best actress of the year for her part in a film written by Brazil's equivalent of Tennessee Williams, *All Nudity Will Be Punished*. During the pre-crusade meetings Darlene Gloria became a Christian and joined a Presbyterian church. On all five nights of the crusade she sang in the choir. On the Monday following, the Rio newspaper *Ultima Hora* carried an article about her, "Now I love God," in which she announced the ending of her career as an actress. The effect on Brazil was such that she could speak about Christ up and down the land, and she gave her time without stint. After marrying in 1975 she devoted herself to work among the very poor in the shanty settlements near Brasilia.

Rehearsals of the crusade choir, under Bill Ichter, were one of the causes of the mounting enthusiasm for the crusade, but even a choir of 10,000 voices would sing into thin air unless the crusade had a stadium. "One of the greatest battles, spiritual and physical," says Harold Renfrow, "was the securing of Maracana."

The largest stadium in the new world, Maracana, was owned by the state of Guanabara and was dedicated to football, Brazil's national game, as totally as any temple to a divinity. It had been leased or loaned for single afternoon rallies (like the Baptist rally which Billy Graham had addressed in 1960) but had never been used at night except for sport. The crusade wanted it for five nights, including the dedication service, and on Sunday afternoon. The committee knew they could not hope to fill it on Wednesday, Thursday and Friday, since Rio's transportation difficulties and the demands of night schooling would keep thousands away. But they rejected, even in face of Walter Smyth's doubts as to the size and expense of Maracana, any idea of going to the smaller Vasco da Gama stadium first. If the crusade had Maracana, everyone in Rio would know where to come on Saturday and Sunday.

The first barrier was the red tape with which any country protects the men at the top. Fanini persisted until he and Renfrow had entree to the state and federal presidents of sport and the governor and vice-governor of Guanabara; the vice-governor, Erasmus Pedro, was in fact a Presbyterian and honorary president of the crusade.

They met refusal. The football clubs would lose too much money. The season would be disrupted. Fanini could have one night, no more.

By radio he called the Believers to prayer. Soon afterward an official promised to telephone the heads of the football clubs one by one, and to his astonishment each graciously surrendered a night. "But," the official told Fanini, "you will have to pay." It would be a huge sum but he agreed, then flew to Brasilia where General Melo, chief of staff, received him. General Melo listened to his story, picked up the telephone and called Governor Chagas of Guanabara. "Governor, we are interested in that crusade. It is for God's honor. Do what you can." Fanini flew back to Rio and went to the governor, who said, "Pastor, I am not going to charge you, except for the janitors and the lighting. The law demands I charge you something but it will be just a symbolic sum."

"It had never happened before," says Fanini. "That was a miracle, with capital letters!"

In 1971 Charles Ward had been in Puerto Rico with Billy Graham and had secured a decision which, three years later, had a profound influence on the buildup to the Rio crusade. Ward, contemporary in age with Graham, had specialized in radio ministry while serving as a missionary in Spanish-speaking South America. In 1962, substituting for a man who was ill, he coordinated Billy's South American tour. When they were in Buenos Aires one of the large industrial concerns bought time for three one-hour television programs, each of a talk by Billy who then answered phoned-in questions. Those programs were named the outstanding TV of that year, and nine years afterward Billy was still declared to have been "the most vigorous and charming personality ever to appear on television in Argentina."

By 1970, asked continually when Billy would return to South America, yet unable to secure a place in his schedule, Ward hit on the idea of bringing him back by television. By then, television had captured the heart of the continent; even the slums of Buenos Aires or Montevideo or Rio were thick with antennae. In January 1971 Ward won Billy to the idea. While staying in a government official's home, among five children, thirteen dogs and a flow of callers, he worked out a series of programs in which he cut a one-hour telecast from an American or overseas crusade to half an hour, had Graham's voice dubbed by a Spanish professional, and removed anything that would not fit the culture.

The experiment proved so fruitful that Ward developed a new ministry for BGEA, preparing programs to show on commercial channels in Korea, Japan, Taiwan, parts of Africa and other language areas, and thereby extending Billy Graham's worldwide television audience. It was extraordinary how Graham's personality and message came through, although the voice was that of another.

The Rio committee dovetailed telecasts into the crusade preparations in July and August 1974, using twenty-six channels that reached a combined population of nearly 65 million potential viewers throughout Brazil at prime time on successive Saturdays. It was the biggest operation this new BGEA ministry had carried out to date. The effect on Brazil was formidable. Billy Graham came across with force. The entire nation suddenly seemed aware of the crusade. Believers heard again and again from converts of the crusade itself that those telecasts had been the first link in the chain.

Thus by late August 1974, little more than a month before the crusade, expectancy grew daily. Protestant leaders had returned from Lausanne impressed by Billy Graham's love for Third World countries like Brazil. Every Home Campaign stood ready to saturate Rio with crusade literature, as they had done in Seoul the previous year. The Roman Catholic church kept benevolently neutral, making no attempt (as in 1960) to mount a counter-attraction. Doors that were usually closed to Protestants were opening: the air force, police, universities, the state-medical association. "Our greatest problem seemed to be to satisfy the demands of a public who wanted to hear and know more about the coming crusade."

General Melo suggested to the commanding officer in Rio of the Fuzilaros, Brazil's Marines, that the troops should hear about it. On the first occasion the commander sent a subordinate to greet the speaker, who found a small audience. Nearer the crusade, the invitation arrived on the commander's personal stationery, and he himself greeted the speaker with a cup of coffee and attended the service. The third time, shortly before the crusade, the commander gave him lunch and then took him to a huge hangar where the whole unit had assembled. Even the Roman Catholic chaplain was present. In introducing the talk he said that every Marine should attend the crusade at least one night.

Prayer meetings took place up and down the land, from the palace of the governor of Rio de Janeiro (Jeremias Fontes, a Protestant) in Niteroi, where he and his family knelt with army officers, cabinet ministers, junior civil servants and domestic staff; to scattered communities such as Centinario in the mountains, where a farmer had put benches around a spring in the shade of old gnarled trees, and his neighbors came after work to join him and his family in prayer for the crusade. Afterward, strengthened by coffee and homemade bread and cheese they would light their way home with torches made of rags soaked in kerosene and stuffed in bamboos.

Then came the prayer vigil. It arose from a remark made by Henry Holley to the general committee on August 28. David Gomes, the Bible society president who had chaired the meeting where the crusade had been born, was chairman for Spiritual Preparation. Using his Bible School of the Air as a chief link he had already achieved much, but "Henry Holley cut my heart into pieces! He didn't mean to hurt me, but he just awakened me when he said, 'I feel the prayer mobilization isn't as good as we expected.'" Gomes said nothing aloud but in his heart he prayed, "Lord, I know he is right. Yet I know I am doing my best. Lord, tell me what to do. I want to do it better."

That night Gomes woke up in the small hours. Unable to sleep again he went into his living room "and I sat on the sofa and I started asking God, 'How can I do it?' And it came to me just as clear as a voice, 'Put the people to pray! Call a watch night for the eve of Billy Graham's arrival. Bind them together in a watch night, and you are going to have results.'"

The next morning he went to his small office near the waterside and made forty telephone calls, "and I did not have a single one who did not accept the idea." The slogans caught on: "Half a Million at Prayer"; "Leave the lamps burning in a thousand churches to prepare the way of the Lord."

At eleven P.M. on Friday 27 September 1974 the churches began their prayer vigil. Right across the nation hundreds of churches kept lights on all night, and thousands of Brazilians were prayed for by name. Fanini's church in Niteroi made a wrought iron replica of the Greek oil lamp of New Testament times, and never let the flame die while more than 1,000 stayed throughout—sometimes forming a prayer chain according to the Brazilian custom, sometimes giving testimonies or singing hymns.

The next day *Ultima Hora* put the prayer vigil across its front page, in story and pictures under the heading, "A Great Search for God," together with news of Graham's coming that afternoon and his picture. The entire edition quickly sold out. Crusade leaders looked on this surprising coverage as proof of the spiritual preparation. "From then on," records Gomes, "we had no more doubts regarding the great victory."

Billy Graham arrived with Grady Wilson in Brasilia, the new capital, with its extraordinarily successful blend of modern architecture and open space. In its setting of natural beauty beside an artificial lake, he planned to spend several days incognito before being received by the president of Brazil.

An alarming cable disrupted his quiet, leading him to believe that Ruth had been seriously injured in a car accident. Fanini helped him get through by telephone to Milwaukee, where Ruth had been staying with Gigi. The facts were serious enough: a swing she was erecting on a tree for her grandchildren had snapped, throwing her fifteen feet. Although she sustained a heavy concussion, five fractures in her left foot, one broken rib and a slight injury to her spine, she was out of danger. Yet throughout the Rio crusade Billy carried the burden of not knowing that she would recover fully, the grief of not being able to hurry to her side.

The visit to President Geisel had great influence on the crusade. It marked Billy Graham in the eyes of all Brazilians as a man of importance whose message must be heard with attention. The president spoke of his gratitude that the crusade came early in his term of office, because Brazil's rapid material growth must be balanced by spiritual growth. He expressed his conviction that the hope of Brazil and the world was the gospel of Christ. He invited Billy to return some day for a crusade in Brasilia. He then broke protocol by speaking a few sentences in English instead of Portuguese, an honor seldom accorded a foreigner. He broke it again by inviting Billy's photographer, Russ Busby, to enter and take pictures alongside his own photographer.

While Billy Graham flew down from Brasilia a comic episode was occurring at Rio. The governors of the two states of Guanabara and Rio de Janeiro[1] had arranged to welcome him at the international airport, a unique honour for a Protestant clergyman. General Melo had secured permission for a covered ceremonial platform to be erected by the state tourist company. Holley had spent many hours over many weeks in many offices agreeing on the exact details. When he arrived about an hour ahead of time and looked for the platform, not a board, not a stitch of red carpet lay in sight. "I just about fell apart!" An hour later Billy's plane could actually be seen as the workmen hammered in the last nails. The governors and welcome committee took up positions on the brand-new platform, the bands played, and Billy stepped onto a red carpet—all perfect in every detail.

The opening night, Wednesday 2 October, drew about 85,000 people. Before the crusade got well underway an incident took place that puzzled the Brazilians. As the platform party filed onto the raised structure, which was placed forward on the turf beyond the dry moat, the crowd's attention focused not on Billy Graham but on a church dignitary with flowing white hair, dressed in what, from a distance under the stadium lights, looked like a red cardinal's robe. "One could sense the apprehension," recalls a veteran British missionary, W. B. Forsyth, "on the part of the thousands of simple Brazilian Believers present, many of them of Pentecostal persuasion and almost militant in their fundamentalism. 'Who is he? A Roman Catholic bishop? Billy Graham invite a Roman bishop to his platform?' "

He was in fact Dr. Michael Ramsey, archbishop of Canterbury, on his final tour before retirement, who in Buenos Aires and in other South American capitals had addressed public meetings drawn from all churches including Roman Catholic. He had hoped to do so in Rio

---

[1] At the time of the crusade the state of Guanabara (which covered the actual city of Rio, the former federal capital, much as the District of Columbia covers Washington) had not yet been absorbed into the state of Rio de Janeiro, which covered the cities and interior of Rio's hinterland. In 1975 the two became one state with Rio as capital.

until Bishop Sherrill pointed out that this could not be arranged because the brief visit coincided with the crusade. Sherrill suggested seeking instead an invitation to the Graham platform. The archbishop agreed, provided he might address the gathering. At a crusade committee on 24 June Bishop Sherrill had approached Henry Holley.

The committee as a whole hesitated, lest a president of the ecumenical movement should unwittingly "disrupt the harmony and the purpose of this crusade." But Billy Graham intervened. At Lausanne in July he said it would be wonderful to have the archbishop bring a brief greeting. He had appeared with Billy once before, at the Hawaii crusade, and the two men had mutual affection. Unlike his predecessor, Archbishop Fisher, Michael Ramsey had not given public support to Graham in London. Yet when Sir Alec Douglas-Home asked his views on Graham, Dr. Ramsey paid tribute to the number of men who joined the Anglican ministry in the wake of each crusade.

The timing and pattern of the opening service in Rio would permit only one sermon, Billy's. Fearing a misunderstanding about this, Holley specifically asked Bishop Sherrill on 10 September "if you would be sure to clarify the archbishop's definition of 'address.' We are thinking of a three-or four-minute 'greeting.' " By the opening night Graham, the Team and the Brazilians believed that this was accepted, but the archbishop, for whatever reason, arrived at Maracana believing differently. He reported to the convocation of the province of Canterbury five days later, that Graham had "invited me to the platform . . . and with great generosity allowed me to speak for as long as I liked."

He had arrived with grave doubts about the whole enterprise, assuming it to be run from outside Brazil and questioning the rightness of the vast expenditure in a land where there is such poverty. But his first impression[2] was of "the great kindness, warmth and humility of Billy himself. He made me feel completely at home by his spirit of outgoing and very humble Christian comradeship. He was at the time worried and distressed by an accident one of his family had had and this was putting a strain on him, but it did not alter his deep Christian serenity."

When Dr. Ramsey rose to speak, the puzzlement in the stands was widespread. Few of the crowd had heard of the title Archbishop of

---

[2] Letter to the author from Lord Ramsey of Canterbury, 8 May 1975.

Canterbury and continued to believe he was a Roman cardinal. Forsyth recalls, "The archbishop began very well with an exposition of the 'feet-washing' in John 13, but when he began to apply his message as though he were addressing a middle-class audience in Britain, consternation and perplexity were general. It was very evident that Dr. Benjamin Moraes was in difficulties. He knew that what was being said would not be understood, or at the best misunderstood, so he took the liberty of glossing over some of the statements that would cause offense to the more simple types of Brazilians present. I heartily endorsed what he was doing and marveled at his skill."

The archbishop, however, weakened his impact by his length, which was inevitably increased by the interpretation into Portuguese. The audience grew restless. The program had to be hastily reorganized to make up time. When Billy Graham rose, writes Forsyth, "we wondered how he would cope. . . . What he did was magnificent. He managed to introduce into his address a reference to what had been said by the archbishop, and to do it in such a way that . . . it became an integral part of the presentation of the truth." In London the next week, when the archbishop spoke of the visit very sympathetically in his valedictory address to the convocation of Canterbury, a profound impression was made on many Anglican leaders not usually favorable to Graham's ministry—that two streams of passionate concern for God's glory should have flowed together on that platform in Rio.

"What impressed those who heard Billy Graham for the first time," recalls David Glass, an Englishman who runs the Evangelical Bookshop in Rio, "was the fact that the Brazilians are accustomed to flowery oratory, and there was nothing of it. It was just simple, straightforward, homely truth."

Billy spoke short, simple phrases which Walter Kaschel of São Paulo interpreted equally simply. This was not the place or time for the carefully argued addresses of Madison Square Garden when, in 1969, millionaires and hippies alike had followed Billy's theme as they sat back in their seats, going deeper with him until he brought them step by step to the point of decision. In Rio "the simplicity of his message was what really made it useful," recalls Josinaldo Agiar Maia, a young lay evangelist at Belem on the lower Amazon, "because he was able to reach every level of society with that kind of preaching. The authority and sureness with which he presented the message seemed so full of the Holy Spirit. His preaching is completely Biblical, and this leads people up, and they have to make a decision." The young evangelist's pastor, 31-year-old Joao Da Silva Cruz, who also came down from Belem to attend the crusade and its school of evangelism, adds, "I think that Billy Graham used simple words and simple phrases in order that he might reach everyone who was there whether rich or poor. To me that seems a wise thing to do."

When Billy gave the invitation the architecture of Maracana prevented a coming forward onto the field. Even if the authorities had allowed the use of the turf, any temporary bridges across the moat would be almost useless because the upper tier of the stadium, where most of the seating was, had no access to the lower tier and thus to the field. On the first night Billy asked that those who had made a decision for Christ should come forward to the rails of their section, where counselors waited; but little movement could be seen from the platform. The absence of aisles hemmed in all but those who happened to be strategically placed. On the second night the platform party, who knew by then that more than 500 decision cards had been received on the previous night, again detected little movement, although in fact nearly double that number of cards came in. After that, Billy Graham told inquirers to stand in their places and wave a handkerchief or hymn sheet, and counselors would come to them.

On that first night those who sat on the platform, far out in the field, remained almost entirely unaware of the effect of Billy's sermon and of the sudden surge of movement in the stands. The story of a Rio office worker who had heard nothing about the crusade until that evening provides an illuminating commentary on what actually happened.

Wilson Martinez Rejala, a lapsed Catholic in his early thirties, had been dying (so his doctor told him) from hepatitis caused by drink. Six weeks before the crusade a Catholic who had been a friend from boyhood brought him a New Testament, telling Rejala that his life had been such that if he died he would go to hell. Reading the Testament alone in his room on 17 August 1974, Rejala was struck by the promise in Matthew 6 that when "you pray, enter into your closet and pray to your Father who sees in secret, and your Father will reward you openly. And so I got down on my knees and prayed. I was afraid to die. I began to cry. I felt something go through my whole body: as though the whole room was full of angels. That lasted about four or five minutes, and then a sensation of joy and peace came over me, just as if someone had thrown a pail of water over me.

"That night I had peace in my heart. And I had a dream. I saw the heavens move. I saw two wagons in gold, and the door to heaven opened, and coming toward me was the Lord Jesus Christ dressed in white clothes. His hair was golden, and he had a crown on his head, and he came with great speed and I could feel the wind as he came by. And I looked to him, and I remembered what is written in the Bible, 'Those that call on the name of the Lord shall be saved.' And so I said to him, 'Lord, save my family.' And at the same time, I was completely healed.

"This was two A.M. I was so happy that I wanted to tell it everywhere, in newspapers, and radio and television and everything. My joy was so great, I didn't know whether I was in heaven or on earth. And so I began to take more and more interest in the Word of God."

On the evening of 2 October he was eating dinner in a restaurant after work when a stranger handed him a Billy Graham tract with a printed invitation to Maracana. That night was Rejala's only free night and he went to the stadium. He had never attended an evangelical church.

"I wept out of pure joy, listening to Billy Graham preach that sermon. I felt he was a man sent of God for the saving of souls. That first message helped me to a greater understanding of what this is all about. When the appeal was made, I went from way back up on the top in the bleachers. I went way down as far as I could get. Many people were moving forward up there at the same time, and when I saw so many people come forward I began to weep. I wanted to talk to Billy Graham himself and tell him about my experience. But of course that was impossible, there were too many people. I really had accepted the Lord before the crusade, but I went forward to confirm it."

Tyndale House, the Illinois publishers of the *Living Bible*, had promised 150,000 free copies of their Portuguese version of the *Living New Testament* to the crusade for use in the follow-up. Months of negotiation with printers, shippers, customs and warehouse men culminated in 6,000 cardboard boxes, holding twenty-five copies each, arriving in Rio at the precise moment when they could be stored under one of the two ramps leading to the upper tier of Maracana, taking an area of some thirty-five feet by twenty.

A team of seminarians and young church people guarded the store of books night and day from pilferers and each day distributed boxes by two Volkswagen minibuses to the points throughout the stadium where counselors could keep them ready.

The young people did more. They emptied boxes from the center first, and before the opening night had carved out a three-foot-wide passage leading to a recess about eight feet square, which they called the Cardboard Chapel (A Capella dé Papelao) in the middle of the great pile of packed Testaments with the ramp for a roof. They left a row of boxes around for seats and stood outside as the crowd surged past. Frequently they would be asked for a free Testament and would explain that it could be given only after the meeting by a counselor to an inquirer. They would then invite the person into the Cardboard Chapel. Very few refused, and their chapel soon held a murmur of voices as the young people read a few verses and answered questions or prayed.

No less than 150 decision cards were signed in the Cardboard Chapel, including one by a man who had said immediately that he was a spiritist witch doctor practicing black magic but had heard about this easily read paraphrase of the New Testament in Portuguese. They took him inside and after a long discussion he left to find a seat in the stadium. "I went in there a witch doctor and I have come out a believer in Jesus Christ," he said.

Farther in behind the Cardboard Chapel they had removed more boxes to make a little inner sanctum which they called a "Prayer Cave." Since they had to watch the books around the clock, they decided also to pray. Throughout every hour one at least would be at prayer, and at night they took turns sleeping, in order to watch and pray.

On the second night they might have been tempted to wonder whether their prayers were being answered. Numbers dropped to about 50,000, partly because of the intrinsic difficulties of bringing large numbers together in Rio on a week night, and partly because few of the nearer city churches had set up delegation programs (Operation Andrew) with hired buses. Walking is not popular, city bus lines are crowded, and although every bus and train stopping near Maracana disgorged Believers, their friends, and thousands of others, many more would have come had groups been specially organized.

The choir turned up in force. On the final nights, however, many members drifted to other parts of the stadium when more counselors were required, or because they were discouraged by not hearing the sermon. The choir section had been particularly affected by the cuts, breakdowns and actual acts of sabotage by Communists which bedeviled the sound system throughout the crusade but on at least one earlier night, so Bill Ichter believes, 11,500 sang.[3] The choir spread over 50 to 60 yards of tiers going far up from the field, so that Ichter on his conducting platform stood about 35 yards from the nearest, yet he never lost them or allowed the beat to go ragged, making such wide movements of his arms that, had he not been a keep-fit devotee, the first two nights would have exhausted him. The sound of at least 4,000 tenors and basses, and then 4,000 trebles and altos, or more, singing the Portuguese version of "Wonderful and Matchless Grace of Jesus" was unforgettable. Contrary to his usual custom, Cliff Barrows had invited Bill Ichter to conduct throughout the crusade, to the choir's delight. Choir and congregation, however, wanted to sing more, and wished that more Brazilians had been chosen as soloists. They appreciated George Beverly Shea and other singers in English, but the enormous applause for their own Feliciano Amaro showed the public's pride and pleasure.

On the third evening, Friday, a steady rain fell on the whole Rio area. Many of the most ardent could not risk damaging their one suit or pair of shoes in the open stands. Others got stuck in traffic jams. On rainy nights the rush hour grinds almost to a halt as streets become clogged with buses and the endless procession of Brazilian-made Volkswagen Beetles and other cars.

Numbers dropped to 30,000. Yet, says Fanini, "it was the best night. The people depended more on God. We had many decisions, but it was tremendous for the Christians. We had big crowds Wednesday, Thursday, but it seems to me that on Friday God put us all together; it was different." A smaller crowd made for easier hearing because there was less noise despite lightning striking the stands. That

---

[3] 11,000 persons filled in choir register blanks, and probably another 2,000 joined the choir without registering—making a potential 13,000 members.

was the night when Billy preached on Belshazzar's Feast, "The Carnival of Death," the sermon best remembered in Rio.

David Glass of the Evangelical Bookshop and his Brazilian wife took in their car two sisters, both Believers, one of whom had brought along a young married woman from her office with an embittered, miserable and complaining character. They got stuck in the traffic jam that rainy night behind Billy Graham's car, which interested this woman particularly. When the others started singing hymns in harmony to pass the time, she listened entranced. She had never heard Christian singing of that kind. During the sermon on the Carnival of Death she paid close attention and at the invitation she stirred hesitantly in her seat. Mrs. Glass said, "If I stand up with you, would you like to make a decision for Christ?" "Yes, I would." Her gloom and resentment seemed to fall away like a discarded garment. "Tonight has been a turning point in my life," she said as they parted afterward. On Sunday they came on her suddenly in the enormous crowd at Maracana, radiant, and she told them laughingly that her husband would not believe her when she said she was going there to find them in all that crowd. She joined a church in Copacabana.

The thumbs-up sign is much used in Brazil. On Saturday morning, when Billy and the Team met the crusade executives and committee members, the atmosphere was thumbs-up. They all felt that the crusade had turned the corner, though no one realized what an exceptional weekend lay ahead.

18 The Glory of Brazil

WHATEVER Saturday and Sunday might bring in Rio, evangelical churches throughout Brazil had been strongly influenced already through the school of evangelism. It has been described as "one of the great permanent benefits of the crusade," yet through an odd lack of communication the idea was put before the committee only a few months before the opening. They decided to hold it in Maracanazinho, which stands next to the stadium and could be adapted to provide covered space for a school numbering, as they hoped, 8,000 out of Brazil's estimated 16,000 Protestant pastors.

Edgar Hallock became coordinator of the school. Kenneth Chafin would come from America to be dean. Unfortunately the men in Rio discovered only at the last minute that Lowell Berry scholarships were available to bring pastors and suitable laymen and women from anywhere in Brazil; the original estimate of 8,000 might have been nearer the mark had that been known sooner, or the school been announced earlier. But since most pastors in Brazil are obliged to have secular employment because churches cannot support them full time, many could not arrange their affairs to travel to Rio for six days. Pre-school registration numbered less than 3,000. Hallock correctly gauged that many would arrive to register at the last minute, expecting to sleep in churches or homes of church people, and that some who attended would not register.

The total attendance was slightly over 3,500. They came from

Amazon rain forests and the cool southern mountains, from the savannahs, from new Brasilia and teeming São Paulo, traveling by country bus along earth roads and then by swift modern buses along the network of highways that link the enormous country. From Recife, with its glorious beaches, a convoy of four buses included most of the Baptist seminary and the women's college for Christian education, both drawing their students from throughout the northeast. They traveled night and day for forty-two hours, to hear "a great and famous preacher," to "learn his methods," to "share in the work of the crusade."

A Belo Horizonte pastor "wanted to learn to evangelize more effectively." Another had heard of these schools "and their good results" elsewhere. A young pastor from the state of Para, even farther from Rio, says that "the real motivation was the crusade. If the crusade had not been going on, probably most of us would never have bothered to go to the school."

The school's program followed the pattern used in the United States, Korea and elsewhere. The Brazilians appreciated every lecture, yet they wished more of their own people had been on the faculty—only two were listed out of fifteen—and counted it a welcome providence when two Americans dropped out and Brazilians substituted for them. The seminars were the high spots. These gave time to talk and discover one another, for most of them knew little or nothing of Christians in other denominations. Pentecostals were suspect of Baptists, and both tended to keep aloof from Methodists and Presbyterians. Lutherans, mainly Brazilians of German extraction, had generally worked alone. The school of evangelism broke down those barriers throughout Brazil, just as the crusade preparations had broken barriers in Greater Rio and had provided opportunity for a fellowship that distance generally prevented. The atmosphere of the school, its spirituality and the seriousness with which it faced the problems of evangelism, heartened pastors and laity, especially the young.

Billy Graham and the crusade itself formed the focal points. When Billy addressed the school, his evangelistic emphasis and his appeal for a deep spiritual life left a strong impression. In the words of a Belo Horizonte pastor, they "could see the love of souls in his face and in his life—in coming all the way over here to teach us how to win souls for Christ."

Some Christian women of Recife counted among the secrets of

Billy's influence that he "places himself completely in God's hand"; "he doesn't work alone: he wants the cooperation of the people"; "there is a chain of prayer, thus his message has power, and God uses him when he preaches."[1] Men and women alike were stirred by the simplicity and force of Graham's sermons. The cassettes they bought to use in evangelism back home in hospitals and schools "were so alive, so full of fire, that you could never tire of them." Month after month cassettes sold widely in bookstores.

A pastor in the rolling uplands of Minas Gerais, living four hours' bus ride from the regional city and forty minutes walk from the bus stop, sums up the school of evangelism like this. "It all really boils down to one thing: I got out of the school of evangelism a passion for souls. You must have a passion for souls to win them, and that's what I came back with. I saw it in the lives of those who spoke, and it touched my life and changed it. Without any doubt, having the crusade at the same time was certainly a stimulus. But even so, in the context of the crusade the school of evangelism was the main step in giving me a desire to win more souls for Christ."

A *Decision* School of Christian Writing took place in a nearby church, with General Mario Barreto Franca, a poet and member of Fanini's congregation, as director. A Southern Baptist missionary, Roberta Hampton from Oklahoma, was coordinator. Since most Brazilians like to write and many believe that they can, General Franca and Senhorita Hampton limited the membership strictly to 135, people whose positions and potentialities suggested they would profit most from it. They selected from the *Decision* curriculum the lectures likely to be of greatest use. All, except for Sherwood Wirt's two addresses, were delivered in Portuguese by Brazilians or missionaries.

As the week wore on, one factor greatly heartened the pastors from the interior, some of whom lived lonely lives serving small scattered churches among a population that despised evangelicals. That factor was "the praise for the crusade we heard from unbelievers: taxi drivers, bus collectors, passengers on buses, and employees in the stores." That comment by a Baptist pastor from the sugar cane country behind

---

[1] Discussing the subject a year later, one of them added, amid peals of laughter, that Brazilians also took to Billy Graham "because he is very, very handsome!"

Recife is echoed by a Rio Pentecostal layman. "Everywhere you went, and whoever you talked to, the subject was always the same: the desire to go and hear Billy Graham in Maracana." "Billy Graham," recalls Isaias Maciel, a Presbyterian leader, "became the password of all the people. Many were asking, 'Who is this Billy Graham?' The word was given back: 'He is a great preacher, a great evangelist, and he brings a message that is positive for our days. Let's go hear him. Let's go to Maracana.' "

Another attraction of the crusade, not to be despised, was the opportunity to get inside Maracana without payment. Thousands who could not afford a ticket to a football game seized the opportunity when the weekend brought freedom from night school and rush hour.

Saturday was Youth Night. Maracana's capacity had been calculated as 187,000 persons, the highest ever recorded for a football game, but stadium authorities believe that on Saturday nearly 200,000 persons were present. When Billy Graham asked those under twenty-five to stand, it seemed that two-thirds of the crowd stood and waved hymn sheets, causing Billy to comment "It looks like snow!"

The closing Sunday afternoon enjoyed beautiful weather. Long before the time of the service the stadium was already as full as on Saturday, yet thousands continued moving up the ramp and along the streets. Three thousand coaches had parked in and around the inadequate lots while others just disgorged passengers. All Rio seemed to converge on Maracana.

When nearly 200,000 persons had entered, again exceeding the official capacity, the colonel in charge ordered the gates shut. At that the chief usher, Eurico Freitas, hurried inside to find Fanini on the platform, and together with Renfrow they held a quick consultation. Then they turned to Erasmo Pedro, honorary chairman of the crusade and vice-governor of the state, which owned the stadium. Pedro wrote an order to the colonel, who reopened the gates. Fanini watched while the outfield between the dry moat and the turf filled up. People then moved into the moat itself, below the level of the ground. "When I saw the stadium so packed," relates Fanini, "I said, 'After this, only heaven! I'm ready, Lord.' "

The colonel allowed another 20,000 or so inside and then, to the distress of those still approaching, the iron gates closed implacably. The turnstiles had clicked to 219,427 and since some 6,000 crusade officials, ushers and choir had entered uncounted, stadium authorities gave the attendance figure as 225,000. Perhaps 25,000 were left outside, able to hear by amplifiers but not to see. Their hammering on the iron gates reverberated inside Maracana at intervals throughout the afternoon, an extraordinary comment on the occasion. The disappointed included several coach loads from distant parts.

Believers *(Crentes)* in Rio in 1974 did not number more than 100,000. They rejoiced that they had achieved the largest evangelistic meeting in the western hemisphere, of which, allowing for Believers from the interior, at least half of those present must have been non-*Crentes,* whether Catholics or spiritists. Most had been brought by the invitation, encouragement, or example of their Believer neighbors. As Cliff Barrows reflected, it was "a moment of triumph for Christ and for the Christians, a triumph that has come at great cost and sacrifice to hundreds and thousands of little people that we ourselves have never known but have been involved as part of God's planning for that particular time."

The 250,000 waiting in or around Maracana to hear Billy Graham that Sunday afternoon formed only a fraction of those about to watch and listen in front of television sets throughout the huge land mass of Brazil (except, by some strange mishap or malevolence, in Para at the mouth of the Amazon, the only state to exclude Billy from the TV screen). For an evangelical meeting to be carried live in Brazil could certainly be claimed as a miracle.

The story goes back to a moment about three weeks earlier when Fanini was praying in the study of his home. He knew the influence of his own nationwide radio program and of the pre-crusade Billy Graham telecasts with dubbed-in Portuguese. "I was praying for God to bless Billy and to use his voice mightily, through all possible means. As I was praying, right then, a light flashed in my mind, telling me that television should be used."

Fanini took Holley to visit Globo, the principal television company (TV in Brazil operates on the American pattern, with sponsors buying time from the companies). "We said, 'We want you to broadcast Sunday afternoon.' And the man said to me, 'How much money have you got?' I asked him how much it would cost, and he said, 'At least a million cruzeiros.' I said, 'But I don't have it.' He said, 'How can you come to talk to me like that?' I said, 'Because the Lord wants us to.' "

Rebuffed, Fanini raised the matter with General Humberto Melo in Brasília on 18 September after Holley and Fanini had been received by the president to fix the details of Billy Graham's visit. The general promptly telephoned Globo Television's owner. Fanini heard the general say, "Roberto, I want you to help us. This crusade is of national interest. I need your help to cover it." The effect on Roberto Marigno was instant: he asked whom he should talk to, and the general said he would send Fanini, whom Marigno knew.

Fanini flew back to Brasilia, but at Globo a secretary said he could not have an appointment with the owner for a month. Fanini asked her to take in a card which the general had given him. "In one minute she rushed back; 'Sir, he is going to attend to you right now!' "

"Roberto," said Fanini, "God wants you to help us to preach the gospel to our people."

"We are ready to help. What do you want?"

"Television on Sunday afternoon, to broadcast Billy's message across the nation."

"But that is impossible!" He named a man in São Paulo who had already bought that hour for his regular Sunday afternoon nationwide show with dancers, contests, and singers.

Senhor Marigno promised to talk with that man. When Fanini was summoned back to Globo a few days later, the owner told him that the show sponsor, a Catholic, had agreed. "For God's work I will give up my time." Globo would send forty men and carry the crusade live in color for one hour, free, across Brazil. Fanini asked if he might pray with Marigno, "and I prayed and I cried. When I finished, he was crying too. He said, 'This is the first time somebody prayed in this office.' "

By then Billy Graham had arrived in Rio, and Fanini drove out to the new Sheraton hotel beyond Leblon beach to give the news, only to find to his astonishment that it distressed Walter Smyth; it conflicted with an axiom of the Team that live television in the immediate area of a crusade would keep people away. But Fanini knew his people. He persuaded Walter and Billy not to miss a miracle.

When that final Sunday afternoon came, 6 October 1974, the Grand Prix motor race at Watkins Glen in the United States, with Brazil's favorite racing star Fittipaldi taking part, would follow on television immediately after the crusade. Innumerable viewers who might have gone to the beaches or the countryside stayed by their sets (and saw Fittipaldi win the Grand Prix.) Globo estimated that at least 25 million persons watched and heard Billy Graham's sermon from Maracana. General Melo, who had brought it all about, sat with three state governors and other dignitaries on the platform.[2]

Inside Maracana, as the service began, the atmosphere was that of a *fest*, bubbling over with joy. "An incredible experience," wrote Sherwood Wirt. "The people joined the platform soloists in their numbers. They applauded after each verse. They sent loud murmurs up to heaven during the prayers. Their bands played (whether or not they were supposed to)."

The people responded warmly to a brief interpreted testimony from Kenneth Cooper, an American physician from Dallas who had trained the Brazilian World Cup soccer team in his keep-fit system (termed Aerobics) in 1969. They credited him with a large share in their retaining the cup. His system had become a craze throughout the country, with keep-fit classes every morning on the beaches. Tracks in sports clubs and parks were laid out for the "Cooper Test." Cooper, a friend of Hallock and Ichter, on his visits always took speaking opportunities, and thus many Brazilians knew he was a Christian.

Billy Graham took as his theme "The Glory of Brazil." Speaking from Paul's words, "God forbid that I should glory save in the Cross of our Lord Jesus Christ," he referred to the cross raised in 1500 on the beach in Bahia on the day of Brazil's discovery by the Portuguese. He spoke of the great statue of Christ the Redeemer on Corcovao, which some of the crowd could see as he spoke—raised with arms outstretched to form a cross. He alluded to the southern cross in Brazil's night sky. Then he led them to contemplate the power of the Cross to transform a human life from that of a sinner to a citizen of heaven. It was the message of redemption and rebirth that he had proclaimed in equally simple terms around the world.

After Billy had given his invitation to decide for Christ, Bill Ichter

---

[2] Parts of the service were seen in a news program sent by international satellite to other parts of the world. Later the videotape was shown at a broadcasting convention in Washington, D.C., and parts were used in a film produced by World Wide Pictures which was telecast across the U.S. in 1976.

raised his arms to the choir. As they began to sing *Tal Qual Estou* (Just as I Am) people throughout the stadium joined in while, in Laurence Olson's words, "Thousands took the decision! It was a magnificent, moving scene when these people began to wave, using the printed programs to make themselves seen by the 10,000 counselors." One counselor, a watchmaker from Belo Horizonte, commented, "I would say the impact was total. We felt that the message really reached its objective. When we went and counseled those people, spoke to them about the Lord Jesus Christ and gave them literature, it was as if a great weight had fallen off their shoulders when they handed their lives over to Jesus Christ." Over 10,000 decision cards were signed in Maracana itself that afternoon.

In the stadium offices a battery of five telephones had been linked to a number shown on television as Billy invited viewers to call by telephone, or write in, if they wanted a free copy of the *Living New Testament*. The moment the program went off the air the telephones began to ring, and with never a pause far into the evening Harold and Nona Renfrow and a team of volunteers counseled callers. A few simply asked for a Testament. Most wanted further help or to tell that they had decided for Christ in front of their television sets. The Renfrows were particularly pleased when their local astrologer came on the line "and said that now he understood what it was to see the light of the world and what Jesus meant when he said, 'I am the way, the truth and the life.'" He became a frequent attender at Fanini's church.

Next morning as Believers went to their places of work (reading in one Rio newspaper that the devil had been defeated by Billy 6–0 and sent off the field by the referee!) they realized at once the impact of the television which the Billy Graham Team had nearly refused. Policeman DeAraujo was surrounded by colleagues: "Everybody said they'd never in all their lives heard a man that could preach like Billy Graham could preach, and the impression was tremendous." Bank clerk Silva's fellow clerks "were always making fun of me. But on Monday they were saying, 'You really had a great preacher there. His personal magnetism attracted us to him.' So then they gave me their congratulations on having defended it all." A non-Believer acquaintance of David Glass paused at the door of the bookshop and shouted, "I saw that program! It was terrific, you're to be congratulated." In São Paulo an Assemblies of God doctor was accosted by three of his colleagues when he arrived at their hospital. "They were mightily impressed by the preaching, the tremendous crowd, the singing, the enthusiasm—they didn't know that the gospel was so wonderful." They asked Dr. Oswaldo to get them each a Bible. And in São Paulo that week, when Perry Ellis, a Texan evangelist who sings and preaches in Portuguese, carried out an extensive visitation program in preparation for his city-wide campaign, "easily 90 percent of all the people I talked with had viewed the broadcast from Maracana." He reckoned it the most useful opportunity ever given the gospel in Brazil.

A Rio military policeman named Joe Alexander Mesquita lives on the outskirts of the suburban city of Nova Iguacu with his wife and their four children. He had been in the barracks on a Saturday some weeks before the crusade when a fellow soldier drew his attention to the dubbed Billy Graham film on television.

Mesquita was a catechist who taught seventy-five children each Sunday. His priest had given him a catechism book and a New Testament, and Mesquita "would find the answer in the New Testament and would tell them what it said. The Padre would always call to my attention that I was not to use the words from the New Testament, I was to use the words from this book. That bothered me a great deal, and so when I went home at night I would ask God, why couldn't I use his words, but had to use the words of the Catholic church. I couldn't understand. Nor was I satisfied with my life."

The sermon on the film had impressed him, so when Billy Graham spoke at Maracana, Mesquita not only watched on television but ran his tape recorder. "I think it was that day I was born again, that I found the transformation of my own life I was looking for." Afterward he wrote down the entire sermon from the tape and took it to the Catholic church to tell his friends that he had found what he was looking for. "But the Catholics didn't understand what I was talking about, and so I sought my neighbor who is a member of the Baptist church of Nova Iguacu, and he told me where to find the pastor. We talked together, and I came to understand what had happened to me."

Mesquita would come back from the Baptist church and tell his wife, an active Catholic, what he had heard "and she became very enthused about it. I told her, 'Now don't you do this just because I have done it. But you must come to know Christ as your Savior. And even though I'm telling you about it, you need to go to church yourself to understand.' She came, and in the second sermon she couldn't resist any longer. She accepted Christ and was born again, and has been extremely happy in this." And so is Mesquita, as his friends and colleagues noticed. A year after the crusade he was summoned by his commanding officer. "He said, 'You're an entirely different man. What has happened to you?' I said, 'I'm reading a Book, and this Book is changing my life, and changing all of my attitudes and my relationships.' He said, 'Yes, we see an entirely different man here! And now we're giving you more responsibility as a result.' I told my wife that our family was so different, that we ought to spend all of our time in prayer at night, thanking God for this new birth."

The Mesquita story is echoed again and again in the evidence of what happened outside and inside Maracana. Pastors were hard pressed to keep up. Because the stadium's design had prevented hundreds, if not thousands, from making proper contact with a counselor, letters, decision cards and requests came week after week, month after month following the crusade. More than 100,000 requests for New Testaments had come by September 1975. A year almost to the day after Billy's closing service two decision cards arrived in the same mail. One was from a convict in São Paulo who had heard the television sermon but delayed a decision until a preacher had visited the prison. The other was from a woman in the state of Minas Gerais who had made her decision in front of her television set but delayed public profession of faith until she had solved her problems of drinking, smoking, and cohabiting with a man who was not her husband. Then she went to a church.

By March 1975, 46,275 decision cards had been received; by October 1975, over 50,000. In August 1976, when Harold Renfrow cleared the box after a six-week absence he found 300 letters and cards, about a third indicating decisions. The rest were requests for literature. The crusade telephone number, which reverted to the denominational office that had loaned it, still received at least a call a week for spiritual counsel or telling about a decision. In December 1977, more than three years after the crusade, Renfrow reckoned that his mail included about a letter a day from people writing as a direct result of it.

The *Evangelical News* newsheet in October 1975 stated: "Churches in the Greater Rio area are experiencing a period of rapid growth, with large numbers of conversions and baptisms. Many churches are feeling the need to expand. The seminaries of all denominations are overflowing, along with the Bible institutes. Many of those enrolling are saying they made their decisions during the Billy Graham crusade. *Servico de Assistencia Social Evangelico,* an evangelical program of social work through hospitals, rest homes, and homes for unwed mothers is experiencing its most rapid growth in this year of 1975." That growing social concern also found outlets which had been opened to non-Catholics by President Geisel.

The Evangelical Bookshop experienced a great upsurge in the sale of evangelical literature. For the first time one denomination exceeded its financial budget, which included support for its missionaries overseas. The crusade put a match to the tinder of Brazilian zeal and brought a revived sense of evangelism, a willingness to work together to bring others to Christ. The varied Protestant churches threw off their old fear that unity in action would trap them into unwanted organic union, and discovered new harmony and cooperation. "This general feeling is now evident throughout Brazil," wrote one leader in 1978. "Together, we're able to do certain things we otherwise could not do."

Evangelicals threw off their sense of inferiority as a minority in a predominantly Catholic nation. The crusade's success gave them self-respect. They had raised the funds, they had drawn a quarter of a million together on one day to hear the evangelical gospel, they had reached the entire country by television. The more perceptive recognized that much more could have been done had they prepared better, united sooner, and raised funds more quickly; or if Billy Graham's Team had involved the Brazilians more closely in the arrangements with the press instead of doing it themselves; or if the follow-up department had been able to draw wider support from laity and pastors. But the crusade had succeeded, and that encouraged the evangelicals to "attempt great things for God, expect great things from God." October 1974 marked a revolution in their outlook.

Matching that came new openness toward the gospel throughout Brazil. The Sunday television, and the message and personality of Billy Graham; the friendly news coverage; the conversion of Darlene Gloria: these factors all contributed to great receptivity. Upper social levels opened. Industrial executives, businessmen, government officials sought Believers, whom they had previously ignored, to ask about their teaching. A pastor in his thirties in Divinopolis who was also learning to be a lawyer "had been speaking about Christ to some of my fellow students in the law school but they did not take religious subjects very seriously. After the crusade, their reaction changed. In the graduation service in our church, there were six professors from the law school, and the church was full of students who all showed the greatest respect and consideration."[3]

At the next federal election an unprecedented number of evangelicals (twenty-seven) reached Congress. In Brasilia the following year it was reported that cabinet ministers now took pains to insure a balance between Roman Catholic and Protestant at the highest executive level of their departments, a change made possible by a Protestant president and by the new atmosphere. It was a foretaste of possible closer working together of the religious communions, once the pain of past unhappy history has worn away.

That new atmosphere has spread to all levels. Pastor Laurence Olson was traveling in the interior some six months after the crusade. Wherever he went he handed out pamphlets of Billy Graham's Maracana addresses in Walter Kaschel's translation. In one area the rumor had gone ahead that Billy Graham himself was going through the countryside, and people crowded in, hoping to see Billy. In the interior and in Rio, said Olson, "I carry these pamphlets in my briefcase, and everyday I give them out to taxi drivers and to people in businesses. I keep asking, 'Did you go to the Billy Graham crusade?' Almost always they will say, 'Yes, I was there,' or 'I heard it on television,' or 'I heard it on the radio.' 'What did you think of it?' 'Wonderful,' they say. I haven't yet found anyone to speak against it. It has had a tremendous effect in opening the doors for preachers, everywhere.

"The results get spread out over such a wide area that it's almost impossible to say just how many have come in directly. My opinion is that the greatest result is not the actual number you can count, the number put down in the church books, but the overall result, and the goodwill toward the gospel."

---

[3] In some cities the crusade presented a problem, in that upper-class people who had been referred to a local church after their decision grew discouraged because the teaching was below their intellectual level.

Nilson Fanini began a regular series of telecasts. He wrote to Billy Graham after they had talked by international telephone on 10 September 1975. "To hear your voice brought many wonderful memories to mind. As a result of what you began here in Brazil, God has seen fit to allow us to reach by color television 40 million people, or 50 percent of the nation each week. In the greater Rio Area of 20 million people there is no other gospel telecast on a regular basis." Before the crusade it would have been impossible to have an evangelical program on television, and Fanini had to make five separate approaches before the Globo TV Company suddenly offered to sell prime time each Sunday. They then demanded a swift answer but on the strength of a substantial promise from BGEA Fanini seized the opportunity.

At the second anniversary of this program, in 1977, a large segment of the crusade choir and some 30,000 people of all Protestant denominations gathered to fill Maracanazinho (where the school of evangelism had been held). By then, plans were already underway for Billy Graham rallies in the great industrial city of São Paulo in 1979, as part of a Eurofest style youth congress for all Brazil.

19 Post-Lausanne

W H E N Billy Graham returned from Brazil in mid-October 1974 he found many letters on his desk showing how Lausanne already had affected different parts of the world.

"Since arriving in the Philippines back from our Lausanne fellowship," runs a typical letter, dated 8 October 1974, "we have organized here in Zamboanga City, in the spirit of Lausanne, a group composed of ministers and laymen of the different churches in this area. . . . The fire of God has touched the lives of these men and women. . . . We are fully committed to the evangelization of the Philippines and of Asia and other parts of the world. This is the main thrust of the leaders of today. . . . If there is anything that has taken our country with great enthusiasm it is the Lausanne Congress."

But unless some permanent world structure emerged, of the kind for which the participants had voted, the good done at Lausanne might evaporate with the passing of time. Much, therefore, hung on the first meeting of the continuation committee which the regional groups at Lausanne had elected. This committee convened in the Hotel Del Prado in Mexico City on the evening of 20 January 1975 where, after dinner, Billy Graham opened with an address that placed their deliberations in the context of history and the future.

During the first of three days of meetings the members' views diverged considerably. Some wished the continuation committee's role to be substantial, some low-powered. John Stott contended that like the

Lausanne Covenant it should exert influence on the entire mission of the church. Billy Graham urged that it should limit itself to a specific task.

Rumors circulated among the press that Stott and Graham were at odds over the social concern of evangelicals, but Graham comments that such an interpretation was wrong. "We share the same social concern. We took a slightly different point of view on 'what was the Lausanne mandate.' Was the mandate to implement the entire Covenant or was it primarily the evangelization of the world? I took the point of view that the mandate of the Congress was to implement the evangelization of the world. The committee compromised, and John and I both supported the compromise. I compromised for the sake of world evangelical unity—the issue was not a basic theological issue. The two of us are closer together than we have ever been in our ministry. We are in constant correspondence with each other. John is a thoroughgoing evangelical with an evangelistic heart and probably one of the most brilliant minds in Christendom today."

Bishop Dain wrote afterward to Billy, "We were facing some tremendous spiritual issues in Mexico City and one recognizes that Satan will not allow this kind of spiritual progress to be made without using every guile to try to frustrate it."

One potential frustration arose over the question of Billy Graham's own position. He had expressed repeatedly his intention not to be on the continuation committee, partly because of his crowded schedule, mainly because he feared it might seem to be one of his own agencies. But an American group at Mexico City urged him to be named as honorary chairman: "We felt that his leadership would do more than anything else to establish the credibility and assure the direction of our work. Billy agreed to pray about it overnight."

He left the room for the discussion. Stott and Dain opposed the motion for his honorary chairmanship, to the surprise of those who expected them to applaud it. The debate grew somewhat heated. "The next morning at our meeting," recalls Robert E. Coleman of Asbury Seminary, "Billy asked for the privilege of speaking first. As he began to open his heart, sharing with us his deep personal feelings, I never witnessed a more magnanimous expression of tenderness and understanding. His insight to the situation, his sensitivity to personalities, amplified by his own transparent humility, literally melted us together. What differences we had were largely resolved in an enveloping sense of trust and purpose. Since that time we have moved forward with remarkable solidarity."

The youngest on the committee, twenty-nine-year-old Ramez Atallah, Egyptian-born director of the Inter-Varsity Christian Fellowship in Quebec, had not known, nor much wanted to know Billy Graham until Lausanne, where he had been impressed by Graham's willingness to let others take the lead. "Then, in the heated debates at the first meeting of the Lausanne continuation committee, I saw his humility, the graciousness of his spirit, and his genuine desire to be open to the Lord and to the counsel of the Lord's people. I became convinced that Dr. Graham actually felt that he had much yet to learn and that he needed the counsel and help of other Christians. For a man in his position actually to reflect that kind of attitude is to me remarkable and a great challenge. He has an incredible capacity of drawing together the broadest spectrum of evangelicals. Many who do not agree with his theology still respect him and are willing to appreciate his contribution."

Jack Dain was disturbed that some suspected a rift between him and Graham. Billy replied to his anxious letter after Mexico City, "I consider you one of the dearest and most beloved friends I have ever had in my ministry. Nothing—nothing, could ever come between us. I hope we can be next-door neighbors in heaven! I feel that I am unworthy to touch your shoe latchet in the gospel ministry."

As a result of the deliberations in Mexico, the continuation of Lausanne was placed in the hands of the committee of forty-eight under the chairmanship of Bishop Dain, who stipulated a term of one year only. In January 1976, at Atlanta, Leighton Ford succeeded him for a two-year period before the next scheduled meeting. A small executive committee of ten, representative of each world region, would meet more frequently, plus an executive secretary. Gottfried Osei-Mensah, Ghanaian pastor of a Nairobi church, accepted that post. His entire secretariat would be himself, his secretary and one deputy executive. A two-hundred strong consultative council, of which Billy Graham was unanimously appointed honorary chairman, would meet every five years. The continuation committee resolved to develop a low profile on a small budget. "It does not wish to duplicate the work of other existing organizations or structures. . . . Its role is primarily to serve as a stimulus and catalyst, to communicate widely what God is doing and what we believe he wants us to do, and to seek to stir God's people to more effective action."

Bishop Dain commented on 18 April 1975, three months after the Mexico meeting: "I have been remarkably impressed by the way in which the Spirit of God has done his own work in Lausanne follow up. Letters reach my desk at the rate of about twenty per week telling of what God is actually doing directly and indirectly as a result of the Congress, and I would just take two that have arrived recently. One from Indonesia speaks of thirteen large cities where there are post-Lausanne groups meeting regularly, seeking to implement under God the vision of the Congress and some of the concerns of the Covenant, as well as a real dynamic outreach in evangelism. The second one comes from Madagascar: they have brought into being throughout the whole of Madagascar, on an interchurch basis, a new coordination committee for evangelism which has derived most of its motivation, drive and imagination from the Congress. This could be repeated again and again in many areas of the world."

Two years later, by April 1978, as the fourth anniversary of the Congress approached, clear worldwide patterns could be discerned.

All Christendom had become aware once again of the integrity and importance of a Biblical theology of evangelization, of its practical implications, and especially of the vigor of theological and evangelistic leadership emerging from the so-called Third World.

Some dozen regional or national congresses on world evangelization, and smaller seminars, had been planned and coordinated. A nine-day seminar for Papua (New Guinea) in June 1976 had included Roman Catholics, one of whom remarked, "It was unthinkable as little as two years ago." A factor leading to this, other than Lausanne, was the crusade tour four years before by Billy Graham's black associate, Ralph Bell, strongly supported by the Roman Catholic archbishop as well as by all Protestant churches.

In September 1976 the first European conference of evangelical theologians at Louvain, Belgium, had discussed "the Kingdom of God and Modern Man." This led to a new fellowship of theologians, with the first three articles of the Lausanne Covenant as doctrinal basis. In Africa that December, another direct result of Lausanne was the Pan-African Christian Leadership Assembly in Nairobi, at which Billy Graham was a speaker.[1]

---

[1] See chapter 22.

The Lausanne Committee had sponsored world study groups on special aspects, such as that in Bermuda in January 1978, when theologians, anthropologists, linguists, missionaries and pastors explored the effect of cultural factors on evangelization. Plans forged ahead for a consultation of evangelists, limited to about 500, to meet somewhere in a Third World country in 1980. It will assess progress since Lausanne and set new directions and priorities.

Lausanne had inspired new agencies for evangelization and numerous evangelistic thrusts, small and great. These included: in Europe, a crusade in Lausanne cathedral itself in 1976, and nation-wide evangelistic programs planned by French Christians for 1978, by Germans for 1979; in Latin America, a Bolivian team had traveled through all countries challenging Christians to evangelize, with such effect that nearly 3,000 new churches have been formed; in Africa, a camel-back team of evangelists reached nomadic tribes in East Africa who had never heard of Christ.

Lausanne had done much, too, to bridge the cleavage between evangelism and social concern in evangelical outlook, both by encouraging close thought about the wholeness of the gospel, and by inspiring projects to help the poor or the deprived.

But far more than any regional, national or interchurch enterprise it is the spirit, the new alignments, the stronger hope that matters. Ten, twenty years must pass before the Lausanne Congress can be assessed for its proper place in history.

The words of a Latin American sum up the probability. "I believe with all my heart that Lausanne was the turning point for a very strong evangelical leadership in the world. It seems to me that the world will not ever be the same after Lausanne." Billy Graham himself, addressing his Team meeting in 1978, ventured a private guess that Lausanne might one day be seen to stand with the three or four decisive moments when church history changed direction.

Certainly Lausanne has brought over the horizon the possibility, which history may discard or confirm, that among all the celebrated men and women of religion in the twentieth century Billy Graham will stand, with Pope John XXIII, as one of its two most decisive figures.

20 Billy and Youth

THE FAMOUS Tournament of Roses at Pasadena, with its Rose Queen, Rose Parade of colorful floats, bands and riders, leading to the east-west college football game in the Rose Bowl, each New Year's Day, is organized by a committee of local businessmen headed by a president whose year of office ends with the four days of festivities. Lewis A. Shingler, a layman of the Nazarene church who had been involved in both Billy Graham Los Angeles crusades, was president back in 1970-71.

He chooses the parade's grand marshal, who is chief speaker at the functions, and the parade theme; and he knows eight years ahead when he will serve. "The very day I was notified of my future honor," writes Shingler, "I determined at the proper time to invite Billy, desiring to buy up this privilege of providing a witness for Christ to the largest TV and personal audience in the world." About three years ahead he secured Billy's acceptance, though the grand marshal's name remains confidential until three months before the parade. It was the first time a man from the religious field had been chosen. "I don't know how a clergyman can fit into this extraordinary event," Billy wrote to Otis Chandler, publisher of the *Los Angeles Times,* in mid-December, "but it will be fun to try!"

After it was over he joked to another friend, "When I accepted the invitation to be the grand marshal three years ago I never dreamed that it would involve an entire week of festivities and twelve addresses. I thought all I had to do was to lead the parade and get a good seat on the 50-yard line at the Rose Bowl! However, it was enjoyable even though it was exhausting." Using the parade theme, *Through the Eyes of a Child*, Billy (in Shingler's words) "presented Christ in a most acceptable and effective manner at every press conference and related function, using Scripture to urge childlike faith and acceptance of Christ's promises."

During the parade itself, as Billy and Ruth rode with Shingler in the presidential car through cheering crowds, estimated at a million and a half people standing shoulder to shoulder, Billy experienced mixed emotions. "I felt a strong upsurge of optimism for America. But at the same time, despite the smiles, fanfare and flag waving I knew in my heart that America and the world were in deep trouble." He could not help being aware, even in this hour, of how many of his own generation had flung away Christian values.

Then he saw young people, by the hundred, mingling in the crowds and making the sign of the "Jesus Revolution." He recalled "that in the past five years something dramatic had happened in my crusades in America. They had become youth crusades," and again he felt hope for the nation. In every Pasadena street he saw placards, *God Is Love, Love Thy Neighbor, Join the Spiritual Revolution Now.* "Wearing bell-bottoms, levis, maxis and hot pants, hundreds of young people carried their Bibles. Suddenly, I felt like getting out of the limousine and joining them. With a singing heart I raised my arm and pointed my index finger upward, and all along that parade route I joined them in their chant, shouting, 'One Way—The Jesus Way.' "

Many of those with banners or booklets in the Pasadena crowd had been trained by Campus Crusade for Christ, the organization founded by Bill Bright. Billy Graham had given CCC its first donation, and Bill Bright, eighteen months later, offered Billy an opportunity that considerably influenced his future work among youth.

Bright had been on the platform as Billy addressed the North American Congress on Evangelism at Minneapolis in the summer of 1969, itself a direct result of the Berlin Congress three years earlier. Bill Bright turned to Akbar Haqq and shared a strong impression that Campus Crusade should sponsor a similar congress for the student world. Haqq, and Graham when he heard, encouraged him.

Bright's International Student Congress on Evangelism, better known by its short title of *Explo '72*, drew 85,000 high-school and college delegates to Dallas for a week in June 1972, with thousands more attending the chief functions in the Cotton Bowl. Graham accepted the post of honorary chairman, and Bright wrote to him afterward: "I am persuaded that thousands of the delegates were here because of you, and your contributions during *Explo* helped to make it by God's grace the success that it was." Paul Eshleman, field director of Campus Crusade and organizer of *Explo '72* has no doubt that it "would not have received such outstanding acceptance nationally by churches of all denominations had not Billy given his endorsement." Many in North America laughed at first at the target of 100,000 young people to be brought together for a week's practical training; because Billy Graham put his weight behind it they began to believe it could happen. He was able, too, to reassure pastors who were worried that the CCC training based on the "Four Spiritual Laws" might prove too slick an evangelism.

"On the eve of *Explo '72*," continues Eshleman, "nearly 2,000 staff members gathered for an evening of prayer, thanksgiving and preparation. The atmosphere was electric as Billy walked in and reported for duty. He said he was available for the whole week to do whatever he could to contribute to *Explo*. With more than 400 press from more than thirty countries, his attendance and contributions to the press conferences were invaluable. When the Cotton Bowl on the first night was ready to break loose because of the sheer excitement and enthusiasm of 85,000 people, a few words from Billy quieted the crowds and prepared them reverently for Dr. Bright's message. His challenge to commitment at the Friday night candlelight service was tremendous."

Explo '72 had a direct effect on the Billy Graham ministry. At the Minneapolis crusade the following year the Team arranged a youth evangelism seminar, *Yes '73*, on Explo lines but on a smaller, less exuberant scale (2,400 students for four days) which they dovetailed into the crusade. As Billy put it, "Teaching sessions in the daytime—crusade at night.... We intend to expand this phase of our ministry."

From *Explo '72* came also *Spre-e '73* in London. Billy Graham's London associate, Maurice Rowlandson, returning from Dallas profoundly touched in his spiritual life, wrote to Billy of his burden "that something of this nature might be held in Britain." He found that others in England, independently, were hoping that Billy Graham would come over to help British teen-agers.

Billy replied encouragingly. The dates offered by Earls Court, site of the 1966 crusade, were the only days he was free, but they left little more than a year to prepare. "I envisage trains coming from every part of Britain bringing thousands of young people," he wrote. The name *Spre-e '73* emerged in the London office with Rowlandson consulting a thesaurus for words meaning a happy assembly. ". . . Spree. A pity we can't have that—but it means a drunken orgy." "Why not?" said Jean Wilson, who was standing in the doorway. On the spur of the moment she suggested "s.p.—"spiritual"; r.e.e.—"re-emphasis." They inserted a hyphen to make the point and *Spre-e' 73* it became.

Rowlandson consulted widely and appeared to receive encouragement from the churches. However a sense that the campaign was imposed from outside, added perhaps to a fear of the unknown, surrounded the plans with criticism. Yet nearly 12,000 young people came for the week's training. Maurice Rowlandson summed up two years later, "For what it was, it was incredibly effective. Everywhere I go, not only in the British Isles but on the Continent of Europe people come up to me and say, *'Spre-e* meant everything to me.' But it had only a shadow of the effect it could have had, because it was so strongly criticized by churches and leaders. If they had come in behind it and backed it, I would not even like to prognosticate what might have happened in this country."

Billy thoroughly enjoyed *Spre-e* but could see and learn from its weaknesses, such as overoptimism in the numbers expected; overspending, so that BGEA in Minneapolis shouldered a sizable deficit; and a level of daytime teaching not as high as could have been wished, nor adapted enough to British ways. The nightly music sessions lasted too long, and most delegates were tired by the time Billy began to preach. As one older observer put it, "We could have done with a little more of Billy and a little less noise." At its closing rally at Wembley stadium, Johnny and June Cash came specially from America. "I do want to thank you most sincerely," wrote Dave Foster, one of the principal organizers, to Billy, "for leaving the security of tried and proven formulas to join us in what became a somewhat controversial pioneer effort. . . . Your ministry fitted our total concept hand-in-glove."

In the months and years that followed *Spre-e,* Maurice Rowlandson continued to receive much evidence of the results, including an exciting telephone call in January 1974 from a mission church at Leigh in Lancashire, where the congregation had dwindled to fifteen; the denomination was about to close it. The church members had sent their six young people to *Spre-e,* and they had returned with such new vision that within weeks they held a mini-crusade of gospel folk-music and Billy Graham films. In January the 300-seat church was full. The minister "could not contain himself," Rowlandson reported to Smyth after the telephone call. "He was absolutely delighted, and beside himself with enthusiasm." Four years later the once moribund church had become well known as a spiritual force in the area.

One of those closely involved in *Spre-e* was British pop singer Cliff Richard. With his understanding of youth and his active concern both for evangelism and the social responsibility of Christians, Cliff Richard's estimate of Billy Graham[1] gives some indication why Graham reaches the new generation.

"My first view of him was in 1966 at Earls Court," he writes. "I had been a Christian for a year or so, and Billy had invited me to testify on one of the youth nights. I thought I would check out the procedure so I went to a meeting a couple of days earlier and was thoroughly impressed by his vocal presence, but when he made his invitation I remember thinking that surely no one would go forward as there had been no emotional stress or pressure . . . if I had been a nonbeliever I would have been impressed by the man but not necessarily moved enough to go forward. To my amazement, hundreds—in fact, I believe it was 3,000 that night—went forward. I mention this first contact because the meeting so obviously proved that the Holy Spirit was using Billy and his words. I consider my sudden understanding of that fact to be part of my own growth, in realising that it is pointless to try and assess a preacher's 'worth,' because when the Holy Spirit is present unaccountable things happen.

"When I met Billy I was rather awed by his physical size, but more by the feeling that one was meeting a man used by God over and over again. Over the years I have been fortunate enough to have met him many times and each occasion is like the first.

"Billy is rather unique because he doesn't just appeal (if that's the

---

[1] In a letter to the author dated 10 March 1975.

right word) to an older generation. *Spre-e '73* showed that young people respect and respond to him, and for me it was one of the finest things Billy had done. I had never before seen him in the role of teacher and yet there he was with that young crowd hanging on his every word. If a man teaches and preaches Jesus, he will always have a huge and attentive audience. Billy does just that!"

Many young continentals crossed the English Channel to *Spre-e,* such as the eighty-three Italians whose leader told Billy they returned "bubbling with what God had done in and through them during the week." They now wanted such an evangelistic congress of their own. Billy, with Dave Foster, whose ministry lay in Europe, Walter Smyth and others, had shared a vision "to learn from our mistakes . . . set it up on a truly international scale at a Continental location. . . . It could affect all Europe and beyond." "I think we have learned some things that may be helpful in the future," Billy wrote shortly after *Spre-e.* "We may have learned that one of the keys to reaching Continental young people may be through music."

At first Graham and Smyth worked on a plan for simultaneous youth events in several countries linked by television and interpreters, with Billy visiting each in turn. But the young people demanded one center where they could learn from each other, and after careful search the Team chose Brussels, where a large exhibition center, Le Palais de Centenaire, stood next to a stadium and to an area suitable for camping and dormitories. Robert P. Evans of the Greater Europe Mission hit on the title *Eurofest,* and it was set for late July 1975.

Billy Graham and the international committee of younger British and European leaders, under Werner Burklin of Germany, were alike determined that *Eurofest*'s faculty should teach more deeply than *Spre-e*'s, and it owed more to the courses worked out at a Minneapolis event, *Yes '73.* The preparations, however, hit the great inflation that followed the oil embargo. Despite the heavily subsidized low charge, the ingenuity of delegates in travelling across Europe, and the simplicity of camp and dormitory, the cost kept many away.

Administrative problems might have throttled the entire enterprise had not the American ambassador given a dinner party for twenty in Billy Graham's honor in December 1974, including the late Louis Camu, president of the Banque de Bruxelles, a devout Roman Catholic who owned the Isle of Patmos where St. John wrote the last book of the Bible. Walter Smyth found himself in spiritual discussion with Camu, who begged another guest to wait, telling her "We are talking about God," and commented to Smyth, "You don't usually get that opportunity nowadays!"

Camu begged Smyth to call if in difficulty, and when, early in 1975, *Eurofest* preparations were hamstrung by the three-week delay in transferring funds from America and other countries, he took Camu at his word. The banker summoned two senior executives and within fifteen minutes foreign funds were designated as available within the hour.

The significance of those nine days at Brussels in the hot summer of 1975 will not be fully known until the passing of the years can demonstrate *Eurofest*'s influence on the next generation of Christian leaders. Numbers were lower than expected, yet the 8,750 young men and women from thirty-nine countries, speaking seventeen languages, were more than enough for the simple facilities and, in fact, placed immense strain on several heads of departments.

Many expected a kind of Christian pop festival. They found instead, amid all the music, that the plenary Bible sessions (taught by Bishop Festo Kivengere from Africa and Luis Palau from South America), the large seminars in the main languages, and the small discussion groups all required study. The practical training in evangelism and the emphasis on social responsibility required action. The Bible sessions, deeper and more theological than at *Spre-e*, revealed great openness to learn and to ask questions. Bishop Festo Kivengere found it remarkable "to see so many young people seriously reading, listening and learning the Bible. . . . The center of *Eurofest* was the living word of Christ." Once the audience remained so absorbed in Bishop Festo's exposition, and the bishop so absorbed in his theme, that he ran far beyond his time. Finally the program director, Richard Bewes from England, in despair at being unable to attract his attention, slithered unseen behind the bank of flowers and shook the episcopal foot. The bishop stopped in mid-sentence.

Billy Graham and his Team did not obtrude. He visited the training sessions—where Richard Bewes observed the extraordinary impact of his presence on the young, most of whom had not heard him before —but he did not want *Eurofest* to seem American-dominated. Moreover, he was in the thick of a crusade to Brussels. *Spre-e* had showed confusion about the role of Billy Graham's sermons: were they extensions of the teaching or were they a crusade to London? In the absence of counselors, he had given no invitation, unaware that all 12,000 *Spre-e* delegates stood ready to counsel. At Brussels the Team had organized separately the proclamation of the gospel to the people of Belgium; at *Eurofest* it was an intrinsic part. To avoid the excessive length of the London meetings, which had blunted the evangelistic thrust, the young people held their musical program after the stadium service. The large numbers heartened the small evangelical minority in Brussels and many came to fresh understanding of the Christian faith.

Eurofest led to a wave of young people's Bible conferences in Europe. And *Spre-e,* by way of *Eurofest,* led directly to *Christival '76* over Whitsuntide (Pentecost) at Essen, where all delegates were German-speaking (except a small English-language section listening by headsets), and under twenty-five. "The language was different but the atmosphere was the same," writes an English observer who had attended the previous events. "There was no mistaking the spirit of friendship and the aura of joy and love." Dormitories, large-scale meals, high caliber music, and a distinguished international faculty recalled *Eurofest.* Billy Graham's part was to conduct a press conference. In reply to one question, "Has not the day of mass evangelism passed?" he observed, "They have said that ever since the apostle Peter preached at Pentecost."

On that sunny Pentecost morning Billy Graham preached at the 35,000-seat Grugastadion, with every seat and all the space around the back filled with young and old to hear and respond to a powerful sermon on the first day of Pentecost.

That summer, back in America, the Team held another important youth event, *Code* (Congress on Discipleship and Evangelism) in conjunction with the San Diego crusade in August. *Code* grew out of the vision of Ken Overstreet, Youth for Christ's executive director in San Diego, who had seen what *Yes '73* and *Eurofest* could mean to youth. More than 2,000 registered from American colleges and high schools, accepting strong demands for Bible study, for commitment and discipleship, with a determination and sacrifice that delighted Billy Graham.

He was delighted, too, by the response of the young at crusades everywhere. He could see on all sides, and especially in America, "a definite swing in the new generation toward Jesus Christ as a person. It is the young people who are coming to crusades. I am sure that my ministry would have diminished years ago had it not been for the tremendous interest among young people."

Graham prefers to hold his crusades in university stadiums, if large enough and well placed geographically. "If I go to a university just for students," he comments, "we have 2,000 or 3,000 out at each of the lectures. If I go and hold a crusade in their football stadium, with the local people attending, there will be many thousands of students. They do not seem to be so conspicuous. They are there to listen to the gospel and have far more of an inclination and a much better climate in responding to the appeal." Statistics disclose that young people usually form the largest sector of inquirers to be followed up—sometimes as high as 70 percent of the recorded decisions. That may stem partly from the enthusiastic youth preparations, forming almost a crusade within a crusade. Young people are trained to reach those whom others might not reach, are encouraged to take part in all the preparation programs of the churches and to work directly themselves in colleges and high schools.

A 1975 incident from Lubbock, Texas, shows the spirit. A senior girl from Esther Carter High School called the office when school resumed a few weeks before opening night and told of plans for a prayer group. She asked for someone "to share a few verses with us and help us to pray for our school; we want to reach it by the crusade." The time would be 7:30 A.M. Franklin Graham, Billy's elder son, volunteered to be there and arrived on campus looking for the handful he expected to have arrived at that hour to pray. He found instead about a hundred students waiting for him. Later that week he returned at noon with the crusade youth director, Lowell Jackson, and they went into the Spanish-style courtyard. On one side stood a crowded cafeteria, on the others the empty classrooms. "About every ten minutes," records Jackson, "about a dozen high school students would come out into the courtyard, meet, have prayer and then leave. We would wait a few minutes and about a dozen more would come and have prayer, in full visibility of the other students. Soon I discerned what was happening. They were cutting their lunch hour short and slipping out of the lunch room for prayer that the Lord would use the crusade to help reach their school for Christ."

"Don't ever stop, Mr. Graham," a girl of seventeen wrote, "because you're one of the few people teen-agers and college kids listen to, and they need salvation as much as everyone else."

21 The Rain Campaign

AFTER Eurofest Billy Graham undertook a ministry among the Chinese. During October and November 1975 he held two five-day crusades, first in Taipei, capital of Taiwan, Republic of China; then in Hong Kong, the British crown colony. Both were extraordinary experiences.

The eleven-month preparation period in Taiwan was difficult because of the cultural, political and religious setting. This large island has beautiful mountains, lush plains, growing cities, and an expanding, vigorous economy. In the mountains, the indigenous animists and former headhunters had become Christians in large numbers during the later years of Japanese rule, despite persecution from police and military. In the plains and cities, the Taiwanese, who form the bulk of the island's population, are descended from Chinese settlers who crossed the Formosa Straits hundreds of years ago. Now they are predominantly Buddhists, following either the Confucian or the Taoist way, mixed with animist folk religion. A small Christian church had emerged from the labors of western Presbyterian missionaries.

Until the Communist victory on the mainland in 1949 Taiwanese Protestants were usually Presbyterian. Afterward their community reflected the denominational loyalties and differences of all China, although Presbyterians remained the largest segment. Disunity was a reproach in the eyes of non-Christians, who therefore were impressed to see them working together with increasing enthusiasm to prepare for a Billy Graham crusade.

Politics, however, cast their shadow. The islanders were not wholly reconciled to the dominant influence of the "mainlanders," the Chinese who had flocked in after President Chiang Kai-shek lost continental China to the Communists. The mainlanders, on the other hand, saw Taiwan as "the island province" of the Republic of China, and looked to the day when the Nationalist government would return to the mainland in triumph. Meanwhile they had led the Taiwanese in impressive progress toward an industrialized modern state. The Taiwanese preferred total independence, resenting the downgrading of their Taiwanese dialect in favor of Mandarin.

For political and religious reasons such as those, which the Billy Graham Team failed to disentangle, the Presbyterian church felt bypassed. The crusade executive elected as their chairman a venerable Taiwanese Presbyterian minister, wholly committed to the crusade but identified more with the mainlanders. Because the Presbyterian church would have preferred its moderator in the chair, they did not enter at once into the preparations with the full energy which they gave, too late, when they realized that the crusade presented the Christian church in Taiwan with its greatest opportunity.

Henry Holley held the hard assignment of directing the Hong Kong and Taipei preparations simultaneously. An enterprise so highly planned went at times against the Chinese grain, and whenever he went to Hong Kong the Taipei committee tended to put aside urgent decisions. Nor did they disturb his peace of mind by disclosing a sudden crisis that arose when the government withdrew their promise of Taipei's largest open-air stadium. Ostensibly it was needed for the national games, but really, so public opinion asserted, cabinet ministers had heeded whispers that Graham was soft on Communism—or wished to prevent a demonstration of Christian strength.

Holley first learned that the crusade would move to a smaller indoor arena when he read in a newspaper that the National Council of Churches in America, which usually tended to criticize Graham, had denounced the cabinet decision as an affront to the religious freedom of the people of Taiwan. Holley immediately told the crusade committee that Graham might wish to reconsider whether he was welcome. Negotiations were reopened with officials, without avail. Finally Holley wrote to the honorary chairman of the crusade, Madame Chiang Kai-shek, known the world over as a Christian. He delivered the letter at

11:30 A.M. At 1 P.M. the telephone rang: the prime minister's office had altered the date of the national games and now placed the city stadium unreservedly at the crusade's disposal, with profuse assurances of welcome to Billy. Henceforth the government showed every consideration.

Six months before the crusade President Chiang Kai-shek died. The whole nation plunged into mourning. All watched on television the Christian funeral, heard the hymns of faith and listened to the sermon preached by his chaplain, Dr. Chow, a Baptist. The president's last will and testament emphasized that he had long been a disciple of Jesus Christ. The Bible and Christian books were placed in the casket. His resting place in the hills became a point of pilgrimage, its cross of fresh flowers placed against the marble in which he lay. People therefore inquired as never before, Who is Jesus Christ? Churches woke to the coming crusade as a providential opportunity to reap where the president had sown.

The funeral of Chiang Kai-shek was a message to the preacher, too. Dr. Chow Lien-hwa now saw the Taiwan field white and ready for harvest. "Before that time I was never too much for mass evangelism, but afterward I thought it was the answer for the longing of the people." Dr. Chow began to plan to preach at mass meetings, and accepted when he was invited to serve as Billy Graham's interpreter. "If I had not changed my views I would not have agreed to interpret."

A brilliant publicity campaign led by Lee Shih-feng, head of the Broadcasting Corporation of China, and whose father had been a China Inland Mission pastor, stoked the widespread curiosity about Christ. By television and radio, street signs and newspaper advertisements, the coming crusade reached the public throughout Taiwan as had no previous Christian endeavor. It stirred those who had lost touch with Christianity since childhood. It created among thousands of non-Christians a willingness to go to the stadium on their own or when invited by church members.

The crusade, however, met a financial barrier. The feeling that Christians formed a poor minority unable to underwrite a costly campaign had discouraged potential treasurers. Man after man refused. Then Henry-Go Wu, the devoted executive secretary, a descendant of the first convert of the pioneer missionary to northern Taiwan, approached E. Tsun Huang, who had been converted some eighteen years before. When Huang realized that many others had refused he said,

"Henry, I am only a very little person. My printing company is small. How can I take this post?" Henry-Go Wu replied, "If it is God's will, it is no matter you are small. God wants to use you and he will help you."

Huang spent many hours on his knees that night. The next morning he accepted, confident that God had prepared the money already and his job was only to collect it and serve as accountant. "I put no faith in man, only in God."

Three weeks before the opening date of the crusade, enough funds had not come in. A long committee meeting nearly cut back from five million new Taiwan dollars to three million, but Huang, Holley, Wu and others, unshaken, prevented the cutback. A mobilization corps of twenty young people traveled all over the island to stir up interest and enroll volunteers for the hundreds of necessary jobs. The financial crisis helped forward the preparations, widened the vision and strengthened the growing unity between the churches. When all was over, the budget had been exceeded by nearly half as much again, leaving a substantial surplus to put to Christian work in Taiwan.

The mobilization corps displayed the mounting enthusiasm of the volunteer workers. "They are the unsung heroes of the crusade," says Frieda Hsu of the crusade office. "Without their quiet work it could never have been successful." She comments especially on "the joy, love and concern between them," and recalls other acts of sacrifice such as that of the man who went daily into a nearby eating place and paid in advance for all their meals.

Billy Graham and his Team arrived in Taipei when expectancy and unity were dominant. The crusade plainly was the most widespread attempt at cooperation in the history of Protestantism in Taiwan. The stadium had been repainted, its entrance lights rearranged to form a huge cross. The city waited. No Christian meeting had ever drawn more than a few thousand people and here they expected 50,000.

Then came the rain. It rained during Billy's days of interviews and consultations while the national games made the stadium a sea of mud. On the day the crusade was to open, rain poured down on the foam rubber seats on the muddy grass, splashed the terraces and blew into the covered stands.

As the evening came, "Every one of us," recalls Frieda Hsu, "was praying, 'Lord, won't you stop the rain? It will hinder many, many people from coming to the crusade.' But it continued to rain. It rained heavily, and it rained lightly. I cannot describe our frustration as we saw it raining. At 7:20 I wanted to go into the arena to see how the crowd was coming but I didn't have the courage! At 7:30 it was time to start. I went in—and tears burst from my eyes. Every seat was filled! Some were standing, some were sitting with their umbrellas out. All our sorrow was gone: our hearts were filled with joy and thanksgiving."

In the speaker's room, with no view of the stadium, Billy Graham agreed with Walter Smyth that not many could be waiting in the downpour, "but if there's anybody there I'll preach!" Smyth recalls, "We left the room and walked through the mud and water and turned into the stadium and we couldn't believe our eyes! There were 40–50,000."

Every night except one, which remained threateningly overcast, the rain drenched the meetings. Variegated umbrellas lent color to the scene. People on the grass upended their foam rubber seats as the mud level rose. The next morning volunteers would wash the rubber, a long dull job. The choir (nearly 5,000, a number that wiseacres had said could never be recruited, though the stadium's size required it) sang unaccompanied—because neither organ nor piano could be kept dry until the last two days. The choir sat under umbrellas, which they closed for special numbers to avoid masking the voice behind. They stood to sing with rain splashing their bodies and music. "It didn't seem to matter at all," recalls one choir member. "Our hearts were so moved, singing with one voice the same song, in such wonderful unity, that tears rolled down our faces and we did not know which were tears and which were raindrops."

By far the largest segment of the audience was young. Billy won many hearts the first night when, after a handshow of those who had attended his previous meeting in Taipei in 1956, he asked, "And who wasn't *born* then?" Thousands of arms shot in the air.

Young people of Taiwan, *of* but not *bound* to Confucian and Buddhist traditions, were open to Christianity. The crusade youth committee had held a series of rallies of which the arrival of Billy Graham was a climax. The majority of the counselors who trained in the crusade school of discipleship were young. The crowds of youth found Graham's message "very much related to young people's thinking," says

Jonathan Chiu, youth chairman. "He was using words that we use," says a young tribal Christian. "Although he was a foreigner we felt very quickly he understood our situation. He was very successful in reaching us." Not surprisingly the great majority of those who swarmed forward through the mud at the invitation were under thirty.[1] The numbers of inquirers so swamped the counseling arrangements that Christians were grateful for the rain keeping away the idly curious or frivolous. In good weather the indoor arena prepared for an overflow would have been used, and the counseling might have lapsed into chaos.

For the Grahams the "rain campaign" was full of memorable incidents. Billy met with Wei Lin Tako, an ancient tribal evangelist and one of the first of the Teroka tribe to become a Christian. Here was a man who had been shut up in a cage by the Japanese in an attempt to stop his preaching. He had come to the crusade and the school of evangelism with a group of ministers, who then returned to the mountains with the fires of faith stoked higher. When introduced, this frail old man gripped Billy's hand tightly, thanking him in broken English for coming to Taiwan and then praying for him on the spot. Both were deeply moved.

Ruth Graham, with her background of childhood and youth in North China, felt she was home. She went to the Sun Yat-sen Memorial Auditorium to address 3,000 women; experienced missionaries and Chinese had said that few women would go to a morning meeting, but the hall was too small for all those who came to hear her. "I'll never forget Ruth trembling before she addressed the women's rally," says William A. Ury of Taipei International Church, "and hearing her ask for prayer. There was no 'professionalism' here but downright need."

Toward the end of the week, carpings and hesitations were forgotten as all churches swung together, saw the hand of God at work and seized the opportunity. James Hudson Taylor, descendant of inland China's pioneer Christian missionary, was one who worked without stint throughout the preparations. "You Christians have done something that no one can ignore: you have never had such a breakthrough into public consciousness." So spoke a leading man in the media to Taylor. Missionaries and pastors from upcountry, often working in

---

[1] Of the 11,619 who came forward, more than 7,000 were between ages 16 and 29. If those between ages 13 and 16 are included, the figure rises to nearly 10,000.

isolation and discouragement, were overwhelmed at seeing thousands singing, listening intently, responding, in the rain.

On the last Sunday afternoon, 2 November, Prime Minister Chiang Ching-kuo, son of Chiang Kai-shek and himself afterward president, refused the use of an umbrella although rain swept into the covered stand and onto the pulpit. Though soaked, he listened throughout a meeting that lasted nearly two hours and culminated in thousands using the soaked foam-rubber cushions as stepping stones. In Walter Smyth's words, "They were literally slipping and sliding in water and mud to come forward to receive Christ."

Of the immediate impact of the Taipei crusade there could be no doubt, especially as government and other officials gave Christianity and the church a deeper respect. Missionaries were moved profoundly. Those who had spent lean years encouraging an indigenous church saw Chinese leaders throwing off fears and hesitations.

In the longer term, Taipei turned into a classic endorsement of a truth at the heart of any Billy Graham crusade: churches that prepare early and fully, and commit themselves to the follow-up, will reap its harvest; those that are slow to grasp their opportunity, or are idle in consolidating, will be disappointed. The follow-up in Taipei was complicated by the chairman's leaving immediately for America (though James Hudson Taylor stepped into the gap) and by the political and cultural tangle peculiar to Taiwan. However much Graham might seek to be nonpolitical and to be an evangelist to all sections of the land, some Taiwanese felt that the crusade had been exploited by mainlanders. Unconsciously Billy Graham brought those problems of national unity into the open, as issues for the churches to face in love.

There were Chinese churchmen, especially among the Presbyterians, who wondered after three months where the 12,000 inquirers had gone. On the other hand a particular follow-up, at Taipei Covenant church, illustrates the difficulties and the joys. That church received twenty-four names. Several could not be traced. In some parts of the world the Billy Graham Team have noticed that a proportion of inquirers will sign fictitious names or give false addresses, since fear of being listed or traced runs deep. Many of these emerge to join a church, although they missed direct follow-up. Others sign twice or more on successive nights.

The young Covenant pastor, Paul Wai, had a clear objective: to see all inquirers become full disciples of Christ. He and his helpers telephoned, visited, enrolled them in a New Believers course which met for one hour on four successive Sundays before worship. Twelve of the twenty-four completed the course, were baptized and joined the church; several of these soon became trainers of others, teaching Bible studies which they had begun as students. Four moved to other locations. One, a seaman, planned to become a pastor. The other seven met together exactly two years after the crusade to describe their experiences.

A businessman named Ruan and his wife, formerly Buddhists, went to the crusade at the suggestion of a teacher at the Christian school she had attended as a child. "I was deeply moved," says Ruan, "to see so many people seeking after the Lord." He had also attended a Christian school, but had remained a Buddhist. "The impression I had of preaching evangelists was that they would say at once, 'You are a sinner'; it turned me off. The beautiful thing about Billy Graham was that instead of condemning you, he brought the truth of Jesus Christ clearly before us; and then left the decision for us to make. Thus I felt an urge, a strong sense of being drawn to go forward." His wife joined him, having already determined to become a Christian believer. They were called on by a member of the church and completed the fifteen hours of the full course. Ruan became a church officer and gave up business to be a teacher. His wife intends to devote all her time to the church when their family is grown.

Mrs. Chen, twenty-nine years old, was an active Buddhist, frequently in the temple to burn joss sticks and to throw down the little wooden blocks to see if they turned up in the way denoting an answered prayer. Her husband, a businessman who was often abroad, had become a Christian, but she refused his invitation to go to the crusade's first night. On the second she forced herself to go to please him. "What impressed me most was the huge crowd sitting in the rain. I sat there silently listening, and after the preaching, during the prayer, my heart became quiet; during the prayer I began to come to Jesus Christ. The third night there was no question, I volunteered to go." She went forward, "and after the crusade a real peace and joy came into my heart." In their letters, wherever he travels on business, "We constantly refer to the presence and joy of the Lord."

Miss Fang came from a Christian home but had no personal faith until she went to the crusade with two office colleagues. All three were much moved to be among the crowd listening in the rain as Billy spoke on the words of Jesus, "I am the way, the truth and the life." She heard that he knocked at the door of her heart and she opened it, as did one of her friends. They brought the other one to church from time to time, and in a service at the end of the year she too believed.

Miss Tsai was a Christian in heart, not in action. "The Billy Graham crusade gave me the opportunity to understand Jesus Christ in a new way. However, it was the follow-up which helped me" and led to her baptism.

Mr. Liang, then a boy of sixteen with strongly Christian parents, had no purpose or discipline until the crusade. He heard Billy say, "Jesus is a Friend, he wants to help you," and the follow-up confirmed Liang's decision. He became an active Christian.

While Taipei's records show hundreds of similar personal stories, the crusade's overall effect spread as years went on. The Christian faith became better known. The church lost its fear of bigness. The crusade heralded a new era of mass meetings and smaller campaigns for evangelism and teaching.

Perhaps the most vital single result was the influence on Dr. Chow, Billy Graham's interpreter, who said, "Working with Dr. Graham and his Team gave me firsthand knowledge of how a good evangelistic campaign should be done. This gave me a great deal of help. As I watched the people respond I knew that if we present the gospel message, people will respond anywhere." With this new assurance Dr. Chow went on to become the foremost evangelist in Taiwan, traveling from city to city. The Taiwanese say his campaigns are, in proportion, more successful than Billy Graham's was. If a national achieves more than a foreigner, that is a result for which Billy Graham works.

After some days of rest in Taipei, where the Grahams had close personal friends, they flew to Hong Kong. There, after crossing the harbor in a junk, they were greeted at a charming ceremony by the crusade committee, a choir and the Anglican bishop of Hong Kong.

The churches had worked hard and long to turn the five-day event in Hong Kong into a true people's crusade. Many difficulties had been surmounted. The colonial government was reluctant to allow use of the two stadiums, side by side, claiming that not even one could be filled. Officials feared disorder. They feared traffic chaos, especially on the night of the Royal Hong Kong Jockey Club races, since the race course uses the same road in that overcrowded island. A high-level meeting chaired by the colonial secretary himself ended in the Jockey Club's graciously changing its date.

In the event, "the police officers involved," writes the commissioner's office, "were impressed by the tremendous organizational ability of Dr. Graham's staff and the exceptional behavior of the very large crowds that attended." The bishop himself had doubted the stadiums could be filled, "but I should have remembered our Lord's reproof to those of little faith."

One important factor in the crusade's success was the interpretation into Cantonese by Daniel Tse, president of the Baptist College, a brilliant physicist. He had at first declined to be Billy's interpreter because of overwork. When asked again he was ill and "I had a perfect excuse. I say 'excuse' because deep in my heart I felt guilty for refusing to serve the Lord in such an important ministry. Then came October. I knew that the committee was still hung up on that matter, and the guilty feeling grew more intense until, one Sunday after the service, I chanced across an article written by a young girl who made a strong appeal to the Christians in Hong Kong to do their part for the crusade. The article settled my struggle. The next day I picked up the phone and called the chairman of the search committee. He had just returned from abroad, and was going to call an emergency meeting that afternoon to discuss the alternative choice of an interpreter. They were running out of waiting time! That same afternoon I surrendered myself and asked that the Lord would forgive me and use me in this great ministry." Daniel Tse prepared as thoroughly as had Billy Kim in Korea or L. H. Chow in Taiwan, and with a similar effect.

At one point Billy had a fever and Tse had a bad cold and cough, yet the stadium crowd remained unaware that either man was not at peak form. "I was very worried," recalls Tse, "because physically I wasn't in shape to do anything of that magnitude and importance. But somehow there was a spiritual uplift and strength that helped me out during the several nights we were standing in the chilly evening on the open field. I didn't cough at all during my interpretation time. But once I stepped off the platform the cough came back. . . . I really forgot myself completely. I was immersed in the whole experience. In that sense I was more an instrument than anything else, part of the channel through which the message was delivered."

The crusade is regarded by the people and government of Hong Kong as a landmark in local religious history. Only the westerners—businessmen, industrialists, officials—stood largely aloof. They gossiped that the huge numbers could be explained by a near total turnout by the Christian community under strict orders from their pastors. This view is rejected by the Christians and disproved by the hundreds of baptisms that followed in the next years. No less than 20,400 persons signed decision cards. Many of those inquirers had no previous formal link with a church; others had attended Christian worship or Christian schools.

Joyce Bennett, the first woman to be ordained priest in the Anglican communion, thirty-one years previously, and now also a member of the executive council of the colony, tells how she and her colleagues at St. Catherine's School asked all girls who had gone forward if they would stay behind after a talk on follow-up. Approximately a hundred, about a tenth of the school, waited to sign up for future classes. "The crusade was undoubtedly a lasting work," she says, "because many of the girls went on to be baptized."

It was above all a youth crusade. The strong participation by students and youth particularly impressed the Hong Kong government. An extraordinarily high proportion of the inquirers were under the age of twenty-five. "I never thought so many people would go to this kind of religious meeting," one girl recalled two years later. "When I saw the crowds inside the football stadium and the great crowd outside, hoping to get in, I felt that God really cares for everyone, his love is so great. I was not 'reached' by Billy Graham's sermon but by the atmosphere of love, salvation and hope. These stirred my heart and made me decide to accept Christ."

Another girl, a Catholic, wrote in neat Chinese characters: "I accepted Christ because of the invisible power that pushed me at that moment. When Billy Graham asked whoever was willing to accept Christ to come down to him, I prayed, 'If you are really God, make me go down.' " She went, and "after God gave me strength to accept Christ, something different happened in my life"—hope, repentance, peace and joy.

22 "I Intend to Keep On ..."

BILLY GRAHAM does not consider himself in a different category from any other minister. He has commented to the present writer: "I believe that God in his sovereignty chose me to do the work that I am doing—just as he chooses another person to do the work that he or she is doing. I believe he gave me the gift of an 'evangelist.' I do not think that my work has been any more successful than the evangelist who has labored in some faraway insignificant place unnoticed by the media. I believe God is going to judge on the basis of faithfulness. I am not sure I have been 'faithful' at all times and on every occasion, as the Lord requires me to be. I am almost afraid of the judgment seat of Christ when I see my thoughts and intents and inner life exposed.

"In this day of publicity and media exposure, people have a tendency to feel that you are 'bigger than life.' Many people put me on a pedestal, on which I do not belong. I am not the holy, righteous prophet of God that many people think I am. I share with Wesley the feeling of my own inadequacy and sinfulness constantly. I am often amazed that God can use me at all."

As the date of his sixtieth birthday, 7 November 1978, drew nearer, Billy knew he must not stop. "We have never had," he told the Team in January of that year, "such an avalanche of invitations for city-wide evangelistic crusades as we are getting right now; places we never expected to go, receptions we never expected to have." He had made his attitude plain at the Team meeting two years earlier. "I intend to keep on going, preaching the gospel, writing the gospel, as long as I have any breath. I hope my last word as I am dying—whether by a bullet wound, by cancer, a heart attack, or a stroke—I hope my dying word will be *Jesus.*"

With his ministry in full flood, any attempt at summing up, any formal assessment of Billy Graham would be quickly outdated. Charles Crutchfield of Charlotte, viewing the matter as a man of the media, could be near the mark when he writes in a personal letter: "I believe that history may very well prove him to be one of the handful of truly indispensable men in this century. Nobody, at this moment, can accurately assess his influence and the impact of his Christian message on our times, but fifty or a hundred years from now I have no doubt that historians will agree that his work and the influence he wielded were essential forces in a republic that was undergoing great social upheaval and was characterized by great doubt and uncertainty as people groped to give meaning and purpose to their lives."

History alone can judge. The perspective remains too short for discussion of developments since 1975. A selection of the more outstanding events can do no more than provide a temporary rounding-off for the story this book has told.

Billy Graham gave the main thrust of his ministry in 1976 to his own country, celebrating the bicentennial of its independence.

He took part at President Ford's side in the religious ceremonies that marked the bicentennial, stressing the Biblical truths on which the nation had been founded. On the night of Independence Day, Sunday 4 July, a coast to coast telecast showed his Festival of Faith held a few days earlier at the College of William and Mary in Colonial Williamsburg in the presence of Governor Godwin. The bishop of Norwich from England, Maurice Wood, led in prayer. The bishop had just concluded a three-week speaking tour where he had "felt the rising tide of idealism in America. It was as though the agonies of Vietnam and the humiliation of Watergate needed to be purged, put aside, and where necessary forgiven, so that the nation could renew itself under God in the beginning of its third century of freedom. Billy Graham caught that mood of the nation, both in his sermon in Washington Cathedral on the Sunday before Independence, when the great national cathedral was packed to the doors, and also at the telecast service itself. Once again, I was struck by his ability to speak to the condition of people and at the same time apply the personal challenge of the gospel, against the background of the political, economic, and social problems he touched upon.

"When Billy Graham gave the invitation to those who desired to give their lives to Christ, the first person forward was a young black boy of perhaps seventeen. The second person was a bearded white youngster of perhaps twenty; then, rather sedately, and surprisingly, a middle-aged Chinese couple; and then from all over the whole place, young and old, black and white, came quietly to the front of the platform. I noticed a black woman counselor standing beside a white woman seeking Christ. This deep sense of oneness in Christ, transcending color, culture and denomination, showed me something of the historic contribution that Billy Graham and his Team are making in their own country as well as across the world."

The first of the three full-length crusades that year also showed the spirit of the times. Seattle had the lowest ratio of church attendance to population in America and though the committee took the new Kingdome covered stadium, the Team expected to use about half the 65,000 seats the first six nights and perhaps nearly fill it on the last two. Preparations, however, revealed widespread interest in Bible study and the prayer program. Whereas in some cities 20,000 or more might begin counselor training classes but a mere 2,000 qualify, in Seattle a record 5,700 qualified. About 8,000 signed up for the choir, an unusual number for an American crusade. The Team sensed "a great spirit of expectancy—people praying, people believing God for something unusual."

The opening night in May nearly filled the stadium. That 51,000 persons should come to a religious service, even to hear Billy Graham, astonished the local newspapers into front-page banner headlines and friendly coverage. They printed Billy's addresses word for word, as at Chicago in 1962, thereby bringing the gospel to most of the population day after day.

On Friday night the doors had to be locked at 7:20 P.M. because all 65,000 seats had filled—as well as every aisle, nook and cranny and the artificial turf outside the counseling area; 77,000 people had passed the turnstiles, more than half under twenty-five. An estimated 10—

15,000 were turned away. Over 2,000 came forward each night. Walter Smyth comments, "It was a very humbling experience. The committee didn't expect it, the Team didn't expect it, but God did it. You get to the place where you realize it is out of your hands: you're not promoting something, you're not trying to get people to come. You're at desperation trying to keep up with what God is doing."

Nearly 18,000 had come forward by the close of what Sterling Huston calls "one of the most blessed and successful meetings we have experienced in North America." In the two years that followed, the Team received encouraging reports of church renewal and strength and a marked rise in the spiritual level of the Seattle region.

San Diego in August was a return, eleven years after Billy's crusade of 1965, and was notable for the Youth Congress on Discipleship and Evangelism already mentioned. The Southeastern Michigan crusade in October proved to be one of the most difficult to prepare. That heavily populated region lacked strong unity or leadership in the churches, the distances created their own problems, the only facility in downtown Detroit was too small; and both blacks and whites on the committee advised against bringing people at night to such an area of high crime. They chose instead the splendid new air-inflated stadium at Pontiac, thirty miles out, although it was not a natural center of gravity for whites or blacks.

Despite all this, the dedication and hard work of local Christians and the Team brought 25,000 the first night, rising to some 75,000 on the last night, when thousands had to walk through the rain owing to inadequate parking. Thousands more were turned away. The response at Detroit rose proportionately higher than at any previous crusade in North America. This, and the estimated two million prayer and Bible study groups, continent-wide, which had sprung up in the past ten years, helped lend substance to Billy Graham's tentative conviction that in this age of rising crime, violence and materialism, the nation might be experiencing simultaneously another Great Awakening.

As for himself, Graham privately had made the three stadium crusades of 1976 a test of whether he should turn to smaller, less demanding meetings which would be televised like the one at Colonial Williamsburg. After Detroit he told the Team, "I believe that God has overwhelmingly showed us we should go on."

During the 1976 presidential election, in which both the principal candidates were his personal friends and of avowed Christian faith, Billy Graham maintained public neutrality. This time he did not reveal his vote. He sent good wishes to both men. Jimmy Carter's acknowledgment came in his own hand during the Detroit crusade. "Thank you for your kind note. I pray that your crusade will be successful and that God will continue to use you grandly in his Kingdom's work. Your friend, *Jimmy.*" In a signed typed note after the election Carter wrote, "I deeply appreciate your support and your prayers. They are very important to me. I will do my best to deserve your confidence. Please let me continue to benefit from your advice and counsel."

Jimmy Carter, ten years earlier, had chaired a Billy Graham film crusade in his own county. Using the normal procedures suggested by the Team, they showed *The Restless Ones* for a week. The number of those who came forward, Jimmy Carter said, "encouraged me to realize that our own efforts cannot be controlled by an indifferent film which is really not of so much moment, or my own faltering efforts, but that the Holy Spirit was there and people were changed." He told a Methodist conference some years later that Graham "has had a great impression and impact on my own life." When, on 30 April 1971, Governor Carter of Georgia sent Billy Graham a personal invitation which led to the Atlanta crusade of 1973, he wrote, 'I know from personal experience the great beneficial impact of your crusades for Christ. It would be a meaningful experience for the people of Georgia if you come here to share with us your commitment to our Lord."

If a future president did not think much of an earlier Billy Graham film, the production released in 1974, *The Hiding Place*, received widespread acclaim and took Christian film making to a new level. Its remote origin lay with Ruth Graham, whom author Elizabeth Sherrill had asked for suggestions. In 1960, while summering in Switzerland with her family, Ruth had met Corrie Ten Boom. From this Dutch Christian woman, Ruth heard how, until their own arrest, she, her father, and sisters had hidden Jews from the Nazis during the German occupation. From the bestseller that followed, with its account of courage, forgiveness and the conquest of bitterness in a concentration camp, Graham's World Wide Pictures created (at Burbank, California and in Holland and England) its most ambitious film. Small gifts sent in by thousands of donors covered the million dollar cost, and hundreds of English Christians gave their services for the crowd scenes which supported the high-caliber professional cast.

The Hiding Place was the first World Wide Pictures production to be distributed commercially on any large scale as well as shown by church sponsorship. By the end of 1977 it had been viewed by ten million people. Although no major distributor in the United States dared risk it, fearing a straight religious theme however sensitively handled, England pioneered a new form of film evangelism when it was accepted by one of the big circuits.

In a schedule stretching from 1977–79, the British Isles saw the film in city and town cinemas, advertised by television and the press and introduced to clergy by previews. These sometimes led to churches buying up the entire seating for a night, in order to treat the showing as a mini crusade. Maurice Rowlandson, Graham's British associate, records that "The commercial distributors have been deeply impressed by the nature of our support for this film and have worked very warmly and closely with us In the trade press it has received excellent reviews." Many letters came from the public, such as one from a Yorkshireman: "I always knew that Christians appeared to have a superfluity of courage, but I imagined this came from a very strong sense of willpower. However, when I went to see the film *The Hiding Place*, I realized that it was not willpower but the power of the Lord Jesus Christ and I have committed my heart and life to him."

The success of *The Hiding Place* made easier the commercial acceptance of the next production, *No Longer Alone*, the story of Joan Winwill, a British actress converted at the Harringay crusade of 1954 and now wife of World Wide's president, William F. Brown. Bill Brown gathered a strong cast which included Wilfred Hyde-White as the 13th Earl of Home and Gordon de Vol as Robert Kennedy.

While his feature films brought the Christian message to millions, Graham's pen had given his ministry yet further influence by the spectacular success of his book *Angels*. Response to a radio sermon he had preached on angels had led him to discover the lack of any commonly known book on a subject of evident public interest. Thus he wrote one himself—and was as astonished as his publisher when *Angels*, though brought out in October, became 1975's number-one nonfiction hardback bestseller in America. By the end of 1976 it had sold more copies in hardback than any book in American history except the Bible. He began next to write *How To Be Born Again,* only to find before completing it that President Jimmy Carter had made the phrase a household word. Inevitably, a book on such a theme by Billy Graham also became a bestseller.

Before the publication of *Angels* Billy had given away the royalties to Wheaton College, to help its new Billy Graham center. In September 1977 he dug the first sod at the ceremonial start of its construction. The idea had been long maturing in Billy's mind to found an institution "from which others, better trained than we, may go out in an ever-widening and deepening stream of influence . . . to communicate the gospel through every means that God has placed at our command." The Billy Graham Center will educate graduates and others from anywhere in the world in subjects that may speed evangelization, strengthen the church and "manifest Christian love in humanitarian needs and social justice." Thus it will be a living memorial to the ideals and principles of the crusades, and also will house the Billy Graham archives. Its story belongs to the future.

A connected ministry, however, grew in importance throughout the 1970s. From his earliest days as an evangelist Billy Graham had found himself entrusted with money from Christians, generally given in small amounts, and he set the highest standards in handling it. "There are many people," he remarked once to a Team meeting, "who read the Bible from cover to cover and do not have integrity or holiness. We must have both." Graham, more than any man, cleansed American evangelism of "Elmer Gantry." Hence he received also many bequests, mostly devised to him personally and absolutely, and for years he had given power of attorney so that they could be put to use without requiring his intervention.

From birth the BGEA took a line unusual in Christian organizations, in not using every penny for its own expanding ministries but giving to other causes devoted to the glory of God. In early days Billy might be theologically unsure of the balance between evangelism and social action, like most evangelicals then, though George Cornell, from the vantage point of his Association Press news desk, holds that the evangelicals' new breadth and awareness concerning a more just society, "is greatly due to Graham's influence." Billy never passed by on the other side. "In all the years I have known Bill," Ruth says, "I have never once seen him presented with a genuine need without doing something about it, either personally or by putting the need in contact with the right source of supply. Then he promptly forgets what he has done."

In 1970, to coordinate and increase that aspect of his ministry Billy Graham founded a trust, later named the World Evangelism and Christian Education Fund, based in Dallas, Texas, separate from BGEA and controlled by businessmen and bankers. It was soon fully stretched by scholarships, grants for theological education in many countries, special needs of missionary organizations; and in helping to finance congresses of evangelism and the building of the Billy Graham Center. The Fund was public from the start, registered with the Internal Revenue Service, its audited reports deposited.

In the summer of 1977 two young *Charlotte Observer* reporters, searching for any matter to Graham's discredit, discovered that through a nominee from Texas he had bought some land near his home (for the site of a future Laymen's Institute; public announcement would raise the price of nearby acreage still to be bought) and this led them to the Fund. In the spirit of America's new investigative journalism they dubbed it a Secret Fund, with the implication that Graham had something to hide. The story rang around the world, some foreign papers insinuating that Graham had salted away for a sinister or selfish purpose the sacrificial gifts of thousands.

No strength is stronger than clear conscience and rockfast integrity. Graham at once went on the offensive with a press conference and an Hour of Decision broadcast, until the facts became self-evident and the *Observer*'s charge collapsed. At the next crusade, Cincinnati, Graham departed from his usual practice and made a spirited defense of his requests for money: he needed far more for the task and was not in the least ashamed to ask. The crusade audience applauded loudly and gave more per person than was usual.

Graham announced that in the future the reports of BGEA would be published, although the law did not require it.

Future historians may well rank Billy Graham's Fund as a prime influence not only on evangelism but on theology. Just as Graham, not himself an academic theologian, has influenced theology throughout the earth by proving, on a scale that no one can ignore, the basic beliefs that secular humanism seeks to devalue, so by his practical encouragement of evangelical scholarship and training he has helped to raise a new generation of thinkers and leaders.

Meanwhile his operations as a channel of philanthropy were becoming known through his relief projects after natural disasters. At the Minneapolis crusade in 1973 he had raised a fund to help relieve a famine in Africa. Early in 1976 he was on vacation in Mexico, writing *How To Be Born Again,* when an earthquake hit Guatemala. He went at once to see for himself and announced substantial aid. In 1977 when a cyclone and tidal wave hit South India, shortly before his rallies in several cities, he flew over the disaster area and increased the gift he had already announced.

The fund did not finance the Graham evangelistic ministries; these depended on the flow of gifts, still mostly small, for the purpose. Rather, all along it forwarded evangelism and met social and educational needs. A colorful example is CHIEF (Christian Hope Indian Eskimo Fellowship) which arose out of the Phoenix crusade (1974) where the American Indian evangelist Tom Claus, of the Turtle Tribe of the Sixth Nation, had brought chiefs of fifteen different tribes to the platform, including one woman chief. They presented Billy Graham with a chief's headdress and honored him with an Indian name, *Natani* ("Warrior of the Great Spirit"). Hundreds of Indians came forward that night.

At Lausanne two months later Claus responded to a strongly felt call to bring together leaders from all the different Native American groups. He put a plan to Billy, who promised a launching sum, with continuing support. The Indians launched CHIEF at a conference held at Albuquerque during the crusade the following March, where Graham told them of his desire to help educate Indian youth to serve their own people in evangelism and social action.

In December 1976 Billy Graham went to Nairobi, Kenya, for the Pan African Christian Leadership Assembly (PACLA), the most representative gathering of Christians ever held on that continent. Before Lausanne this had been "prayed for as a dream, a wonderful thought." The phrase is Bishop Festo Kivengere's. He and Michael Cassidy and others were sharply aware of Africa's problems despite the rapid expansion of Christianity in the past twenty years. They believed that if leaders from every land could discover their ties of brotherhood and share their plans, evangelization would accelerate.

Lausanne, by the contacts made and by the new spirit, brought that dream into reality by the hard work of Africans, black and white. DCEA's part was limited to a "characteristically generous" (Cassidy's phrase) donation to expenses.

Graham, one of the few non-Africans invited, set the tone. "Let us be clearly conscious of the fact that only the Word of God can bring true peace and true liberty to hearts and nations. Only the Word of God, preached by the power of God, can bring the love of God and unselfish brotherhood to individuals and communities." Michael Cassidy described the address as "pure Billy, with a very strong affirmation of the Bible's authority and the necessity for this to be appreciated by a leader. I was struck after the meeting by the extraordinary desire of so many of the African delegates simply to meet him and shake his hand. And of course, in spite of all the staff trying to whisk him out of the conference hall, he was enormously patient and gracious in giving time to those who wanted to chat with him."

Halfway through the conference Kenya's independence day brought an opportunity for a public evangelistic rally. At that time Nairobi's Uhuru Park, which slopes down from the Anglican cathedral toward the city center, became a dense mass of Africans from throughout the country. One observer estimated the crowd to be merely average for a Billy Graham rally "but by anyone else's standards it would have been a prodigious meeting." Billy was told that it was probably the largest crowd of black Africans to hear the gospel in the history of the missionary movement. It was broadcast live on radio and televised by videotape the following Sunday, President Jomo Kenyatta himself being a viewer.

During the conference Graham and Walter Smyth discussed with Archbishop Luwum of Uganda his hope that Billy could hold a crusade in Kampala later that year to celebrate the centenary of Christianity's coming. A few weeks later the archbishop was martyred, Festo Kivengere was an exile, and in other parts of Africa (such as the Horn) many delegates and their churches were under pressure or persecution—but were strengthened by the invisible brotherhood which PACLA had openly expressed.

Back in America immediately after Christmas 1976 Graham joined more than 17,000 students at Inter-Varsity Christian Fellowship's missionary conference at Urbana, Illinois. When the organizers had invited him to give the mid-conference address, "Responding to God's glory," which would be the only one to close with an invitation to commitment, Billy had replied, "I am not at all sure that I am God's man for the job, but I will come on my knees." In the intervening months he had written or called Director David Howard for advice and prayer more than had any other of the fifteen intended speakers. Howard "sensed a real apprehension as he seemed to question his ability to communicate any longer to the present student generation." Ruth, too, noticed Billy's apprehension.

On the third day of Urbana, 29 December 1976, he was scheduled for a question hour. The students greeted him with great warmth and repeated applause. "The concise, clear tone of his answers," writes David Howard, "and their eager reception was indicative of God's hand upon him. I said later, 'I hope, Billy, you are now disabused of your feeling that you can no longer communicate with students.' He chuckled in a noncommittal way."

Two evenings later Billy spelled out the cost of discipleship in an address of strong conviction with absence of emotion. At the close he gave two invitations: first for those to stand who wished to receive Christ as Savior. Although this was a conference of students with missionary concern, about 500 stood. He made the second invitation very difficult, explaining that he did not wish people to stand unless willing to commit themselves "totally" for whatever God's call to them might be. It was to be a deliberate personal transaction with God. Billy gave that invitation briefly and without pressure.

At once the vast auditorium of the University of Illinois seemed to vibrate with a quiet shuffling. Thousands of students stood. Some of the press put the figure as high as 15,000, and all the evidence that reached Howard and his staff confirmed that decisions were intellectual and determined, not emotional and heedless.

Such a response amazed Billy—and supported his growing belief about America's new Great Awakening. He himself had remained on his feet, though not simply as the speaker in charge. He admitted publicly the next day to the students that "I was standing because God was dealing with me on some personal issues. Several times I have gone back to my room this week and wept before the Lord as he has spoken to me about areas of my life."

The night after his address Billy was seized with sharp pains in a leg. The next morning doctors summoned a specialist, but T. W. Wilson had difficulty persuading Billy to leave the platform as he listened intently to John Stott. The specialist diagnosed a serious attack of thrombophlebitis, summoned an ambulance and flew him at once to the Mayo Clinic. There, Billy was touched to receive personal telephone calls from three presidents of the United States in one day: the incumbent President Ford, President-elect Carter, and former President Nixon. In less than two weeks Billy was due at Gothenburg, Sweden, for his first full campaign in Scandinavia . . .

23 "...And On"

"**I** WOULD have cancelled Sweden—the doctors didn't want me to go—but I felt I could trust the Lord and I went; and I think that God greatly honored it because the people of Sweden were not even conscious of the crusade very much until I got sick. . . . And I would say that the crusade made as great an impact on Sweden as Harringay did on Britain 23 years ago."

Billy returned from Gothenburg in January 1977 deeply moved. Swedish ministers and laypeople had seen their traditionally cool and unemotional countrymen experience a touch of revival. Sweden had been somewhat hostile to Graham for years, being rather anti-American. In 1975 before preaching at the Baptist World Alliance public rally in Stockholm Billy had confronted one of the most difficult press conferences of his career, more difficult even than London's before Harringay. But, as in London, his answers wrought a total reversal, and from that hour the Swedish media became his friends.

Gothenburg, city of Volvo cars, and its neighboring southwest coast were known as the most religious region of a nation where ninety percent of the population are members of the Church of Sweden, yet few worship. It was the small vigorous assortment of Free Churches that mounted the Billy Graham campaign ("crusade" is a disliked term) and, though the bishop of Gothenburg showed personal friendliness, few of his Lutherans joined the preparations early. Larry Turner, the Team's director, had hard ground to till.

Billy had accepted the invitation in April, and from May to September most citizens disappear to the seaside and mountains, driving in to work. Church life slips into somnolence. That left the committee a bare four months. Different churches discovered each other's qualities, their members took up Operation Andrew (15,000 people, at least, asked one or more friends), skilled volunteers built the special platform in the city's new ice hockey arena, the Scandinavium, and the youth put on an immense procession to publicize the campaign.

Billy limited his engagements and stayed under doctor's orders: providentially the campaign chairman, Sven Ahdrian, not only was senior pastor of a thriving Pentecostal church but was one of the city's leading physicians.

The Christians had prayed for mild weather whereas Billy rather hoped for a real Scandinavian snow scene. As it developed, the worst weather for ten years, bitter cold with deep snow and frequent snowstorms, left several hundred empty seats in the arena on the first night. The Christians hardly noticed. They were thrilled to see 12,000 packed in to hear the gospel, when no such crowd had ever gathered for that purpose in Gothenburg.

The audience did not seem too responsive. It endured the overlong greetings and moderately enjoyed the hymns. Billy preached. They listened carefully. He gave the invitation, knowing that the very idea of making a public spectacle of themselves ran counter to the Swedes' sense of propriety. Committee members and Lutheran ministers had warned him not to expect the open response he evoked in other parts of the world.

Billy carefully explained to his audience, when you married, you took your vows openly before witnesses; in the New Testament, when Jesus gave an invitation he gave it publicly, for public response.

No one moved. Billy momentarily wondered whether for the first time in his ministry none would respond. He stood calmly without another word. Then they came—not in the numbers common to America but enough to humble the committee and counselors. "I had not believed that so many would get up and give themselves to God," one younger layman recalls. "It was truly a sight to behold, the people streaming from all corners, all the way up from the balcony and down to the platform to ask for prayer."

Next night, again the snowstorms, again not quite full, again a sense of spiritual battle. Yngve Nillson, schoolmaster-pastor and campaign secretary, describes what happened. "Suddenly these cold Swedes sitting there a bit critical-looking, watching Billy Graham, suddenly their hearts are wide open! It was like a whirlwind through the arena, and after that it was just as if heaven was open to Gothenburg." A committee man recalls it as too thrilling to describe. "Brother Graham made a very simple altar call, and people started to get up. One here; a mother with her daughter over there; a father with a son. Soon hundreds were flocking around us who were on the platform." Counselors watched with tears down their cheeks. "They didn't believe it to be true, that this could happen in Sweden," recalls Roland Hellsten, their chairman. Many of those going forward were in tears, too, and counselors and inquirers stood weeping together.

The next morning about five A.M. Billy woke in his hotel room convinced that he should stay for a longer campaign, thrombophlebitis notwithstanding, if they could secure the arena. He summoned the Team to his room for prayer and about seven A.M. he called Nillson, who arranged an emergency committee meeting to follow the civic reception at noon.

An American pop star had taken the arena for a one-night concert on Monday; except for that one night the management offered the next three weeks. The pop star wanted his own special platform, and his agent refused to use the campaign's. To dismantle and rebuild was impracticable. Sadly, the emergency committee decided against buying out the pop star for 75,000 kronen. They could find the money but to extinguish an eagerly awaited pop concert would antagonize Gothenburg.

On Friday and the remaining nights the bishop of Gothenburg sat on the platform. Cautious Church of Sweden ministers now urged their people to attend and take friends. The bishop himself said that if Billy came again the church's admiration for the spiritual preparation and the campaign itself would insure full support.

On Saturday some 2,000 people were still lined up when every seat had filled. The cold prevented outside amplification as in Rio, so all who waited received a reserved ticket for Sunday. The whole city was stirred. An English radio journalist recalls "a real sense of something spontaneous; it was not organized. The Swedes began to see that God was really at work. There was a revival atmosphere, more so than I have experienced anywhere else in Billy Graham's crusades."

The campaign had brought the spiritual hunger into the open. "I had been seeking God since I was little," recalls a young nursemaid who had come after reading newspaper advertisements. "The message was easy to understand, and when the invitation was given I started to cry. When I stood in front with all the others, I felt the presence of God. . . . I have always felt alone, but now I know I need not feel that way anymore. I have received a Friend who will never leave me." "I have always had a longing to come into contact with God," says a beauty shop owner, thirty-two years old, whose boyfriend had Christian ideals. She went forward. "When I stood up there I didn't experience any heavenly emotional feelings, rather simply that now I have made a decision. I wanted to make it definite. I didn't want to remain seated, surrounded by pious thoughts about myself; rather, I wanted to be submissive to God's will and to be a messenger to tell of this beauty which I had experienced."

A husband and wife in their thirties, neither from religious homes but recently in touch with Christian neighbors, listened to Billy. Kenneth "found his preaching challenging. It made me think a good deal. When the invitation came, my first thought was 'No, I could never step forward in front of all these people.' But I couldn't resist, I had to go." Inge-Marie felt the call to go forward but remained seated. "I fought against going forward. Afterward we left with good friends. They asked if they could pray with and for me, but I resisted. We went home and to bed, but then I felt I couldn't let another second pass before I accepted Jesus. We prayed and cried out to God. On Saturday we drove to the campaign again so that I consciously could go forward and seal my decision to follow Jesus."

That was happening everywhere, and then it was all over. After five nights, just as the campaign was taking off, it stopped. London's Harringay crusade of 1954 had been extended and extended again until it lasted nearly three months and touched all England. Billy believed that Gothenburg, though brief, made a similar impact on Sweden.

So it has proved, if not quite in the way first expected. In some churches the campaign brought great accessions of strength (one pastor eight months later counted 250 newly active, whether without previous church links, or hitherto idle) but the total of listed inquirers did not reflect the true number because Sweden had lately known a political campaign against computerizing the population. Hundreds refused to give their names and addresses, yet pastors continually meet people who ask to join a church because of what they first heard from Billy Graham, whether or not they went forward. Many other inquirers were not followed up because churches had spurned or skimped the preparation.

What counted was the change of atmosphere. In schools and the university, where many students had been antagonistic to religion, Christian workers now note a new openness. Clergy find a willingness to listen, to talk about religion, a new respect for the faith.

Gothenburg was a beginning. Like Harringay it opened a nation and led straight to the Stockholm campaign scheduled for September 1978, with fifteen closed-circuit television relays in Sweden (Gothenburg had only one, to Stockholm) and Norway. That was a thorough reversal from 1970 when Swedish television had refused to allow them from Dortmund.

Graham's domestic crusades in 1977 were at Asheville, South Bend and Cincinnati.

The Western Carolina crusade at Asheville near his home originated with an approach by twenty-five black ministers, appreciative of their neighbor's work for evangelism and for race relations. Graham promised to come, provided the committee would represent both black and white communities. Several years passed, however, before Asheville completed its convention facilities, including a new civic auditorium, to offer a suitable location. Even with four overflow halls connected by closed circuit TV the crusade had to be small in comparison with those in stadiums of great metropolitan centers, but Graham took special delight in preaching among his own people—and they in him. That happiness could be felt by the millions who saw the crusade later on television. One of the overflow halls at Asheville was St. Laurence Roman Catholic church. The parish priest opened its every corner and said, "You can put them on the chandeliers if you want to!"

Roman Catholic territory provided the site for Billy's next crusade at South Bend, held on the campus of Notre Dame. Christians of the small industrial cities of southwestern Michigan, northeastern Illinois and northern Indiana had been praying for nineteen years that Graham would come. A factor in his acceptance undoubtedly was the opportunity to preach at a Catholic university, but also the excellent facilities formed in effect the region's civic auditorium. The Roman church showed a warm neutrality which thousands of their faithful, on and off campus, interpreted by taking full part—though final examinations that week prevented a large turnout of students from Notre Dame and St. Mary's. In the follow-up, eleven percent of the response gave their denomination as Catholic.

The third crusade, Cincinnati, in October 1977, had an unusual origin. Five years earlier Esther Wilmes, who had never attended a church since youth, was converted to Christ through watching a crusade telecast and listening to Billy Graham. Talking about her new faith to colleagues in the Hartman Electric Company, she discovered two other committed Christians in the office. The three banded together to pray that Graham would come to Cincinnati, one of the few important cities where he had never held a crusade. According to Billy Sunday in his day, it was the graveyard of evangelists.

Esther Wilmes began calling pastors with such persistence that the senior minister of a downtown church summoned a luncheon meeting of clergy in October 1972. Esther died of pneumonia the following February but thanks to her faith and telephone a group of pastors became sure that God was leading them toward a crusade. Their threefold vision was that a Billy Graham crusade should renew their city and region by bringing the churches together, by proclaiming Christ, and by applying the love of Christ to some of the community's hurts and ills. Billy accepted, knowing that unity grew from preparations for his proclamation of the gospel, and that a crusade usually sparked practical love within a community to help heal social ills.

Cincinnati's downtown auditorium, on the Ohio river, seated only 17,500. The nearby stadium was unavailable for a closing rally. Since the region had a much higher population than those of his previous two 1977 crusades, Billy agreed, a little reluctantly, to preach for ten days, more than his usual practice for some years past. Afterward he said, "I wish we could have stayed for a month; because when we stopped we were just getting started." Strong civic and media support, the intimate setting, the success of Operation Andrew and a consequent high ratio of inquirers without previous church connection all contributed to a growing awareness of what the crusade offered. More and more pastors and laypeople rallied to the opportunity, and the people of Cincinnati pressed in. Graham helped forward the vision that the crusade would heal local hurts by telling the audience one night that no offertory would be taken that service. All should give instead to their own church, earmarked "to help needs and hurts where you live." "I have never sensed the presence and power of God this year as I sensed it at Cincinnati," Billy told the Team at year's end.

During Cincinnati Graham made a brief dash to Atlanta between services to receive from the American Jewish Committee their first national interreligious award. In presenting it, Rabbi Tanenbaum declared that most of the progress in Protestant-Jewish relations in the past quarter century had been due to Graham, thus echoing the sentiments of the former prime minister of Israel, Mrs. Golda Meir. A long-time friend of Graham's, she spoke of him as a "great human being, an outstanding spokesman for peace and real brotherhood among men. I shall always remember his deep understanding of Israel's problems and his support for our struggle for peace for all nations in our area."[1]

Graham's reply at Atlanta stands high among the major addresses he has given down the years, with its clear statement of his personal commitment to the beliefs of the New Testament because of "meeting Jesus Christ face to face, a Jew who was born in Bethlehem and reared in Nazareth"; its opening up of problems common to Jew and Christian; and its call for a national spiritual awakening that would influence social and political life and meet the needs of the young. The Jewish audience gave him a prolonged standing ovation.

Soon after Cincinnati the Grahams left on the first leg of their tour to the Orient. The year that had begun with Scandinavia ended with the Metro Manila crusade in the Philippines and the Good News festivals in India. Any extended account must wait a longer perspective, although memories crowd in for the Grahams and the Team. Metro Manila (four cities and thirteen municipalities, with the crusade meetings broadcast live throughout the Philippines and South East Asia) had been prepared with vigor and imagination. For the first time the two main church councils of the Protestant denominations came together for an evangelistic effort, a direct result of Lausanne. Protestants

---

[1] In a letter to the author dated 4 May 1975.

are a small minority in that predominantly Roman Catholic nation. Still, the cardinal archbishop, without officially lending support, showed his warm sympathy, although he was out of the country throughout the crusade.

The president of the Philippines and his wife, Imelda Marcos, virtually placed the crusade under presidential patronage. On 23 November 1977 Mrs. Marcos addressed the first session of the school of evangelism (more than 5,000 pastors and laypeople had registered) in the fine new convention hall on Manila Bay. "We are grateful," Mrs. Marcos said, "for Dr. Graham's presence in the Philippines, for his love and eloquence, for his goodness and kindness. We are appreciative of the bountiful harvest that awaits the Filipino people this week. . . . We can never, never have enough divine leadership and its spiritual fulness. Dr. Billy Graham, Madame Ruth Graham and their crusade are here to remind us that Christ is our guardian and our sanctuary, and that amid all our worldly endeavors, it is only those who are Christ-informed and Christ-conscious who are strong."

Later President and Mrs. Marcos, following a crusade service, gave a state dinner at which the president said, "We are happy that you have come to preach to us. You come at a time when we in the Philippines are moving toward seeking a New Society, a society of compassion. But unless we have a new sense of values, that society will never be obtained. There is something joyful and good in the message of a man who comes in the freshness of the Spirit." In his reply Graham stressed the spiritual foundations of the Christian state. To speak again after preaching at a crusade was an unusual burden, though lightened because English is the official language. The dinner ended long after midnight, yet by eight A.M. the next day both president and evangelist, and a somewhat sleepy Team, sat at the presidential prayer breakfast which both addressed.

The crusade took place in the open air at Rizal or Luneta Park, centered on the grandstand at the seaward end, far enough from the roar of Manila's traffic. In theory two million people could gather in the park, which stretches deep into the city's heart, and Henry Holley, the director, longed a little bit to see Korea out-millioned. In fact some 150,000 came to the last service on Sunday afternoon, a happy, attentive crowd.

The Filipinos and missionaries had trained their counselors to work unhurriedly. Most spent twenty or thirty minutes with each inquirer, sometimes up to an hour. On Sunday, response was so great that each counselor needed to handle several inquirers, some sitting in a circle, others individually, without stint of time. Inquirers lined up with patience, a proof of their genuine spirit of commitment. When darkness fell suddenly, as it does at that latitude, two hours after Billy had given the invitation, hundreds of counselors and inquirers were still together. As the follow-up chairman said, "The gospel is preached to multitudes, but people come to Christ one by one."

No less than 60 percent of the 22,512 inquirers of the five-day crusade were found to have had no previous contact with a Protestant church; they were placed in nurture groups in which trained layleaders took responsibility for ten or twelve persons each. The follow-up committee "faced a gigantic task. . . . For fifteen days we worked around the clock," in two shifts, to insure that every inquirer received literature and that every name went to a pastor. The crusade's general secretary, Castro, who provided office space, was not only a pastor but a restaurant owner and sent up generous snacks for the workers. He also gave a wonderful dinner to the Team after the Saturday service.

Only years will tell what the crusade did for the leaders, the clergy and the people of the Philippines.

Billy Graham reached India early in December 1977, two weeks after the most devastating cyclone and tidal wave in its history. The country was ripe for the proclamation of the Good News at festivals prepared by the Christian community over many months.

Akbar Haqq, the Indian Associate evangelist on the Billy Graham Team, had grown more and more aware that many Hindus and Muslims were moving toward Christ. When Billy spoke in Calcutta, in a specially designed colorful *shamiana* or great tent, where at the second meeting the crowd spilled over into the surrounding school grounds, nearly half the audience were reckoned to be non-Christian. Of the 2,013 inquirers who filled in cards, 481 declared in effect their desire to leave the worship of other gods.

At Hyderabad-Secunderabad, inland capital of the cyclone-stricken state, leaders of both Catholic and Protestant communities sat on the platform as Graham preached to some 125,000 in warm sunshine in the Gymkhana Grounds. Then the counseling committee undertook the immense task of following up all who stood. A longer festival, with Akbar Haqq, was immediately planned for 1978. At Kottayam in Kerala, with its strong Christian minority, center of the Syrian Orthodox and Mar Thoma churches as well as Protestant and Catholic, Billy was back in the college grounds where he had preached in 1956. Crowds were even greater, and just as orderly and eager.

The largest festival, climax of Billy Graham's visit, followed at Madras. He handed one of the five services to Haqq in order to tour the devastated areas by government helicopter, then increased his emergency fund's gift after seeing the sorrow and ruin.

The Nehru stadium filled up on the last Sunday with the largest crowd in its history. Billy did not make commitment an easy step. "I tried to spell out the *cost* of following Christ," he said afterward, "night after night, so that they would not come under false pretences." When he gave the invitation an extraordinary surge forward swamped the counseling arrangements. Hundreds may have been moved by a desire to see Billy closer, to show their affection, to touch him if they could. But hundreds, too, as the follow-up showed, wanted nothing but Christ.

24 New Fields

"**N**OW IS the moment to proclaim the gospel," Graham said to the Team after returning from India. "Lives are groping. There is fear. Loneliness. Guilt. Now is the moment." Graham's schedule had crusades at home and abroad for 1978 and three weeks at Sydney, Australia, in 1979 (twenty years after his earlier crusade there). The stopping place in a biography of an active contemporary man or woman must be arbitrary.

Without doubt, however, though the full story must wait, the most significant events for Graham in 1977 and 1978 were the visits to Hungary and Poland—the start of a remarkable ministry in eastern Europe.

When Billy and Ruth Graham, Cliff Barrows, and other Team members met in a Vienna hotel on 3 September 1977 before taking the plane to Budapest, their prayers were somewhat apprehensive.

An official invitation from the Council of Free Churches of Hungary, cleared by the Hungarian government, had arrived suddenly a few weeks before, the result of five years' patient diplomacy by Alexander Haraszti of Atlanta, a Hungarian-American physician, surgeon, and pastor. Dr. Haraszti had practiced medicine in Budapest and taught theology at the Baptist seminary there during the postwar years when the Communist government strongly opposed religion. He had translated Billy Graham's *Peace with God,* presenting it as Notes for

Students on Homiletics by a world-famous preacher. It cleared the censorship. After the Hungarian revolution he emigrated with his wife and five children because of an inner call to go out as a medical missionary, an impossible ambition if he had stayed in Hungary. Problems beyond his control stopped Haraszti from becoming a full-time missionary but he added to his Atlanta medical practice and pastorate the work of secretary of the Hungarian Baptist Union of America. Thus he kept close ties with his native land.

Alexander Haraszti's background, education, and professional experience[1] was remarkably apt for the role that opened up to him. He had been trained to understand Marxist philosophy, which was a prerequisite for a man who could open Communist eastern Europe to Billy Graham.

As far back as 1957 Billy Graham had promised a Hungarian-American churchman, George Balla of New York, that he would drop all engagements if invited to preach in Hungary. At that time the Communist government had refused permission, but Haraszti brought a visiting deputation of free church leaders to the Cleveland crusade in 1972; there Graham renewed his promise, this time to the president of the Council of Free Churches of Hungary, Sandor Palotay, and to the president of the Baptist Church of Hungary, Janos Laczkovski.

Five years passed. Haraszti made many visits to Budapest and was unwearying in telephone calls and correspondence. Slowly he won the confidence of the Team; Graham appointed him his adviser in Eastern European affairs, a status that eased negotiations with the Hungarian authorities, whose trust Haraszti won as well.

State officials in Budapest had made plain that Hungary would need the consent of the other Warsaw Pact countries. Haraszti removed misconceptions about Graham's attitudes and motives and made a telling point: since Graham never went where strings were placed on his message, the government should admit Billy Graham and allow him to preach—if they wanted the western press to acknowledge the existence of religious liberty in Hungary. (It is not the liberty

---

[1] In Hungary he had earned degrees in theology and a Ph.D. in linguistics. From Budapest University Medical School he had an M.D., with special training in obstetrics and gynecology in Hungary and Switzerland. From Emory University Medical School, Atlanta, he had an M.D. and had specialized in surgery and gynecology. He had also been a professor at the International Baptist Seminary in Zurich.

enjoyed in the West, however; the cost of being an open believer is higher.) In earlier years the rulers had aimed to eliminate Christianity, while churchmen had looked to the day when Communism would vanish. More recently each had accepted the fact that Communist rule and Christian devotion would continue to exist in Hungary.

In April 1977 negotiations had advanced far enough for Haraszti to take Walter Smyth with him. Finally the door opened, with a written invitation brought by the hand of Haraszti, from Sandor Palotay. Traditionally, three quarters of the population were Roman Catholic, one quarter Protestant. Of these, most were Reformed (Calvinist) and a lesser number, Lutheran; eight small denominations formed the Council of Free Churches, of which the Baptists were largest with 20,000 members.

Billy had no idea how the Hungarian people, after thirty-two years of Communism, would respond. He could not tell whether the government would be friendly, though it would not cold-shoulder him; President Carter had entrusted him with oral messages of good will. He knew, too, that this week would open or close his ministry to the other Socialist countries of eastern Europe, the one large area of humanity, other than mainland China, where he had never preached. One third of the world's population lives in Communist countries. Although some of his countrymen might accuse him of compromise with Communism, this was a risk to be accepted. Christ had died for men and women in Communist lands, as elsewhere. He could not refuse to minister to them because they lived under a different political ideology.

Billy Graham's objectives for the remaining years of his life, as he described them in his letter of acceptance to Palotay, were twofold: "One is to proclaim the gospel of Christ to as many people as possible, and the other is to help establish bridges of understanding between the peoples of the world. I am confident that such a visit to Hungary at this time in history would have a great meaning to peoples of all backgrounds as they search for peace on earth."

"At the Budapest airport a delegation of church leaders put us at ease," runs Billy's diary of the trip. "We felt among friends." He saw at once that this was to be no inconspicuous visit. A high-ranking official of the Hungarian state office for church affairs officially welcomed him as an envoy of good will in the presence of the American ambassador, Philip M. Kaiser, in the state visitors' lounge. The government had given visas for an ample support Team and a large corps of western press and television crews, together with the Hungarian press. Billy soon found himself in the familiar setting of a press conference.

The Grahams reached their hundred-year-old hotel on Margaret island in the Danube encouraged and pleased by their warm reception from Hungarian people, church officials, and press. On Sunday 4 September, "we were up early for a day of surprises, and a day of preaching the gospel," continued Billy in his diary. With the American ambassador and his wife in the convoy, the Grahams were motored to the Baptist Youth camp at Tahi, sixteen miles north of Budapest "for our first public service. There had been no formal announcement, nothing in the press, and we were told that perhaps 3,000 persons were expected for the outdoor service. To reach the camp, we drove up a steep dirt road for a mile or two. All along the road were people walking to the camp: old, young, some with their best Sunday finery, some peasant women in black stockings, black full skirts, and shawls." Special public buses and street cars had carried loads of people every two minutes to a place close to the dirt road. No police were in sight except to direct the heavy traffic.

Since religious meetings are permitted only on church grounds, the occasion was the closing service of the summer youth recreational program of the Baptist church. Hungary's Protestants and Catholics, however, had pushed aside denominational lines. News of the meeting had spread by word of mouth, and believers spent hours on long distance telephone calls. By train, plane, or car, a thousand people came from nearby Czechoslovakia; others came from Poland, Rumania, Bulgaria; a top-level Baptist delegation came from Moscow; thousands upon thousands arrived from all parts of Hungary, many bringing nonbelievers.

About half the audience may have been under twenty-five, although the turnout of all ages surprised the authorities. Press reports were low key; newspaper figures varied between 5,000 and 15,000. Some believers counted no less than 6,000 cars parked along the Danube bank, which coincided with the police estimate that 30,000 or more people squeezed into the twelve-acre camp site, and even beyond its fences, under the poplar and locust trees.

It was Hungary's largest gathering for a preaching service since

World War II, which made it an hour of great encouragment to Protestants and Catholics, young and old. As Billy and Ruth, surprised at the size of the crowd, walked to their places they received prolonged applause.

"The choir was glorious," continued Billy. "The Hungarians love music and sing beautifully. A simple platform of split poles had been constructed, and when I began to preach, the sun beat down unmerci-fully. A plump lady with a big smile slipped onto the platform and handed Ruth an umbrella for shade. I preached on John 3:16, outlining as clearly as possible the fact of God's love for us, regardless of our backgrounds." Impeccably translated by Dr. Haraszti, Billy began by referring to his hope of building bridges between peoples. "I come from a different social system," he said, "but we are bound together as brothers and sisters in Christ." He then turned to his Bible and read his text, commenting that no matter what system you live in, God loves you.

His homely illustrations amused and warmed the crowd and he preached Christ plainly, for a verdict, just as in Nagaland, Korea, South Africa, and in America North or South. "At the end of the sermon," continues Billy, "I asked people to raise their hands if they sincerely wanted to commit themselves to Christ, and thousands showed their hands all over the hillside."

The Grahams lunched at Hotel Sylvanus overlooking the Danube and the castle-clad mountains beyond, in company with church leaders and Ambassador Kaiser, who is Jewish, and his wife, a Unitarian. They returned to Budapest by leisurely riverboat, watching as picturesque villages, churches, and farms slipped by. It was dusk when they came upon the splendid view of central Budapest, with the floodlit parliament house on the left bank and the royal palace and St. Mathias cathedral high on Castle Hill on the right.

They went immediately to Sun Street Baptist Church. "As we neared the church we could see the courtyard and the street packed with people who could not get inside. Loudspeakers carried the service to those outside and to several other churches which were also filled. The service was long, and the crowded church hot, but the people were attentive, hungry for the gospel." Graham's official host, Dr. Palotay, welcomed him with a long address, and Billy was especially touched by a warm speech of welcome from Bishop Tibor Bartha of the Reformed

Church, president of the ecumenical council and of the Hungarian Bible Council, who addressed the congregation in Hungarian, then spoke to Graham in English. "Let us demonstrate what we have in common: our commitment to Jesus Christ." Before Billy's arrival Bishop Bartha had been doubtful, but he said afterward, "I was deeply impressed by his warmth, his Christian spirit, his honesty, and his humility in saying, 'I have come to learn.' I took him to my heart immediately." Likewise Bishop Kaldy of the Lutherans abandoned prejudice and turned distrust into support and friendship.

When church leaders had finished their necessary statements about social justice, and Graham had responded at length in a prepared statement (which included an expression of his desire to learn and his prayer that one day there would be one world, without wars hot or cold), the simple preaching of the gospel could begin. The people had waited patiently. "I was tired after a long day," Billy wrote, "but God gave me strength as I spoke about the meaning of faith in Christ.

"At the end of the service there were soft sounds all over the church, as if people were clicking their tongues. We were told later that it was from dozens of tape recorders being turned off." Tapes were copied, recopied, and sent all over Hungary and other eastern bloc lands. Thus Graham's voice and Haraszti's translation became familiar to thousands who had not attended that service.

On Monday morning Graham met Jewish leaders at their head-quarters: this meeting was the one request he had attached to his acceptance of the invitation to Hungary. He found it "an informative and deeply moving experience." They told him how for the first time in Hungarian history Jews were free of discrimination. They spoke of past sufferings and of their huge synagogue which they believed to be the world's largest. Dr. Haraszti noticed how "a warm personal rapport developed very soon between the evangelist and Jewish leaders," and long afterward some of them recalled the love they had sensed in Graham. "What comes from the heart reaches the heart," one said.

That afternoon the Grahams, with Haraszti as interpreter, called on the cabinet minister in charge of the State Office for Church Affairs, Imre Miklos, who had been at the center of the long negotiations. "At first," noted Billy, "the meeting was very formal, but His Excellency broke into a warm smile and produced a lovely bouquet of roses for Ruth, which broke the ice. From then on we talked as if we were old friends. I spoke frankly about my faith in Christ, and how I had come to believe that only God could solve the basic problem of the human heart and of society."

Haraszti recalls: "He said it in simple words, boldly, and without apologies. Imre Miklos was evidently touched himself and so was his staff. Then he told Dr. Graham, how he, a Roman Catholic by birth, had drifted away from a church which, in his opinion, was interested only in political power and landholdings. 'I joined the Communist Party during World War II and became a member of the underground movement. Then, little by little I became an atheist. After World War II, I started fighting a church which did not represent Christianity, in my opinion. Is it not a sad thing that we Communists had to teach the Roman Catholic Church to preach the gospel and to represent the true Church of Jesus Christ? I have no quarrels with churches now,' he continued, 'because they have learned the lesson which was forced upon them by history. I have many believer friends whom I appreciate because they are good workers also. I prefer a believer for a friend who is an honest worker, to an atheist who is a loafer.' "

Graham could not help admiring Miklos's dedication "even if I disagreed with his philosophy. It is sobering to meet someone who has been turned off because of the lives of Christians who did not live up to the teaching of their Master."

"Time passed swiftly and we talked longer than we had planned. Mr. Miklos was apologetic to Ruth, who was scheduled to speak to a group of ministers' wives. He asked if he could do anything to help make it up to her. She smiled. 'Can you sing,' she asked, and he broke into laughter. Then, as we were saying goodbye, Ruth shook his hand and said one of the few Hungarian phrases she knew: 'Isten aldja meg (God bless you),' and he laughed again. Ruth said as we were leaving, 'God's sun shines on atheists also, even if they don't know it.' We had had a good visit and we left feeling we had established a friendship in spite of wide differences."

The Grahams went to their separate meetings for Free Church ministers and for ministers' wives. The next day, with Palotay, Haraszti, several of the Team, and followed by the press corps, expert drivers took the Grahams at an alarming pace to Debrecen in eastern Hungary, a Reformed stronghold.

During the 150-mile journey they visited Hortobagy national park and lunched at the ancient thick-walled Csarda in the center; once a tavern for cowherds, horse shepherds, and vagrant outlaws, it now served delicious goulash cooked in a large pot over an open flame. Graham was taken by buggy two or three miles on the Great Plain to a horse farm where *csikos* demonstrated their skills in herding horses. Billy delighted them when "they insisted that I mount one of the horses, which I did after considerable pushing and pulling by my friends—since the saddle was nothing but a strip of leather with stirrups on each end. Hungarian horsemen ride without benefit of girths. I'm glad that the horse was patient with me." Billy had been a natural horseman as a boy but his opportunities since have been limited.

There in the national park a worker grabbed Billy's arm and said with tears of emotion, "I am a believer!" Billy had several such experiences during the week: a parking lot attendant; a journalist who lingered behind, seemed lost for words, and then said in English, "There are many believers in Hungary, Dr. Graham. I am one of them."

At Debrecen, Graham toured the Reformed Theological Academy which had been founded in 1538 in the early years of the Reformation and now was beautifully renovated. He preached nearby in a small Baptist church, where a crowd of some 5,000 overflowed into the square outside. The deacons had worried lest there be disturbance, but not a sound could be heard except the preaching coming over the loudspeakers.[2]

Billy had to return to Budapest but Cliff Barrows and Denton Lote stayed for singing and preaching, far into the night.

Wednesday began with a reception. Leaders of all Protestant groups, forming the ecumenical council, attended. "Bishop Bartha," runs Billy's diary, "challenged Christians in the nonsocialist countries to work for the cause of world peace and brotherhood. It could have been a political address, but instead it was the sincere testament of a Christian leader deeply sensitive to the problems of a divided world. He also acknowledged the need of Hungarian churches to be more evangelistic in their outreach. . . . I outlined some of the differences

---

[2] One of the most charming of the many stories told the present writer a year later, when he visited Debrecen with Dr. Haraszti, was of a nearby householder who had gone to his loft to feed his pigeons. He heard the loudspeakers and stayed up in the loft listening until his wife came to see what had happened. She too listened to the end.

between our background and theirs, and how we can learn from each other. It is hard to express the feeling of love and mutual devotion we all felt in that meeting. Those men represent churches and people from a much different background, and yet we all sensed our oneness because of a common faith in Christ."

That afternoon, Billy, Smyth, and Haraszti drove south to Pecs, where a Roman Catholic cathedral stands on fourth-century foundations: martyrs were buried there long before the heathen Magyars came in from the east. The bishop of Pecs, Joseph Cserhati, was secretary of the bishops' council. Patient negotiation had led him to speak up for Graham at the council and agree to meet him; and, though he would not offer the cathedral for preaching, he helped remove Catholic caution.

Cserhati received Graham in his chancery, surrounded by lesser prelates, close advisers, and the Baptist minister of Pecs. He spoke in an open moving manner of the problems and opportunities of Christians in a socialist land. Graham was "interested to note that there is very little sense of competition or rivalry between Protestants and Catholics. Both face a secular society, and know that they have more in common than they have in division." The bishop described the dialogue he had initiated with Communists for Hungary's good, but pointed out that Communism has no answer to the deepest human needs.

While the bishop took Billy on a tour of the cathedral and into the catacombs, he spoke of the liberty of Hungarian Christians and the price they pay in discrimination or unpopularity. Graham "thought of Christians of the first century who lived in a Roman civilization which was unchristian, and yet they did all they could to be 'salt of the earth' and 'light in the world.' The sincerity and dedication of present-day Hungarian Christians is a challenge to Christians throughout the world."

As they said goodbye the bishop pointed to the wide sweep of cathedral grounds falling gently to the square. Many thousands of people could stand there, on church property. Next time, the bishop promised, Graham should preach from the cathedral steps.

That night Graham preached in the small Baptist church at Pecs, where loudspeakers carried his voice to the overflow again crowding the street. The bishop did not attend but a year later he said that Graham had stimulated the bishop's own evangelism, and had helped it, too, by preparing the ground.

Graham and his party began the night-time drive back. As they left the town their car was flagged down by a policeman and ordered to draw to the side of the road "because a great churchman is coming." When told that Graham was in that very car, the policeman stepped back and saluted.

Thus a week of overwhelming hospitality, brotherhood, and mutual discovery drew toward its close. On Thursday, Graham addressed an opening joint session of the new academic year for Budapest theological seminaries. Originally only Free Church schools were expected, but the past few days had created an urge to hear Graham. Reformed and Lutheran students came also, and Graham jettisoned his prepared text to speak instead on communicating the gospel to unbelievers. The students "were very open and receptive. Bishop Zoltan Kaldy, leader of the Lutheran Church, gave a magnificent address before me. He was very warm and friendly and I feel I made a new friend." Kaldy, who had spoken on confessional outlook and dedication to an ecumenical spirit, had stopped being a critic and became an admirer of Graham's courage, openness, and spirituality.

During his last days in Hungary Graham first had a cordial and unexpectedly long interview with Deputy Prime Minister Gyorgi Aczel, Hungary's leading Marxist theorist and a member of the Communist Politburo, and then attended a reception given by the American ambassador in Graham's honor. Many of the diplomatic corps as well as religious leaders and state officials came, and Graham had a friendly useful discussion with the Rumanian ambassador. Graham and Imre Miklos then withdrew for a further confidential talk. Miklos intimated that the week had been only the beginning of Graham's ministry to eastern Europe, as indeed it proved: Graham's visit to Poland in October 1978 arose directly from the Hungarian tour.

Miklos hinted also that Graham would be invited back. Having said that Graham might be accused of returning from Hungary brainwashed, he added, "And I shall be accused of joining the Christian church! This is not so. You have not joined the Communist party and I have not become a Christian. You probably would not expect me to."

Billy Graham answered, gently but affirmatively, that it was his prayer and hope that Miklos would rejoin Christianity. Miklos said, as they parted, "It is not enough for friends to meet only once."

Friday morning Billy visited the Tungsram electric appliances factory. All work stopped and the workers listened enthralled to Archie Dennis singing. The man in charge asked if Dennis might remain afterward to record songs on a cassette so that the general manager, absent that day, might hear them—this, among the proletariat of an officially atheistic state. Then the workers presented Billy with an electric light bulb as a souvenir.

Billy thanked them and said, "This light bulb will be shining in my home and will remind me of Hungary, an unforgettable experience in my life. I have also brought a souvenir for you, my dear friends, something that shines much brighter than this light bulb. I have brought to you the light of the world, Jesus Christ." Workers standing around were weeping openly. "This," notes Haraszti, "was the very first time in Communist Hungary that any minister preached about Jesus Christ in a state-owned factory." Following a rather emotional closing service, again at the Sun Street Baptist church, and a presentation, Billy Graham left Hungary on the morning of Saturday, 10 September 1977.

Despite the briefest of mentions of the visit in the media, the country had been touched. A month later, when driving a Hungarian Baptist minister to the airport, a truck driver asked, "Reverend, have you hear of Dr. Graham? . . . His ministry in Hungary has made a tremendous change in public opinion. He has called attention to the Bible, and it is no more a strange thing in factories to speak about salvation."

Eternity will reveal that ministry's converts, direct and indirect. For Graham and the Team, Hungary had been a breakthrough into a new dimension with new perspectives, since Communist eastern Europe, with its heritage of a thousand years of Christianity, differs from non-Christian lands as much as it differs from the West.

Looking back on Graham's visit, Imre Miklos, the Hungarian cabinet minister, remarked that chronologically it had been the third most significant event in Hungary's church history since World War II. The partial Concordat of 1969 with the Vatican, Communist party leader Janos Kadar's visit with the Pope in June 1977, and Billy Graham's coming had each marked a stage in the improvement of relation between the Communist state and Christians. As a Marxist, Miklos recognized only the impersonal outworking of historical forces, Christians saw the working of God's Providence.

A year later in Poland, God's design for Eastern Europe seemed yet more apparent in Billy Graham's preaching tour of October 1978, for it effected an extraordinary breakdown of barriers between the predominent Roman Catholic majority and the non-Roman minorities; it strengthened freedom of religion; and it ended a few hours before the election of a Polish cardinal as Pope.

Billy had been invited to poland in 1966 by the Polish Baptist Union, one of the smallest of the many denominations represented on the non-Roman Polish Ecumenial Council, but the govenrment had refused permission. A visit then would have been of little significance to the Polish people, since ninety-four percent were practicing Catholics and any interchurch cooperation, except in certain social causes, was almost unknown at that time. Following the success in Hungary, Dr. Haraszti was received in Warsaw in January 1978 by Tadeusz Dusik, director of non-Catholic affairs at the State Office for Church Affairs, in the presence of leaders of the Baptist Union and the Ecumenical Council.

Haraszti explained Graham's theology and methods and emphasized that his work in any country encouraged Christians to be true followers with a renewed responsibility towards the society in which they live. Graham would also encourage nonprofessing Christians to accept Christ. Haraszti spoke of Graham's desire to build bridges between peoples and to promote the cause of peace.

Without the Communist government's consent and cooperation no visit could have taken place; and the State Office gave approval to an official invitation to Billy Graham, dated 24 February 1978, signed by the president of the Polish Baptist Union, Michal Stankicwicz, and the general secretary, Adam Piasecki, for a ten-day visit in October. In April, Haraszti and Walter Smyth had fruitful discussions with President Witold Benedyktowicz of the Ecumenical Council, Metropolitan Bazyli of the Polish Autocephalic Orthodox Church, and Bishop Janusz Narzynski of the Polish Lutheran Church. The Ecumenical Council invitation followed on 24 May.

In July the two Americans, with the Polish Baptist leaders, were received in turn by two key officials of the Roman Catholic hierarchy, Bishop Bronislaw Dabrowski and Bishop Wladislaw Misiolek, and to

Baptist astonishment, the Catholics offered the use of their cathedrals and churches. Cardinal Wojtyla, soon to be Pope John Paul II, had been foremost in offering his cathedral in Cracow when other bishops hesitated.

Thus Graham had the unique privilege, never previously granted to a visiting churchman, of an opportunity "to share my faith within Protestant, Roman Catholic, and Orthodox churches and institutions."

Excitement mounted, with invitations to more cities than Graham could possibily visit. Walter Smyth spent almost all September in Poland supervising preparations. The Polish branch of the Bible Society published 100,000 copies of John's Gospel for distribution during the crusade; the Baptist Union published Polish editions of Graham's books, *Peace with God* and *The Secret of Happiness*, and a biography, with sermon excerpts. Throughout the country, posters of invitation went up outside churches of all denominations and church journals featured his upcoming visit until all Poland was expectant.

Billy and Ruth Graham came to Poland immediately after the crusade in Stockholm (which itself will be an exciting story to tell). Their plane touched down at Warsaw in heavy rain on Friday, 6 October 1978, the last day, as it proved, of a long wet spell. As the Poles said, Billy "brought the sunshine." The welcome at the airport showed the spirit abroad in the land. "We open the gates of our churches for you," said Bishop Miziolek, Chairman of the Roman Catholic episcopate's committee on ecumenism. The bishop brought greetings from Stefan Cardinal Wyszynski, head of the Church in Poland, and expressed pleasure that Graham would preach in cities "where the overwhelming majority of listeners will be Catholic." Graham commented that this represented a new spirit of cooperation which was a constructive example for Christians in other nations.

In his arrival speech Graham said he felt as if he were treading on sacred ground, because so much of historical and spiritual significance had happened in the Polish nation. During more than 1,000 years the Poles had shown an indomitable spirit, refusing to succumb to adversity. "I understand you have fought much in your history, not because you love war but because you love peace and freedom. I want to observe at first hand your social system and to see the results of your cooperative efforts." He spoke of peace and goodwill on earth, and stressed his conviction that "the lord of the Church, who is also Lord of history, is still at work in our world, sometimes in ways we can never foresee."

The ten days that followed were packed with incident. What follows can be only a temporary footnote, as it were; but certain features stand out.

One is Billy Graham's diplomacy. He was received by Deputy Prime Minister Jozef Techjma, by the Secretary for Foreign Relations of the Central Committee of the governing Polish United Socialist Workers Party, Ryszard Frelek, and by the Director of the State Office for Church Affairs, Kazimierz Kakol. A profoundly Christian land ruled by Communists has inevitable tensions between Church and State, which were discussed frankly, as was the historical friendship between the United States and Poland, dating back to the Polish patriots who helped Americans secure their independence. And Graham did not hesitate to affirm that a nation, whatever its social system and ruling ideology, needs a spiritual dimension; Deputy Prime Minister Techjma agreed.

As a Finnish counterpart of *Newsweek* commented: "There are two Billy Grahams one preaches an extremely plain and simplified message of the decision between God and man; the other builds peace and understanding by the delicate means of international politics."

This increased the significance of the Grahams' visits to the concentration camps, with their memorials to four million victims of the Nazis. At Auschwitz the infamous gas chambers are a shrine where the horror is not allowed to be forgotten; Graham was touched to tears. After laying a wreath, the Grahams knelt in prayer, and when Billy turned to address the people he was so emotionally overcome that he was almost unable to speak. He delivered his lengthy prepared address, however, which was quoted widely by media throughout the world. He urged Christians to remind mankind that all are accountable to God, and he called upon world leaders, "regardless of their political ideology, to learn the lessons of Auschwitz." He ended by saying that Christians must not isolate themselves: "Let us make this a moment to rededicate ourselves to the Lord Jesus Christ, to the cause of peace, to reconciliation among all the races and nations."

The Polish Crusade contributed much to ecumenical relations. The luncheon reception given in Graham's honour by the Lutheran bishop and the Orthodox metropolitan, the meetings with Jewish leaders, and the visit to the shrine of the Black Madonna at Czestochowa indicated the new spirit which the visit fostered. The Shrine, which contains a painting of the Virgin traditionally ascribed to the hand of St. Luke, stands in a monastery high on a crag famous in Poland's wars. Of great national and religious significance, it had been strictly barred to non-Catholics until recently. Billy Graham, accompanied by some of his staff, was the first Protestant leader to be entertained by the abbot, who invited him to return in 980 and preach to the several hundred thousand pilgrims who would attend its 600th anniversary.

But it was the crusade's spirit of mutual cooperation for Christ which astonished and delighted Catholics, Protestants, and Orthodox alike. Working together to make the great evangelistic services a success, they discovered the depth of their brotherhood. As was said at the time, even the greatest Roman Catholic could not bring Poles of different church loyalties together as equals, but Billy Graham could.

He preached in Baptist, Roman Catholic, and Lutheran churches in Warsaw, all crowded to the doors; and in the open air outside the Baptist church in the industrial city of Bialystok, near the Soviet border. He was brilliantly interpreted throughout the tour by Dr. Zdzislaw Pawlik, general secretary of the Polish Ecumenical Council. At Poznan, in Western Poland, the church of the Dominican order overflowed with 3000 men and women of all ages, including many hundreds of students. The people stood shoulder to shoulder, for these great churches do not contain many seats; they stood in side chapels, the churchyard, or wherever they could hear, with priests and seminarians doing all they could to assist. "We have met here in the Holy Spirit," said the rector, opening the service, "and He will unite us and hold us closer together." The Warsaw and Bialystok Baptist choirs led the singing under Cliff Barrows's direction, and Myrtle Hall sang "How Great Thou Art" in English and invited the congregation to join the chorus in Polish; they sang hesitantly at first, then the sound swelled to a crescendo.

Graham had officiated at weddings in Roman Catholic churches, but a few years earlier neither he, nor his Catholic hosts at Poznan, nor the Baptists of Poland would have dreamed that he would conduct a mixed evangelistic crusade in a Catholic sanctuary anywhere in the world.

He preached on the Cross. Cliff Barrows, sitting near Graham, saw the hunger on the faces of the intent listeners. At the end, when

Graham asked those who wished to decide for Christ to raise their hands, the response was prompt. Among the 200 or so who responded were twenty priests and some nuns, solemnly rededicating themselves to God.

The Team drove on through a countryside harvesting potatoes and sugar beets to Wroclaw (Dresden), where the Polish National Catholics were hosts in a great church with vaulted ceilings and flying buttresses. Again the people stood shoulder to shoulder. The church had been full four hours before, and many had stood the entire time.

Another night he preached in Cracow, in the 700-year-old church of St. Anne's, gorgeous in painted ceilings and marble columns. Cardinal Wojtyla, Archbishop of Cracow, having given warm permission, had planned to meet Graham but then left for the conclave which a few days later elected him Pope. The church leaders in Cracow showed intense interest in Graham's preaching, and the Team could not fail to be impressed by the eagerness of hundreds after the service to learn how to pray, to read the Scriptures, and to share their faith.

Busloads of people came from other Communist Eastern European countries. The total of men, women, and children who heard Billy Graham preach in Poland was estimated at around 60,000. Far greater were the numbers—approximately 110 million in Poland and beyond its borders in the Ukraine and elsewhere—who, understanding Polish, could hear the sermons on tape or read them in print: a new dimension of great potential for Billy's ministry in Communist countries.

Perhaps the high point came on the evening when Graham preached in Poland's largest sanctuary, the modern cathedral of Christ the King at Katowice, a coal-mining and steel-making city of Silesia. Once again every corner was filled. Detailed research after the tour estimated the congregation at 13,000 inside the cathedral and 5,000 outside, with most of this 18,000 Roman Catholic. It was an unprecedented ecumenical occasion. Up to this time in Poland Billy Graham had not used a counseling area such as he used in the West, but that night in Katowice he asked those who wanted counsel to go to the crypt. A Baptist pastor and a Roman priest shepherded them down to where trained counselors waited.

And as the singing dies away in the cathedral of Christ the King, this book must close. Billy Graham had been evangelist to five continents; his ministry to Eastern Europe made him evangelist to the world. He had met dedicated Christians in Eastern Europe, "with a depth of commitment which puts me to shame." Negotiations were in progress for a public evangelistic visit to yet another Communist land.

"My commander-in-chief, Jesus Christ, has ordered me to go and proclaim the gospel all over the world. My goal is to proclaim the gospel to as many people as possible and to build bridges of friendship and peace regardless of political or economic systems. I believe my ministry is one way of bringing peace and understanding as I proclaim the gospel of Jesus Christ, the Prince of Peace."

APPENDIX

One Man's Furrow

ON A November Monday in 1949 thirty-one-year-old Billy Graham and his wife Ruth boarded a train in Los Angeles. He was exhausted yet thrilled. An evangelistic campaign in a tent had extended from three weeks to eight. An unbelievably large crowd of more than 9,000 had attended the final night. And the national press had actually made front-page news of Christian evangelism.

The train conductor, to the Grahams' surprise, treated him as a celebrity. At Kansas City reporters badgered him. At Minneapolis he found a hero's welcome. Only then did the Grahams realize that Billy had catapulted into fame. And he wrote: "I feel so undeserving of all the Spirit has done, because the work has been God's, not man's. I want no credit or glory. I want the Lord Jesus to have it all."

That first extraordinary response at Los Angeles brought new hope as Americans found afresh that the great truths of the Christian gospel had power to transform lives not merely by ones or twos but by hundreds—and later by thousands. Nobody can fully explain why one man, however dedicated and disciplined, should suddenly achieve on a large scale what others had been doing in small ways for decades past. One of his team put it well during the Boston awakening in January, 1950: "It was the sovereignty of God in answer to the prayers of all these people."

Graham's thirty years of preparation had been hard, from the

Abridged from the article by John Pollock in *Christianity Today*, 13 September 1974, reproduced by kind permission.

Carolina dairy farm to the presidency of a Midwest college. The "country boy" image given by the press had never been wholly correct; if it had, the swift rise in the early 1950s to a measure of national fame and influence might have toppled Billy Graham, as cynical commentators expected. Even allowing for the vital factor of the hand of Providence, it is a wonder more mistakes or misjudgments did not occur. Graham and the team were preserved by their complete sincerity, by their roots in devotional life, and by Graham's firm grasp of the basic truths of the faith.

Graham has always emphasized that his is a team ministry. Cliff Barrows and George Beverly Shea had joined before Los Angeles and so had Grady Wilson. George M. Wilson (no relation) organized the Billy Graham Evangelistic Association to meet the expanding opportunities. As the ministry grew, the team grew. Graham could pick the right man. In those early days each crusade seemed to add someone. Willis Haymaker, the veteran Carolinian who organized the Colombia crusade in 1950, thereafter joined the team and taught them much about preparation and mobilizing lay workers and prayer. And at Shreveport in 1951 Graham brought in Dawson Trotman, founder of Navigators, to fashion a way by which those coming forward could be more adequately helped and followed up and turned over to the pastoral care of the churches. The early, somewhat haphazard methods gradually developed into the Schools of Discipleship, which have perhaps done more than any other feature to foster local evangelism.

As the numbers attending the crusades and making decisions increased, Graham refused paths that might have led to a personal following. The team members are the servants of the churches—in the Apostle Paul's words, "your servants for Jesus' sake." In consequence the Billy Graham crusades have brought the churches into the sowing and reaping of evangelism on a scale never previously seen, not even in the greatest days of D. L. Moody.

Graham broke into the printed word with his bestselling *Peace With God* (1953) and his daily syndicated column, "My Answer." And into films, with *Mr. Texas.* Graham books and films have had immense influence over the past quarter-century. Yet an equally important opening was not obvious immediately. It took persistent effort by Walter Bennett and Fred Dienert before the evangelist dared to launch his weekly radio "Hour of Decision."

The year 1954 lifted the Billy Graham ministry to a new level through the historic events of Harringay Arena. Few who lived in England at that time can forget the atmosphere that came over the land. The Greater London crusade opened under suspicion and opposed by the press. It ended three months later with Graham flanked by the archbishop of Canterbury and the lord mayor of London in the largest outdoor stadium, as he preached the same unaffected gospel message. The response of England to this hitherto unknown American was beautifully summed up by a greatly loved national figure (whose name still may not be revealed) in a private letter thanking Billy Graham for "the spiritual rekindling you have brought to numberless Englishmen and women whose faith has been made to glow anew by your addresses."

Graham was flooded with requests that he stay on. Britain was hungry for the gospel of Christ. He now believes he should have stayed that summer of 1954. Undoubtedly Harringay, and the All Scotland Crusade the following year, and the landline relays and the great Good Friday nationwide television broadcast, gave British Christianity a new impetus throughout the later 1950s. Too many churches, however, held back, debating the pros and cons of this evangelism instead of recognizing their own opportunity. Had they grasped it, the sixties might have been as different for Britain nationally, despite the flooding in of secularism, as they were for the thousands who through the crusades of 1954–5 found faith or vocation (the number of ordinands and missionary recruits shot up in the years following Harringay and Kelvin Hall).

Billy Graham was now one of the most famous people on earth. Whether he preached under the starlight in South India by interpretation to huge, attentive crowds, or in the pulpit of the University Church in Cambridge, England, or for sixteen weeks in the sticky heat of the old Madison Square Garden in New York, ordinary people found themselves understanding the issues of commitment to Christ. Theologians might debate the crusades, sociologists might analyze them, but Graham reached the masses, and hundreds discovered that Christ is alive.

If the Graham team was a vehicle of blessing to a land or region, each land contributed to the team's collective skill and understanding. Thus the British introduced the landline relays, and Operation Andrew, which ensured that very many of those attending would come in the company of friends who had already found the Lord Jesus. The ideas of one country would be used in the next and absorbed into the general pattern of future crusades.

The year 1959 made a fitting tenth anniversary, being the year of the first Australian and New Zealand crusades. Graham's impact on the churches of Australia is a matter of history.

The 1960s widened and deepened the Graham ministry. He had been one of the founders of CHRISTIANITY TODAY, which from the start was entirely independent. To complement its theological and scholarly approach he now founded *Decision,* his own devotional magazine. Without advertising revenue, which is supposed to be an economic necessity for periodicals, its circulation climbed in the next thirteen years past the five million mark, far beyond that of any other religious magazine, with several foreign-language editions. As a by-product *Decision* produced the Schools of Christian Writing. These years saw also the vast increase of the television ministry, the means of Graham's greatest single impact on his own country.

From Tokyo in 1968 Graham went to Australia in 1969, where many converts of '59 served as counselors; and then to New York again, in the new Madison Square Garden, with the crusade shown later each night on television all down the Eastern seaboard. The crusade penetrated the city. I recall the intent faces in New York, of all types and ages, and the variety of the nightly crowds who came reverently forward. That autumn Billy returned to southern California for his third crusade in Los Angeles and its neighborhood.

Japan, New York, California; then the European television crusade of 1970. . . .

What Graham said to a skeptical press before Harringay may surely be quoted as his aim for the years to come: "I am going to present a God who matters, and who makes claims on the human race. He is a God of love, grace and mercy, but also a God of judgment. When we break his moral laws we suffer; when we keep them we have inward peace and joy. . . . I am calling for a revival that will cause men and women to return to their offices and shops to live out the teaching of Christ in their daily relationships. I am going to preach a gospel not of despair but of hope—hope for the individual, for society and for the world."

Index

Aczel, Gyorgi, 305
Adams, Lane, 44n, 105, 131
Africa crusades in, 7, 27–42, 162, 194;
    Lausanne congress and, 32, 196, 205–206,
    213, 252, 253, 282–283
Agard, Clarence, 126
Ahdrian, Sven, 287
Akers, John, 151
Albert Hall, 81, 86–90, 98, 152
Alberts, Louw, 30, 40
Amaro, Feliciano, 234
American Jewish Committee, 292
Amin, Idi, 213
Angami, Nihulie, 21
Angels (Billy Graham), 279–280
Anibal, Senhor, 223
Ao, Bendang, 22–23
Ao, Longri, 4–26 *passim*
Apartheid, 27, 28, 29, 33–42, 205–206
Asian Center for Theological Studies and
    Mission, 66
Asia and Euro 70, 72; and Lausanne
    congress, 203, 206, 211, 252, 292. *See
    also* Cambodia; China; India; Japan;
    Korea; Philippines; Vietnam war
Asia-South Pacific Congress on Evangelism,
    5, 189
Assemblies of God, in Brazil, 218, 219
Atallah, Ramez, 251
Attendance statistics in Brazil, 233–234,
    236–237, 239–240; in Europe, 73–74,
    77–78, 287, 299, 311; in Glasgow, 62; in
    Hong Kong, 273; in Korea, 47–48, 55,
    60–61, 62; in Nagaland, 17, 19, 23–24,
    25; in Philippines, 293; in Taiwan, 267; at
    U.S. crusades, 62, 107, 120, 169,

276–277, 313; at youth congresses, 256,
    257, 260, 261
Australia Blinco in, 120; crusades in, 138,
    296, 316, Dain in, 189–190, 191, 193;
    and Euro 70, 72; and plane flight in, 12;

Baines, Samuel, 170
Balla, George, 297
Baptist churches in Bangkok, 14; in Brazil,
    217, 218–219, 237, 244–245; in Hungary,
    296, 297, 298, 299, 300, 303; in India, 4,
    5, 8, 14, 25; in Korea, 49; in Moscow, 95,
    299; in Poland, 307, 308, 310; in
    Yugoslavia, 81
Baptist World Congress, 81, 127, 216, 223,
    286
Barnes, David, 118–119
Barnhouse, Don, 151
Barr, Dave, 84
Barrows, Bonnie, 114–115
Barrows, Cliff, 111, 119, 134–135, 160,
    203n, 314; in Asia, 11n, 12, 13, 15, 16,
    19, 21, 44n, 55; and Brazil, 234, 240; in
    Europe, 75, 77, 83, 296, 303, 310; at
    Knoxville, 108; and Lausanne congress,
    201
Bartha, Tibor, 300–301, 303–304
Bazyli, Metropolitan, 307
Believers *(Crentes)*, 218–247 *passim*
Bell, Nelson, 139–140, 143, 149, 150,
    187
Bell, Ralph, 44n, 252
Bell, Virginia, 139–140, 143
Benedyktowicz, Witold, 307
Bennett, Joyce, 273
Bennett, Walter, 114, 314

Berlin, 73, 74. *See also* World Congress on Evangelism
Berry, Lowell, 131, 132, 236
Berryman, Barry, 208
Bewes, Richard, 260
Beyerhaus, Peter, 212
Billy Graham Center, 280, 281
Billy Graham Day, 142, 174–175
Billy Graham Evangelistic Association (BGEA), 71; and congresses, 187, 188, 189, 191, 194, 211, 257, 283; finances of, 25, 136, 187, 188, 189, 191, 194, 221, 257, 280–281, 283; members of, 127, 135–136, 314
Bizo, L., 14–15, 16
Black Madonna shrine, 309–310
Blessitt, Arthur, 93–95
Blinco, Joe, 120
Bob Jones University, 49–50
Books by Billy Graham, 279–280, 308. *See also Peace with God*
Boston, 313
Brandt, Willi, 79
Bright, Bill, 193, 255–256
Brooks, Frederick, 132–133
Brown, William F. (Bill), 279
Buddhism, 44, 210, 263, 267, 270
Burklin, Werner, 259
Burnett, Bill, 35
Busby, Russ, 228

Calcutta, 3, 6, 11, 13, 15–18; crusades at, 5, 294; Mother Teresa in, 18, 211
California, 131, 183, 261, 277. *See also* Los Angeles; Rose Bowl Parade
Cambodia, 107, 108, 155, 210
Campus Crusade for Christ (CCC), 54n, 255–256
Camu, Louis, 259–260
Cardboard Chapel, 233
Carlson, Frank, 165
Carter, Jimmy, 278, 280, 285, 298
Cash, Johnny, 106, 257
Cash, June, 106, 257
Cassidy, Michael, 27–30, 35, 37, 39–40, 282–283
Castro, Fidel, 204
Catholics in Asia, 293, 294; in Brazil, 217, 218, 220–221, 225, 244; in Germany, 78–79; in Hungary, 298, 299, 302, 304; in Ireland, 91–102; in Italy, 130; in New Guinea, 252; in Poland, 307–308, 310, 311; in U.S., 129, 290–291; in Yugoslavia, 81, 82, 83, 85
Chafin, Kenneth (Ken), 131–132, 205, 236
Chambers, Irv, 158
Chandler, Otis, 254
Chiang Ching-kuo, 269
Chiang Kai-shek, 264, 265, 269

Chiang Kai-shek, Madame (Soong Mei-ling), 11, 264–265
Chicago: 1962 crusade in, 131, 276; 1971 crusade in, 113–114, 122, 124–125, 145
China, 11, 26, 203, 263–273
Chiu, Jonathan, 268
Cho, Dong Jin (David), 43n, 47–48, 55, 58, 60, 66
Chow Lien-hwa, 265, 271, 272
Christian Hope Indian Eskimo Fellowship (CHIEF), 282
Christianity Today, 156, 316; Bell (Nelson) and, 149, 187; and Chicago crusade, 125; and Hollywood Bowl crusade, 216; and Raleigh crusade, 129; and Watergate, 179, 180; and world congress, 187, 188
Christian Life and Witness course, 116, 222
Christival '76, 261
Church growth, 314; in Asia, 4, 62–63, 65–66; in Brazil, 218; in Britain, 258; in Sweden, 289–290
Churchill, Winston, 90
Church of Sweden, 286, 288
Clarkson, Margaret, 201
Claus, Tom, 282
Coe, Douglas, 160
Coleman, Robert E., 194, 250
Communists, 298, 312; in Brazil, 217; in Hungary, 296, 297–298, 302, 304, 305, 306; in Korea, 66; in Poland, 307, 309; in Yugoslavia, 74, 81, 83
Confucianism, 44, 58, 263, 267
Congresses: African, 28–37, 252, 282–283; Baptist, 81, 127, 216, 223, 286; on evangelism, 5, 28–37, 80, 187–191, 255, 256, 259. (*See also* World Congress on Evangelism); on evangelization, *see* Lausanne International Congress on World Evangelization; youth, 54, 255–261, 277, 283–284
Congress on Discipleship and Evangelism (*Code*), 261, 277
Connally, John, 167
Conway, William, 96–97
Cooper, Kenneth, 242
Cornell, George, 153, 162, 176, 177, 280
Corr, Edmond (Ed), 12, 14
Corts, John, 112, 115
Council of Free Churches of Hungary, 296, 298, 305
Counselors, 6, 120–121, 122; in Australia, 316; in Brazil, 222, 231, 233, 243, 245; in India, 6, 21, 294–295; in Korea, 51, 57, 61–62; in Philippines, 293–294; in Poland, 311; in South Africa, 36; at *Spre-e '73*, 261; in Sweden, 288; in Taiwan, 267–268; at U. S. crusades, 120–121, 133, 276
Cousins, Jack, 113, 114, 124
Cox, Tricia Nixon, 145, 172
Coy, Frank, 135–136

Crutchfield, Charles, 174, 175, 275
Cruz, Joao Da Silva, 231
Cserhati, Joseph, 304
Cunville, Rleweh Robert, 7–25 passim

Dabrowiski, Bronislaw, 307
Dain, Jack and Lausanne congress, 189–213
    passim; and Lausanne continuation
    committee, 250, 251, 252
Daley, Richard, 114
Dallas crusade at, 110, 115, 170; Explo '72
    at, 54, 256; life threat at, 8; World
    Evangelism and Christian Education
    Fund based in, 281
Damaskinos, Archbishop, 82–83
De-Camp, Elizabeth, 51
De-Camp, Otto, 45, 51
Decision cards, 121, 122; in Asia, 21, 25,
    62, 273, 294; in Brazil, 231, 233, 243,
    245. See also Response statistics
Decision magazine, 316; crusades publicized
    in, 113; and Euro 70, 77; in Nagaland, 5;
    Schools of Christian Writing,.238, 316;
    Wirt and, 45, 75
De Gruchy, John, 35
Demonstrators in Germany, 76, 78; in U.S.,
    108, 109, 124–125, 175
Dempsey, J. F., 98
Dennis, Archie, 11n, 20, 24, 306
de Vol, Gordon, 279
Dienert, Fred, 32, 114, 314
Dienert, Mildred, 32, 114, 116, 198–199
Dienert, Ruth Graham (Bunny), 139, 141,
    142, 143, 145
Dienert, Ted, 139
Dortmund, 71–80, 84, 105
Douglas, Jim D., 208, 209
Duncan, George, 213
Dusik, Tadeusz, 307
Dutch Reformed Church (DRC), in South
    Africa, 28, 29, 30, 31, 42

Earls Court, 71–72, 74, 114, 257, 258
Ecumenical Council, Polish, 307
Eisenhower, Dwight D., 164–167, 172
Eisenhower, John, 166
Eisenhower, Julie Nixon, 171, 172, 178–179,
    183
Ellis, Perry, 244
Elsner, Theodore, 114, 203n
Elson, Ed, 166
Ervin, Sam, 175
Eshleman, Paul, 256
Eurofest, 259–261
Europe (continent): congresses in, 80,
    187–191, 252, 259–261. (See also
    Lausanne International Congress on
    World Evangelization; World Congress
    on Evangelism); preaching in, 71–85, 253,
    285, 286–290, 296–312, 316

European Broadcasting Union, 74, 75
Euro 70, 71–85, 316
Evangelical Bookshop, Rio, 230, 235, 243,
    246
Evangelism, 25, 28, 49–50, 110–117,
    119–120; congresses on, 5, 28–37, 80,
    127, 187–191, 255, 256, 259. (See also
    World Congress on Evangelism); Europe
    and, 79, 81; Korea and, 49–50, 63–64, 66;
    schools of, 56–57, 63, 66, 130–132, 150,
    236–238, 293; and social concerns, 25,
    187–188, 190, 197, 201, 207, 213, 250,
    253, 260, 280–281
Evans, Robert P. (Bob), 81, 188, 189, 193,
    259
Explo '72, 54, 256

Fanini, Nilson de Amaral, 217–248
    passim
Featherstone, Bob, 151
Ferm, Lois, 150
Ferm, Robert O. (Bob), 131, 132, 149,
    150–151
Films, 125, 135, 278–279, 314; of Brazil,
    242n; of Euro 70, 84–85; of Korea, 58; at
    Lausanne congress, 204
Finances, 280–282; for American Indians,
    282; of BGEA, 75, 136, 187, 188, 189,
    191, 194, 221, 257, 280–281, 283; in
    Brazil, 220–221; for congresses, 187, 188,
    189, 191, 194, 198, 199, 257, 260, 281,
    283; for Euro 70, 72–73; for Hiding
    Place, 278–279; in Korea, 46, 51, 66; in
    Nagaland, 9, 22; for natural disasters, 282,
    295; in South Africa, 30, 34; in Taiwan,
    265–266
Fisher, Archbishop, 229
Fisher, Betty, 150
Fisher, Lee, 57, 149–150
Fitch, Thomas, 86, 93
Fitch, William (Bill), 86–101 passim
Follow-ups, 6, 120–122, 314; in Brazil, 222,
    231, 232–233, 243, 245; in Chicago, 125;
    in India, 21, 25, 295; in Korea, 62–63; of
    Lausanne, 249–253; in Philippines, 294;
    in South Africa, 36; at South Bend, 291;
    in Taiwan, 269–271, 273. See also
    Counselors
Fontes, Jeremias, 226
Ford, Gerald, 182, 275, 285
Ford, Jean Graham, 161, 175
Ford, Leighton, 118, 119, 149, 161; at
    Knoxville, 109; and Lausanne congress,
    192, 193, 208, 209, 211, 251; in South
    Africa, 37
Forsyth, W. B., 228, 230
Foster, Dave, 257, 259
Franca, Mario Barreto, 238
Free Churches in Hungary, 296, 298, 305;
    in Sweden, 286

Freitas, Eurico, 239
Frelek, Ryszard, 309
Frost, David, 97–98
Frost, Ralph, 110
Fuller, Charles E., 28

Gandhi, Indira, 24
Gatu, John, 34
Geisel, Ernesto, 217, 227–228, 246
German Evangelical Alliance, 71, 79
Germany, West, 71–82, 84, 105, 253, 261. *See also* World Congress on Evangelism
Glass, David, 230, 235, 243
Globo Television, 240–242, 248
Gloria, Darlene, 223, 246
Goddard, Jean, 32
Goddard, Trevor, 31, 32, 41
Godwin, Governor, 275
Goldwater, Barry, 145
Gomes, David, 219, 226, 227
Goode, Pearl, 113
Goodman, Lord, 89
Gore, Albert, 107
Graham, Anne. *See* Lotz, Anne Graham
Graham, Nelson Edman (Ned), 139, 140, 145
Graham, Ruth Bell, 137, 150, 152, 156, 159; accident of, 227; and films, 135, 278–279; and funding, 280–281; and Goode, 113; home life of, 139–140, 141, 142, 143–145, 146, 147, 148–149, 154; and Hungary, 296, 299, 300, 301, 302; and Inter-Varsity conference, 284; and Ireland, 101; at Knoxville, 108; and Korea, 50, 52, 53, 54, 55, 58, 59; and Lausanne congress, 195, 198, 201, 211; in Los Angeles, 313; and Mother Teresa, 18; in Philippines, 293; in Poland, 308; at Rose Bowl Parade, 255; in Taiwan, 268; and U.S. presidents, 165, 168–169, 170, 178–179, 181, 184
Graham, Ruth (daughter). *See* Dienert, Ruth Graham
Graham, Virginia. *See* Tchividjian, Virginia Graham
Graham, William Franklin, Jr. (Franklin), 140, 141, 144–145, 211, 262
Greater Chicago Evangelistic Association, 125
Gregory, Marnie, 13, 14
Gregory, Richard E., 13
Grist, Walter, 6, 11n
Guinness, Os, 207
Gustavson, Luverne, 149

Hahn, Keysun, 48
Hall, Myrtle, 310
Hallock, Edgar, 221, 236, 242
Hamilton-Reid, Margaret, 98

Hampton, Roberta, 238
Han, Kyung Chik, 43–49, 59, 62, 63, 66
Haqq, Akbar and Campus Crusade congress, 255; and India crusades, 5, 6, 10, 11, 16, 294, 295; in Ireland, 101; in Korea, 44n
Haraszti, Alexander, 296–297, 300–307
Harringay arena, 215, 315; Cassidy at, 27; Goode and, 113; and Gothenburg, compared, 286, 289, 290; invitation at, 120; publicity about, 7, 315; Rennie and, 74; Schneider and, 73; Shippam at, 88, 152; Winwill at, 279
Harvey, Paul, 173
Hatfield, Mark, 172, 178, 180
Haymaker, Willis, 314
Healings, in India, 22–23
Health of Billy Graham, 147–148, 157; in Britain, 89; in Hong Kong, 272; and Korea, 44, 46, 157; at Lausanne congress, 182, 194, 201, 214; and South Africa, 30, 37, 39–40; in Sweden, 286; at Urbana, 285
Heineman, Gustav, 79
Hellsten, Roland, 288
Helms, Senator, 178
Helza, Dona, 222
Henry, Carl, 187, 188, 192
Hill, Edward V. (Ed), 128
Hilton, Conrad, 165
Hoey, Clyde, 171
Höfliger, Tony, 203
Hoke, Donald E. (Don), 191–197, 202, 203, 204
Holley, Henry and Brazil, 219, 221, 226, 228, 229, 240, 241; and Hong Kong, 264; in Korea, 45–46, 47, 49, 51, 53; in Philippines, 293; and Taiwan, 264, 266
Holt, A. D., 109
Home, Alec Douglas-, 162, 229
Hopkins, Nan, 35, 36
Horak, Josip, 76, 81, 82–83, 84
Hour of Decision, 32, 113, 135, 149–150, 203n, 314; in Nagaland, 5; and Watergate, 176; and World Evangelism and Christian Education Fund, 281
House, Dennis, 31, 37
Howard, David, 284
How To Be Born Again (Billy Graham), 280, 282
Hsu, Frieda, 266–267
Huang, E. Tsun, 265–266
Hudson, Noel, 34
Humphrey, Hubert, 169
Hungarian Baptist Union of America, 297
Hunt, Carroll, 45, 53, 54
Hunt, Everett, 53
Huston, Sterling, 110–113, 116, 138, 277
Hyderabad-Secunderabad, 294–295
Hyde-White, Wilfred, 279

Ichter, Bill, 223, 234, 242–243
India: cyclone and tidal wave in, 282, 294; Dain in, 190; Good News festivals in, 292, 294–295; and Lausanne congress, 206, 211; Nagaland crusade in, 3–26, 194
Indians, American, 282
Institute of Directors conference, 86, 87–90, 98
International congresses. See Explo '72; Lausanne International Congress on World Evangelization; World Congress on Evangelism
Interpreters at Euro 70, 76, 81; in Hong Kong, 272; in Hungary, 300, 301–302; in Korea, 45, 49, 56; in Nagaland, 20; in Poland, 310
Inter-Varsity Christian Fellowship, 283–284
Invitation to decision, 119–120. See also Response statistics
Irish Council for International Christian Fellowship (ICI), 98, 99
Irish Republican Army (IRA), 94, 96, 99–100
Italy, 130, 259

Jookoon, Lowell, 262
Johannesburg, 30–32, 37–42, 206
Johnson, Arthur, 202
Johnson, Lady Bird, 168, 169, 170
Johnson, Lyndon B., 106, 107, 147, 160, 167–171, 174
Johnston, J. R., 86
Jones, Bob, Jr., 50
Jones, Cornelius (Neal), 3, 14–15
Jones, Glacefield Rosebud, 22n
Jones, Grace, 14–15
Jones, Howard, 33, 37, 44n, 127, 161, 221

Kadar, Jonos, 306
Kaiser, Philip M., 299, 300
Kakol, Kazimiez, 309
Kaldy, Zoltan, 301, 305
Kaschel, Walter, 230, 247
Kennedy, John F., 20, 167, 173, 187
Kennedy, Joseph, 167
Kennedy, Robert, 167, 279
Kenyatta, Jomo, 283
Key 73, 119
Kim, Helen, 58
Kim, Jang Whan (Billy), 49–64 passim, 272
Kim, Ok Kil, 58
Kim, Trudy, 49, 50
King, Martin Luther, 127, 128
Kissinger, Henry, 107, 183
Kivengere, Festo, 28, 205, 213–214, 260, 282–283
Kucharsky, David, 156

Lacey, Graham, 92–95
Laczkovski, Janos, 297
Landry, Tom, 110, 115
Latin America, 7, 167, 189, 216–253, 282, 314
Lausanne Covenant, 206, 207–210, 212, 250, 252
Lausanne International Congress on World Evangelization, 184, 191–215; Africans and, 32, 196, 205–206, 213, 252, 253, 282–283; American Indians and, 282; Brazil and, 225; continuation committees of, 249–253; Graham speeches at, 151, 202, 214; Philippines and, 249, 292; preparations for, 162, 178, 182, 189–201, 208
Laustade, 211–212
Lee Shih-feng, 265
Lincoln, Abraham, 156
Lindsell, Harold, 189, 200, 202
Little, Paul E., 162–163, 192–193, 197, 202, 211
Living Bible, 148, 232
Living New Testament, 232–233, 243
Loane, Marcus, 190
London: Albert Hall gatherings in, 81, 86–90, 98, 152; Earls Court crusade at, 71–72, 74, 114, 257, 258; and Ireland crusade, 91–92, 97–98; Ramsey and, 229, 230; Spre-e '73 in, 256–259, 260–261. See also Harringay arena
Los Angeles, 71; crusades in, 127–128, 215, 216, 254, 313, 316; Lausanne preparations in, 191, 192
Lote, Denton, 303
Lotz, Anne Graham, 129, 139–145 passim, 156, 158
Lotz, Daniel, 129, 139, 141
Lotz, Jonathan, 144
Lundquist, Carl, 128
Lutheran churches in Brazil, 237; in Germany, 79; in Hungary, 298, 301, 305; in Poland, 307, 309, 310
Luwum, Archbishop, 196, 283

McCormick Place, 113–114, 124–125
Macdonald, Jimmie, 75
McGavran, Donald, 202
Maciel, Isaias de Souza, 219, 220, 239
Madison Square Garden, 28, 71, 162, 230, 316
Maia, Josinaldo Agiar, 230–231
Malan, Gabrielle, 31
Malan, Jan, 31, 41–42
Maracana stadium, 223–224, 228–245 passim
Marcos, Ferdinand, 293
Marcos, Imelda, 293

Marigno, Roberto, 241
Marxism, 66, 297. *See also* Communists
Mathis, Jim, 122
Matthews, Gordon, 17, 18
Mayer, Eric, 151
Mayo Clinic, 30, 157, 182, 201, 285
Meir, Golda, 292
Melo, Humberto, 217, 224, 225, 228, 241, 242
Mesquita, Joe Alexander, 244–245
Mhasi, Lhousuchie (Suchie), 6, 12, 16, 23
Miklos, Imre, 301–302, 305–307
Minneapolis, 313 congresses in, 255, 256, 259; crusades in, 119, 120, 128, 282. *See also* Billy Graham Evangelistic Association
Misiolek, Wladislaw, 307, 308
Moffett, Sam (junior), 54, 62
Moffett, Samuel (senior), 47
Moll, Sue, 41
Montreat, 71, 105–106, 139–141, 150, 155, 157
Moody, D. L., 139, 314
Mooneyham, Stan, 188, 189, 191, 208
Moraes, Benjamin, 219, 230
Mother Teresa, 18, 211
Moynihan, Daniel, 127
Muggeridge, Malcolm, 211
Muhammad Reza Shah Pahlevi, 24

Narzynski, Janusz, 307
Nehru, B. K., 26
Neill, Mrs., 93, 99
Nelson, Dotson, 133
Nelson, Victor, 131, 188, 189, 191, 211
Newspapers, 148; in Brazil, 223, 227; in Charlotte, 136, 281; in Chicago, 39, 149, 276; column in, 149, 150, 177, 314; in Ireland, 100; in London, 39, 87, 89, 148; in New York, 148, 149, 176, 179, 181; in Seattle, 276; in South Africa, 36, 37–39; in Taiwan, 265; on Watergate, 176, 179, 181. *See also* Press coverage
New York (city) Eisenhower meeting in, 166; 1957 crusade in, 28, 62, 122, 127, 142, 150, 162, 166, 192, 219; 1969 crusade in, 71, 230, 316
Niebuhr, Reinhold, 157
Nillson, Yngve, 288
Niteroi, 218, 219, 226, 227
Nixon, Patricia, 107, 178, 182
Nixon, Richard M., 171–184, 285; and Cambodia, 107, 108, 155; inauguration of, 170; in Knoxville, 106–109; in Moscow, 95; at Richardson's funeral, 167; and Watergate, 176–184
North East India Christian Council, 5, 6–7

Ockenga, Harold, 189, 214
O'Dalaigh, Cearbhal, 100
Ogden, Bruce, 203
Oh, Chae Kyung, 45, 47, 63
O'Herron, Edward M., 175
Olford, Stephen, 214
Olson, Laurence, 218, 219, 220, 243, 247
Olson, Warwick, 193
Oo, Mun Sun, 60
Operation Andrew, 114–115, 117, 233, 287, 291, 315–316
Orthodox churches in Poland, 307, 309; in Yugoslavia, 82, 83, 85
Osei-Mensah, Gottfried, 251
Overstreet, Ken, 261

Paisley, Ian, 96
Pak, Seung Wan, 51
Palais de Beaulieu, 195, 201, 203, 208, 210
Palau, Luis, 260
Palotay, Sandor, 297, 298, 300
Pan-African Christian Leadership Assembly (PACLA), 252, 282–283
Pant, K. C., 8
Pawlik, Zdzislaw, 310
Payne, Edward (Brother Ted), 220
Peace with God (Billy Graham), 149, 314; in Cambodia, 210; in Hungary, 296–297; in Ireland, 101; in Nagaland, 5; in Poland, 308
Pedro, Erasmus, 224, 239
Pentecostal churches in Brazil, 218, 219, 237; in Sweden, 287
Phillips, Frank, 135
Piasecki, Adam, 307
Pierce, Bob, 166
Player, Gary, 31, 39
Poland, 296, 299, 305, 307–311
Pope John XXIII, 253
Pope John Paul II, 307, 308, 311
Powell, Richard, 86, 87, 88–89, 90
Prayer, 111, 113–117, 226–227; in Brazil, 226–227, 233–234; in Korea, 58–59; for Lausanne congress, 198–199; in Nagaland, 14, 17, 19; in South Africa, 32; in Taiwan, 268; in U. S., 113–114, 115–116, 262; women's groups for, 32, 58, 114–116, 268
Preaching, 20, 56–57, 119–120, 149–152
Preparation, crusade, 110–117, 134–135; in Brazil, 222–227, 233–234; in Britain, 315–316; in Hong Kong, 271–272; in Korea, 51–52; in South Africa, 31–32; in Sweden, 286–287; in Taiwan, 265–266, 268–269; in U.S., 110, 113–114, 115–116, 262, 291
Presbyterian churches in Brazil, 218, 219, 237; in Korea, 43, 46, 47, 48, 49, 50, 64, 65–66; in Taiwan, 263, 264, 269; in

Ulster, 93; in Washington, D.C., 165–166
Presidents, U. S., 164–184, 285; Carter, 278, 280, 285, 298; Eisenhower, 164–167, 172; Ford, 182, 275, 285; Kennedy, 20, 167, 173, 187; Truman, 164. *See also* Nixon, Richard M.
Press coverage, 156, 183–184, 280, 313–314; in Brazil, 223, 227, 245–246; in Chicago, 276; at *Christival '76*, 261; at Euro 70, 77; on finances, 136, 281; in Hungary, 299; in Ireland, 100; at Lausanne, 207, 212–213; in London, 7, 87, 89, 315, in Los Angeles, 313; and Nagaland, 13, 16, 19, of presidential associations, 164, 166, 173, 176, 177, 179, 181, 182; on race issues, 36, 37–39, 42, 126; at Rose Bowl Parade, 255; in Seattle, 276; in South Africa, 36, 37–39, 42; in Taiwan, 265; in Yugoslavia, 82

Race issues, 157; in South Africa, 28, 29, 33–42, 205–206; in U. S., 38, 93, 126–128, 166, 290
Radio in Africa, 31, 37, 40–41, 283; in Asia, 5, 64–65, 265; in Europe, 78, 84, 288–289; in Ireland, 101; in London, 87; in South America, 220, 224; in U.S., 107, 115. *See also* Hour of Decision
Ramsey, Michael, 228–230
Rayburn, Sam, 167
Rees, Jean, 114
Rees, John, 29, 35
Reformed churches in Hungary, 298, 300–301, 302, 303, 305; in South Africa, 28, 29, 30, 31, 42
Rejala, Wilson Martinez, 231–232
Renfrow, Harold, 218–219, 221–224, 239, 243, 245
Renfrow, Nona, 243
Rennie, David, 71, 72, 74, 75, 77, 78
Response statistics in Korea, 57, 62–63; in South Africa, 36; in Taiwan, 268n; in U.S., 120, 129, 284. *See also* Church growth; Decision cards
Richard, Cliff, 89, 258
Richardson, Sid, 164–165, 167
Riggs, Charlie, 137; in Asia, 6, 7, 13, 14, 16, 17, 21; in U.S., 113–114, 115, 122
Rio de Janeiro, 216, 217, 219–220, 221–226, 228–248
Roberts, Oral, 188
Rodeheaver, Homer, 149
Rogers, Roy, 74
Rowlandson, Maurice, 256–257, 258, 279

Safire, William, 178
Sanders, Cheryl, 221
Sanders, Norman, 113, 221
Sanford, Terry, 129

São Paulo, 216, 220, 222, 243–244, 245, 248
Schmidt, Dominie, 41
Schneider, Peter, 71–79 *passim*
Schools of Christian Writing, 238, 316
Schools of evangelism, 130–132, 150; in Brazil, 236–238; in Korea, 56–57, 63, 66; in Philippines, 293
Secret of Happiness (Billy Graham), 308
Serafim, Senhor, 222
Sermons, 20, 56, 57, 119–120, 149–152
Shah of Iran, 24
Shea, George Beverly, 55, 118, 134, 234, 314
Sherrill, Edmund, 219, 229
Sherrill, Elizabeth, 278
Shillong Agreement, 26
Shingler, Lewis A., 254, 255
Shippam, Ernest, 88, 90, 152
Sikakane, Ebenezer, 32, 33
Simms, Archbishop, 96, 97
Singing, 134; at Euro 70, 77, 80; in Hungary, 300, 306; at Lausanne, 201–202; in Nagaland, 6, 11n, 20; in Poland, 310; at U.S. crusades, 118, 276.
Smith, Oswald J., 20
Smith, Tedd, 11n, 20, 21, 75, 201
Smyth, Walter, 111, 113, 117, 137, 154; and Africa, 29, 30, 37, 283; and Brazil, 217, 219, 220, 221, 223, 241; and Europe crusades, 72–73, 75, 298, 304, 307, 308; and India, 6, 11, 12, 13, 16; and Ireland, 91, 92–93, 95, 99–100; and Korea, 45, 46, 53, 58, 61, 63; and Lausanne congress, 195, 210, 211; and Seattle, 277; and Taiwan, 267, 269; and youth congresses, 258, 259, 260
Social concerns, 7; and evangelism, 25, 187–188, 190, 197, 201, 207, 213, 250, 253, 260, 280–281; Lausanne and, 190, 197, 201, 205–207; and politics, 177; WCC and, 187–188, 190, 197, 201. *See also* Race issues
Soper, Franjo, 82
South Africa, 27–42, 194, 205–206
South African Broadcasting Commission (SABC), 31, 40–41
South African Congress of Mission and Evangelism, 28–37
South African Council of Churches (SACC), 28–29
Spre-e '73, 256–259, 260–261
Spurgeon, Charles Haddon, 82
Stadiums vs. auditoriums, 119; university, 107–109, 129, 130, 262, 290–291
Stankiewicz, Michal, 307
Stott, John, 153, 190, 207, 208–210, 249–250, 285
Sunday, Billy, 149, 291

Sweden, 74–75, 205, 285, 286–290
Switzerland, 77, 178, 187, 278

Tabb, Don, 114
Tam, David, 195, 198
Tapes in Hungary, 301; in Korea, 63; in
    Poland, 311
Taylor, Clyde, 188, 189
Taylor, James Hudson, 268, 269
Tchividjian, Stephan, 139, 195
Tchividjian, Virginia Graham (Gigi),
    139–145 passim, 163, 195, 201, 227
Techjma, Jozef, 309
Telecasts, 32, 119, 135, 154; in Africa, 283;
    in Asia, 54, 265; in Britain, 71–72, 74,
    87, 97–98, 315; in Europe, 71–73, 74–80,
    290, 316; in Ireland, 97–98; in South
    America, 221, 224–225, 240–242,
    243–244, 245, 246, 248; in U.S., 126,
    176, 216, 242n, 275, 276, 290, 291, 316
Ten Boom, Corrie, 278
Tennessee, 71, 105–109, 126, 174, 175
Texas, 71, 115, 169, 170, 262. See also
    Dallas
Thielman, Calvin, 151
Tolbert, William Richard, Jr., 81
Trotman, Dawson, 314
Truman, Harry S., 164
Tse, Daniel, 272–273
Turner, Larry, 111, 286

Uganda, 28, 196, 205, 206, 213, 283
Ultima Hora, 223, 227
Umbanda, 217, 222, 223
United States, 118–133; bicentennial of,
    275; and Euro 70, 72, 77; and Ireland
    crusade, 91; and Lausanne congress, 162,
    191, 192, 251; and race issues, 38, 93,
    126–128, 166, 290; telecasts in, 126, 176,
    216, 242n, 275, 276, 290, 291, 316; youth
    congresses in, 54, 255–256, 259, 283–284.
    See also Presidents, U.S.
University of North Carolina, 129
Upper Mid-West crusade, 119, 120, 123,
    128
Ury, William A., 268

Veritas, 81
Vesnik, 82
Vietnam war, 76, 108, 118, 142, 155

Wai, Paul, 270
Wanderers cricket ground, 31, 39, 40, 41,
    42
Wang, Leland, 148
Ward, Charles, 216–217, 224–225
Washington, D.C., 45, 160, 164, 165, 189,
    275–276
Watergate affair, 118, 175, 176–184
Waters, Ethel, 109

Wei Lin Tako, 268
Wesley, John, 90
White, John Wesley, 44n, 57, 96, 149
Whitefield, George, 152
Williams, Bob, 121
Williams, Christie, 125–126
Williams, Harry, 111
Williams, Howard, 125–126
Williams, John W., 127
Williams, Katie, 110, 125–126
Williams, Ralph, 149
Wilmes, Esther, 291
Wilson, George M., 135–136, 156, 211, 314
Wilson, Grady, 136–137, 151, 152, 159,
    162, 314; in Brazil, 227; in Chicago,
    124–125; in Korea, 44n; and U.S.
    presidents, 167, 169
Wilson, Jean, 77, 257
Wilson, Jim, 155–156
Wilson, T. W., 136, 152, 155; in Asia, 11,
    12, 13, 15, 16, 21, 58; in Chicago,
    124–125; in Ireland, 96; and Johnson
    (Lyndon), 169; and Knoxville, 106; in
    South Africa, 37, 40; at Urbana, 285
Wimbush, John, 150
Winwill, Joan, 279
Wirt, Sherwood, 45, 75, 238, 242
Wojtyla, Karol, 307, 308, 311
Women's prayer groups, 32, 58, 114–115,
    268
Wood, Maurice, 275
World Congress on Evangelism (Berlin),
    191, 197, 208, 255; BGEA and, 188–189;
    Cassidy at, 28; and Europe, 75; Koreans
    at, 44, 50; representation in, 191, 204
World Council of Churches (WCC), 7;
    Lausanne and, 187–188, 190, 197, 200,
    201, 207
World Evangelism and Christian Education
    Fund, 281–282
World Literature Crusade, 51, 225
World Wide Pictures, 58, 135, 242n,
    278–279
Wu, Henry-Go, 265–266
Wyszynski, Stefan, 308

Yes '73, 256, 259
You, Ook Chun, 64–65
Youth congresses of, 54, 255–261, 277,
    283–284; and crusades, 79, 261–262, 266,
    267–268, 273
Youth for Christ (YFC), 30, 31, 37
Yugoslavia, 74, 77, 81–85

Zagreb, 74, 77, 81–85
Zamboanga City, 249
Zerda, Dona, 222, 223
Zulu, Alpheus, 33, 36
Zulus, 32, 33–34, 36, 42